D1232554

STRUCTURAL ELEMENTS FOR ARCHITECTS AND BUILDERS

Design of columns, beams, and tension elements in wood, steel, and reinforced concrete

Second Edition

Jonathan Ochshorn

Structural Elements for Architects and Builders

Design of columns, beams, and tension elements in wood, steel, and reinforced concrete

Second Edition

Jonathan Ochshorn

Common Ground Publishing 2015

First published in 2015 in Champaign, Illinois, USA
by Common Ground Publishing LLC
As part of the Constructed Environment book imprint

Copyright © Jonathan Ochshorn 2015

All rights reserved. Apart from fair dealing for the purposes of study, research, criticism or review as permitted under the applicable copyright legislation, no part of this book may be reproduced by any process without written permission from the publisher.

Library of Congress Cataloging-in-Publication Data

Ochshorn, Jonathan, author.
  Structural elements for architects and builders : design of columns, beams, and tension elements in wood, steel, and reinforced concrete / Jonathan Ochshorn. -- Second edition.
     pages cm
  Includes bibliographical references and index.
  ISBN 978-1-61229-801-6 (pbk : alk. paper) -- ISBN 978-1-61229-802-3 (pdf : alk. paper)
  1. Structural design. 2. Architectural design. 3. Building materials. I. Title.

  TA658.O29 2015
  624.1'772--dc23

                            2015026075

Disclaimer: The author and publisher assume no liability for any injury and/or damage to persons or property arising from the use or application of the methods or instructions contained in this book: it is intended only for a preliminary understanding of structural behavior and design; a competent professional should be consulted for the design of actual structures.

Cover Photo: Schwartz Auditorium in Rockefeller Hall, Cornell University
Photo © Susan Schwartz 2015

All drawings and figures were created by the author except for Figure 4.6 (Fair Store in Chicago by Jenney & Mundie), a public domain item in the collection of the Ryerson & Burnham Libraries at the The Art Institute of Chicago: RBA Digital File name: 000000_121127_016.jpg. All photographs were taken by the author, some screen captured from the author's online video series on the construction of Milstein Hall at Cornell University (http://impatientsearch. com/milstein/).

Table of Contents

PREFACE TO FIRST EDITION

As is well known, architects and builders rarely design the structural elements and systems within their buildings, instead engaging the services of (and, it is to be hoped, collaborating with) structural engineers, or relying upon standard practices sanctioned by building codes. Where architects or builders wish to be adventurous with their structures, some knowledge of structural behavior and the potential of structural materials is certainly useful. On the other hand, where they are content to employ generic structural systems — platform framing in wood, simple skeletal frames in steel or reinforced concrete — one can get by with little actual knowledge of structural design, relying instead on the expertise of structural consultants and the knowledge of common spans, heights, and cross-sectional dimensions around which many ordinary buildings can be planned.

The heroic stage of modernism, in which architects often sought to reconcile structural behavior and overall building form — some finding inspiration in the structural frame or the load-bearing wall — was also the heroic stage of structural education for architects: it was hardly necessary, in that context, to explain why architects needed to learn about structures. Some of the same excitement about the potential of structure in architecture still remains, but it is also true that a "mannerist" tendency has emerged, interested not necessarily in renouncing the role of structure in architecture, but rather reveling in its potential to distort, twist, fragment, and otherwise subvert modernist conventions and the architectural forms they support.

Yet all structures, whether hidden from view or boldly expressed, follow the same laws of equilibrium, are exposed to the same types of forces, and are constrained by the same material properties and manufacturing practices. It is therefore appropriate for architects and builders to study structures in such a way that the basic principles underlying all structural form become clear. This can be accomplished in three phases: first, by studying the concepts of statics and strength of materials; second, by learning how these concepts are applied to the design of common structural elements fabricated from real materials; and third, by gaining insight into the design of structural systems comprised of structural elements interconnected in a coherent pattern.

Much of the material presented in this text can be found elsewhere; the basic conditions of equilibrium, historical insights into structural behavior that form the basis for structural design, and recommendations for design procedures incorporated into building codes, are all widely disseminated through industry-published manuals, government-sanctioned codes, and academic texts. Many excellent structures texts have been written specifically for architects and builders. The question therefore naturally arises: Why write another one?

The primary motivation for writing this text is to organize the material in a manner consistent with the structures curriculum developed within the Department of Architecture at Cornell University, based on the three sequential "phases" described above — structural concepts, elements, and systems. While this text does contain a concise introduction to structural concepts (statics), it is primarily concerned with the design and analysis of structural elements: columns, beams, and tension members, and their connections. This material is organized into a single volume that is concise, comprehensive, and self-sufficient, including all necessary data for the preliminary design and analysis of these structural elements in wood, steel, and reinforced concrete.

A second motivation for writing this text is to present material in a manner consistent with my own priorities and sensibilities. Every chapter contains insight, speculation, or forms of presentation developed by the author and generally not found elsewhere. Additionally, the Appendices included at the end of the text contains numerous tables and graphs, based on material contained in industry publications, but reorganized and formatted especially for this text to improve clarity and simplicity — without sacrificing comprehensiveness.

Methods for designing structures and modeling loads are constantly being refined. Within the last several years, important changes have occurred in the design of wood, steel, and reinforced concrete structures, as well as in the modeling of loads. These changes include revised procedures for beam and column design in wood; the replacement of the standard specification for 36-ksi steel with a new standard based on 50-ksi steel for wide-flange sections; a major modification in the load factors used in reinforced concrete design, aligning them with those recommended by SEI/ASCE 7 and already used in the design of wood and steel structures; and numerous refinements in the modeling of environmental loads. These changes have all been incorporated into this text.

Finally, a disclaimer: this text is intended to be used only for the preliminary (schematic) design and understanding of structural elements. For the design of an actual structure, a competent professional should be consulted.

Preface to Second Edition

Unlike laws of equilibrium, which remain unchanged year after year, the application of structural concepts to the design of actual structures using real materials and accepted methods changes on a fairly regular schedule. Material-centric institutes periodically revise their suggestions for building code language; these are referenced in model building codes, and the various states of the union eventually get around to adopting these model codes, turning them into legal mandates that reflect evolving standards for structural design.

This fact alone would make it necessary to update the first edition of Structural Elements, and I have indeed incorporated recommendations from the latest versions of all four primary references (i.e., from the AF&PA/AWC, AISC, ACI, and ASCE) into this second edition, including revised values for Southern Pine lumber that became effective in 2013.

In addition, I have reorganized the material in this second edition around the idea of materials rather than based on structural actions. In other words, while the first edition considered tension, compression, and bending as the primary "subjects" (with wood, steel, and reinforced concrete discussed for each of these structural behaviors), the second edition organizes the content around wood, steel, and reinforced concrete (with the various structural actions — tension, compression, and bending — included within each "material" chapter). Doing so has allowed me to add new content concerning structural systems and material properties for each of the primary structural materials, and to integrate the discussion of connections within the particular material chapters to which they apply. In this way, the organization of the book reflects curricular changes within the building technology area of the architectural curriculum at Cornell.

J. Ochshorn, Ithaca, NY
January, 2015

LIST OF EXAMPLES

Chapter 4: Steel

Chapter 5: Reinforced Concrete

LIST OF APPENDICES

CHAPTER 1

Introduction to structural design

The study of structural behavior and structural design begins with the concept of load. We represent loads with arrows indicating direction and magnitude. The magnitude is expressed in pounds (lb), kips (1 kip = 1000 lb), or appropriate SI units of force; the direction is usually vertical (gravity) or horizontal (wind, earthquake), although wind loads on pitched roofs can be modeled as acting perpendicular to the roof surface (Figure 1.1).

Where loads are distributed over a surface, we say, for example, 100 pounds per square foot, or 100 psf. Where loads are distributed over a linear element, like a beam, we say, for example, 2 kips per linear foot, or 2 kips per foot, or 2 kips/ft (Figure 1.2). Where loads are concentrated at a point, such as the vertical load transferred to a column, we say, for example, 10 kips or 10 k.

STATICS

Finding out what the loads are that act on a structure and how these loads are supported is the prerequisite to all structural design. There are two main reasons for this. First, the fact that a structural element is supported at all means that the supporting element is being stressed in some way. To find the magnitude of the reactions of an element is thus to simultaneously find

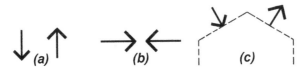

Figure 1.1: Direction of loads can be *(a)* vertical; *(b)* horizontal; or *(c)* inclined

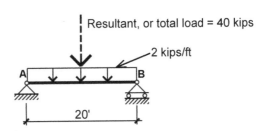

Figure 1.2: Distributed loads on a beam

the magnitude of the loads acting on the supporting element. Each action, or load, has an equal reaction; or, as Newton said in defense of this third law: "If you press a stone with your finger, the finger is also pressed by the stone."

The second reason for finding reactions of the structural element is that doing so facilitates the further analysis or design of the element itself. That is, determining reactions is the prerequisite to the calculation of internal loads and internal stresses, values of which are central to the most fundamental questions of structural engineering: Is it strong enough? Is it safe?

TRIBUTARY AREAS

When loads are evenly distributed over a surface, it is often possible to "assign" portions of the load to the various structural elements supporting that surface by subdividing the total area into tributary areas corresponding to each member. In Figure 1.3, half the load of the table goes to each lifter.

In Figure 1.4, half the 20-psf snow load on the cantilevered roof goes to each column; the tributary area for each column is 10 ft × 10 ft, so the load on each column is 20(10 × 10) = 2000 lb = 2 kips.

Figure 1.5 shows a framing plan for a steel building. If the total floor load is 100 psf, the load acting on each of the structural elements comprising the floor system can be found using appropriate tributary areas. Beam *A* supports

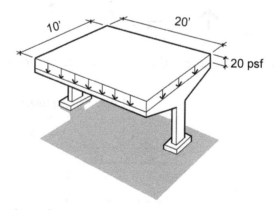

Figure 1.3: Tributary areas divide the load among the various supports

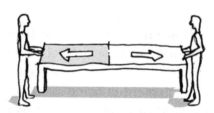

Figure 1.4: Distributed load on a floor carried by two columns

a total load of 100(20 × 10) = 20,000 lb = 20 kips; but it is more useful to calculate the distributed load acting on any linear foot of the beam — this is shown by the shaded tributary area in Figure 1.6a and is 100(1 × 10) = 1000 lb = 1 kip. Since 1000 lb is acting on a 1-ft length of beam, we write 1000 lb/ft or 1.0 kip/ft, as shown in Figure 1.6b.

As shown in Figure 1.7a, Beam B (or Girder B) supports a total tributary area of 17.5 × 20 = 350 ft². The load at point a is not included in the beam's tributary area. Rather, it is assigned to the edge, or spandrel, beam where it goes directly into a column, having no effect on Beam B. Unlike Beam A, floor

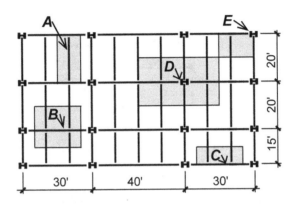

Figure 1.5: Framing plan showing tributary areas for beams, girders, and columns

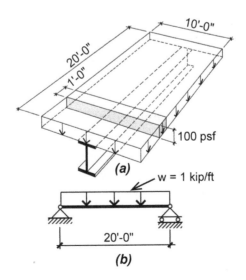

Figure 1.6: Distributed load on a steel beam, with (a) one linear foot of its tributary area shown; and (b) load diagram showing distributed load in kips per foot

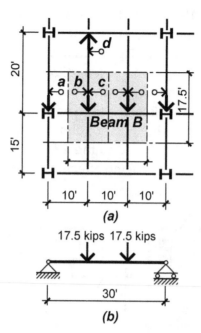

Figure 1.7: Concentrated loads on a girder *(a)* derived from tributary areas on framing plan; and *(b)* shown on load diagram

loads are transferred to Beam *B* at two points: each concentrated load corresponds to a tributary area of 17.5 × 10 = 175 ft²; therefore, the two loads each have a magnitude of 100 × 175 = 17,500 lb = 17.5 kips. The load diagram for Beam *B* is shown in Figure 1.7*b*.

Spandrel girders

Beam *C* (or spandrel girder *C*), shown in Figure 1.5, is similar to Beam *B* except that the tributary area for each concentrated load is smaller, 7.5 × 10 = 75 ft², as shown in Figure 1.8*a*. The two concentrated loads, therefore, have a magnitude of 100 × 75 = 7500 lb = 7.5 kips, and the load diagram is as shown in Figure 1.8*b*.

There are three reasons spandrel girders are often larger than otherwise similar girders located in the interior of the building, even though the tributary areas they support are smaller. First, spandrel girders often support cladding of various kinds, in addition to the floor loads included in this example. Second, aside from the added weight to be supported, spandrels are often made bigger so that their deflection, or vertical movement, is reduced. This can be an important consideration where nonstructural cladding is sensitive to movement of the structural frame. Third, when the girders are designed to be part of a moment-resisting frame, their size might need to be increased to account for the stresses introduced by lateral forces such as wind and earthquake.

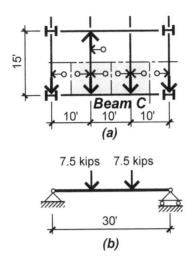

Figure 1.8: Concentrated loads on a spandrel girder *(a)* derived from tributary areas on framing plan; and *(b)* shown on load diagram

Columns

One way or another, all of the load acting on the floor must be carried by columns under that floor. For most structures, it is appropriate to subdivide the floor into tributary areas defined by the centerlines between columns so that every piece of the floor is assigned to a column.

It can be seen from Figure 1.9 that typical interior columns carry twice the load of typical exterior columns, and four times the load of corner columns. However, two of the conditions described earlier with respect to the enlargement of spandrel girders can also increase the size of exterior and corner columns: the need to support additional weight of cladding and the possibility of resisting wind and earthquake forces through rigid connections to the spandrel girders.

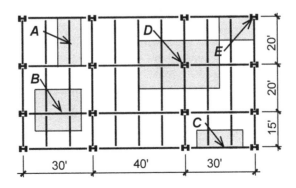

Figure 1.9: Framing plan showing tributary areas for columns (one floor only)

Column D supports a tributary area of $35 \times 20 = 700$ ft^2 so that the load transferred to Column D from the floor above is $100 \times 700 = 70,000$ lb = 70 kips, assuming that the floor above has the same shape and loads as the floor shown. But every floor and roof above also transfers a load to Column D. Obviously, columns at the bottom of buildings support more weight than columns at the top of buildings, since all the tributary areas of the floors and roof above are assigned to them. As an example, if there are nine floors and one roof above Column D, all with the same distributed load and tributary area, then the total load on Column D would be, not 70 k, but $(9 + 1) \times 70 = 700$ kips.

In practice, the entire load as previously calculated is not assigned to columns or to other structural elements with large total tributary areas. This is because it is unlikely that a large tributary area will be fully loaded at any given time. For example, if the live load caused by people and other movable objects is set at 60 psf, and one person weighed 180 lb, then a tributary area of 7000 ft^2 (as in the example of Column D) would have to be populated by more than 2000 people, each occupying 3 ft^2, in order to achieve the specified load. That many people crowded into that large a space is an unlikely occurrence in most occupancies, and a live load reduction is often allowed by building codes. As the tributary area gets smaller, however, the probability of the full live load being present increases, and no such reduction is permitted. Permanent and immovable components of the building, or dead loads, have the same probability of being present over large tributary areas as small tributary areas, so they are never included in this type of probability-based load reduction. Calculations for live load reduction are explained in the next chapter.

The path taken by a load depends on the ability of the structural elements to transfer loads in various directions. Given the choice of two competing load paths such as (1) and (2) in Figure 1.10, the load is divided between the two

Figure 1.10: Competing load paths on a corrugated steel deck

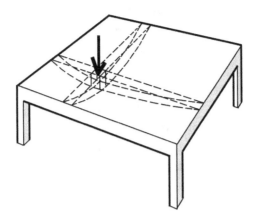

Figure 1.11: Competing load paths on a two-way slab

paths in proportion to the *relative stiffness* of each path. Since the corrugated steel deck shown in Figure 1.10 is much stiffer in the direction of load path (1), and, in fact, is designed to carry the entire load in that direction, we neglect the possibility of the load moving along path (2).

For "two-way" systems, generally only used in reinforced concrete (Figure 1.11), or for indeterminate systems in general, the assignment of loads to beams and columns also becomes a function of the relative stiffness of the various components of the system. Stiffer elements "attract" more load to them, and the simplistic division into tributary areas becomes inappropriate, except in certain symmetrical conditions.

Equilibrium

Where loads or structural geometries are not symmetrical, using tributary areas may not accurately predict the effects of loads placed on structures, and other methods must be used. We can determine the effects of loads placed on statically determinate structures by assuming that such structures remain "at rest," in a state of equilibrium. The implication of this condition, derived from Newton's second law, is that the summation of all forces (or moments) acting on the structure along any given coordinate axis equals zero. For a plane structure — i.e., one whose shape and deflection under loads occurs on a planar surface — three equations uniquely define this condition of equilibrium: two for loads (forces) acting along either of the perpendicular axes of the plane's coordinate system and one for moments acting "about" the axis perpendicular to the structure's plane. Some examples of plane structures are shown in Figure 1.12.

In words, the equations of equilibrium state that the sum of all "horizontal" forces is zero; the sum of all "vertical" forces is zero; and — take a deep breath here — the sum of all moments about any point, including those resulting from any force multiplied by its distance (measured perpendicular to the "line of action" of the force) to the point about which moments are being taken, is zero.

"Horizontal" and "vertical" can be taken as any perpendicular set of coordinate axes. Where x is used for the horizontal axis and y for the vertical, moments in the plane of the structure are acting about the z-axis. This conventional way of representing coordinate systems for the consideration of equilibrium is inconsistent with the labeling typically used to distinguish

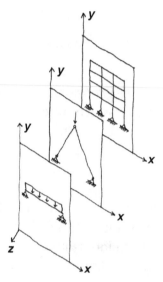

Figure 1.12: Examples of plane structures: simply-supported beam, three-hinged arch, and rigid (moment-resisting) frame

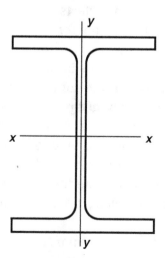

Figure 1.13: Coordinate axes for a steel W-shape

between axes of bending. Compare the typical axes of bending shown in Figure 1.13 with the "equilibrium" coordinate axes in Figure 1.12. Written symbolically, the equations are:

$$\Sigma F_x = 0$$
$$\Sigma F_y = 0 \qquad (1.1)$$
$$\Sigma M_{pt.} = 0$$

For any plane, rigid-body structure (just "structure" or "structural element" from now on) subjected to various loads, the three equations of equilibrium provide the mathematical basis for determining values for up to three unknown forces and moments — the reactions of the structure to the loads. Structural elements of this type are statically determinate because the magnitudes of the unknown reactions can be determined using only the equations of static equilibrium.

Free-body diagrams

Any structure (or part of a structure) so defined can be represented as a free-body diagram (FBD). All "external" loads acting on the FBD, all unknown "external" moments or forces at the points where the FBD is connected to other structural elements (i.e., all reactions), and all unknown "internal" moments or forces at points where a FBD is "cut" must be shown on the diagram.

Single or multiple reactions occurring at a given point are often represented by standard symbols. These pictures graphically indicate the types of forces and moments that can be developed (Figure 1.14). Other combinations of forces and moments can be represented graphically; the three symbols shown, however, cover most commonly encountered conditions.

Where an FBD is "cut" at a point other than at the reactions of the structural element, an internal moment as well as two perpendicular internal forces are typically present, unless an internal constraint, such as a hinge, prevents one or more of those forces (or moments) from developing.

Where there are more reactions than equations of equilibrium, the structure is said to be statically indeterminate, and equilibrium alone is insufficient

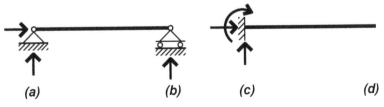

Figure 1.14: Abstract symbols for reactions, including: *(a)* hinge or pin-end, *(b)* roller, *(c)* fixed, and *(d)* free end

to determine the values of the reactions; other techniques have been developed to find the reactions of indeterminate structures, but these are beyond the scope of this text.

REACTIONS

The following examples show how the equations of equilibrium can be used to find reactions of various common determinate structures. The procedures have been developed so that the equations need not be solved simultaneously. Alternatively, where determinate structures are symmetrical in their own geometry as well as in their loading (assumed to be vertical), reactions can be found by assigning half of the total external loads to each vertical reaction.

Example 1.1 Find reactions for simply supported beam

Problem definition. Find the three reactions for a simply supported beam supporting a distributed load of 100 kips/ft over a span of 20 ft. Simply supported means that the beam is supported by a hinge and a roller, and is therefore determinate.

Solution overview. Draw load diagram with unknown forces and/or moments replacing the reaction (constraint) symbols; use the three equations of equilibrium to find these unknown reactions.

Problem solution
1. Redraw load diagram (Figure 1.15*a*) by replacing constraint symbols with unknown forces, H_A, R_A, and R_B, and by showing a resultant for all distributed loads (Figure 1.15*b*).

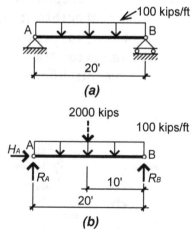

Figure 1.15: Load diagram for simply-supported beam for Example 1.1 showing *(a)* constraint symbols and *(b)* unknown forces replacing constrain symbols, and resultant corresponding to distributed load

2. The solution to the horizontal reaction at point A is trivial, since no horizontal loads are present: $\Sigma F_x = H_A = 0$. In this equation, we use a sign convention, where positive corresponds to forces pointing to the right and negative to forces pointing to the left.

3. The order in which the remaining equations are solved is important: moment equilibrium is considered before vertical equilibrium in order to reduce the number of unknown variables in the vertical equilibrium equation. Moments can be taken about any point in the plane; however, unless you wish to solve the two remaining equations simultaneously, it is suggested that the point be chosen strategically to eliminate all but one of the unknown variables. Each moment is the product of a force times a distance called the moment arm; this moment arm is measured from the point about which moments are taken to the "line of action" of the force and is measured perpendicular to the line of action of the force.

    Where the moment arm equals zero, the moment being considered is also zero, and the force "drops out" of the equation. For this reason, it is most convenient to select a point about which to take moments that is aligned with the line of action of either of the two unknown vertical reactions so that one of those unknown forces drops out of the equation of equilibrium. The sign of each moment is based on an arbitrary sign convention, with positive used when the moment causes a clockwise rotation of the beam considered as a free-body diagram and negative when a counterclockwise rotation results (the opposite convention could be chosen as well). In the equation that follows, each product of two numbers represents a force times a distance so that, taken together, they represent the sum of all moments acting on the beam. Any force whose moment arm is zero is left out.

    $$\Sigma M_B = R_A(20) - 2000(10) = 0$$

    Solving for the vertical reaction at point A, we get: $R_A = 1000$ kips.

4. Finally, we use the third equation of equilibrium to find the last unknown reaction. Another sign convention is necessary for vertical equilibrium equations: we arbitrarily choose positive to represent an upward-acting force and negative to represent a downward-acting force.

    $$\Sigma F_y = R_A + R_B - 2000 = 0$$

    or, substituting $R_A = 1000$ kips:

    $$1000 + R_B - 2000 = 0$$

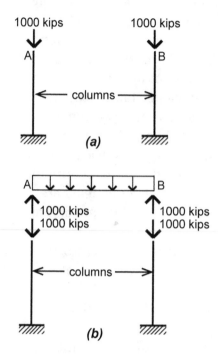

Figure 1.16: Support for the beam from Example 1.1 showing *(a)* load on column supports and *(b)* reactions from beam corresponding to load on column supports

Solving for the vertical reaction at point *B*, we get R_B = 1000 kips.

The two vertical reactions in this example are equal and could have been found by simply dividing the total load in half, as we did when considering tributary areas. Doing this, however, is only appropriate when the structure's geometry and loads are symmetrical.

If the reactions represent other structural supports such as columns or girders, then the "upward" support they give to the beam occurs simultaneously with the beam's "downward" weight on the supports: in other words, if the beam in Example 1.1 is supported on two columns, then those columns (at points *A* and *B*) would have load diagrams as shown in Figure 1.16*a*. The beam and columns, shown together, have reactions and loads as shown in Figure 1.16*b*. These pairs of equal and opposite forces are actually inseparable. In the Newtonian framework, each action, or load, has an equal reaction.

Example 1.2 Find reactions for three-hinged arch

Problem definition. Find the reactions for the three-hinged arch shown in Figure 1.17*a*.

Solution overview. Draw load diagram with unknown forces and/or moments replacing the reaction (constraint) symbols; use the three equations of equilibrium, plus one additional equation found by considering the equilibrium of another free-body diagram, to find the four unknown reactions.

Problem solution

1. The three-hinged arch shown in this example appears to have too many unknown variables (four unknowns versus only three equations of equilibrium); however, the internal hinge at point C prevents the structure from behaving as a rigid body, and a fourth equation can be developed out of this condition. The initial three equations of equilibrium can be written as follows:

    a. $\Sigma M_B = R_A(60) - 20(30) = 0$, from which $R_A = 10$ kips.

    b. $\Sigma F_y = R_A + R_B - 20 = 0$; then, substituting $R_A = 10$ kips from the moment equilibrium equation solved in step *a*, we get $10 + R_B - 20 = 0$, from which $R_B = 10$ kips.

    c. $\Sigma F_x = H_A - H_B = 0$.

    Sign conventions are as described in Example 1.1. This last equation of horizontal equilibrium (step *c*) contains two unknown variables and

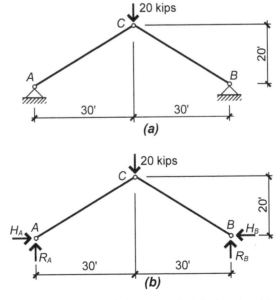

Figure 1.17: Load diagram for 3-hinged arch for Example 1.2 showing *(a)* constraint symbols and *(b)* unknown forces replacing constrain symbols

cannot be solved at this point. To find H_A, it is necessary to first cut a new FBD at the internal hinge (point C) in order to examine the equilibrium of the resulting partial structure shown in Figure 1.18.

2. With respect to this FBD, we show unknown internal forces H_C and V_C at the cut, but we show no bending moment at that point since none can exist at a hinge. This condition of zero moment is what allows us to write an equation that can be solved for the unknown, H_A:

$$\Sigma M_C = 10(30) - H_A(20) = 0$$

from which $H_A = 15$ kips.

Then, going back to the "horizontal" equilibrium equation shown in step c that was written for the entire structure (not just the cut FBD), we get:

$$\Sigma F_x = H_A - H_B = 15 - H_B = 0$$

from which $H_B = 15$ kips.

While the moment equation written for the FBD can be taken about any point in the plane of the structure, it is easier to take moments about point C, so that only H_A appears in the equation as an unknown. Otherwise, it would be necessary to first solve for the internal unknown forces at point C, using "vertical" and "horizontal" equilibrium.

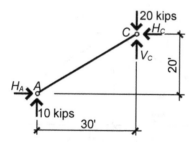

Figure 1.18: Free-body diagram cut at internal hinge at point C, for Example 1.2

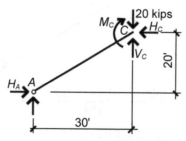

Figure 1.19: Free-body diagram for a two-hinged arch (with internal moment at point C)

If there were no hinge at point C, we would need to add an unknown internal moment at C, in addition to the forces shown (Figure 1.19). The moment equation would then be $\Sigma M_C = 10(30) - H_A(20) + M_C = 0$. With two unknown variables in the equation (H_A and M_C), we cannot solve for H_A. In other words, unlike the three-hinged arch, this two-hinged arch is an indeterminate structure.

Example 1.3 Find reactions for a cable

Problem definition. Find the reactions for the flexible cable structure shown in Figure 1.20*a*. The actual shape of the cable is unknown: all that is specified is the maximum distance of the cable below the level of the supports (reactions): the cable's sag.

Solution overview. Draw load diagram with unknown forces and/or moments replacing the reaction (constraint) symbols; use the three equations of equilibrium, plus one additional equation found by considering the equilibrium of another free-body diagram, to find the four unknown reactions.

Problem solution
1. The cable shown in this example appears to have too many unknown variables (four unknowns versus only three equations of equilibrium); however, the cable's flexibility prevents it from behaving as a rigid body, and a fourth equation can be developed out of this condition. The three equations of equilibrium can be written as follows:
   a. $\Sigma M_B = R_A(80) - 10(65) - 20(40) = 0$, from which $R_A = 18.125$ kips.

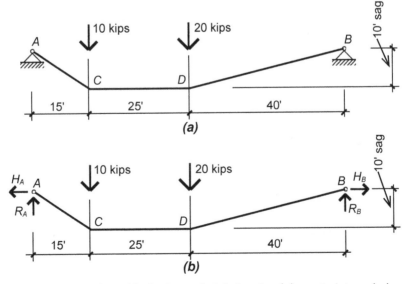

Figure 1.20: Load diagram for cable for Example 1.3 showing *(a)* constraint symbols and *(b)* unknown forces replacing constraint symbols

b. $\Sigma F_y = R_A + R_B - 10 - 20 = 0$; then, substituting $R_A = 18.125$ kips from the moment equilibrium equation solved in step *a*, we get $18.125 + R_B - 10 - 20 = 0$, from which $R_B = 11.875$ kips.

c. $\Sigma F_x = H_A - H_B = 0$.

Sign conventions are as described in Example 1.1. This last equation of horizontal equilibrium (step *c*) contains two unknown variables and cannot be solved at this point. By analogy to the three-hinged arch, we would expect to cut an FBD and develop a fourth equation. Like the internal hinge in the arch, the entire cable, being flexible, is incapable of resisting any bending moments. But unlike the arch, the cable's geometry is not predetermined; it is conditioned by the particular loads placed upon it. Before cutting the FBD, we need to figure out where the maximum specified sag of 10 ft occurs: without this information, we would be writing a moment equilibrium equation of an FBD in which the moment arm of the horizontal reaction, H_A, was unknown.

2. We find the location of the sag point by looking at internal vertical forces

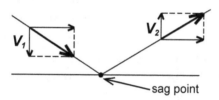

Figure 1.21: Sag point occurs where the vertical component of internal cable forces changes direction (sign), for Example 1.3

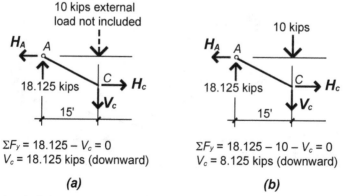

Figure 1.22: Vertical component of cable force for Example 1.3 is found *(a)* just to the left of the external load at point *C* and *(b)* just to the right of the load

within the cable. When the direction of these internal vertical forces changes, the cable has reached its lowest point (Figure 1.21). Checking first at point *C*, we see that the internal vertical force does not change direction on either side of the external load of 10 kips (comparing Figure 1.22*a* and Figure 1.22*b*), so the sag point cannot be at point *C*.

However, when we check point *D*, we see that the direction of the internal vertical force does change, as shown in Figure 1.23. Thus, point *D* is the sag point of the cable (i.e., the low point), specified as being 10 ft below the support elevation.

We can also find this sag point by constructing a diagram of cumulative vertical loads, beginning on the left side of the cable (Figure 1.24). The sag point then occurs where the "cumulative force line" crosses the baseline.

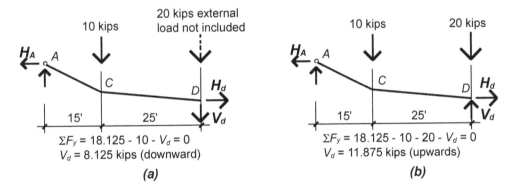

Figure 1.23: Vertical component of cable force for Example 1.3 is found *(a)* just to the left of the external load at point D and *(b)* just to the right of the load

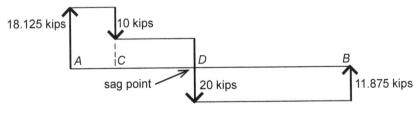

Figure 1.24: Diagram of cumulative vertical loads, for Example 1.3

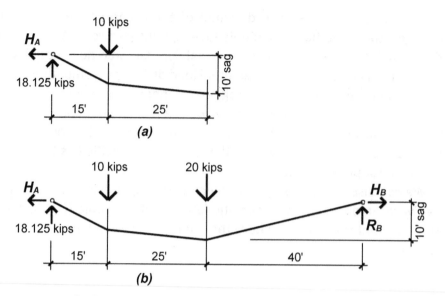

Figure 1.25: Free-body diagram cut at the sag point for Example 1.3

3. Having determined the sag point, we cut an FBD at that point (Figure 1.25*a*) and proceed as in the example of the three-hinged arch, taking moments about the sag point: $\Sigma M_D = 18.125(40) - 10(25) - H_A = 0$, from which $H_A = 47.5$ kips.

Once the location of the sag point is known, a more accurate sketch of the cable shape can be made, as shown in Figure 1.25*b*.

Then, going back to the "horizontal" equilibrium equation shown in step 1*c* that was written for the entire structure (not just the cut FBD), we get $\Sigma F_x = H_A - H_B = -47.5 + H_B = 0$, from which $H_B = 47.5$ kips. In this last equation, the value of H_A is written with a minus sign since it acts toward the left (and our sign convention has positive going to the right).

We have thus far assumed particular directions for our unknown forces — for example, that H_A acts toward the left. Doing so resulted in a positive answer of 47.5 kips, which confirmed that our guess of the force's direction was correct. Had we initially assumed that H_A acted toward the right, we would have gotten an answer of −47.5 kips, which is equally correct, but less satisfying. In other words, both ways of describing the force shown in Figure 1.26 are equivalent.

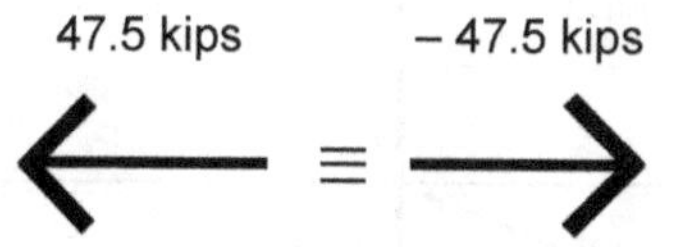

47.5 kips   − 47.5 kips

$\Longleftarrow \quad \equiv \quad \Longrightarrow$

Figure 1.26: Negative and positive signs on force arrows going in opposite directions represent equivalent loads

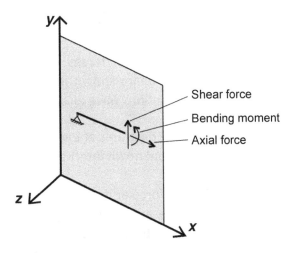

Figure 1.27: Internal shear and axial forces, and internal bending moment

INTERNAL FORCES AND MOMENTS

Finding internal forces and moments is no different than finding reactions; one need only cut an FBD at the cross section where the internal forces and moments are to be computed (after having found any unknown reactions that occur within the diagram). At any cut in a rigid element of a plane structure, two perpendicular forces and one moment are potentially present. These internal forces and moments have names, depending on their orientation relative to the axis of the structural element where the cut is made (Figure 1.27). The force parallel to the axis of the member is called an *axial force*; the force perpendicular to the member is called a *shear force*; the moment about an axis perpendicular to the structure's plane is called a *bending moment*.

In a three-dimensional environment with *x*-, *y*-, and *z*-axes as shown in Figure 1.27, three additional forces and moments may be present: another shear force (along the *z*-axis) and two other moments, one about the *y*-axis and one about the *x*-axis. Moments about the *y*-axis cause bending (but bending perpendicular to the two-dimensional plane); moments about the *x*-axis cause twisting or torsion. These types of three-dimensional structural behaviors are beyond the scope of this discussion.

Internal shear forces and bending moments in beams

Where the only external forces acting on beams are perpendicular to a simply supported beam's longitudinal axis, no axial forces can be present. The following examples show how internal shear forces and bending moments can be computed along the length of the beam.

Example 1.4 Find internal shear and bending moment for simply supported beam with "point" loads

Problem definition. Find internal shear forces and bending moments at key points along the length of the beam shown in Figure 1.28, i.e., under each external load and reaction. Reactions have already been determined.

Solution overview. Cut free-body diagrams at each external load; use equations of equilibrium to compute the unknown internal forces and moments at those cut points.

1. To find the internal shear force and bending moment at point A, first cut a free-body diagram there, as shown in Figure 1.29.

    Using the equation of vertical equilibrium, $\Sigma F_y = 5 - V_A = 0$, from which the internal shear force $V_A = 5$ kips (downward).

    Moment equilibrium is used to confirm that the internal moment at the hinge is zero: $\Sigma M_A = M_A = 0$. The two forces present (5 kips and $V_A = 5$ kips) do not need to be included in this equation of moment equilibrium since their moment arms are equal to zero. The potential internal moment, M_A, is entered into the moment equilibrium equation as it is (without being multiplied by a moment arm) since it is already, by definition, a moment.

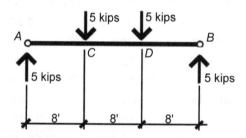

Figure 1.28: Load diagram for Example 1.4

Figure 1.29: Free-body diagram cut at left reaction for Example 1.4

2. Shear forces must be computed on "both sides" of the external load at point C; the fact that this results in two different values for shear at this point is not a paradox: it simply reflects the discontinuity in the value of shear caused by the presence of a concentrated load. In fact, a truly concentrated load acting over an area of zero is impossible, since it would result in an infinitely high stress at the point of application; all concentrated loads are really distributed loads over small areas. However, there is only one value for bending moment at point C, whether or not the external load is included in the FBD. In other words, unlike shear force, there is no discontinuity in moment resulting from a concentrated load.

   a. Find internal shear force and bending moment at point C, just to the left of the external load, by cutting an FBD at that point as shown in Figure 1.30a. Using the equation of vertical equilibrium: $\Sigma F_y = 5 - V_C = 0$, from which the internal shear force $V_C = 5$ kips (downward). Using the equation of moment equilibrium, $\Sigma M_C = 5(8) - M_C = 0$, from which $M_C = 40$ ft-kips (counterclockwise).

   b. Find internal shear force and bending moment at point C, just to the right of the external load by cutting a FBD at that point, as shown in Figure 1.30b. Using the equation of vertical equilibrium: $\Sigma F_y = 5 - 5 - V_C = 0$, from which the internal shear force $V_C = 0$ kips. Using the equation of moment equilibrium, $\Sigma M_C = 5(8) - M_C = 0$, from which $M_C = 40$ ft-kips (counterclockwise), as before.

3. Find shear and moment at point D.

   a. Find internal shear force and bending moment at point D, just to the left of the external load by cutting an FBD at that point, as

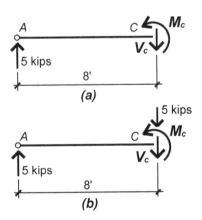

Figure 1.30: Free-body diagram for Example 1.4 *(a)* cut just to the left of the external load at point C and *(b)* just to the right of the load

shown in Figure 1.31a. Using the equation of vertical equilibrium: $\Sigma F_y = 5 - 5 - V_D = 0$, from which the internal shear force $V_D = 0$ kips. Using the equation of moment equilibrium, $\Sigma M_D = 5(16) - 5(8) - M_D = 0$, from which $M_D = 40$ ft-kips (counterclockwise).

b. Find internal shear force and bending moment at point D, just to the right of the external load by cutting an FBD at that point, as shown in Figure 1.31b. Using the equation of vertical equilibrium, $\Sigma F_y = 5 - 5 - 5 - V_D = 0$, from which the internal shear force $V_D = -5$ kips (downward), which is equivalent to 5 kips (upward). Using the equation of moment equilibrium, $\Sigma M_D = 5(16) - 5(8) - M_D = 0$, from which $M_D = 40$ ft-kips (counterclockwise), as before.

4. Find shear and moment at point B by cutting a free-body diagram just to the left of the reaction at point B, as shown in Figure 1.32. Using the equation of vertical equilibrium, $\Sigma F_y = 5 - 5 - 5 - V_B = 0$, from which the internal shear force $V_B = -5$ kips (downward), which is equivalent to 5 kips (upward).

Moment equilibrium is used to confirm that the internal moment at the hinge is zero: $\Sigma M_B = 5(24) - 5(16) - 5(8) - M_B = 0$, from which $M_B = 0$. The internal shear force, V_B, does not need to be included in this equation

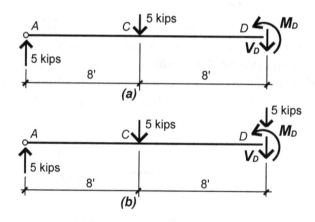

Figure 1.31: Free-body diagram for Example 1.4 *(a)* cut just to the left of the external load at point *D* and *(b)* just to the right of the load

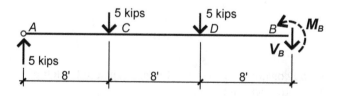

Figure 1.32: Free-body diagram cut just to the left of the reaction at point *B* for Example 1.4

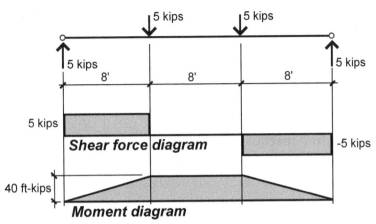

Figure 1.33: Load, shear, and moment diagrams for Example 1.4

of moment equilibrium since its moment arm is equal to zero.

The forces and moments can be graphically displayed as shown in Figure 1.33, by connecting the points found earlier.

Some important characteristics of internal shear forces and bending moments may now be summarized: (1) Internal axial forces are always zero in a horizontally oriented simply supported beam with only vertical loads. (2) Moments at hinges at the ends of structural members are zero. Only when a continuous member passes over a hinge can the moment at a hinge be nonzero. (3) A shear force acting downward on the right side of an FBD is arbitrarily called "positive"; a bending moment acting counterclockwise on the right side of an FBD is arbitrarily called "positive." Positive bending corresponds to "tension" on the bottom and "compression" on the top of a horizontal structural element.

General strategy for finding internal shear forces and bending moments

Shear and moment diagrams can also be drawn by noting the following rules: (1) At any point along the beam, the slope of the shear diagram equals the value of the load (the "infinite" slope of the shear diagram at concentrated loads can be seen as a shorthand approximation to the actual condition of the load being distributed over some finite length, rather than existing at a point). (2) Between any two points along a beam, the change in the value of shear equals the total load (between those points). (3) The slope of the moment diagram at any point equals the value of the shear force at that point. (4) The change in the value of bending moment between any two points equals the "area of the shear diagram" between those points. These rules are derived by applying the equations of equilibrium to an elemental slice of a beam, as shown in Appendix Table A-1.1.

Example 1.5 Find internal shear and bending moments for a simply supported cantilever beam with distributed loads

Problem definition. Find the distribution of internal shear forces and bending moments for the beam shown in Figure 1.34, first by using FBDs and then by applying the rules from Appendix Table A-1.1.

Solution overview. Find reactions using the equations of equilibrium; find internal shear force and bending moment at key points (at reactions and at location of zero shear).

Problem solution

1. Find the resultant of the distributed load, equal to 1 kip/ft × 25 ft = 25 kips.
2. To find reactions, first take moments about either point A or point B; we choose point B: $\Sigma M_B = R_A(20) - 25(12.5) = 0$, from which $R_A = 15.625$ kips. Next, use the equation of vertical equilibrium to find the other reaction: $\Sigma F_y = R_A + R_B - 25 = 15.625 + R_B - 25 = 0$, from which $R_B = 9.375$ kips.
3. Find shear and moment at point A.
   a. Find internal shear force and bending moment at point A, just to the left of the reaction by cutting an FBD at that point, as shown in Figure 1.35a. Using$_A$the equation of vertical equilibrium, $\Sigma F_y = -5 - V_A = 0$, from which the internal shear force, $V_A = -5$ kips (downward) or 5 kips (upward). Using the equation of moment equilibrium, $\Sigma M_A = -5(2.5) - M_A = 0$, from which $M_A = -12.5$ ft-kips (counterclockwise) or 12.5 ft-kips (clockwise).
   b. Find internal shear force and bending moment at point A, just to the right of the reaction by cutting an FBD at that point, as shown in Figure 1.35b. Using the equation of vertical equilibrium, $\Sigma F_y = 15.625 - 5 - V_A = 0$, from which the internal shear force $V_A = 10.625$ kips (downward). Using the equation of moment equilibrium, $\Sigma M_A = -5(2.5) - M_A = 0$, from which $M_A = -12.5$ ft-kips

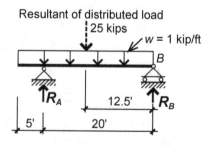

Figure 1.34: Load diagram for Example 1.5

(counterclockwise) or 12.5 ft-kips (clockwise), as before.

    The moment at point A is not zero, even though there is a hinge at that point. The reason is that the beam itself is continuous over the hinge. This continuity is essential for the stability of the cantilevered portion of the beam.

4. Find shear and moment at point B by cutting a free-body diagram just to the left of the reaction at point B, as shown in Figure 1.36. Using the equation of vertical equilibrium, $\Sigma F_y = 15.625 - 25 - V_B = 0$, from which the internal shear force $V_B = -9.375$ kips (downward), which is equivalent to 9.375 kips (upward). Moment equilibrium is used to confirm that the internal moment at the hinge is zero: $\Sigma M_B = 15.625(20) - 25(12.5) + M_B = 0$, from which $M_B = 0$. The internal shear force, V_B, does not need to be included in this equation of moment equilibrium since its moment arm is equal to zero.

5. The internal shear forces can be graphically displayed as shown in Figure 1.37, by connecting the points found earlier. The slope of the shear dia-

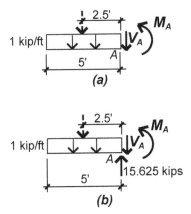

Figure 1.35: Free-body diagram for Example 1.5 *(a)* cut just to the left of the reaction at point A; and *(b)* just to the right of the reaction

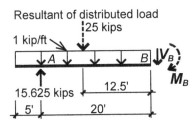

Figure 1.36: Free-body diagram cut just to the left of the reaction at point B for Example 1.5

gram at any point equals the value of the load; since the load is uniformly distributed, or constant, the slope of the shear diagram is also constant.

The bending moment cannot be adequately diagrammed until one more point is determined and analyzed: the point somewhere between the two reactions where the shear is zero. Since the slope of the moment diagram at any point equals the value of the shear force, a change from positive to negative shear indicates at least a "local" minimum or maximum moment (Figure 1.38).

This key point, labeled C in Figure 1.39, can be located by dividing the value of shear just to the right of the reaction at point A by the distributed load: the distance of point C from point A, then, is $x = 10.625/1.0 = 10.625$ ft.

The length, x, can also be found using similar triangles: $x/10.625 = 20/20$. Solving for x, we get the same value as earlier: $x = 10.625$ ft.

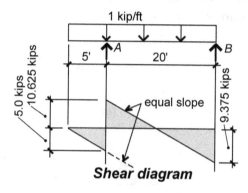

Figure 1.37: Load and shear diagrams for Example 1.5

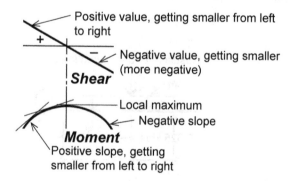

Figure 1.38: Relationship between value of shear diagram and slope of moment diagram

The moment at this point can be found by cutting an FBD at point *C*, as shown in Figure 1.40, and applying the equation of moment equilibrium: ΣM_C = 15.625(10.625) − 15.625(7.8125) − M_C = 0, from which M_C = 43.9 ft-kips (counterclockwise).

6. Alternatively, shear and moment diagrams may be drawn based on the rules listed in Appendix Table A-1.1, and illustrated in Figure 1.41. The critical points of the shear diagram are derived from the load diagram based on Rule 2: the "areas" of the load diagram (with concentrated loads or reactions counting as areas *b* and *d*) between any two points equal the change in shear between those points. These "area" values are summarized in the box between the load and shear diagrams. Connecting the points established using Rule 2 is facilitated by reference to Rule 1: the slope of the shear diagram equals the value of the load at that point. Therefore, where the load diagram is "flat" (i.e., has constant value), the shear diagram has constant slope represented by a straight line that has positive slope for positive values of load, and negative slope corresponding to negative values of load. Since almost all distributed loads are downward-acting (negative value), shear diagrams often have

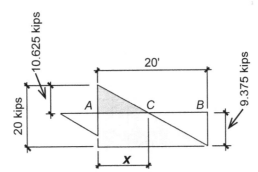

Figure 1.39: Shear diagram for Example 1.5, showing distance from reaction at point *A* to the point where the shear diagram crosses the baseline, going from positive to negative value

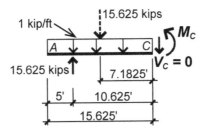

Figure 1.40: Free-body diagram for Example 1.5, cut at the point of zero shear (where the shear diagram crosses the baseline, going from positive to negative value)

the characteristic pattern of negative slope shown in Figure 1.41.

Once the shear diagram has been completed, and any critical lengths have been found (see step 5), the moment diagram can be drawn based on Rules 3 and 4 of Appendix Table A-1.1. Critical moments are first found by examining the "areas" under the shear diagram, as described in Rule 4 of Appendix Table A-1.1. These "areas" — actually forces times distances, or moments — are shown in the box between the shear and moment diagrams in Figure 1.41 and represent the change in moment between the two points bracketed by the shear diagram areas — not the value of the moments themselves. For example, the first "area e" of −12.5 ft-kips is added to the initial moment of zero at the free end of the cantilever, so that the actual moment at point A is 0 + −12.5 = −12.5 ft-kips. The maximum moment (where the shear is zero), is found by adding "area f"

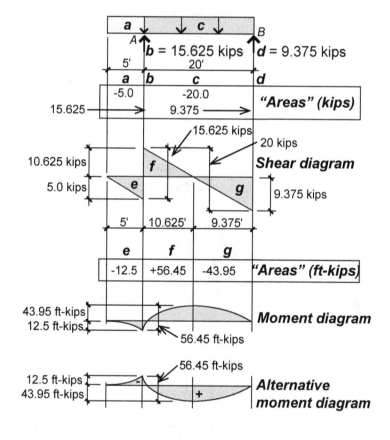

Figure 1.41: Load, shear, and moment diagrams for Example 1.5, using load diagram "areas" to find shear values, and shear diagram "areas" to find moment values

to the moment at point *A*: 56.45 + −12.5 = 43.95 ft-kips, as shown in Figure 1.41. Finally, slopes of the moment diagram curve can be determined based on Rule 3 of Appendix Table A-1.1: the slope of the moment diagram is equal to the value of the shear force at any point, as illustrated in Figure 1.38.

In drawing the moment diagram, it is important to emphasize the following: (1) The area under the shear diagram between any two points corresponds, not to the value of the moment, but to the change in moment between those two points. Therefore, the triangular shear diagram area, *f*, of 56.45 ft-kips in the Example 1.5 does not show up as a moment anywhere in the beam; in fact, the maximum moment turns out to be 43.95 ft-kips. (2) The particular curvature of the moment diagram can be found by relating the slope of the curve to the changing values of the shear diagram. (3) The moment and shear diagrams are created with respect to the actual distribution of loads on the beam, not the resultants of those loads, which may have been used in the calculation of reactions. The location of the maximum moment, therefore, has nothing to do with the location of any resultant load but occurs at the point of zero shear. (4) Moment diagrams can also be drawn in an alternate form, as shown at the bottom of Figure 1.41, by reversing the positions of negative and positive values. This form has the benefit of aligning the shape of the moment diagram more closely with the deflected shape of the beam (although it still remains significantly different from the deflected shape), at the expense of being mathematically inconsistent. (5) Finally, it may be important in some cases to account for both positive and negative moments, and not just the maximum moment. In this example, the maximum positive moment is 43.95 ft-kips, while the maximum negative moment is 12.5 ft-kips.

Internal axial forces in trusses, arches, and cables

There is a class of determinate structures that cannot sustain internal shear forces or bending moments, either because their component elements are pinned together or because they are inherently flexible. We will examine three types of these axial-force structures. Trusses are made from individual elements organized in a triangular pattern and assumed to be pinned at the joints so that they may be analyzed using only equations of equilibrium. Reactions of trusses are found just like the reactions of beams, while the reactions of three-hinged arches and cables — the other two axial-force structures already examined — require special treatment. In general, the axial forces within trusses, three-hinged arches, and cables are found using the three equations of equilibrium. The following examples illustrate specific techniques and strategies.

Example 1.6 Find internal axial forces in a truss (section method)

Problem definition. Find the internal axial forces in truss bars *C-F*, *C-E*, and *D-E* for the truss shown in Figure 1.42. Assume pinned joints, as shown.

Solution overview. Find reactions; then, using the so-called section method, cut a free-body diagram through the bars for which internal forces are being computed. As there are only three equations of equilibrium, no more than three bars may be cut (resulting in three unknown forces); use equations of equilibrium to solve for the unknown forces.

Problem solution
1. *Find reactions:* by symmetry, $R_A = R_B = (10 + 10 + 10)/2 = 15$ kips. Alternatively, one could take moments about point *A* or *B*, solve for the unknown reaction, and then use the equation of vertical equilibrium to find the other unknown reaction.
2. Cut a free-body diagram through the bars being evaluated (cutting through no more than three bars) as shown in Figure 1.43. Bar forces are labeled according to the nodes that are at either end of their bars, so, for example, F_{CF} is the force between nodes *C* and *F*.
   a. Show unknown axial forces as tension forces; a negative result indicates that the bar is actually in compression. Tension means that

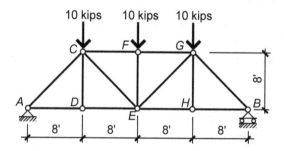

Figure 1.42: Loading diagram for, and geometry of, truss, for Example 1.6

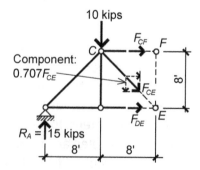

Figure 1.43: Free-body diagram cut through bars based on the section method, for Example 1.6

the force is shown "pulling" on the bar or node within the free-body diagram.

b. Use equilibrium equations, chosen strategically, to solve for unknown bar forces. To find F_{CF}: $\Sigma M_E = 15(16) - 10(8) + F_{CF}(8) = 0$; solving for the unknown bar force, we get $F_{CF} = -20\,\text{k}$ (compression).

c. To find F_{DE}: $\Sigma M_C = 15(8) - F_{DE}(8) = 0$; solving for the unknown bar force, we get $F_{DE} = 15\text{k}$ (tension).

d. Finally, to find F_{CE}: find force "components" of inclined internal axial force F_{CE}. The components can be found using principles of trigonometry, based on the geometry of the triangle determined by the 8 ft × 8 ft truss panels. For example, the vertical (or horizontal) component equals $F_{CE} \times \sin 45° = 0.707 F_{CE}$. We then use the equation of vertical equilibrium: $\Sigma F_y = 15 - 10 - 0.707 F_{CE} = 0$; solving for the unknown bar force, we get $F_{CE} = 7.07$ kips (tension).

The assumption that only axial forces exist within a truss is valid when the following conditions are met: (1) all bar joints are "pinned" (hinged), and (2) external loads and reactions are placed only at the joints or nodes. Under these circumstances, no internal shear forces or bending moments are possible. In practice, modern trusses are rarely pinned at each joint; nevertheless, the assumption is often used for preliminary design since it facilitates the calculation of internal forces. What is more, actual bar forces in indeterminate trusses (i.e., where the members are continuous rather than pinned) are often reasonably close to the approximate results obtained by assuming pinned joints.

Example 1.7 Find internal axial forces in a three-hinged arch

Problem definition. Find the internal axial force in bar *AC* of the three-hinged arch analyzed in Example 1.2.

Solution overview. Cut a free-body diagram through the bar in question, as shown in Figure 1.44*a*; label the unknown bar force as if in tension; use the

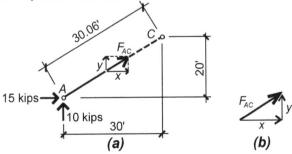

Figure 1.44: Internal bar force for Example 1.7 shown *(a)* in free-body diagram and *(b)* as a "force" triangle with components *x* and *y*

equations of equilibrium to solve for the unknown force.

Problem Solution

1. Because the far force, F_{AC}, is inclined, it is convenient to draw and label its horizontal and vertical component forces, x and y. Using the equations of vertical and horizontal equilibrium, we can find these component forces directly: $\Sigma F_y = 10 + y = 0$, from which $y = -10$ kips; $\Sigma F_x = 15 + x = 0$, from which $x = -15$ kips. In both cases, the negative sign indicates that our initial assumption of tension was incorrect; the bar force is actually in compression, as one would expect in such an arch.

2. To find the actual bar force, F_{AC}, the most direct approach is to use the Pythagorean theorem, with the unknown force being the hypotenuse of a right triangle, as shown in Figure 1.44b. Therefore, $F_{AC} = \sqrt{x^2 + y^2} = \sqrt{15^2 + 10^2} = 8.03$ kips. The signs of the forces are omitted in this calculation.

Example 1.8 Find internal axial forces in a cable

Problem definition. Find the internal axial force in segment AC of the cable analyzed in Example 1.3.

Solution overview. Cut a free-body diagram through the segment in question, as shown in Figure 1.45; label unknown cable force as if in tension; use the equations of equilibrium to solve for the unknown force.

Problem solution

1. Because the cable force, F_{AC}, is inclined, it is convenient to draw and label its horizontal and vertical component forces, x and y. Using the equations of vertical and horizontal equilibrium, we can find these component forces directly: $\Sigma F_y = 18.125 - y = 0$, from which $y = 18.125$ kips; $\Sigma F_x = -47.5 + x = 0$, from which $x = 47.5$ kips. In both cases, the positive

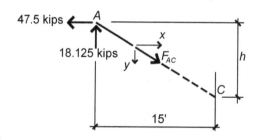

Figure 1.45: Bar force for Example 1.8 shown in free-body diagram with components x and y

sign indicates that our initial assumption of tension was correct, as one would expect in any cable structure.

2. To find the actual cable force, F_{AC}, the most direct approach is to use the Pythagorean theorem, with the unknown force being the hypotenuse of a right triangle. Therefore, $F_{AC} = \sqrt{x^2 + y^2} = \sqrt{47.5^2 + 18.125^2} = 50.84$ kips. The signs of the forces are omitted in this calculation.

3. Since the cable is flexible, the height, h, is initially unknown and, in fact, will change if the loads are changed. To find h, we can use the fact that the "force triangle" and "geometry triangle" are similar; therefore, the ratio of their sides must be equal: $h/15 = y/x = 18.125/47.5$, from which $h = 5.72$ ft. Because the height will change if the loads change, the cable is an unstable structure.

INDETERMINATE STRUCTURES

Where there are more reactions, or constraints, than there are equations of equilibrium, a structure is said to be statically indeterminate or redundant. Each added constraint adds one degree of indeterminacy or redundancy to the structure, making it that much more difficult to solve mathematically. To understand the basis of the mathematical solution to indeterminate structures, we will examine a simply supported beam with a single concentrated load that has been made 1-degree redundant (indeterminate) by adding a hanger at midspan: the structure now has four unknown reactions (constraints), and only three equations of equilibrium are available, as shown in Figure 1.46.

The key to the solution is to find an additional equation that includes one or more of the structure's constraint variables; that equation will not be concerned with equilibrium, but rather with the compatibility of structural deformations or deflections. Looking at the simply supported beam and the tension hanger separately, it is possible to write equations relating the loads acting

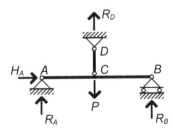

Figure 1.46: Load diagram for a simply supported beam with an added hanger at midspan

on them to their deflection. For now, we will simply note that $\Delta_1 = P_1 S_1$, and $\Delta_2 = P_2 S_2$ as shown in Figure 1.47, where Δ_1 and Δ_2 are the deflections of the beam and hanger, respectively; P_1 and P_2 are the loads assumed to act separately on the beam and hanger; and S_1 and S_2 are deflection constants that include the length or span of the elements as well as their stiffness (i.e., their resistance to deformation).

These deflections, calculated separately for the beam and hanger, must actually be equal in the real structure, and the loads P_1 and P_2 that correspond to these equal deflections are actually only the parts of the total load, P, that the beam and hanger separately resist. In other words, $\Delta_1 = \Delta_2$; and P_1 and $P_2 = P$. This can be rewritten as follows:

$$P_1 S_1 = P_2 S_2 \qquad (1.2)$$

$$P_1 = P - P_2 \qquad (1.3)$$

Solving Equation 1.2 for P_1, and substituting the result into Equation 1.3, we get:

$$\frac{P_2 S_2}{S_1} = P - P_2 \qquad (1.4)$$

Solving for P_2, we get:

$$P_2 = \frac{P}{S_1/S_2 + 1} \qquad (1.5)$$

Since the load P and coefficients S_1 and S_2 are all known, the force P_2 can be determined from Equation 1.5. Then, from Figure 1.47b, it can be seen that the vertical reaction, $R_D = P_2$. With this "fourth" reaction solved, the other vertical reactions at A and B can easily be determined using the equations of equilibrium.

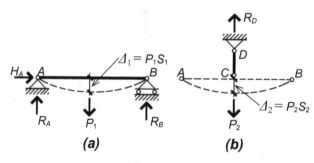

Figure 1.47: Deflection diagrams for the two components of the structure shown in Figure 1.46: *(a)* a simply-supported beam with a concentrated load, P_1, and *(b)* a tension hanger with load P_2

Equation 1.5 also clarifies the relationship between the element load-deformation constants, represented by S_1 and S_2, and the overall behavior of the structure. For example, if the constants are equal, it can be seen that $P_2 = P/2$; i.e., half the load is resisted by the hanger and half by the beam. On the other hand, if S_1 is small compared to S_2 (i.e., if the hanger is more effective in resisting deformation than the beam), then P_2 approaches the value of P, and the hanger begins to resist virtually all of the total load, with the beam's share approaching zero. This is of crucial importance in understanding the behavior of indeterminate structures: loads tend to follow the path of greatest stiffness, or, put another way, loads follow various competing load paths in proportion to the stiffness of those paths. In these formulations, "stiffness" is used as shorthand for the load-deformation relationship, which includes both the actual element stiffness (involving only material and cross-sectional properties) as well as element length or span.

For highly redundant structures, a greater number of equations, based on compatibility of deformations, needs to be solved simultaneously. While this becomes unwieldy if done by hand, structural analysis software has been developed to solve such problems: the designer need only indicate the geometry of the structure (including lengths and spans), the nature of each constraint (hinged, fixed, etc.), and the relative stiffness of each element. This last requirement presents a bit of a dilemma, since relative member stiffnesses must be assumed before the structure can be designed. The stiffnesses assumed for the structure determine how the structure will respond to its loads, unlike determinate structures, whose internal forces and moments are independent of member cross sections and material properties. For this reason, experience, trial and error, or a bit of both are crucial in the design of indeterminate structures.

Once internal forces and moments have been determined, however, the same strategies for the design of structural elements outlined in this book can be used, whether the structure is statically determinate or indeterminate.

MATERIAL PROPERTIES

Wood, steel and concrete are actually extraordinarily complex materials. Of the three, wood was used first as a structural material, and some of the otherwise inscrutable vocabulary of structural analysis derives from this fact: the notion of an "outer fiber" of a cross section, or even the concept of "horizontal shear" are rooted in the particular material structure of wood.

Only certain material properties are of interest to us here — specifically, those that have some bearing on the structural behavior of the elements under consideration. The most obvious, and important, structural properties are those relating force to deformation, or stress to strain. Knowing how a material sample contracts or elongates as it is stressed up to failure provides a crucial model for its performance in an actual structure. Not only is its ultimate stress (or strength) indicated, but also a measure of its resistance to strain (modulus of elasticity), its linear (and presumably elastic) and/or nonlinear (plastic) behavior, and its ability to absorb energy without fracturing (ductility).

Ductility is important in a structural member because it allows concentrations of high stress to be absorbed and redistributed without causing sudden, catastrophic failure. Ductile failures are preferred to brittle failures, since the large strains possible with ductile materials give warning of collapse in advance of the actual failure. Glass, a non-ductile (i.e., brittle) material, is generally unsuitable for use as a structural element, in spite of its high strength, because it is unable to absorb large amounts of energy, and could fail catastrophically as a result of local stress concentrations.

A linear relationship between stress and strain is an indicator of elastic behavior — the return of a material to its original shape after being stressed and then unstressed. Most structural materials are expected to behave elastically under normal "service" loads; but plastic behavior, characterized by permanent deformations, needs to be considered when ultimate, or failure, loads are being computed. Typical stress-strain curves for wood, steel and concrete are shown in Figure 1.48. The modulus of elasticity, E, is the slope of the curve — i.e., the change in stress, σ, divided by the change in strain, ε. For linear materials:

$$E = \sigma/\varepsilon \qquad\qquad (1.6)$$

The most striking aspect of these stress-strain curves shown in Figure 1.48 is the incredibly high strength and modulus of elasticity (indicated by the slope of the curve) of steel relative to concrete and wood. Of equal importance is the information about the strength and ductility of the three materials in tension versus compression. For example, structural carbon steel, along with its high strength and modulus of elasticity, can be strained to a value 60 times greater than shown in Figure 1.48 in both tension and compression, indicating a high degree of ductility. Concrete, on the other hand, has very little strength in tension, and fails in a brittle (nonductile) manner in both tension and compression. Wood has high tensile strength compared to concrete, but also fails in a brittle manner when stressed in tension; in compression, however, wood shows ductile behavior.

Aside from this stress-strain data, material properties can also be affected by environmental conditions, manufacturing processes, or the way in which loads are applied. These material-dependent responses are discussed in the chapters that follow.

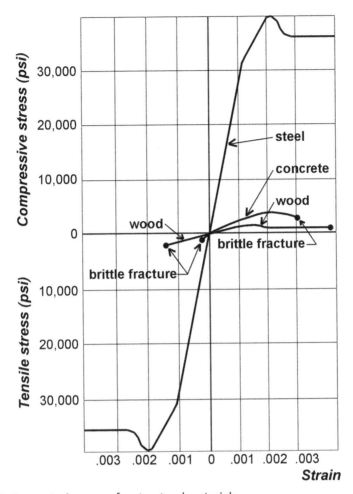

Figure 1.48: Stress-strain curves for structural materials

Sustainability

Sustainability is a notoriously inadequate term, as its use in both casual speech as well as in green building guidelines has no consistent relationship to the ongoing maintenance (or rather, degradation) of human life and natural resources on planet Earth. Nevertheless, facts relating to at least one aspect of global environmental welfare — the production of greenhouse (global warming) gases — can be established for wood, steel, and concrete.

A tree, as is well known, extracts CO_2 from the atmosphere as part of the photosynthesis process; carbon — formerly in the atmosphere — is sequestered in the material of the tree itself until the wood is left to decay, at which time it releases the carbon back into the atmosphere in the form of CO_2. To the extent that trees are "farmed" on plantations, i.e., planted and harvested like any other agricultural crop, there is neither a net loss nor gain in greenhouse gases from the material itself. There are, however, greenhouse gases emitted from the cutting, transportation, and especially the drying of wood in kilns. Other greenhouse gases, e.g., formaldehyde, are associated with the glues used in various engineered wood products such as plywood. It is difficult, however, to find data about the overall impact of forest products on global warming.

Information is more readily available for steel and concrete, as both of these materials leave a significant mark on greenhouse gas emissions. The manufacture of steel releases CO_2 at an average rate of 1.8 tonnes per tonne of steel produced (where 1 metric ton, or *tonne*, equals 1000 kilograms, which in turn equals 2205 lb or about 1.1 ton). This corresponds to about 6.7% of overall global CO_2 emissions generated by humans (and results from about 1.6 billion tonnes of steel being produced annually). Much of this CO_2 is due to the persistence of less-efficient steel production technology in many parts of the world: old-fashioned and inefficient *open hearth furnaces* are still in use, for example, in Russia and Ukraine, while other inefficient technologies have been developed or persist because they exploit regionally available materials or expertise. In the U.S., steel is produced in *electric arc furnaces* (having the least global warming impact) or *basic oxygen furnaces* (with the next least global warming impact).

Concrete's large contribution to global warming comes about for two reasons. First, more concrete is consumed than any other material on earth, discounting water. Second, it turns out that heating limestone to obtain calcium — a necessary ingredient in portland cement — releases quite a bit of CO_2, as does the burning of fossil fuels to create the heat needed to drive this process of *calcination*. While "only" 1 tonne of CO_2 is produced for every tonne of cement (compared with 1.8 tonnes of CO_2 for every tonne of steel), the 2.35 billion tonnes of concrete produced annually result in about 5% of the world's human-generated CO_2. These statistics are, of course, subject to change, and reflect approximate values from the years 2010–2014.

STRENGTH OF MATERIALS

The magnitude of internal forces and bending moments do not, by themselves, give any indication as to whether a particular structural element is safe or unsafe. Instead, the load or moment that an element can safely resist can only be determined when information about the element's cross section and material properties is considered: clearly, a large cross section is stronger than a small one. But "large" in what way? The cross-sectional properties relevant to the determination of structural safety and serviceability are different for tension elements, columns, and beams and are, therefore, discussed more fully in their appropriate context. What follows is a brief overview and summary of the major cross-section properties encountered in structural analysis and design, followed by a discussion of tension, compression, and bending.

Area

Cross-sectional areas are easily determined: for rectangles, the area $A = B \times H$ (Figure 1.49a) and for circles, $A = \pi R^2$ (Figure 1.49c). What may not be as immediately clear is that the I-shaped cross section (Figure 1.49b) has an area, $A = (B \times H) - (b \times h)$, and the circular ring (Figure 1.49d) has an area, $A = \pi R^2 - \pi r^2$, where R is the outer and r is the inner radius.

Moment of inertia

The moment of inertia, I_x, is defined as the sum of all elemental areas above or below the centroid (x-axis) of the cross section multiplied by the square of the distance from each of the individual elemental centroids to the centroid of the cross section as a whole, or

$$I_x = \int_{-H/2}^{H/2} y^2 dA \qquad (1.7)$$

where y is the distance from each elemental area (the elemental areas being $dA = width \times dy$) to the centroid of the cross section, while $H/2$ and $-H/2$ represent the limits over which the integral is taken for the rectangle and I-shaped section shown in Figure 1.49 (the same equation holds for the circu-lar sections as well, except with the integral taken from $R/2$ to $-R/2$).

This property is useful in understanding the stiffness of a cross section when bent. It can be seen that placing a good deal of the cross-sectional material away from the centroid — as in the I-shaped section or, to a lesser extent, in the circular ring — increases the moment of inertia, and therefore the stiffness, since more "area" is multiplied by the square of a greater distance from the centroidal axis. Equation 1.7 can be solved as follows for rectangular and circular shapes:

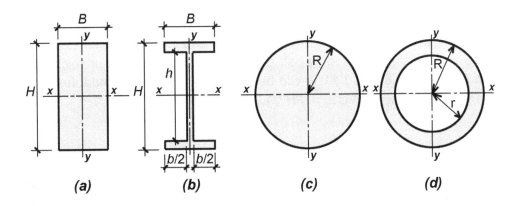

(a)   (b)   (c)   (d)

Figure 1.49: Cross sections typically encountered as structural elements include (a) rectangles, (b) I-shaped sections, (c) circles, and (d) circular rings

$$I_x = \frac{BH^3}{12} \text{ (rectangles)}; \quad I_x = \frac{\pi R^4}{4} \text{ (circles)} \quad\quad (1.8)$$

Moments of inertia for the I-shaped section and circular ring can be easily found by subtracting the smaller rectangle (or circle) from the larger one: for the I-shaped section, $I_x = BH^3/12 - bh^3/12$; for the circular ring, $I_x = \pi R^4/4 - \pi r^4/4$.

For moments of inertia taken about the y-axis, the equations for rectangles and circles are easily modified:

$$I_y = \frac{HB^3}{12} \text{ (rectangles)}; \quad I_y = \frac{\pi R^4}{4} \text{ (circles)} \quad\quad (1.9)$$

Moments of inertia for circular rings (Figure 1.49d) are determined as before: by subtracting the moment of inertia of the smaller from that of the larger circle. For the I-shaped section, however, it is not possible to simply subtract the smaller rectangles from the larger, as was done when computing the moment of inertia about the x-axis, since the centroids of the various parts being subtracted do not coincide. Instead, one must add the three moments of inertia of the two flanges and web, as shown in Figure 1.50, each taken about the y-axis:

$$I_y = \frac{t_f B^3}{12} + \frac{h t_w^3}{12} + \frac{t_f B^3}{12} \quad\quad (1.10)$$

Section modulus

The elastic section modulus, S_x, is a single parameter that measures a cross section's strength in bending. For symmetrical sections, such as those shown in Figures 1.49a and 1.49b:

$$S_x = \frac{I_x}{(H/2)} \quad\quad (1.11)$$

For the circular shapes, $S_x = I_x/R$ (Figures 1.49c and 1.49d). In each case, the moment of inertia is divided by half the cross-sectional height, or thickness. From Equations 1.8 and 1.11, it can be seen that the section modulus for a rectangular cross section is $S_x = (BH^3/12)/(H/2) = BH^2/6$.

Plastic section modulus

The plastic section modulus, Z_x, is used to determine the limit state of steel beams, defined as the point when the entire cross section has yielded. This property is unique to steel, since neither of the other materials we are considering (wood and reinforced concrete) has the necessary ductility to reach this state. Unlike the elastic section modulus, S_x, the plastic section modulus has no fixed relationship to the moment of inertia of the cross section. Rather, it is defined as the sum of all elemental areas above or below the centroid (x-axis) of the cross section multiplied by the distance from each of the individual elemental centroids to the centroid of the cross section as a whole. The plastic section modulus for a rectangular cross section can be determined by multiplying each section half (e.g., the shaded area shown in Figure 1.51) by the distance from its centroid to the centroid for the whole section: $Z_x = B(H/2)(H/4) + B(H/2)(H/4) = BH^2/4$.

Radius of gyration

The radius of gyration of a cross section, r or ρ, is a distance — but one without any obvious physical meaning. It measures the cross section's resistance to buckling, when compressed, and is defined as follows:

$$r_x = \sqrt{\frac{I_x}{A}} \qquad (1.12)$$

where I_x is the moment of inertia about the x-axis, and A is the cross-sectional area. Since buckling might occur about either of the cross-sectional axes, it is the cross section's smaller radius of gyration, taken about the y-axis (the weaker axis), that is often critical:

$$r_y = \sqrt{\frac{I_y}{A}} \qquad (1.13)$$

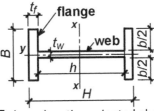

Figure 1.50: Dimensions of an I-shaped section oriented about its y-axis, for the calculation of moment of inertia

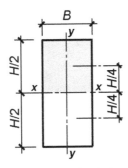

Figure 1.51: Rectangular cross section showing shaded area and distance from centroid of shaded area to centroid of the whole cross section, for calculation of plastic section modulus, Z_x

From Equation 1.9, the moment of inertia about the y-axis used to compute the minimum radius of gyration for a rectangular cross section is $I_y = BH^3/12$.

Tension elements

Elements subjected to tension provide us with the simplest mathematical model relating internal force and stress:

$$\text{axial stress} = \frac{\text{force}}{\text{area}} \qquad (1.14)$$

This equation is simple and straightforward because it corresponds to the simplest pattern of strain that can develop within the cross section of a structural element. As shown in Figure 1.52, this strain is assumed to be uniformly distributed across the entire cross section; for this reason, the stress can be defined as force per unit area. Classical "strength of materials" texts use the symbol, σ, for axial stress, so that we get:

$$\sigma = \frac{P}{A} \qquad (1.15)$$

where P is the internal force at a cross section with area, A. By axial stress, we mean stress "acting" parallel to the longitudinal axis of the structural element, or stress causing the element to strain in the direction of its longitudinal axis. Tension is an axial stress causing elongation; compression is an axial

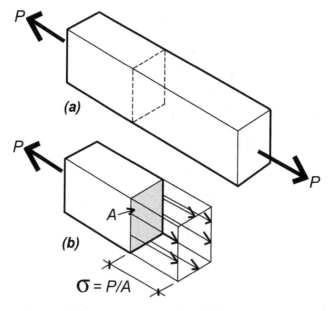

Figure 1.52: Illustrations of (*a*) tension element; and (*b*) free-body diagram cut at any cross-section with area, A.

stress causing shortening or contraction.

Where bolt holes reduce the cross-sectional area of a tension element, the remaining area at the cross section, A_n, is called the net area. Failure or "rupture" of an element stressed in tension occurs at a failure surface defined by the location and quantity of such bolt holes. Where the holes are arrayed in an orthogonal grid, as shown in Figure 1.53a, the failure surface is easily determined. For staggered rows of bolts, as shown in Figure 1.53b, more than one possible failure surface may exist: the net area in each case can be determined by multiplying the net width of the section by its thickness, t. This net width is found by subtracting from the gross width, W, the sum of hole diameters, d_h, and then adding spacing-gage terms, $s^2/(4g)$, for each diagonal line in the failure surface. In these calculations, s is the spacing between bolt centerlines parallel to the direction of load, and g is the "gage," or spacing between bolt centerlines perpendicular to the direction of load.

When we discuss particular structural materials, stresses are often represented by the letter F rather than σ, and capitalized when referring to allowable, yield or ultimate stresses in timber and steel. For example, F_y refers to the yield stress of steel; F_u refers to the ultimate stress of steel (the highest stress, or "strength," of steel reached within the strain-hardening region); while F_t symbolizes allowable tensile stress in both timber and steel. Lowercase f, with appropriate subscripts, is often used to refer to the actual stress being computed. An exception to this convention occurs in reinforced concrete strength design, where the yield stress of reinforcing steel (F_y in steel design) is given a lowercase designation, f_y (as is the cylinder strength of concrete, f_c') In any case, for axial tension in steel and wood, allowable stress design requires that:

$$f_t \leq F_t \qquad\qquad (1.16)$$

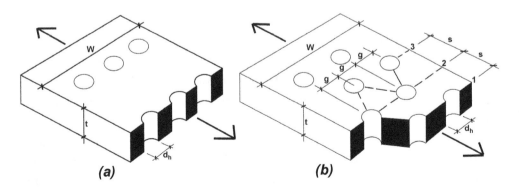

(a)   **(b)**

Figure 1.53: Net area of a cross section, shown in black, with (a) one possible failure surface when bolt holes are arrayed in orthogonal grid; and (b) multiple possible failure surfaces when bolt holes are staggered

The elongation of an element in tension can be computed based on the definition of modulus of elasticity given in Equation 1.6; since $E = \sigma/\varepsilon$, and substituting P/A for σ and (elongation)/(original length) for ε, we get:

$$E = \frac{(P \times \text{original length})}{(A \times \text{elongation})} \qquad (1.17)$$

Solving for elongation, and letting L = original length, the equation becomes:

$$\text{elongation} = \frac{PL}{AE} \qquad (1.18)$$

Example 1.9 Find elongation in tension element

Problem definition. Compute the elongation, or change in length, for a steel bar with a cross-sectional area of 4 in², 3 ft in length, with E = 29,000,000 psi, subjected to a tensile load of 10 kips.

Solution overview. Find elongation = $(PL)/(AE)$. Units must be consistent.

Problem solution
From Equation 1.18, elongation = $(PL)/(AE)$ = (10 kips × 36 in.)/(4 in² × 29,000 ksi) = 0.0031 in.

Columns

Columns are vertical elements subjected to compressive stress; nothing, however, prevents us from applying the same design and analysis methods to any compressive element, whether vertical, horizontal or inclined. Only axially-loaded compression elements (with no bending moments present) will be considered here.

Compression is similar to tension, since both types of structural action result in a uniform distribution of axial stress over a cross section taken through the element. But allowable stress in compression is often limited by the phenomenon of buckling, in which the element deforms out of its axial alignment at a stress that may be significantly lower than the stress causing compressive crushing.

To understand why an axially-loaded column will buckle rather than simply compress, consider the case of an eccentrically-loaded column, as shown in Figure 1.54. Unlike a beam whose internal bending moments are not influenced by load-induced deflections (Figure 1.55), the eccentrically-loaded column will deflect more than might be expected if only the initial moment, M_1, is considered, since the "initial deflections" increase bending moments throughout the column, in turn causing further deflection, as shown in Figure 1.54b. What the mathematician Leonard Euler (1707–1783) figured out was that these deflections increase rapidly in the vicinity of a particular ("critical") load, at which point the column is assumed to fail, and that the value of this load is independent of the initial eccentricity. In other words, even with the smallest imaginable deviation from axiality, a column is assumed to buckle at some critical load. Since no perfectly axial columns (or loads) can exist, all columns behaving elastically are assumed to buckle at the critical buckling stress derived by Euler:

$$\sigma_{cr} = \frac{\pi^2 E}{(KL/r)^2} \tag{1.19}$$

where

E = the modulus of elasticity

K = a coefficient that depends on the column's end constraints (see Appendix Table A-1.2)

L = the unbraced length of the column

r = the radius of gyration with respect to the unbraced length (sometimes given the symbol, ρ), equal to $\sqrt{I/A}$, where I is the moment of inertia and A is area of the cross section

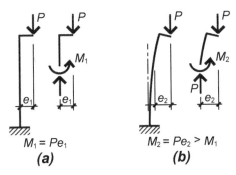

Figure 1.54: Increase of bending moment in a column due to load-induced deflection

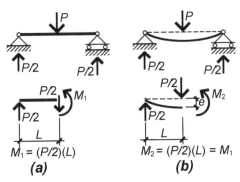

Figure 1.55: No increase of bending moment in a beam due to load-induced deflection

For the typical case in which the unbraced length is the same for both axes of the column, r (or I) is taken as the smaller of the two possible values, i.e., r_{min} (or I_{min}). The term L/r, or KL/r, is called the column's *slenderness ratio*. Although this formulation for buckling is widely used, it is actually an approximation of a more accurate equation derived by Euler which does not indicate any catastrophic buckling point at all. Instead, as may be confirmed by physically buckling a slender piece of wood or other material, the initiation of buckling (at a stress approximated by Equation 1.19) leads to a gradually increasing lateral deflection up until the point of failure, which is initiated when the stresses in the material exceed the material's strength. Certainly, the capacity of such a column is thereby reduced (compared with a hypothetical case in which the column remains perfectly straight), and Euler's approximate formula does give a conservative value for the point at which such failure occurs; however, it is incorrect to imagine the actual behavior of a compression element as failing catastrophically and suddenly at a precise "critical buckling" point.

The strength of wood and steel columns is limited in two ways: either they will crush at their maximum compressive stress, or buckle at some critical stress that is different from, and independent of, their strength in compression. Euler's equation for critical buckling stress works well for slender columns, but gives increasingly inaccurate results as the slenderness of columns decreases and the effects of crushing begin to interact with the idealized conditions from which Euler's equation was derived. Figure 1.56 shows schematically the relationship between Euler critical buckling stress, crushing strength, and test results for columns with different slenderness ratios. It can be seen that only for slender columns can the Euler curve be used as a basis for design.

Beams

Like all structural elements, beams are both stressed and subject to deformations when loaded. Both of these considerations must be accounted for in the

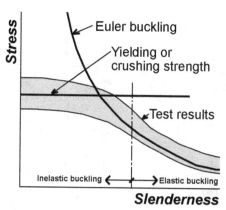

Figure 1.56: Schematic relationship between critical stress and column slenderness

design of beams.

Deflection. While the elongation or contraction of axially-loaded members along their longitudinal axes is usually of little consequence, beams may experience excessive deflection perpendicular to their longitudinal axes, making them unserviceable. Limits on deflection are based on several considerations, including minimizing vibrations, thereby improving occupant comfort; preventing cracking of ceiling materials, partitions, or cladding supported by the beams; and promoting positive drainage (for roof beams) in order to avoid ponding of water at midspan. These limits are generally expressed as a fraction of the span, L (Appendix Table A-1.3). Formulas for the calculation of maximum deflection are included in the appendices for the wood and steel chapters, while values for recommended minimum beam depth are included in the appendix for reinforced concrete. The maximum (midspan) deflection, Δ, of a uniformly loaded simple span can also be found from the equation:

$$\Delta = \frac{5wL^4}{384EI} \tag{1.20}$$

where w = distributed load (lb/in. or kips/in.); L = span (in.); E = modulus of elasticity (psi or ksi); and I = moment of inertia (in⁴). When using Equation 1.20 with L in feet, w in lb/ft or kips/ft, E in psi or ksi (compatible with load, w), and I in in⁴, as is most commonly done, multiply the expression by 12^3 to make the units consistent.

Bending stress. Beams are stressed when they bend because the action of bending causes an elongation on one side, resulting in tension, and a shortening on the other side, resulting in compression. By exaggerating the curvature of the beam as it bends, this elongation and shortening can be visualized. Exactly where the tension and compression are depends on how the beam is loaded and how it is supported.

For *simply-supported beams* with downward-acting loads (i.e., with gravity loads), the beam is stretched on the bottom (tension) and shortened on the top (compression) as shown in Figure 1.57.

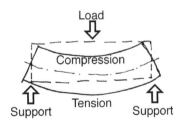

Figure 1.57: Behavior of a simply supported beam

For *cantilevered beams* fixed at one end, with downward-acting loads, the beam is stretched on the top and shortened on the bottom (Figure 1.58).

For *continuous beams* spanning over several supports, the changing curvature causes the position of tension and compression zones to reverse a number of times over the length of the beam, as illustrated in Figure 1.59.

The relative position of tension and compression within the beam's cross section is directly related to the sign of the bending moment at that cross section. As can be seen from Figure 1.60*a*, a counterclockwise moment on the

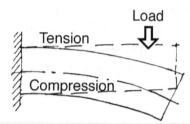

Figure 1.58: Behavior of a cantilevered beam

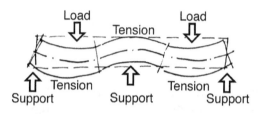

Figure 1.59: Behavior of a continuous beam

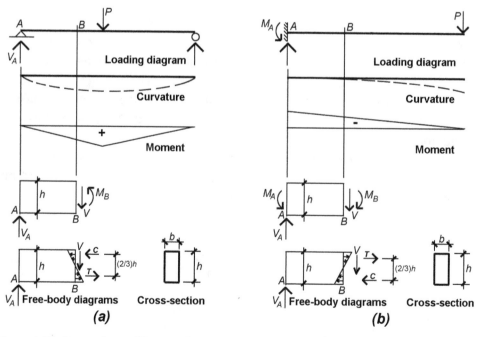

Figure 1.60: Comparison of "positive" and "negative" bending in (*a*) a simply-supported beam, and (*b*) a cantilevered beam

right side of a free-body diagram is equivalent to a distribution of bending stress with compression on the top and tension on the bottom of the beam: so-called "positive" bending (and "positive" bending moment). Figure 1.60*b* shows a free-body diagram cut through a cantilever beam with "negative" bending — i.e., tension on the top and compression on the bottom corresponding to a clockwise moment as shown. The reversing curvature of a continuous beam, such as that shown in Figure 1.59, corresponds precisely to a reversal in the sign of the bending moment. As shown in Figure 1.61, points of inflection (points where the curvature changes) always occur at points of zero moment.

Bending stresses within these beams can be computed if we assume that the stretching and shortening that take place at any cross section are linear; i.e., a straight line connecting a stretched point with a shortened point on any cross-sectional cut will accurately describe the shape of the beam throughout the entire cross section (Figure 1.62).

Three observations can be made, once this assumption is accepted: (1) maximum elongation and shortening occur at the top and bottom of the beam (the "extreme fibers"); (2) a surface exists somewhere between the extreme fibers that is neither elongated nor shortened — this "plane" is called the "neutral axis" or "neutral surface"; and (3) strain can be defined as the elongation or shortening of any portion of the beam, divided by its original (unloaded) length. Since the original length is a constant, a strain diagram has the same shape as an "elongation-shortening diagram." For materials with linear stress-strain relationships (where stress equals strain times a constant

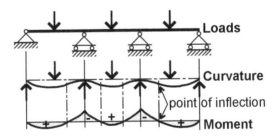

Figure 1.61: Continuous beam showing correspondence of points of inflection (change from positive to negative curvature) and points of zero moment

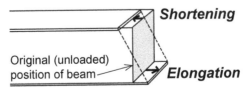

Figure 1.62: Shortening and stretching (compression and tension) at a typical beam cross-section

modulus of elasticity), a stress diagram will also have the same shape as the strain or "elongation-shortening diagram." Figure 1.63 compares these diagram shapes for materials with linear stress-strain relationships.

For materials with nonlinear stress-strain relationships, a stress diagram can be pieced together by plotting points from a stress-strain curve for the material. Thus, a steel beam stressed beyond its elastic region would have stress and strain distributions as shown in Figure 1.64. The elongation and shortening, shown in Figure 1.64*a*, and therefore the strain, shown in Figure 1.64*b*, is assumed to remain linear even when the stress, shown in Figure 1.64*d* through Figure 1.64*f*, becomes nonlinear. In Figure 1.64*c*, the stress at

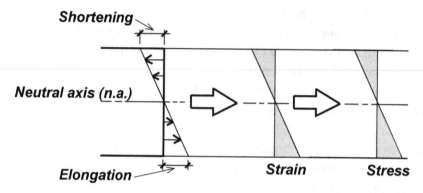

Figure 1.63: Elongation, strain, and stress diagrams for a linear, elastic material

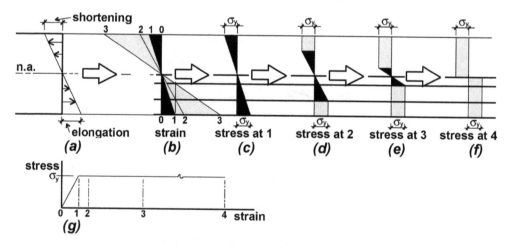

Figure 1.64: Elongation, strain, and stress diagrams for an elastic-plastic material such as steel showing (*a*) elongation and shortening of the actual material; (*b*) strain diagrams; (*c*) stress diagram at the point where the outer fiber has just yielded; (*d*) stress diagram corresponding to strain just beyond the elastic limit; (*e*) stress diagram corresponding to continued strain beyond the elastic limit; (*f*) stress diagram corresponding to the plastic moment (where the entire cross-section has yielded); and (*g*) stress-strain diagram

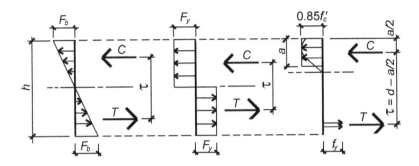

Figure 1.65: Bending stresses acting on rectangular cross sections corresponding to the (*a*) allowable moment for wood; and the limit states (maximum moment at failure) for (*b*) steel; and (*c*) reinforced concrete

the extreme fibers of the cross section just reaches the limit of elastic behavior (with stress, σ_y) which corresponds to the so-called *elastic moment*, M_e. In Figure 1.64f, the strain at the outer fiber is extremely large (theoretically infinite), and the entire cross section is assumed to have yielded at the stress σ_y, i.e., moved past the linear-elastic yield strain labeled "1" in Figure 1.64g. This condition represents the limit state for a steel beam, and corresponds to the so-called *plastic moment*, M_p. For reinforced concrete, a nonlinear stress-strain relationship is most often assumed for design; special procedures have been developed to simplify the construction of these stress diagrams.

The shape of the stress diagram is a key element in determining the magnitudes of stresses within the beam: when combined with the cross-sectional shape, the requirements of equilibrium can be used to find the magnitudes of the stresses. Typical stress diagrams are shown in Figure 1.65 corresponding to the allowable moment for wood and the limit states for steel and reinforced concrete.

Allowable stress design. As an example of how the stress-moment relationship is computed using the allowable stress design method, consider a free-body diagram cut from a rectangular cross section of width, *b*, and height, *h* (assuming a linear stress-strain relationship resulting in a linear stress diagram), as shown in Figure 1.65a. From the requirements of horizontal equilibrium, the total compressive force, *C*, must equal the total tension force, *T*. For this to occur, the neutral axis must be at the center of the beam, and the maximum compressive stress must equal the maximum tension stress. Any other linear distribution of stresses would be inconsistent with these requirements of equilibrium. The couple of equal and opposite forces represented by *C* and *T*, multiplied by the moment arm between them, must equal the bending moment, *M*, caused by the loads acting on the beam. The basic bending stress equation derives from this simple fact: M equals C (or T) times the moment arm, τ; that is:

$$M = C \times \tau \qquad (1.21)$$

Accounting for beam width, b, $C = (\frac{1}{2})(F_b)(h/2)(b)$ and $\tau = (\frac{2}{3})(h)$; substituting these values into Equation 1.21, we get:

$$M = F_b \frac{bh^2}{6} = F_b \frac{bh^3/12}{h/2} \qquad (1.22)$$

Defining "$bh^2/6$" as the *section modulus*, S, and "$bh^3/12$" as the *moment of inertia*, I, for a rectangular cross section, and solving for the maximum allowable stress, F_b, we get the basic bending stress equations for allowable stress design:

$$F_b = \frac{M}{S} = \frac{Mc}{I} \qquad (1.23)$$

where F_b is the allowable bending stress for the material (psi or ksi), M is the bending moment (in-lb or in-kips), S is the required section modulus (in³); I is the required moment of inertia (in⁴), and $c = h/2$ is the distance from the neutral axis to the extreme fiber (in.).

Stress-moment relationships. Equation 1.23 shows the relationship between bending stress, bending moment, and section modulus for a material stressed within its linear-elastic range. It is the basis for wood beam design. Steel and reinforced concrete, however, are no longer designed on the basis of assumed linear-elastic behavior. Even so, the basic relationship between moment, stress, and some sort of section modulus property remains essentially the same for all three materials, as can be seen by comparing the stress and resultant force diagrams shown in Figure 1.65. While specific derivations will be covered in the chapters that follow, the requirements of horizontal equilibrium ($C = T$) and rotational equilibrium ($M = C \times \tau = T \times \tau$) lead to design equations with essentially the same form for all three materials: Equation 1.24 (solving for the required section modulus, S, in Equation 1.23) applies to allowable stress design in wood; Equation 1.25 to allowable strength design in steel; and Equation 1.26 to strength design in reinforced concrete.

$$S_{req} = M/F_b' \qquad (1.24)$$

$$Z_{req} = M_a \, \Omega/F_y \qquad (1.25)$$

$$bd^2 \geq M_u/(\phi R) \qquad (1.26)$$

In each case, the section modulus term (S, Z, or bd^2) must be greater or equal to the bending moment divided by a bending stress term. The stress terms in Equations 1.24, 1.25, and 1.26 vary: for wood, an adjusted allowable stress, F_b', is used directly; for steel, the yield stress, F_y, is used; for reinforced concrete, the stress term, R, is more complex as it must account for the limit state of both concrete (in compression) and steel (in tension), as well as the ratio of steel to gross area within the beam cross section. Factors of safety are also handled differently for the three materials: in wood "allowable stress" design, the factor of safety is hidden within the stress term, F_b'; in steel "allowable strength" design, the factor of safety, Ω (normally 1.67 for bending), is applied, not to the stress, but to the plastic moment capacity of the cross section in order to determine its "available strength"; in reinforced concrete "strength" design, the factor of safety, ϕ (normally 0.9 for bending), is a strength reduction factor applied to the moment capacity of the section. Load safety factors are also included within the reinforced concrete design moment, M_u.

The triangular stress distribution in allowable stress design for wood corresponds to the elastic section modulus, $S = bd^2/6$, defined in Equation 1.22 for rectangular cross sections. For steel, the plastic section modulus, Z, is used, and is equal to $bd^2/4$ for a rectangular section — this is easily derived from the equilibrium of stresses shown in Figure 1.65b, although it should be noted that rectangular solid shapes are virtually nonexistent in steel beams. The term, bd^2, used in reinforced concrete Equation 1.26, has no official status as a "section modulus," yet it consists of the same basic variables and has the same units as wood's S and steel's Z.

Bending design methods. Equations 1.24, 1.25, and 1.26 are "design" equations, since they provide guidance for the size and shape of bending elements that are capable of resisting a given bending moment. In practice, after bending moments are determined (for example, by the construction of load, shear, and moment diagrams; from moment value tables; or with the use of structural analysis software), the required section modulus term is calculated, and a cross section is then selected. In the case of wood and steel, tables of standard cross sections and their corresponding section moduli facilitate the direct selection of appropriate shapes. The design of a reinforced concrete beam is less direct, since the ratio of steel to concrete may vary, producing a range of acceptable bd^2 terms, each of which may sponsor a range of choices for cross-sectional dimensions b and d.

Shear stress. Internal forces perpendicular to the longitudinal axis of beams may also exist along with bending moments at any cross section, consistent with the requirements of equilibrium (see, for example, the force V shown in the free-body diagrams within Figure 1.60). These *shear forces* are distributed over the cross-sectional surface according to the equation:

$$\tau = \frac{VQ}{Ib}$$

(1.27)

where τ = shear stress at a distance, y, from the extreme fiber (psi or ksi); V is the total shear force at the cross section (lb or kips); Q is the "static moment" of the partial cross-sectional area (from the extreme fiber to the distance, y) about the neutral axis of the cross section (in³); I is the moment of inertia of the cross section (in⁴); and b is the width of the cross section at a distance, y, from the extreme fiber (in.).

Rectangular sections. For rectangular cross sections, the maximum shear stress, which occurs at the neutral axis, becomes:

$$\tau_{max} = \frac{1.5V}{bh}$$

(1.28)

where h is the height of the rectangular cross section; all other variables are as defined above for Equation 1.27. Alternatively, one can solve for the required cross-sectional area, $A_{req} = bh$ (in²) as the basis for designing or analyzing a rectangular beam for shear, corresponding to an allowable shear stress, τ_{allow} (psi or ksi) for maximum shear force, V (lb or kips). In this case, one gets:

$$A_{req} = \frac{1.5V}{\tau_{allow}}$$

(1.29)

This is the basis for checking shear in timber beams, which are almost always rectangular (Figure 1.66). Reinforced concrete beams behave in a more complex manner, and special procedures for dealing with shear, or diagonal tension, have been developed.

In the vicinity of supports, loads are transferred by compression directly to those supports (Figure 1.67), and the maximum shear force is therefore

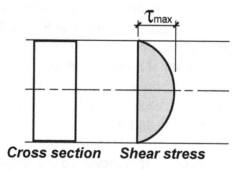

Cross section   **Shear stress**

Figure 1.66: Distribution of shear stress on a rectangular cross-section

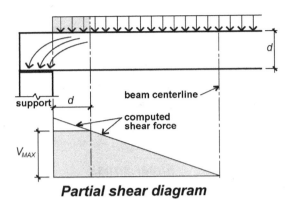

Partial shear diagram

Figure 1.67: Reduction of shear force, V_{max}, in the vicinity of the beam's reaction (support)

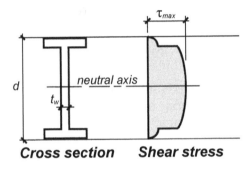

Cross section **Shear stress**

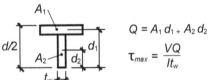

Figure 1.68: Distribution of shear stress on a flanged cross-section, and calculation of maximum shear stress, τ_{max}

somewhat less than the computed maximum value. In the design of wood and reinforced concrete beams, the shear force within a distance, d, of the face of the supports can be considered equal to the value of the shear force at that distance, d. For wood beams, d is the total beam height; for reinforced concrete, it represents the effective depth, measured to the centerline of the tension reinforcement.

Wide-flange sections. For steel wide-flange sections, the maximum shear stress, also at the neutral axis, can be found by computing the static moment, Q, of the partial area (above the neutral axis) about the neutral axis and solving Equation 1.27, as shown in Figure 1.68. For steel wide-flange shapes, simplified

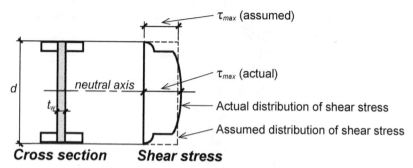

Figure 1.69: Comparison of actual and assumed maximum shear stress, τ_{max}, for a steel wide-flange beam

procedures have been developed, based on the average stress on the cross section, neglecting the overhanging flange areas; that is:

$$\tau_{max} = \frac{V}{dt_w} \tag{1.30}$$

where τ_{max} = the maximum shear stress within the cross section, V = the total shear force at the cross section, d = the cross-sectional depth, and t_w = the web thickness (see Figure 1.69).

SECTIONAL PROPERTIES

The behavior of structural elements is conditioned by the particular shapes into which these materials are formed, as well as the particular material qualities selected. Wood, steel and reinforced concrete structures can be fabricated from elements having an enormous range of strength, stiffness, size and geometric configurations, subject only to the constraints imposed by manufacturing technologies, transportation and handling, and the requirements of safety and serviceability.

In practice, though, the usual range is smaller, limited to standard shapes and sizes endorsed by industry associations. Typical standards for wood, steel, and reinforced concrete elements are described in the chapters that follow, but a few general observations can be made. For wood and steel, standard cross-sectional shapes are promulgated by industry associations for two primary reasons. First, especially for steel, there is a huge infrastructural investment in the machinery that creates particular shapes and sizes and — in spite of advances in numerical controlled manufacturing processes — it remains impractical to routinely produce custom designs. Second, properties of standard cross-sectional shapes can be easily complied and tabulated, facilitating structural design. Not only that, a whole assortment of subtle structural requirements can be verified in advance by controlling the proportions of these cross sections.

In the case of site-cast reinforced concrete, only reinforcing bars are man-ufactured in standard sizes. However, even in this case, the concrete must still be cast within forms, and these forms tend to be deployed in standard increments for a variety of reasons. Of course, it is always possible to create custom designed structural shapes, and some notable instances of this prac-tice can be found. Such instances are beyond the scope of this book. Specific requirements for wood, steel, and reinforced concrete are discussed in the chapters that follow.

CONSTRUCTION SYSTEMS

Structural systems can be extremely complex, and their behavior and design can be incredibly nuanced and sophisticated. However, at a basic level, there are really only two relevant aspects to the design of structural systems: with respect to floors, the structure must accommodate the human need for *hor-izontal surfaces* upon which to walk, sit, sleep, and so on; with respect to roofs — in particular, long-span roofs where there is no such requirement for horizontal walking surfaces — an efficient structure must "find a form" that prioritizes axial stresses, reduces bending stresses, and maximizes the overall depth (height) of the spanning geometry. This last point bears repeat-ing. To the extent that the structural system is made "deep" in the direction of applied loads, internal stresses will be reduced, making constituent struc-tural elements that comprise the system that much smaller. This is true not only of long-span roof structures (Figure 1.70*a*), but also of tall buildings or

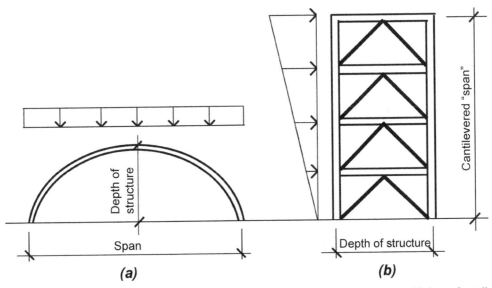

Figure 1.70: Increasing the "depth" of a structure, whether of a long-span roof (a) or of a tall building (b), reduces internal stresses

towers subjected to lateral (wind or seismic) loads. For such tall buildings, the "depth" is really the building width where the building itself is modeled as a vertical span cantilevered out of the ground, subjected to lateral forces (Figure 1.70b).

Floor structures are inherently inefficient because it rarely makes sense to increase the depth of the floor in order to increase structural efficiency — doing so might reduce stresses in the floor, but would create enormous inefficiencies in the overall building form. We therefore typically use ordinary beams, girders, slabs, and decks to make floors, rather than using deeper, and potentially more efficient, spanning elements. For long-span roofs or tall buildings, however, efficiency becomes paramount, especially because deflections increase proportionally with the *fourth power* of the span (Equation 1.20).

The structural elements described in this book — tension elements or hangers, columns, and beams — are assembled into structural systems that must provide strength, stiffness, and stability. *Strength* refers to the ability to resist internal stresses up to a limit state modified (reduced) by a factor of safety. *Stiffness* refers to the resistance to movement, whether axial deformation in the case of tension elements and columns, or deflection in the case of beams. *Stability* is required in compressive elements so that they don't buckle, but more generally in structural systems as a whole so that they maintain their intended geometry even when loaded. Because vertical loads (live and dead "gravity" loads) can most often be transferred to a building's foundation without adversely affecting the stability of the building as a whole, whereas horizontal ("lateral") loads originating with wind or seismic events can often challenge a building's stability (think of a house of cards), a *lateral-force-resisting system* not only must be part of every structural system but is the key to the structure's stability.

Aside from the design of innovative long-span or tall-building geometries, this last requirement is actually what makes structural design most interesting: whereas adequate strength and stiffness can be achieved simply by making structural elements as large as required — by calculating their size — the stability of a structural system must be adequately conceptualized *before* any calculations are made. Fortunately, there really are only three alternative strategies for the design of such lateral-force-resisting systems: shear walls, triangulation (trusses, braces, buttresses, etc.), or rigid (moment-resisting) joints (Figure 1.71).

Masonry and reinforced concrete walls can serve as shear walls, as can wood "diaphragms" consisting of vertical studs, horizontal plates, and sheathing boards (Figure 1.71a). To the extent that such "solid" surfaces resist deformation, they keep a building stable. Where such systems are already used to support the live and dead loads of floors and roofs, it usually makes sense to take advantage of their inherent lateral stability as well.

Placing diagonal elements within the rectangular geometry of framed structures (i.e., structures otherwise consisting of columns and beams, rather than walls) is probably the most efficient way to achieve stability (Figure 1.71*b*). Triangles are inherently stable forms, in that they cannot be deformed without changing the length of their bounding elements in both compression and tension. In contrast, rectangular frames can be deformed into parallelograms without changing the length of any of their bounding elements, especially when the joints between these elements offer little or no resistance to rotation.

In fact, where the joints between columns and beams in a rectangular geometry are made rigid (moment-resisting) so that rotation is prevented, we get the third, and least-efficient, strategy for stability: the rigid, or moment-resisting, frame (Figure 1.71*c*). The reason for the relative inefficiency of such rigid frames can best be understood by comparing a triangulated and rigid frame structure, each modeled as a 1-story, 1-bay building subjected to a single 2000 kip horizontal load at the "roof" and consisting of rectangular 10 in. × 20 in. vertical and horizontal structural elements (Figure 1.72). Using truss analysis (see Example 1.6, section method), it can be seen that the maximum axial force in the triangulated structure is 2000 kips (in the horizontal "roof" element closest to the load). Since the cross-sectional area of that horizontal element is assumed to be 10 × 20 = 200 in^2, the axial compressive stress (Equation 1.15) = force/area = 2000/200 = 10 ksi.

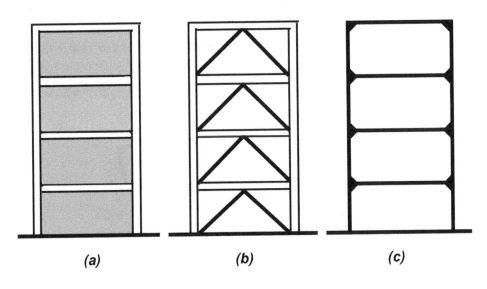

(a)   (b)   (c)

Figure 1.71: Lateral-force-resisting systems can consist of (*a*) shear walls, (*b*) triangulated elements, or (*c*) rigid (moment-resisting) frames

Now let's examine the stress within the rigid frame, subject to the same 2000 kip horizontal load. Because this is an indeterminate structure, we will make some simplifying assumptions so that it can be analyzed using only the three equations of equilibrium: first, that points of inflection (with zero bending moment) occur at the midpoints of all elements as the rigid frame deforms under the load; second, that the two horizontal shear forces at these inflection points split the 2000 kip external load equally between them; and third, that the frame dimensions are 10 ft high and 20 ft across. With these assumptions, we can cut the frame into four free-body diagrams and solve for the unknown axial and shear forces, starting with the top, left section (Figure 1.73). The bending moment at the top-left corner, point B, is therefore $500 \times 10 = 5000$ ft-k or, multiplying by twelve, 60,000 in-k. The section modulus (see the derivation for rectangular sections immediately after Equation 1.11) of the 10×20 cross section is $10 \times 20^2/6 = 666.67$ in^3. The bending stress (Equation 1.23) is therefore equal to $M/S = 60,000/666.67 = 90$ ksi. The axial stress in the horizontal member = force/area = $1000/200 = 5$ ksi, so the total maximum stress is actually 95 ksi.

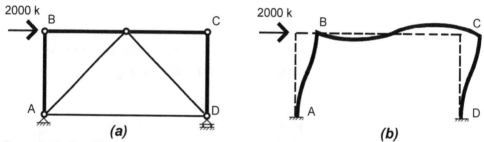

Figure 1.72: Simplified 1-story, 1-bay buildings with (*a*) triangulated and (*b*) rigid (moment-resisting) frame lateral-force-resisting systems

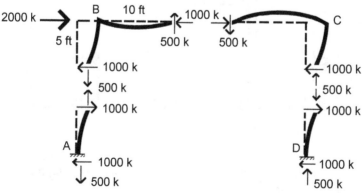

Figure 1.73: The rigid frame shown in Figure 1.72*b* is cut into four free-body diagrams at assumed inflection points, allowing for the calculation of internal shears and axial forces

In other words (even ignoring the axial component), stresses in the rigid frame (90 ksi) are *nine times greater* than stresses in the triangulated structure (10 ksi) in this admittedly simplified example. Looked at in another way, the horizontal and vertical elements would need to have a section modulus *nine times greater* than the required section modulus of the structural elements in the triangulated structure in order to keep internal stresses at the same levels — resulting in cross-sectional dimensions of about 20 in. × 40 in. instead of 10 in. × 20 in. Not only that, lateral movement (deflection) in the more flexible rigid frame will also be much greater than in the triangulated structure. The rigid frame is inefficient as a lateral-force-resisting system because the magnitude of its internal stresses and its tendency to deflect are primarily determined by the "depth" (actually the section modulus, or moment of inertia in the case of deflection) of individual framing elements, rather than by the "depth" of the structural system as a whole.

A final point about lateral-force-resisting systems: they are typically deployed along two structural lines in each of two orthogonal directions. Two lateral-force-resisting elements are used in each orthogonal direction because a single element would have difficulty dealing with torsional (twisting) movements of the structure as a whole if the resultant of the applied load were not perfectly aligned with it. Such pairs of lateral-force-resisting elements are placed in each of two orthogonal directions since lateral forces (wind or seismic) can come from any direction. If such a lateral force arrives at an angle different from either of the two orthogonal axes, that force can be resolved into two orthogonal components aligned with the lateral-force-resisting elements — such components will always be smaller than the original force, so that a design based on the assumption that lateral forces may arrive in either of the two orthogonal directions is generally safe.

However, just providing a lateral-force-resisting system is not enough: somehow, all the *other* structrural elements in the building must be adequately connected to the lateral-force-resisting system so that they, too, remain stable. This is often accomplished by considering the floor structures, consisting of beams, girders, slabs, and decks, as rigid (or semi-rigid) diaphragms that — because they are attached to the lateral-force-resisting system — keep the rest of the structure in its intended alignment (Figure 1.74).

For long-span structures, the concept of a *funicular shape* — one that resolves all external loads into internal axial forces — is useful, since we have already seen in the case of the rigid frame that a strategy of resisting internal bending moments is inherently inefficient. A cable will always find its funicular shape, since it is incapable of resisting anything other than internal axial tension forces; therefore, optimal compressive shapes can be visualized by literally modeling them in tension and then "flipping them" over into compressive forms. Such idealized axial forms can then be used to gain insight into

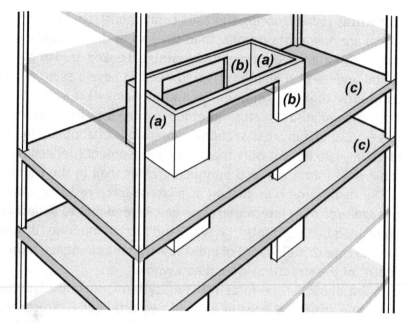

Figure 1.74: Shear walls, or triangulated braces, are typically organized into two orthogonal pairs, (*a*) and (*b*); their stability is extended throughout the structure by the rigid or semi-rigid diaphragm action of floors slabs or decks (*c*)

non-ideal geometries, since any geometric deviation from the ideal form corresponds to the magnitude of internal bending moments that would result, and therefore to the requirement for an increased section modulus in proportion to the geometric deviation (Figure 1.75).

The concept of the funicular curve also explains why floor structures are almost always structurally inefficient: the idealized form under a floor's uniformly distributed load, as in the curve shown in Figure 1.75*a*, would be a parabolic vault or arch (think of the cable shape supporting the horizontal roadway of a suspension bridge), a shape not at all consistent with the efficient stacking of habitable space in multi-story buildings.

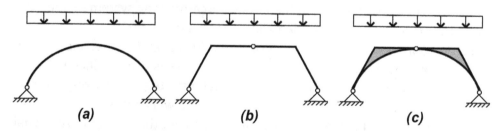

Figure 1.75: (*a*) The ideal funicular curve under a uniformly distributed load is a parabola; (*b*) a 3-hinged arch formed out of straight segments deviates from this ideal form; (*c*) to accommodate bending moments in this non-ideal form, the cross-section must become "deeper" in proportion to the deviation of the real from the ideal at all point along its length

In spite of the potential complexity of structural systems — especially indeterminate systems subject to, and designed to account for, dynamic loads such as those caused by wind or seismic events, or geometrically complex 3-dimensional structures like hyperbolic paraboloids, whose behavior cannot easily be translated into 2-dimensional diagrams — the discussion of simple structural elements remains relevant. In the final analysis, even the most complex systems are often composed of structural elements subject to tension, compression, and bending moments, and so the procedures developed in this book are, in principle, applicable to the design of individual elements comprising more complex systems. Of course, the actual design and analysis of such complex systems, typically accomplished with structural analysis software, is beyond the scope of this book, but insights gained into the behavior and design of the simpler elements from which they are assembled is a useful first step.

Connections

Structural elements are connected to form structural systems; the connections thus constitute an intermediate condition between elements and systems, and are not, strictly speaking, part of the elements themselves. Such connections, however, do have a direct bearing on the types of assumptions made when the individual elements (or systems) are analyzed. Specifically, when the various elements of structure — columns, beams, and so on — are considered individually, we show them either as constrained by hinges and rollers, free to translate and rotate, or fixed in such a way that all relative movement is prevented.

These abstract constraints are models of the actual conditions encountered by such elements when they are connected within actual structural systems. For example, beams are attached to girders, walls, or columns; columns are attached to foundations, transfer girders, or other columns; and tension elements are hung from beams, or inserted within truss systems. It may seem surprising that the conventional means of attaching structural elements to each other with nails, screws, bolts, welds, and reinforcing bars corresponds to the abstract hinges, rollers, or fixed constraints that will be encountered in the discussion of individual elements of wood, steel, or reinforced concrete (or as discussed earlier in this chapter): we rarely see connections in typical building structures that look anything like the diagrammatic representation of the constraints shown in Figure 1.14.

In fact, the relationship between the reality of a connection and the abstract modeling of it as hinge, roller, etc. is quite interesting. On the one hand, it is possible to design a real connection so that it both appears and behaves just like the abstract model. More commonly, however, one starts with a convenient means for connecting real materials, and then chooses a constraint model that approximates the behavior of this connection. Of course, such typical and "convenient" connections have evolved over time so that their behavior is in line with the assumptions we make about the types of movement, and the magnitude of forces and moments transmitted, between the elements being connected.

It is the latter group of typical connection strategies that will be discussed in the chapters about wood, steel, and reinforced concrete. These connections must resist the same sort of forces already encountered in the design of the structural elements themselves: direct compression and tension, as well as shear. Bending does not often show up directly in the design of fasteners, as it can usually be resolved into the other forces already mentioned.

CHAPTER 1 APPENDIX

Table A-1.1: Derivation of rules for drawing shear and moment diagrams[1]

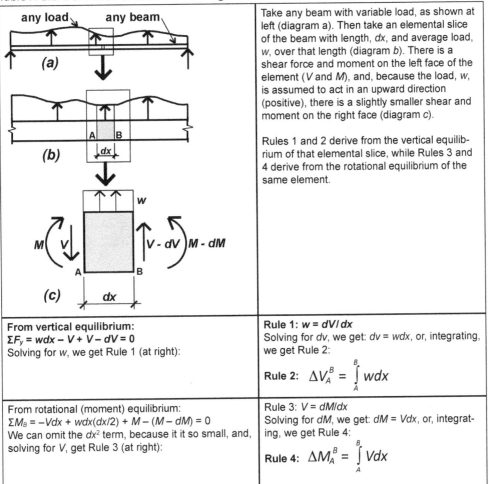

any load, any beam (a) (b) A B dx (c) M V $V - dV$ $M - dM$ w dx	Take any beam with variable load, as shown at left (diagram a). Then take an elemental slice of the beam with length, dx, and average load, w, over that length (diagram b). There is a shear force and moment on the left face of the element (V and M), and, because the load, w, is assumed to act in an upward direction (positive), there is a slightly smaller shear and moment on the right face (diagram c). Rules 1 and 2 derive from the vertical equilibrium of that elemental slice, while Rules 3 and 4 derive from the rotational equilibrium of the same element.
From vertical equilibrium: $\Sigma F_y = wdx - V + V - dV = 0$ Solving for w, we get Rule 1 (at right):	**Rule 1: $w = dV/dx$** Solving for dv, we get: $dv = wdx$, or, integrating, we get Rule 2: **Rule 2:** $\Delta V_A^B = \int_A^B wdx$
From rotational (moment) equilibrium: $\Sigma M_B = -Vdx + wdx(dx/2) + M - (M - dM) = 0$ We can omit the dx^2 term, because it it so small, and, solving for V, get Rule 3 (at right):	Rule 3: $V = dM/dx$ Solving for dM, we get: $dM = Vdx$, or, integrating, we get Rule 4: **Rule 4:** $\Delta M_A^B = \int_A^B Vdx$

Note:

1. The four rules are expressed mathematically in the Table A-1.1; they may also be expressed in words, as follows:

Rule 1: At any point along a beam, the slope of the shear diagram equals the value of the load (the "infinite" slope of the shear diagram at concentrated loads can be seen as a shorthand approximation to the actual condition of the load being distributed over some finite length, rather than existing at a point).

Rule 2: Between any two points along a beam, the change in the value of shear equals the total load (between those points).

Rule 3: The slope of the moment diagram at any point equals the value of the shear force at that point.

Rule 4: The change in the value of bending moment between any two points equals the "area of the shear diagram" between those points.

Table A-1.2: Effective length coefficient, K, for wood and steel columns

Descrip-tion	Pinned at both ends	Fixed at one end; pinned at the other	Fixed at one end; only horizontal translation allowed at the other end	Fixed at both ends	Fixed at one end; free at the other end (cantile-ver)	Pinned at one end; only horizontal translation allowed at the other end
"Ideal" K	1.0	0.7	1.0	0.5	2.0	2.0
"Code" K	1.0	0.8	1.2	0.65	2.1	[1]2.0 - 2.4

Note:

1. Use 2.0 for steel columns; 2.4 for wood columns

Table A-1.3: Allowable deflection for span, L[1]

A. Live, snow, or wind load only	
Floor beams	**Roof beams**
Basic: $L/360$	No ceiling: $L/180$ Non-plaster ceiling: $L/240$ Plaster ceiling: $L/360$

B. Combined live and dead load	
Floor beams	**Roof beams**
Basic: $L/240$	No ceiling: $L/120$ Non-plaster ceiling: $L/180$ Plaster ceiling: $L/240$

Note:

1. Use span, L, in inch units for allowable deflection in inch units; for cantilevers, use twice the actual cantilevered span for L.

CHAPTER 2

Loads

There are three broad categories of loads on building structures: dead loads, live loads and "environmental" loads.

DEAD LOADS

Dead loads consist of the weight of the building itself, including structure, partitions, cladding, roofing materials and permanent interior finishes such as carpet, ceiling systems, etc. These gravity loads are always downward-acting, and can be calculated with a reasonable degree of accuracy, being the summation of various building material weights, which are easily determined and quite predictable. That being said, it is sometimes prudent to anticipate unpredictable scenarios which call for additional dead load, so that future building modifications (such as the addition of a heavy tile floor, or a change from a mechanically attached to a ballasted roof) can be made without major structural modifications.

Dead loads are calculated by multiplying the unit weight of the materials by their quantity. Weights of some common materials and assemblies are listed in Appendix Table A-2.1.

Example 2.1 Calculate dead loads

Problem definition. Assume a typical steel structure with corrugated steel deck and concrete slab, tile floor, suspended ceiling system, and allowances for partitions and mechanical ducts, as shown in Figure 2.1. The spandrel girders

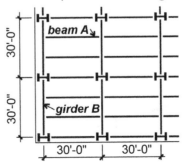

Figure 2.1: Framing plan for Example 2.1

carry an additional cladding load consisting of a brick and block cavity wall, 12-ft high from floor to floor. Find the dead load distribution on beam *A* and spandrel girder *B*.

Solution overview. Find weights of building elements; compute total dead load on beams and girders.

Problem solution
Beam A

1. From Appendix Table A-2.1, find weights of building elements:
   a. steel deck, finish floor, ducts and ceiling system = 47 psf.
   b. partitions = 8 psf.
   c. subtotal = 55 psf.
2. Compute weight per linear foot of beam by multiplying unit weight by tributary area on one linear foot of the beam: 55 × 10 = 550 lb/ft.
3. From Appendix Table A-2.1, assume weight of beam: 40 lb/ft.
4. Add beam weight to superimposed dead load to get total dead load, *D* = 550 + 40 = 590 lb/ft, as shown in Figure 2.2.

Girder B

1. Find concentrated dead loads at third points caused by typical beam re-actions, equal to the distributed load on the beam times the beam span divided by two: *P* = 590(30)/2 = 8850 lb.
2. From Appendix Table A-2.1, find weight of cladding = 1000 lb/ft.
3. From Appendix Table A-2.1, assume weight of girder: 80 lb/ft.
4. Add girder weight to cladding weight = 80 + 1000 = 1080 lb/ft.
5. The dead load on the girder consists of the distributed load in addition

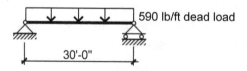

590 lb/ft dead load

30'-0"

Figure 2.2: Beam *A* load diagram for Example 2.1

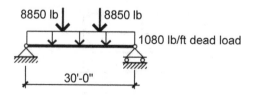

8850 lb   8850 lb

1080 lb/ft dead load

30'-0"

Figure 2.3: Girder *B* load diagram for Example 2.1

to the concentrated loads transferred by typical beams, as shown in Figure 2.3.

Dead loads also figure prominently in the evaluation of various environmental loads, such as those caused by wind and earthquakes. Seismic loads, for example, are directly proportional to the inertial mass of the building, so that large dead loads are associated with large seismic forces. The effects of wind, on the other hand, can often be mitigated by the addition of dead load, since overturning and uplift — tendencies that act opposite to the force of gravity — are reduced as the building's weight increases.

LIVE LOADS

Live loads are nonpermanent, or movable, loads within buildings caused by the weight of people, furnishings, storage of objects, etc. They are relatively unpredictable, vary over time, and are often dynamic, rather than static, in their application. Since it is not possible to measure these loads absolutely, a probabilistic approach is used: values are assigned to various types of occupancies based on "worse case" expectations, taking into consideration actual observed loading conditions and the historical record of structural failures.

Since these determinations are generic to various occupancy classifications, and are not unique to each structure, the problem of determining live loads is taken out of the hands of building designers altogether, and appears as a mandate of government in the form of building codes. Within these codes, the actual complex behavior of live loads is reduced to an array of uniformly distributed values, one for each type of occupancy. Examples of these live load values are listed in Appendix Table A-2.2.

As floor areas become larger, it becomes increasingly improbable that the full live load will ever be present; therefore, a reduction in live load is generally permitted for structural elements "influenced" by relatively large floor areas. These so-called influence areas are different from the tributary areas used to compute "unreduced" loads — they are, in fact, four times larger for columns and two times larger for beams (Figure 2.4). For this reason, a single reduction equation based on tributary areas cannot be derived for both columns and beams; instead, such a formula is written in terms of what used to be called the influence area, A_I, but is now defined in terms of the tributary area, A_T (ft^2), times a "live load element factor," K_{LL}:

$$\text{live load reduction coefficient} = 0.25 + \frac{15}{\sqrt{K_{LL}A_T}} \qquad (2.1)$$

Live loads are thus calculated by multiplying the tabulated values from

Appendix Table A-2.2 by the area-dependent reduction coefficients (Equation 2.1), where K_{LL} is defined in Appendix Table A-2.2, but equals 2.0 for most beams and 4.0 for most columns. The reduction coefficient is subject to the following limitations: (1) no reduction is allowed for values of $K_{LL}A_T$ smaller

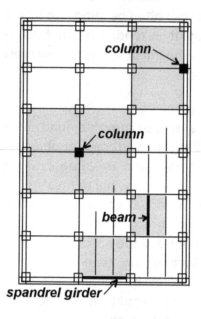

Figure 2.4: "Influence areas" for beams and columns

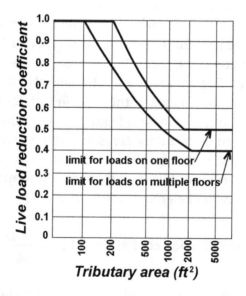

Figure 2.5: Live load reduction coefficient graph

than 400 ft^2; (2) no live load reduction is permitted for elements supporting a single floor with live loads greater than 100 psf (and for elements supporting more than one floor with live loads greater than 100 psf, no reduction greater than 20% is permitted); (3) no reduction coefficient smaller than 0.5 is allowed for ordinary beams or columns supporting one level only; and (4) no reduction coefficient smaller than 0.4 is allowed for any other condition, i.e., for columns or beams supporting more than one level.

Live load reduction coefficients are plotted in Figure 2.5 for various tributary areas, shown separately for beams and columns. Notice that as the tributary area gets larger (and the likelihood of the full live load being present decreases), the live load reduction increases — i.e., the reduction *coefficient* decreases.

There are a few obvious exceptions to the rules governing live load reductions, most importantly for structural elements supporting large areas which are expected to be fully loaded. In such cases, for example in places of public assembly or in garages, no live load reduction is allowed. Additionally, reductions are restricted for one- and two-way slabs since the failure mode of such slabs is not directly a function of tributary area, but rather corresponds more closely to the pattern of reinforcing bars. These are minimum values for live loads: other than exposing oneself to the potential wrath of developers, owners, project managers and contractors, nothing prevents a designer from using larger, or unreduced, values if warranted by the particular conditions of the project.

Example 2.2 Calculate live loads

Problem definition. Find the live loads for typical Beam *A* and Girder *B* in the 6-story office building shown in Figure 2.6. What is the live load on first floor interior column *C* (ignoring roof loads)?

Solution overview. Find unreduced live loads; apply live load reduction coefficient where applicable.

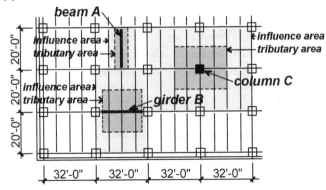

Figure 2.6: Framing plan for Example 2.2

Problem solution
Beam A

1. From Appendix Table A-2.2, the unreduced live load for office occupancy = 50 psf. The load on a linear foot of the beam, found by multiplying the unit load by the tributary area on 1 linear foot of the beam, is 50(8) = 400 lb/ft (as shown in the shaded region of Figure 2.7).

2. From Appendix Table A-2.2, consider live load reduction, based on the beam's tributary area, $A_T = 8 \times 20 = 160$ ft² and a live load element factor, $K_{LL} = 2$. Since $K_{LL}A_T = 2(160) = 320$ ft² ≤ 400 ft², no reduction is allowed, and the loading diagram remains as shown in Figure 2.8.

Girder B

1. Find the unreduced live load on the girder, applied at the quarter-points by the reactions of the beams, each of which equals the unit load on the beam times its span divided by two, or 400(20)/2 = 4000 lb. Since two beams frame into the girder at each point, the unreduced live load is 4000(2) = 8000 lb at each of the quarter-points.

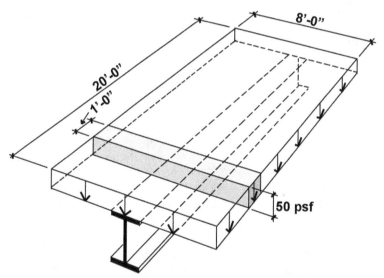

Figure 2.7: Tributary area for live load on one linear foot of beam for Example 2.2, with shaded "stress block" volume of 50 × 8 × 1 = 400 lb/ft being the unreduced live load on one linear foot of the beam

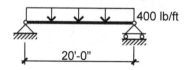

Figure 2.8: Beam A load diagram for Example 2.2

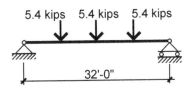

Figure 2.9: Girder *B* load diagram for Example 2.2

2. Consider live load reduction:
   a. Find $K_{LL}A_T$ = 2(20 × 32) = 1280 ft². The tributary area is taken as 20 ft × 32 ft rather than 20 ft × 24 ft since the loads placed outside the middle 24 ft will have a structural effect on the girder.
   b. From Equation 2.1, apply a reduction coefficient of: 0.25 + 15/√1280 = 0.67. The concentrated live loads at each quarter-point become: 0.67 × 8000 = 5354 lb = 5.4 kips as shown in Figure 2.9.

Column C, 1st floor

1. Find the unreduced live load on the column: Since the 1st-floor column of a 6-story building supports 5 floors (not including the roof), and the tributary area of each floor is 32 × 20 = 640 ft², the total tributary area supported by the column is 5 × 640 = 3200 ft². This results in an unreduced live load of 50 × 3200 = 160,000 lb.
2. Consider live load reduction:
   a. Find $K_{LL}A_T$ = 4(3200) = 12,800 ft².
   b. From Equation 2.1, apply a reduction coefficient of: 0.25 + 15/√12,800 = 0.38. Since the minimum reduction coefficient for columns supporting more than one level is 0.4, we use a total live load of 0.4(160,000) = 64,000 lb = 64 kips.

ENVIRONMENTAL LOADS

Environmental loads are those due to snow, wind, rain, soil (and hydrostatic pressure) and earthquake. Unlike live loads, which are assumed to act on all floor surfaces equally, independent of the geometry or material properties of the structure, most of these environmental loads depend not only upon the environmental processes responsible for producing the loads, but upon the geometry or weight of the building itself. For snow, wind and earthquake loads, the "global" environmental considerations can be summarized by location-dependent numbers for each phenomenon: ground snow load for snow, basic wind speed for wind, and maximum ground motion (acceleration) for earthquake (Appendix Table A-2.3). Considerations specific to each building are then combined with these "global" environmental numbers to establish the magnitude and direction of forces expected to act on the building. Like live loads, the actual procedures for calculating environmental loads are not derived independently for each building, but are mandated by local building codes. For the actual design of real buildings in real places, the governing building code must be consulted; for the preliminary design of real or imaginary buildings, the following guidelines will do.

Snow loads

Determining the weight of snow that might fall on a structure starts with a ground snow load map, or a ground snow load value determined by a local building code official. These values range from zero to 100 psf for most regions, although weights of up to 300 psf are possible in locations such as Whittier, Alaska. Some typical ground snow load values are listed in Appendix Table A-2.3. Flat roof snow loads are generally considered to be about 30% less than these ground snow load values, and both wind and thermal effects — as well as the "importance" of the structure — are accounted for in further modifying this roof load. A thermal factor, $C_t = 1.2$, is included in the flat roof load for unheated structures ($C_t = 1.0$ for heated structures and 1.1 for heated structures with ventilated roofs protected with at least R-25 insulation below the ventilated plenum or attic); we will assume a nominal value of 1.0 for both wind ("exposure") and "importance." Other possible values for the snow load importance factor, I_s, are listed in Appendix Table A-2.4. However, the major parameter in determining snow loads is the slope of the surface expected to carry the load. As the slope increases, more snow can be expected to slide off the roof surface, especially if the surface is slippery, and if the space immediately below the surface is heated. The slope-reduction factor, C_s, which is multiplied by the flat roof snow load to obtain the actual roof snow load, takes these factors into account:

    a. $C_s = 1.0$ for roof angles from 0° to A°.

    b. $C_s = 1.0 - \dfrac{\text{roof angle} - A°}{70° - A°}$ for roof angles from A° to 70°.   (2.2)

    c. $C_s = 0$ for roof angles greater or equal to 70°.

The parameter A (degrees Fahrenheit) depends on how slippery the roof surface is, and whether that surface is allowed to become warm or cold: $A = 5°$ for warm, slippery roofs (where the R-value must be at least 30 for unventilated roofs, and at least 20 for ventilated roofs); 30° for warm, not slippery roofs (or for slippery roofs not meeting the R-value criteria); 15° for cold, slippery roofs; 45° for cold, not slippery roofs; and, for the intermediate condition where a roof remains somewhat cold because it is ventilated (with at least R-25 insulation below the ventilated space), $A = 10°$ for slippery roofs; and 37.5° for not slippery roofs. Neglecting variations due to exposure, the snow load can be written as:

$$0.7C_sC_tI_s(\text{ground snow load}) \tag{2.3}$$

For low-slope roofs (i.e., hip, gable, or monoslope roofs with slopes less than 15°), the roof snow load cannot be taken less than $I_s \times$ ground snow load or $I_s \times 20$ lb/ft^2, whichever is less.

As an example, for "ordinary" buildings ($I_s = 1.0$) with nonslippery (e.g., asphalt shingle) roofs having slopes no greater than 37.5°, kept cold by proper ventilation (with at least R-25 insulation below the ventilated space), the sloped roof snow load, deployed on the horizontal projection of the inclined structural roof members, becomes:

$$0.7(1.0)(1.1)(1.0)(\text{ground snow load}) \tag{2.4}$$

Judgment should be used where the building geometry provides opportunities for drifting snow to accumulate on lower roofs, or when sliding snow from higher roofs might fall on lower roofs. Most building codes provide guidelines for these situations.

To account for the effects of wind acting simultaneously with snow on hip- or gable-type roofs, it is necessary to also check a so-called unbalanced snow load, caused by wind blowing snow from the windward to the leeward portion of the roof. In old building codes, this unbalanced load was computed by taking 1.5 times the snow load acting on the leeward side of the gable, with zero snow load on the windward side. Contemporary codes have a more complex strategy for computing such loads, but only applicable to hip and gable roofs with slopes between 2.38° (i.e., ½:12) and 30.26° (i.e., 7:12). Steeper or shallower roofs are not affected by wind-blown snow in the same way and so the calculation of such unbalanced loads is not required in these cases. For residential-scale buildings — i.e., where the horizontal distance from ridge to eave is not greater than 20 ft — the unbalanced snow load is taken as $I_s \times$ ground snow load on the leeward side, with zero snow load on the windward side.

For larger buildings with ridge-to-eave horizontal distances greater than 20 ft, the unbalanced snow load calculations are more easily performed using a spreadsheet or other software. A load is first computed for the windward side, taken as 0.3 × roof snow load. In addition, there are two loads computed for the leeward side: the first is just the roof snow load taken over the entire leeward surface; the second has a magnitude of $h_d\gamma/\sqrt{S}$, but is placed on only part of the leeward roof, specifically, that rectangular portion on the leeward side extending from the ridge a distance, measured horizontally, of $(\frac{2}{3})h_d\sqrt{S}$. In these calculations, h_d (ft) is the height of a snow drift = $0.43(l_u^{1/3})$(ground snow load +10)$^{1/4}$ − 1.5; l_u is the length of the roof upwind of the drift (ft), taken here as the horizontal distance from ridge to eave measured on the windward part of the roof; γ = the so-called snow density, taken as (0.13 × ground snow load) + 14 but no greater than 30 pcf; and S is a measure of the roof slope, taken as the horizontal run for a rise of 1.

Example 2.3 Calculate snow loads

Problem definition. Find the snow load on a house in Portland, ME with a conventional roof with a 7:12 slope, i.e., with an angle = $\tan^{-1}(7/12) = 30.26°$. The roof is kept cold by having a ventilated attic, with R-30 insulation separating the ventilated attic space from the heated house below. Calculate for both asphalt shingles and metal roofing.

Solution overview. Find ground snow load; compute roof snow load.

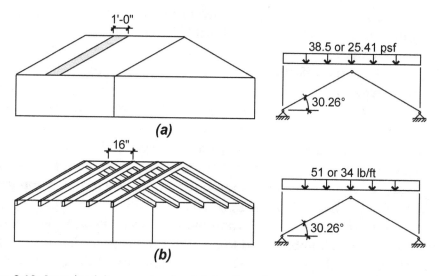

Figure 2.10: Snow load diagram showing (*a*) distributed snow load; and (*b*) snow load on a typical rafter, for Example 2.3

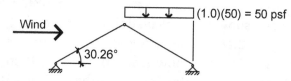

Figure 2.11: Unbalanced snow load for Example 2.3

Problem solution.
1. From Appendix Table A-2.3, the ground snow load = 50 psf.
2. Find the roof snow load:
   a. *Nonslippery surface (asphalt shingles)*: From Equation 2.4, for this condition only, the snow load = 0.7(1.1)(1.0)(ground snow load) = 0.7(1.1)(1.0)(50) = 38.5 psf.
   b. *Slippery surface (metal roofing)*: From Equation 2.2, find the co-efficient, C_s for roof angles from $A°$ to 70°, where $A = 10°$ for cold, slippery roofs (kept cold by ventilation). In this case, C_s = $1.0 - (\text{roof angle} - A°)/(70° - A°) = 1.0 - (30.26 - 10)/(70 - 10) = 0.66$. From Equation 2.3, the snow load = $0.7C_sC_t$ (ground snow load) = 0.7(0.66)(1.1)(50) = 25.41 psf.
3. For rafters (sloped roof beams) spaced at 16 in. on center, the snow load on each rafter becomes:
   a. 38.5($^{16}\!/_{12}$) = 51 lb/ft for the non-slippery roof.
   b. 25.41($^{16}\!/_{12}$) = 34 lb/ft for the slippery roof.
4. Both of these loading diagrams are shown in Figure 2.10.
5. To account for the effects of wind acting simultaneously with snow on ga-ble-type roofs, we also check the unbalanced snow load. Since the 30.26° slope of this roof falls between 2.38° and 30.26°, the unbalanced snow load on the leeward side must be computed. For residential-scale build-ings — i.e., where the horizontal distance from ridge to eave is not greater than 20 ft — the unbalanced snow load is taken as $I_s \times$ ground snow load, with zero snow load on the windward side. For this example, the unbal-anced snow load diagram is shown in Figure 2.11.

Wind loads

Building codes take one of two approaches to the mathematical calculation of wind pressure on building surfaces: either these pressures are simply given as a function of height, or they are calculated as a function of the basic wind speed, modified by numerous environmental and building-specific factors.

The Building Code of the City of New York historically took the first ap-proach, specifying a 30 psf horizontal wind pressure on the surfaces of build-ings over 100 ft tall. This number was actually reduced to 20 psf in the 1930s and 1940s. Then, as buildings grew consistently taller and more data was as-sembled about wind speed at various elevations above grade, wind pressure began to be modeled as a discontinuous function, increasing from 20 psf be-low 100 feet to 40 psf above 1000 feet (Figure 2.12).

In contrast to this approach, wind pressure can also be calculated directly from wind speed: the relationship between the velocity or "stagnation" pres-sure, q, and the basic wind speed, V, is derived from Bernoulli's equation for streamline flow:

$$q = 0.5pV^2 \qquad\qquad (2.5)$$

where p is the mass density of air. Making some assumptions about air temperature to calculate p, and converting the units to pounds per square foot
(psf) for q and miles per hour (mph) for V, we get:

$$q = 0.00256(K)K_d K_t V^2 \qquad\qquad (2.6)$$

where K accounts for heights above ground different from the 10 m above
ground used to determine nominal wind speeds as well as different "boundary layer" conditions, or exposures, at the site of the structure; $K_d = 0.85$ is
used only when computing the effects of load combinations (see section below on *design approaches*) to account for the lower probability that an actual
wind direction will produce the worst-case outcome when the effects of load
combinations — not just wind alone — are simultaneously measured; and K_t

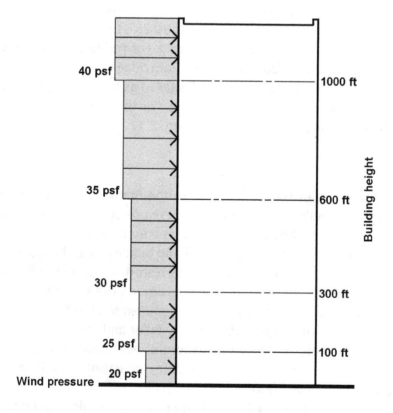

Figure 2.12: Historic values for wind loads, based on 1969 – 1981 New York City
Building Codes

is a factor used only in special cases of increased wind speeds caused by hills, ridges, escarpments, and similar topographic features. The importance factor, formerly included in this equation to account for relative hazards to life and property associated with various types of occupancies, is now incorporated directly into wind speed maps — that is, it shows up as part of V.

For a building with normal occupancy at a height of 10 meters above grade in open terrain, i.e., with $K = K_d = K_t = 1.0$, a wind speed of 115 mph corresponds to a velocity pressure equal to:

$$q = 0.00256(1.0)(1.0)(1.0)(115^2) = 33.0 \text{ psf} \qquad (2.7)$$

The external design wind pressure, p_e, can be found at any height, and for various environmental and building conditions by multiplying the velocity pressure, q, by a series of coefficients corresponding to those conditions:

$$p_e = qGC_p \qquad (2.8)$$

where q is the velocity pressure as defined in Equation 2.6; G accounts for height-dependent gustiness; and C_p is a pressure coefficient accounting for variations in pressure and suction on vertical, horizontal and inclined surfaces. Combining Equations 2.6 and 2.8, we get:

$$p_e = 0.00256(K)K_d K_t GC_p V^2 \qquad (2.9)$$

where:

p_e = the external design wind pressure (psf)

V = the basic wind speed (mph)

K = the velocity pressure exposure coefficient

K_d = 0.85 is a wind directionality factor (for use only when computing load combinations)

K_t = a topography factor (can be taken as 1.0 unless the building is situated on a hill, ridge, escarpment, etc.)

G = a coefficient accounting for height-dependent gustiness

C_p = a pressure coefficient accounting for variations in pressure and suction on vertical, horizontal and inclined surfaces

Some values for these coefficients — for buildings in various terrains (exposure categories) — are given in Appendix Table A-2.5 (except that wind velocities, V, for various cities and risk categories, are found in Appendix Table A-2.3). The resulting distribution of wind pressures on all exposed surfaces of a generic rectangular building (with a sloped roof) is shown in Figure 2.13.

Only on the windward wall of the building does the wind pressure vary with height above ground. On all other surfaces, the coefficient K is taken at mean roof height for the entire surface, resulting in a uniform distribution of wind pressure (whereas for the windward wall, the coefficient K is taken at the height at which the pressure is being computed). This is consistent with the results of wind tunnel tests, which show a much greater variability (related to height) on the windward wall than on any other surface.

Changes in the building's *internal* pressure as a result of high winds can increase or decrease the total pressure on portions of a structure's exterior "envelope." This internal pressure, p_i, is normally taken as 18% of the roof-height velocity pressure for enclosed buildings, but can be as high as 55% of the roof-height velocity pressure for partially-enclosed buildings The total design pressure, p, is therefore:

$$p = p_e + p_i \qquad\qquad (2.10)$$

The actual behavior of wind is influenced not only by the surface (or boundary layer) conditions of the earth, but also by the geometry of the building. All sorts of turbulent effects occur, especially at building corners, edges, roof eaves, cornices, and ridges. Some of these effects are accounted for by the pressure coefficient C_p, which effectively increases the wind pressure at critical regions of the building envelope. Increasing attention is also being given to localized areas of extremely high pressure, which are averaged into the total

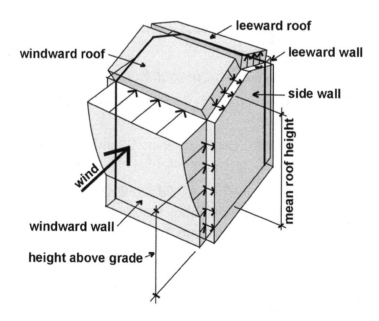

Figure 2.13: Wind pressure on buildings

design pressures used when considering a structure's "main wind-force resisting system" (MWFRS). These high pressures need to be considered explicitly when examining the forces acting on relatively small surface areas, such as mullions and glazing, plywood sheathing panels, or roofing shingles. Building codes either stipulate higher wind pressures for small surface elements like glass and wall panels, or provide separate "component and cladding" values for the external pressure coefficients and gust response factors.

Since both external and internal pressures can be either positive (i.e., with the direction of force pushing on the building surface), or negative (i.e., with a suction-type force pulling away from the building surface), the total design pressure on any component or cladding element is always increased by the consideration of both external and internal pressures. For certain MWFRS calculations, however, the internal pressures on opposite walls cancel each other so that only external pressures on these walls need to be considered.

As an alternative to the analytic methods described above, three other methods are also permitted: a simplified tabular method for certain buildings no more than 160 ft high, a simplified analytic procedure for enclosed, more-or-less symmetrical low-rise (no more than 60-feet high) buildings; and physical testing of models within wind-tunnels to determine the magnitudes and directions of wind-induced pressures.

Example 2.4 Calculate wind loads

Problem definition. Find the distribution of wind load on the windward and leeward surfaces of a 5-story office building located in the suburbs of Chicago (assume typical "suburban" terrain, or Exposure Category B). Since $K_d = 0.85$, the results can be combined with other loads; $K_t = 1.0$, since no peculiar topographic features are present, and wind speed is found based on a "risk category" of II corresponding to normal occupancy. A typical section is shown in Figure 2.14. Plan dimensions are 100 ft × 100 ft. Neglect internal pressure.

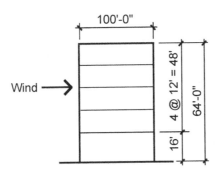

Figure 2.14: Schematic section through building for Example 2.4

Solution overview. Find basic wind speed; compute external design wind pressures.

Problem solution

1. From Appendix Table A-2.3, the basic (ultimate) wind speed, $V = 115$ mph.
2. *Windward wall:* From Equation 2.9, the external design wind pressure, $p_e = 0.00256(K)K_d K_t GC_p V^2$; where values for K, G, and C_p are found in Appendix Table A-2.5 (K_d and K_t, are given in the problem statement). It is convenient to organize the solution in tabular form, as shown below in Table 2.1. The value of K at mean roof height (64 ft) is found by interpolation between the value at 60 ft and the value at 70 ft:

$$\frac{K - 0.85}{0.89 - 0.85} = \frac{64 - 60}{70 - 60}$$

from which $K = 0.87$. The value for K_t equals 1.0 and is not included in the table.

Table 2.1: Calculation of external design windward wall pressure for Example 2.4

Height	0.00256	K	K_d	G	C_p	V^2 (mph)	p_e (psf)
70	0.00256	0.89	0.85	0.85	0.8	115 x 115	17.42
64	**0.00256**	**0.87**	**0.85**	**0.85**	**0.8**	**115 x 115**	**17.02**
60	0.00256	0.85	0.85	0.85	0.8	115 x 115	16.63
50	0.00256	0.81	0.85	0.85	0.8	115 x 115	15.85
40	0.00256	0.76	0.85	0.85	0.8	115 x 115	14.87
30	0.00256	0.70	0.85	0.85	0.8	115 x 115	13.70
20	0.00256	0.62	0.85	0.85	0.8	115 x 115	12.13
0 - 15	0.00256	0.57	0.85	0.85	0.8	115 x 115	11.15

3. *Leeward wall:* From Equation 2.9, the external design wind pressure for the leeward wall can be found (there is only one value for the entire

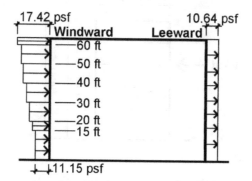

Figure 2.15: Distribution of wind pressure on windward and leeward surfaces for Example 2.4

leeward wall, based on K at the mean roof height). From Appendix Table A-2.5, $C_p = -0.5$ (since the ratio $L/B = 100/100 = 1.0$); $K = 0.87$ (at mean roof height: see step 2); $G = 0.85$; $K_d = 0.85$; and $K_t = 1.0$. The external wind pressure on the leeward side of the building is:

$$p_e = (0.00256)(0.87)(0.85)(0.85)(-0.5)(115^2) = -10.64 \text{ psf}$$

The negative sign indicates that this leeward pressure is acting in "suction," pulling away from the leeward surface.

4. The distribution of wind pressure on the building section is shown in Figure 2.15. The direction of the arrows indicate positive pressure (pushing) on the windward side and negative pressure (suction) on the leeward side. Rather than connecting the points at which pressures are computed with straight lines (which would result in triangular stress blocks over the surface of the building), it is common to use the more conservative assumption of constant pressure from level to level, which results in a discontinuous, or stepped, pattern of wind pressure, as shown in Figure 2.15.

When computing the magnitude of wind loads that must be resisted by a building's lateral-force-resisting system, internal pressures can be neglected (as they act in opposite directions on the two interior faces of the building, canceling out), leaving only the windward and leeward pressures to be considered for each orthogonal plan direction.

Seismic loads

A building riding an earthquake is like a cowboy riding a bull in a rodeo: as the ground moves in a complex and dynamic pattern of horizontal and vertical displacements, the building sways back and forth like an inverted pendulum. The horizontal components of this dynamic ground motion, combined with the inertial tendencies of the building, effectively subject the building structure to lateral forces that are proportional to its weight. In fact, the earliest seismic codes related these seismic forces, F, to building weight, W, with a single coefficient:

$$F = CW \qquad\qquad (2.11)$$

where C was taken as 0.1.

What this simple equation doesn't consider are the effects of the building's geometry, stiffness and ductility, as well as the characteristics of the soil, on the magnitude and distribution of these equivalent static forces. In particular, the building's fundamental period of vibration, related to its height and type of construction, is a critical factor. For example, the periods of short, stiff buildings tend to be similar to the periodic variation in ground accelera-tion characteristic of seismic motion, causing a dynamic amplification of the forces acting on those buildings. This is not the case with tall, slender buildings having periods of vibration substantially longer than those associated with the ground motion. For this reason, tall flexible buildings tend to perform well (structurally) in earthquakes, compared to short, squat and stiff buildings.

But stiffness can also be beneficial since the large deformations associ-ated with flexible buildings tend to cause substantial nonstructural damage. The "ideal" earthquake-resistant structure must therefore balance the two contradictory imperatives of stiffness and flexibility.

In modern building codes, the force F has been replaced with a "design base shear," V, equal to the total lateral seismic force assumed to act on the building. Additionally, the single coefficient relating this shear force to the building's weight ("seismic dead load") has been replaced by a series of coef-ficients, each corresponding to a particular characteristic of the building or site that affects the building's response to ground motion. Thus, the base shear can be related to the building's weight with the following coefficients, using an "equivalent lateral force procedure" for seismic design:

$$V = C_s W = \left[\frac{S_{DS}}{(R/I_e)}\right] W \tag{2.12}$$

where:

V = the design base shear

C_s = the seismic response coefficient equal to $S_{DS}/(R/I_e)$

W = the effective seismic weight (including dead load, permanent equip-ment, a percentage of storage and warehouse live loads, partition loads, and certain snow loads)

S_{DS} = the design elastic response acceleration at short periods

R = a response modification factor (relating the building's lateral-force-resisting system to its performance under seismic loads)

I_e = the seismic importance factor (with somewhat different values than the equivalent factors for wind or snow)

The coefficient C_s has upper and lower bounds that are described in Ap-pendix Table A-2.6 part H, so it will only correspond to the value defined in Equation 2.12 when it falls between the two bounding values. The response modification factor, R, is assigned to specific lateral-force-resisting systems — not all of which can be used in every seismic region or for every type of occupancy; Appendix Table A-2.6, part D, indicates which structural systems are either not permitted, or limited in height, within specific seismic design categories.

To approximate the structural effects that seismic ground motion produces at various story heights, seismic forces, F_x, are assigned to each level of the building structure in proportion to their weight times height (or height raised to a power no greater than two) above grade:

$$F_x = \frac{V w_x h_x^k}{\Sigma w_i h_i^k} \qquad (2.13)$$

where:

V = the design base shear, as defined above in Equation 2.12

w_i and w_x = the portions of weight W at, or assigned to, a given level, i or x

h_i and h_x = the heights from the building's base to level i or x

k = 1 for periods ≤ 0.5 s and 2 for periods ≥ 2.5 s (with linear interpolation permitted for periods between 0.5 s and 2.5 s) and accounts for the more complex effect of longer periods of vibration (defined in Table A-2.6, part E) on the distribution of forces

The Σ symbol in Equation 2.13 indicates the *sum* of the product of $(w_i h_i^k)$ for i ranging from 1 to n, where n is the number of levels at which seismic forces are applied.

A typical distribution of seismic forces resulting from the application of this equation is shown in Figure 2.16. It can be seen that Equation 2.13 for F_x guarantees that these story forces are in equilibrium with the design base shear, V.

By considering both a building's occupancy category (see Appendix Table

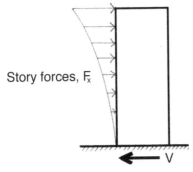

Figure 2.16: Typical distribution of equivalent seismic story forces on a building

A-2.6, part *F*) and the expected ground motion at the building's site, a Seismic Design Category, or SDC, can be determined. Criteria for a building's SDC are found in Appendix Table A-2.6, part *G*. For structures that are in the lowest-risk SDC *A*, it is not necessary to consider the design of *nonstructural* components for seismic resistance. On the other hand, for the highest-risk SDCs *C*, *D*, *E*, and *F*, increased scrutiny is required: issues of slope instability, liquifaction, settlement, surface displacement, and — for SDCs *D*, *E*, and *F* only — lateral pressure on basements must be considered. Such issues are beyond the scope of this chapter. Buildings with the most extreme SDCs *E* and *F* are not permitted where the ground surface might be ruptured by a known active fault.

Building codes require that larger seismic forces be used for the design of individual building elements, and for the design of floor "diaphragms." The rationale for the separate calculation of these forces is similar to the logic behind the calculation of larger "component and cladding" loads in wind design: because the actual distribution of seismic forces is nonuniform, complex, and constantly changing, the average force expected to act upon the entire lateral-force-resisting structural system is less than the maximum force expected to occur at any one level, or upon any one building element.

The "equivalent lateral force analysis" method described above is but one of several alternate procedures developed for seismic force calculations. In addition to a "simplified analysis" method for most non-hazardous and nonessential low-rise structures, more sophisticated alternate methods have been developed that can be used for any structure in any seismic region. These methods include modal response spectrum analysis as well as both linear and nonlinear response history analysis, all beyond the scope of this text.

Whatever the method of analysis, designers in seismically-active regions should carefully consider the structural ramifications of their "architectural" design decisions, and provide for ductile and continuous load paths from roof to foundation. Following are some guidelines:

1. Avoid "irregularities" in plan and section. In section, these irregularities include soft stories and weak stories that are significantly less stiff or less strong than the stories above; and geometric irregularities and discontinuities (offsets) within the structure. Plan irregularities include asymmetries, reentrant corners, discontinuities and offsets that can result in twisting of the structure (leading to additional torsional stresses) and other stress amplifications. Buildings articulated as multiple masses can be either literally separated (in which case the distance between building masses must be greater than the maximum anticipated lateral drift, or movement), or structurally integrated (in which case the plan and/or sectional irregularities must be taken into account).

2. Provide tie-downs and anchors for all structural elements, even those that seem secured by the force of gravity: the vertical component of seismic ground acceleration can "lift" buildings off their foundations, roofs off of walls, and walls off of framing elements unless they are explicitly and continuously interconnected. Nonstructural items such as suspended ceilings, mechanical and plumbing equipment must also be adequately secured to the structural frame.

    The explicit connection of all structural elements is also necessary for buildings subjected to high wind loads, since uplift and overturning moments due to wind loads can pull apart connections designed on the basis of gravity loads only. But unlike seismic forces, which are triggered by the inertial mass of all objects and elements within the building, wind pressures act primarily on the exposed surfaces of buildings, so that the stability of interior nonstructural elements is not as much of a concern.

3. Avoid unreinforced masonry or other stiff and brittle structural systems. Ductile framing systems can deform inelastically, absorbing large quantities of energy without fracturing.

Example 2.5 Calculate seismic loads

Problem definition. Find the distribution of seismic story loads on a 5-story office building located in San Francisco. Plan dimensions are 60 ft × 80 ft; assume that an "effective seismic weight" of 75 psf can be used for all story levels above grade, including the roof (primarily due to the dead load). The structure is a steel special moment-resisting frame and is built upon dense soil. The typical building section is shown in Figure 2.17.

Solution overview. Find the effective seismic weight, W and the seismic response coefficient, C_s; compute the base shear, V, and the story forces, F_x.

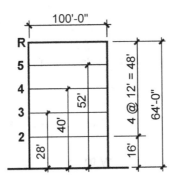

Figure 2.17: Schematic section through building, showing story heights, for Example 2.5

Problem solution

1. *Find W:* The effective seismic weight for each story is the unit weight times the floor area = 75(60 × 80) = 360,000 lb = 360 kips per floor; the total weight, *W*, for the entire building (floors 2 – 5 plus roof) is therefore 5 × 360 = 1800 kips.

2. *Find V:*

   a. From Appendix Table A-2.3, find S_s, S_1 (maximum considered earthquake ground motion at short and long periods, respectively), and T_L (long-period transition period) for San Francisco: $S_s = 1.5$; $S_1 = 0.638$; $T_L = 12$.

   b. From Appendix Table A-2.6 parts *A* and *B*, find site coefficients F_a and F_v: using dense soil (corresponding to Site Class *C*) and the values of S_s and S_1 found in step *a*, we find that $F_a = 1.0$ and $F_v = 1.3$.

   c. From Appendix Table A-2.6 part *C*, find the design elastic response accelerations: $S_{DS} = (\frac{2}{3})(F_a S_s) = (\frac{2}{3})(1.0)(1.5) = 1.0$; $S_{D1} = (\frac{2}{3})(F_v S_1) = (\frac{2}{3})(1.3)(0.638) = 0.553$.

   d. From Appendix Table A-2.6 part *D*, the response modification factor, *R* = 8 (for special steel moment frames). There are no height limits or other restrictions for this structural system category; otherwise, it would be necessary to check which seismic design category the building falls under, from Appendix Table A-2.6 part *G*.

   e. From Appendix Table A-2.6 part *E*, the fundamental period of vibration, *T*, can be taken as $C_T h_n^x = 0.028(64^{0.8}) = 0.78$ second, where h_n = 64 ft is the building height; and the values used for C_T and *x*, taken from Appendix Table A-2.6 part *E*, correspond to steel moment-resisting frames.

   f. From Appendix Table A-2.6 part *F*, the importance factor, I_e equals 1.0 for ordinary buildings.

   g. It is now possible to find the seismic response factor, C_s. The provisional value for $C_s = S_{DS}/(R/I_e) = 1.0/(8/1.0) = 0.125$. However, this must be checked against the upper and lower limits shown in the table: since $S_1 = 0.638 \geq 0.6$ and $T = 0.78 < T_L = 12$, the lower limit for C_s is the greater value of $0.044S_{DS}I_e = 0.044(1.0 \times 1.0) = 0.044$, or 0.01, or $0.5S_1/(R/I_e) = 0.5(0.638)/(8/1.0) = 0.040$; i.e., the lower limit is 0.044 and the upper limit for $C_s = S_{D1}/(TR/I_e) = 0.553/(0.78 \times 8/1.0) = 0.089$. The upper limit governs in this case, so we use $C_s = 0.089$.

   h. From Equation 2.12, the base shear, $V = C_s W = 0.089(1800) = 160.2$ kips.

3. From Equation 2.13, the story forces can be determined as follows:

$$F_x = \frac{V w_x h_x^k}{\Sigma w_i h_i^k}$$

In this equation, since the period, T = 0.78 seconds, is between 0.5 and 2.5, and the limiting values of the exponent, k, are set at 1.0 for $T \leq 0.5$ and 2.0 for $T \geq 2.5$, our value of k is found by linear interpolation:

$$\frac{k - 1.0}{2.0 - 1.0} = \frac{0.78 - 0.5}{2.5 - 0.5}$$

from which k = 1.14. The seismic weight at each story, w_i = 360 kips (see step 1), and the various story heights can be most easily computed in tabular form (as shown below in Table 2.2).

Table 2.2: Calculation of story forces for Example 2.5

Story level	Story height, h_x (ft)	$h_x^{1.14}$	$F_x = 0.471 h_x^{1.14}$ (kips)
Roof	64	114.56	53.94
5	52	90.42	42.57
4	40	67.04	31.56
3	28	44.64	21.02
2	16	23.59	11.11
Sum of story forces, F_x = base shear V =			160.2

Once the values for $h_x^{1.14}$ have been determined for each story level, Equation 2.13 can be re-written as:

$$F_x = \frac{(160.2)(360)h_x^{1.14}}{(360)(23.59 + 44.64 + 67.04 + 90.42 + 114.56)} = 0.471 h_x^{1.14}$$

and values for $F_x = 0.471 h_x^{1.14}$ can then be added to the table. Finally, their distribution on the building can be sketched, as shown in Figure 2.18. The sum of all the story forces, F_x, equals the design base shear, V, as it must to maintain horizontal equilibrium.

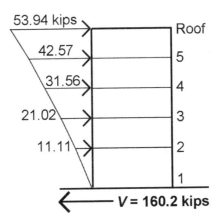

Figure 2.18: Distribution of story forces, F_x, for Example 2.5

DESIGN APPROACHES

Structural engineering prescriptions tend to be written in the form of unambiguous mathematical relationships. In fact, the seeming authority of these formulations masks a rather different reality: the entire subject area of structures is littered with fundamental uncertainties. These uncertainties include not only the nature of loads and the strength and stiffness of structural materials in resisting these loads; but also the appropriateness of mathematical models used in design and analysis, and the degree to which actual built structures conform to the plans and specifications produced by their designers. The basic requirements of safety, serviceability and economy depend on how well designers maneuver within this probabilistic environment.

Allowable Stress Design

Structural design approaches can be characterized by the extent to which these uncertainties are made explicit. The simplest approach to designing structures uses a single factor of safety to define allowable stresses for a particular material. If actual (i.e., calculated) stresses do not exceed these allowable stresses, the structure is considered to be safe. Rather than using allowable stress, it is also possible to use allowable strength, measured in moment or force units. The allowable, or "available," strength is defined by applying a safety factor to the structural element's so-called "limit state," i.e., to the maximum moment or force it can sustain. Then, the element is designed such that its available strength (the limit state divided by a safety factor) is greater or equal to its required strength (the computed force or moment resulting from the application of loads).

In some cases, the factor of safety is actually given. In steel design, for example, the available strength is determined by dividing the limit-state moment or force by a safety factor. In other cases, for example in timber design, the allowable stress is simply presented as a property of the material, and the degree of safety is hidden from the designer. In all cases, however, it is not possible to "fine tune" the structure's design by considering the relative uncertainty of various load types.

In allowable stress (or allowable strength) design, dead and live loads are simply added together, in spite of the fact that dead loads can be predicted with a higher degree of certainty than live loads. Thus, if two structures carry the same total load, but one structure has a higher percentage of dead load, the structures will have different degrees of safety if designed using the allowable stress method. In fact, the structure with more dead load will be statistically safer, since the actual dead load acting on the structure is more likely to correspond to the calculated dead load than is the case with live load. Allowable stress design is sometimes called working stress design, since the loads used in the method ("service loads") represent what we expect to actually "work" with during the life of the structure.

To account for the improbability of multiple loads simultaneously acting on a structure at their maximum intensity, most codes provide load reduction factors for various combinations of load types. For example, where several loads are being considered, the "non-dead" loads may be multiplied by 0.75, as long as the total thus calculated does not exceed the dead load together with the largest single additional load considered in the calculations (earthquake loads are sometimes excluded from this provision). The reduction of live loads on relatively large influence areas was discussed previously in this chapter.

Strength Design

A more recent approach to the design of structures explicitly considers the probabilistic nature of loads and the resistance of structural materials to those loads. Instead of regulating the design of structural elements by defining an upper limit to their "working stresses," strength design considers both the limit state of the structural element — typically the strength at which the element fails or otherwise becomes structurally useless — as well as the relative uncertainty of the various loads acting on that element.

Using this method, the required strength of a structural element, calculated using loads multiplied by load factors (that correspond to their respective uncertainties), must not exceed the design strength of that element, calculated by multiplying the strength of the structural element by resistance factors (that account for the variability of stresses, and the consequences of failure). If Q represents the loads and their effects on a structural element, and R represents the resistance, or strength, of that element, then strength design can be schematically represented as follows:

$$\lambda \Sigma (\gamma_i Q_i) \leq \phi R_n \qquad\qquad (2.14)$$

where γ_i are the load factors (mostly greater than 1.0); ϕ is the strength reduction factor (smaller than 1.0); and λ is an additional factor (smaller than 1.0) that can be used when multiple load types are assumed to act simultaneously, in which case the likelihood of all loads being present at their maximum intensities is reduced.

For reinforced concrete designed with the strength method, some commonly used factored load combinations are listed in Appendix Table A-2.7. Multiple combinations of loads are less likely to occur simultaneously at full magnitude; the load factors listed in Appendix Table A-2.7 account for these variable probabilities. The load factor for dead load is sometimes less than zero, since this can represent the more dangerous condition (i.e., the more conservative assumption) where wind or earthquake forces cause overturning or uplift.

Strength design is similar to Load and Resistance Factor Design (LRFD in wood or steel), or "limit state design." In the U.S., strength design is now used almost exclusively in reinforced concrete design; beginning to be widely used in steel design; and not yet commonly used in timber design. In this text, we will use strength design for reinforced concrete, allowable stress design for timber and allowable strength design for steel.

Example 2.6 Load combinations (Part I)

Problem definition. For the "light manufacturing" structure shown in Figure 2.19, assume that the dead load consists of the reinforced concrete floor structure. The weight of the reinforced concrete can be taken as 150 pcf. Find the distributed "design" load on a typical beam for both strength design and allowable stress design.

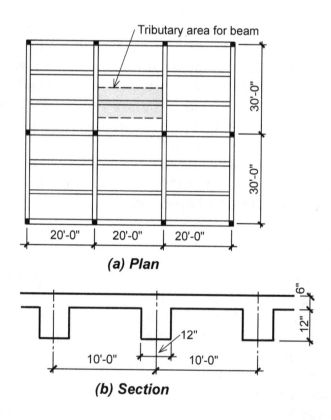

Figure 2.19: (*a*) Framing plan and (*b*) section for Example 2.6

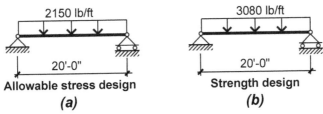

Figure 2.20 Load diagrams for Example 2.6 using (*a*) allowable stress design; and (*b*) strength design

Solution overview. Find dead and live loads; add loads together for allowable stress design; apply load factors for strength design (strength design is used almost exclusively for the design of reinforced concrete structures).

Problem solution
1. From Appendix Table A-2.2, find live load: L = 125 psf; or, considering the distributed load on a typical beam, L = 125 × 10 = 1250 lb/ft.
2. Find dead load.
   a. Slab: (150)($\frac{5}{12}$)(10) = 750 lb/ft.
   b. Beam: (150)($\frac{12}{12}$)($\frac{12}{12}$) = 150 lb/ft.
   c. Total dead load = 750 + 150 = 900 lb/ft.
3. *Allowable stress design:* Total load = $D + L$ = 900 + 1250 = 2150 lb/ft (Figure 2.20*a*).

4. *Strength design:* From Appendix Table A-2.7, the total load = 1.2D + 1.6L = 1.2(900) + 1.6(1250) = 3080 lb/ft (Figure 2.20*b*).

Example 2.7 Load combinations (Part II)

Problem definition. Now, repeat Example 2.6, except change the occupancy to that of a restaurant, and add ceramic tile (weighing 25 psf) to the surface of the slab.

Solution overview. Find dead and live loads; add loads together for allowable stress design; apply load factors for strength design.

Problem solution
1. From Table A-2.2, find live load: L = 100 psf; or, considering the distributed load on a typical beam, L = 100 × 10 = 1000 lb/ft.
2. Find dead load.
   a. Slab: concrete + tile = ($\frac{5}{12}$)(150)(10) + 25(10) = 1000 lb/ft.
   b. Beam: ($\frac{12}{12}$)($\frac{12}{12}$)(150) = 150 lb/ft.
   c. Total dead load = 1000 + 150 = 1150 lb/ft.

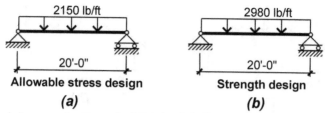

Figure 2.21: Load diagrams for Example 2.7 using (*a*) allowable stress design; and (*b*) strength design

3. Allowable stress design: Total load = $D + L$ = 1150 + 1000 = 2150 lb/ft (Figure 2.21*a*).
4. Strength design: From Table A-2.7, the total load = $1.2D + 1.6L$ = 1.2(1150) + 1.6(1000) = 2980 lb/ft (Figure 2.21*b*).

Examples 2.6 and 2.7 were admittedly rigged to make a point: even though the total unfactored loads are the same in both cases, the factored loads used in strength design are different, since the proportion of live to dead loads has changed. The allowable stress procedure would result in exactly the same beam design in both cases, whereas the strength method would permit a smaller beam for the restaurant in Example 2.7 (since the total design loads are smaller). However, according to the probabilistic logic of strength design, even though the restaurant beams are smaller, the degree of safety would be the same for both beams.

Example 2.8 Load combinations (Part III)

Problem definition. Assuming strength design, find the various combinations of load acting on the 9th- and 10th-floor columns shown in Figure 2.22. Assume that the dead load for each floor level is 40 psf, the live load for the 10th floor is 60 psf, the roof live load, L_r (maintenance, etc.), is 20 psf, and the wind load acting on the roof is 30 psf (acting upward). The tributary area is 25 × 10 = 250 ft² per floor, as shown in Figure 2.22.

Solution overview. Find loads (including live load reduction coefficient); compute load combinations; identify critical (governing) combinations.

Problem solution
10th-floor column:

1. Find loads:
   a. D = 250(40) = 10,000 lb = 10 kips.
   b. L_r = 250(20) = 250(20) = 5000 lb = 5.0 kips.

c. $W = 250(-30) = -7500$ lb $= -7.5$ kips.

2. From Table A-2.7 (strength design), compute load combinations:
   a. $1.4D = 1.4(10) = 14$ kips.
   b. $1.2D + 1.6L + 0.5(L_r$ or $S) = 1.2(10) + 0 + 0.5(5) = 14.5$ kips.
   c. $1.2D + 1.6(L_r$ or $S) + (0.5L$ or $0.8W) = 1.2(10) + 1.6(5) + 0.8(-7.5) = 14$ kips.
   d. $1.2D + 1.6W + 0.5L + 0.5(L_r$ or $S) = 1.2(10) + 1.6(-7.5) + 0 + 0.5(5) = 2.5$ kips.
   e. $1.2D + 1.0E + 0.5L + 0.2S = 1.2(10) + 0 + 0 + 0 = 12$ kips.
   f. $0.9D + 1.6W = 0.9(10) + 1.6(-7.5) = -3$ kips.
   g. $0.9D + 1.0E = 0.9(10) + 0 = 9$ kips.

3. Conclusions: For the 10th-floor column, the critical load combinations are 14.5 kips from live and dead load plus roof live load (combination *b*); and −3 kips from dead and wind load (combination *f*). The negative force due to wind uplift must be considered since it places the upper level column in tension. In equations *c*, *d*, and *e*, the live load factor is taken as 0.5 (see Note 2 in Appendix Table A-2.7).

9th-floor column:

1. Find loads:
   a. $D = 250 (40) \times 2$ floors $= 20,000$ lb $= 20$ kips.
   b. $L_r = 250(20) = 250(20) = 5000$ lb $= 5.0$ kips.

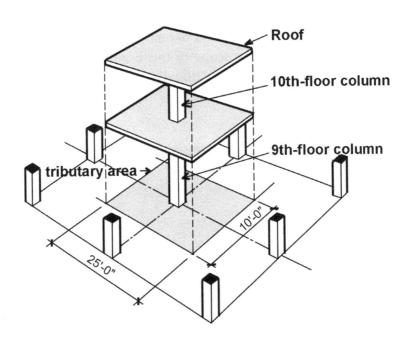

Figure 2.22 Tributary floor areas for Example 2.8

c. The live load reduction coefficient can be found from Table A-2.2 and is equal to: $0.25 + 15/\sqrt{4 \times 250} = 0.72$.

d. $L = (250 \times 60)$(reduction coefficient) $= (250 \times 60)(0.72) = 10,800$ lb $= 10.8$ kips.

e. $W = 250(-30) = -7500$ lb $= -7.5$ kips.

2. From Table A-2.7 (strength design), compute load combinations:

a. $1.4D = 1.4(20) = 28$ kips.

b. $1.2D + 1.6L + 0.5(L_r \text{ or } S) = 1.2(20) + 1.6(10.8) + 0.5(5) = 43.78$ kips.

c. There are two choices here:

(1) using W: $1.2D + 1.6(L_r \text{ or } S) + (0.5L \text{ or } 0.8W) = 1.2(20) + 1.6(5) + 0.8(-7.5) = 26.0$ kips; or

(2) using L: $1.2D + 1.6(L_r \text{ or } S) + (0.5L \text{ or } 0.8W) = 1.2(20) + 1.6(5) + 0.5(10.8) = 37.4$ kips.

d. $1.2D + 1.6W + 0.5L + 0.5(L_r \text{ or } S) = 1.2(20) + 1.6(-7.5) + 0.5(10.8) + 0.5(5) = 19.9$ kips.

e. $1.2D + 1.0E + 0.5L + 0.2S = 1.2(20) + 0 + 0.5(10.8) + 0 = 29.4$ kips.

f. $0.9D + 1.6W = 0.9(20) + 1.6(-7.5) = 6$ kips.

g. $0.9D + 1.0E = 0.9(20) + 0 = 18$ kips.

3. Conclusions: For the 9th-floor column, the critical load combination is 43.78 kips from live and dead load plus roof live load (combination *b*). No combination of loads places the column in tension. In equations *c*, *d*, and *e*, the live load factor is taken as 0.5 (see Note 2 in Appendix Table A-2.7).

In a reinforced concrete structure, columns typically are also subjected to bending moments due to their continuity with beams, girders or slabs. Where the combined effects of axial loads and bending moments are accounted for — something that is beyond the scope of this book — the axial loads computed from other load combinations (together with the bending moments associated with them) might turn out to be critical.

Chapter 2 Appendix

Table A-2.1: Dead loads

A. Basic volumetric weights in pounds per cubit foot (pcf)	
Stone:	
Sandstone	144
Granite	165
Marble	173
Brick/CMU/concrete	100 – 145
Normal-weight reinforced concrete	150
Metals:	
Aluminum	165
Steel	492
Lead	710
Glass	160
Wood	25 – 50
Water	64
Earth:	
Dry clay	63
Silt, moist and packed	96
Wet sand and gravel	120
Insulation:	
Glass fiber batts	0.8
Expanded polystyrene boards	0.9 – 1.8
Extruded polystyrene boaards	2.2
Polyisocyanurate boards	2.0
Fiberboard	1.5

B. Distributed loads in pounds per square feet (psf)	
Wood floor system: 2 × 10 joists at 16 in. on center, wood finish floor and subfloor, gypsum board ceiling	10.5
Steel floor system: 4½ in. corrugated steel deck with concrete slab, tile floor, mechanical ducts, suspended tile ceiling	47
Concrete floor system: 6 in. reinforced concrete slab, tile floor, mechanical ducts, suspended tile ceiling	80
Floor-ceiling components:	
Harwood finish floor, ⅞ in.	4.0
Wood subfloor, ¾ in.	2.5
Acoustical tile with suspended steel channels	
Mechanical duct allowance	3.0
Steel stud partition allowance	4.0
	8.0
Sheathing:	
Plywood, per ⅛ in. thickness	0.40
Gypsum board, per ⅛ in. thickness	0.55

(continued)

Table A-2.1 continued (Part *C*)

C. Linear loads in pounds per foot (lb/ft)	
Steel beam, ordinary span and spacing	30 – 50
Steel girder, ordinary span and spacing	60 – 100
Wood joist, 2 × 10	4.0
Brick-CMU cavity wall, 12 ft high	1000

Table A-2.2: Live loads

A. Typical live loads based on occupancy (psf)	
Assembly areas with fixed seats	60
Assembly areas with movable seats	100
Lobbies, corridors (first floor)	100
Dining rooms and restaurants	100
Garages for passenger cars	40
Libraries, reading rooms	60
Libraries, stack areas (not less than)	150
Manufacturing, light	125
Manufacturing, heavy	250
Office buildings	50
Dwellings and hotels (except as noted below)	40
Note: Residential sleeping areas	30
Schools (classrooms)	40
Schools (corridors above first floor)	80
Stadium and arena bleachers	100
Stairs and exitways	100
Stores, retail (first floor)	100
Stores, retail (upper floors)	75
Stores, wholesale (all floors)	125

B. Live load reduction coefficient[1,2,3,4]
Live load reduction coefficient = $0.25 + \dfrac{15}{\sqrt{K_{LL}A_T}}$

Notes for Part *B*:

1. K_{LL} is the live load element factor and is defined as follows for selected common beam and column configurations:

K_{LL} = 4 for columns without cantilever slabs

K_{LL} = 3 for edge columns with cantilever slabs

K_{LL} = 2 for corner columns with cantilever slabs

K_{LL} = 2 for beams (except as noted below)

K_{LL} = 1 for one-way and two-way slabs, edge beams with cantilever slabs, and anything else not previously mentioned — and note that A_T for one-way slabs cannot be taken as more than 1.5 × (slab span)^2

(continued)

Table A-2.2 continued (Notes)

2. A_T is the tributary area of the element being considered (ft^2)

3. No live load reduction applies when $K_{LL}A_T \leq 400$ ft^2 or when the element supports a single floor with live load > 100 psf (for an element supporting more than one floor with live loads > 100 psf, a reduction no greater than 20% is permitted)

4. Reduction coefficient cannot be taken greater than 1.0; nor can it be smaller than 0.5 for elements supporting a single floor level; or smaller than 0.4 for all other conditions.

Table A-2.3: Environmental loads[1]

City, State	Ground Snow Load (psf)	Basic (Ultimate) Wind Speed, V (mph)			Seismic Ground Motion[2]		
		Risk Category I	Risk Category II	Risk Category III or IV	S_s	S_1	T_L
Boston, MA	40	118	128	140	0.217	0.069	6
Chicago, IL	25	105	115	120	0.133	0.062	12
Little Rock, AR	10	105	115	120	0.405	0.164	12
Houston, TX	0	128	136	145	0.072	0.039	12
Ithaca, NY	40	105	115	120	0.126	0.056	6
Miami, FL	0	157	169	181	0.042	0.020	8
New York, NY	20	105	115	123	0.278	0.072	6
Philadelphia, PA	25	105	115	120	0.202	0.060	6
Phoenix, AZ	0	105	115	120	0.171	0.057	6
Portland, ME	50	108	118	127	0.241	0.078	6
San Francisco, CA	0	100	110	115	1.500	0.638	12

Notes:

1. Approximate values taken from snow, wind, and seismic maps. Various web-based applications are available to find environmental loads at specific locations in the U.S. See, for example:

   SNOW: http://www.groundsnowbyzip.com/ [Johannessen & Leone Associates]

   WIND: http://www.atcouncil.org/windspeed/ [Applied Technology Council]

   SEISMIC: http://earthquake.usgs.gov/hazards/designmaps/ [United States Geological Survey]

2. S_s and S_1 are, respectively, the maximum considered earthquake ground motions of 0.2 s (short) and 1 s (long) spectral response acceleration (5% of critical damping) for site class B, measured as a fraction of the acceleration due to gravity. T_L is the so-called "long-period transition period" (seconds).

Table A-2.4: Snow load Importance factor, I_s

Category	Description	Factor
I	Low hazard (minor storage, etc.)	0.8
II	Regular (ordinary buildings)	1.0
III	Substantial hazard (schools, jails, places of assembly with no fewer than 300 occupants)	1.1
IV	Essential facilities (hospitals, fire stations, etc.)	1.2

Table A-2.5: Wind coefficients

A. Velocity pressure coefficient, K^1			
Height above grade[2], z (ft)	Exposure B[3]	Exposure C[4]	Exposure D[5]
500	1.57	1.78	1.90
400	1.47	1.69	1.82
300	1.35	1.59	1.73
200	1.20	1.46	1.62
100	0.99	1.27	1.43
90	0.96	1.24	1.41
80	0.93	1.21	1.38
70	0.89	1.17	1.35
60	0.85	1.14	1.31
50	0.81	1.09	1.27
45	0.79	1.07	1.25
40	0.76	1.04	1.22
35	0.73	1.01	1.19
30	0.70	0.98	1.16
25	0.67	0.95	1.13
20	0.62	0.90	1.08
0 - 15	0.57	0.85	1.03

Notes for Part A:

1. Values of K are based on the following equation, where z is the height above grade (ft); $a = 7.0$ for Exposure B; 9.5 for Exposure C, and 11.5 for Exposure D; and $z_g = 1200$ for Exposure B; 900 for Exposure C; and 700 for Exposure D:

$$K = 2.01 \left[\frac{z}{z_g} \right]^{2/a}$$

When using tabular values for K, linear interpolation between values is permitted.

2. When computing pressures on windward surfaces, use height z corresponding to height for which pressure is being computed; for all other surfaces, use $z = h$ (mean roof height: i.e., use this single value of z for the entire surface). See Table A-2.5 Part H for graphic explanation of building geometry parameters.

3. Exposure B refers to urban or suburban areas, wooded areas, etc.

4. Exposure C refers to open terrain with scattered obstructions, excluding water surfaces in hurricane regions.

5. Exposure D refers to flat, unobstructed areas like mud flats, salt flats, or water, both inside or outside of hurricane regions.

B. External pressure coefficient for walls, C_p^1			
Orientation	$0 < L/B \leq 1$	$L/B = 2$	$L/B \geq 4$
Windward	0.8	0.8	0.8
Leeward	−0.5	−0.3	−0.2
Side	−0.7	−0.7	−0.7

Note for Part B:

1. L and B are the plan dimensions of the rectangular building, with B being the dimension of the windward and leeward walls, and L the dimension of the side walls. See Table A-2.5 Part H for graphic explanation of building geometry parameters.

(continued)

Table A-2.5 continued (Part *C*)

C. External pressure coefficient on windward slope of roof, C_p, for wind direction normal to ridge[1,2,7]			
Roof angle, θ (deg)	$h/L \leq 0.25$	$h/L = 0.50$	$h/L \geq 1.0$
[6]θ < 10 $0 < D \leq h/2$	−0.9, -0.18	−0.9, -0.18	[3]−1.3, -0.18
$h/2 < D \leq h$	−0.9, -0.18	−0.9, -0.18	−0.7, -0.18
$h < D \leq 2h$	−0.5, -0.18	−0.5, -0.18	−0.7, -0.18
$2h < D$	−0.3, -0.18	−0.3, -0.18	−0.7, -0.18
[6]θ = 10	−0.7, -0.18	−0.9, -0.18	[3]−1.3, -0.18
θ = 15	−0.5, 40.0	−0.7, -0.18	−1.0, -0.18
θ = 20	−0.3, 0.2	−0.4, 40.0	−0.7, -0.18
θ = 25	−0.2, 0.3	−0.3, 0.2	−0.5, 40.0
θ = 30	−0.2, 0.3	−0.2, 0.2	−0.3, 0.2
θ = 35	[4]0.0, 0.4	−0.2, 0.3	−0.2, 0.2
θ = 45	0.4	[4]0.0, 0.4	[4]0.0, 0.3
[5]θ ≥ 60	0.01θ	0.01θ	0.01θ

Notes for Part *C*:

1. Where two values are given, either may apply, and both must be considered. Interpolation between adjacent values is permitted, but must be between numbers of the same sign; where no number of the same sign exists, use 0.0.

2. Values are used with *K* taken at mean roof height. Units of length for *D*, *h*, and *L* must be consistent with each other. For roof angles less than 10°, *D* refers to the range of horizontal distances from the windward eave (edge) for which the value of C_p applies; *h* is the height of the eave above grade for roof angles no greater than 10°, otherwise, *h* is the mean roof height above grade; *L* is the horizontal length of the building parallel to the wind direction. See Table A-2.5 Part *H* for graphic explanation of building geometry parameters.

3. Value of −1.3 may be reduced depending on the area it is acting on: for areas no greater than 100 ft², no reduction; for areas of 200 ft², multiply by 0.9; for areas no smaller than 1000 ft², multiply by 0.8; interpolate between given values.

4. Values of 0.0 are used only to interpolate between adjacent fields.

5. Roof angles over 80° are treated as windward walls, with $C_p = 0.8$.

6. See Note 2 for roof height, *h*, where roof angle is no greater than 10°.

7. Negative numbers indicate "suction," i.e., forces acting away from the building surface; positive numbers indicate forces "pushing" against the building surface.

(continued)

Table A-2.5 continued (Part *D*)

D. External pressure coefficient on leeward slope of roof, C_p, for wind direction normal to ridge[1,2,3]			
Roof angle, Θ (deg)	$h/L \leq 0.25$	$h/L = 0.50$	$h/L \geq 1.0$
$\theta = 10$	−0.3	−0.5	−0.7
$\theta = 15$	−0.5	−0.5	−0.6
$\theta \geq 20$	−0.6	−0.6	−0.6

Notes for Part D:

1. The height *h* is measured to the eave for roof angles equal to 10°, otherwise, *h* is the mean roof height above grade; *L* is the horizontal length of the building parallel to the wind direction. See Table A-2.5 Part *H* for graphic explanation of building geometry parameters.

2. For roof angles less than 10°, the roof is considered to be flat, and no leeward pressures are computed. Instead, use the values in Table A.2.4 Part *C* for the entire roof.

3. Interpolation is permitted between values.

4. Negative numbers indicate "suction," i.e., forces acting away from the building surface; positive numbers indicate forces "pushing" against the building surface.

E. External pressure coefficient roof, C_p, for wind direction parallel to ridge, for all roof angles[1,2,4,5]			
Applicable Roof Area	$h/L \leq 0.25$	$h/L = 0.50$	$h/L \geq 1.0$
$0 < D \leq h/2$	−0.9, −0.18	-0.9, −0.18	[3]-1.3, −0.18
$h/2 < D \leq h$	−0.9, −0.18	−0.9, −0.18	−0.7, −0.18
$h < D \leq 2h$	−0.5, −0.18	−0.5, −0.18	−0.7, −0.18
$2h < D$	−0.3, −0.18	-0.3, −0.18	−0.7, −0.18

Notes for Part *E*:

1. Where two values are given, either may apply, and both must be considered. Interpolation between adjacent values is permitted, but must be between numbers of the same sign.

2. Values are used with *K* taken at mean roof height. Units of length for *D*, *h*, and *L* must be consistent with each other. For all roof angles, *D* refers to the range of horizontal distances from the windward eave (edge) for which the value of C_p applies; *h* is the height of the eave above grade for roof angles no greater than 10°, otherwise, *h* is the mean roof height above grade; *L* is the horizontal length of the building parallel to the wind direction. See Table A-2.5 Part *H* for graphic explanation of building geometry parameters.

3. Value of −1.3 may be reduced depending on the area it is acting on: for areas no greater than 100 ft², no reduction; for areas of 200 ft², multiply by 0.9; for areas no smaller than 1000 ft², multiply by 0.8; interpolate between given values.

4. Roof angles over 80° are treated as windward walls, with $C_p = 0.8$.

5. Negative numbers indicate "suction," i.e., forces acting away from the building surface; positive numbers indicate forces "pushing" against the building surface.

F. Gust effect factor, G
In lieu of more complex calculations, use $G = 0.85$ for so-called "rigid" buildings: such buildings are in most cases no more than 4 times taller than their minimum width, and have a fundamental frequency of at least 1 Hz (1 cycle per second).

(continued)

Table A-2.5 continued (Part *G*)

G. Importance factor, I_w		
Category	Description	Factor[1]
I	Low hazard (minor storage, etc.)	—
II	Regular (ordinary buildings)	—
III	Substantial risk to human life or major economic impact, with or without significant disruption of daily life	—
IV	Essential facilities (hospitals, fire stations, etc.)	—

Note for Part *G*:

1. Importance factors for wind are no longer used directly in calculations; instead, consideration of importance (risk) has been incorporated within basic wind speed maps and wind speed values.

H. Graphic definition of building parameters[1]

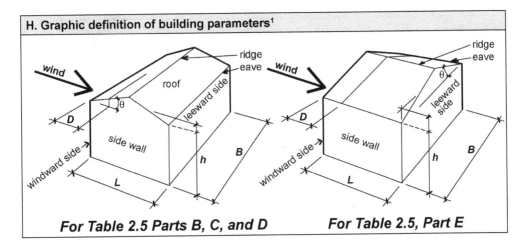

For Table 2.5 Parts B, C, and D   **For Table 2.5, Part E**

Note for Part *H*:

1. When using Table A-2.5 Parts *C*, *D*, and *E*, the roof height, *h*, is measured to the mean roof elevation, except for roof angles less than or equal to 10°, in which case *h* is measured to the eave, as indicated by the dotted line.

Table A-2-6: Seismic coefficients

A. Site coefficient, F_a

Site class	S_s				
	≤ 0.25	0.5	0.75	1.0	≥ 1.25
A = hard rock	0.8	0.8	0.8	0.8	0.8
B = rock	1.0	1.0	1.0	1.0	1.0
C = dense soil or soft rock	1.2	1.2	1.1	1.0	1.0
D = stiff soil	1.6	1.4	1.2	1.1	1.0
E = soft soil	2.5	1.7	1.2	0.9	0.9
F = liquifiable soils, etc.	Need site-specific investigation				

B. Site coefficient, F_v

Site class	S_1				
	≤ 0.25	0.5	0.75	1.0	≥ 1.25
A = hard rock	0.8	0.8	0.8	0.8	0.8
B = rock	1.0	1.0	1.0	1.0	1.0
C = dense soil or soft rock	1.7	1.6	1.5	1.4	1.3
D = stiff soil	2.4	2.0	1.8	1.6	1.5
E = soft soil	3.5	3.2	2.8	2.4	2.4
F = liquifiable soils, etc.	Need site-specific investigation				

C. Design elastic response acceleration, S_{DS} and S_{D1}

[1]$S_{DS} = \frac{2}{3}(F_a)(S_s)$	[1]$S_{D1} = \frac{2}{3}(F_a)(S_1)$

Note for Part C:

1. See Table A-2.3 for selected values of S_s and S_1. See Table A-2.5, Parts A and B for F_a and F_v respectively.

(continued)

Table A-2.6 continued (Part *D*)

D. Response modification coefficient, *R* (including height and other limitations based on seismic design category[1])	
Bearing wall systems	
01. Special reinforced concrete shear walls ([1,2]categories *D, E* limited to 160 ft; *F* limited to 100 ft)	5
02. Ordinary reinforced concrete shear walls ([1]not permitted in categories *D – F*)	4
03. Detailed plain concrete shear walls ([1]not permitted in categories *C – F*)	2
04. Ordinary plain concrete shear walls ([1]not permitted in categories *C – F*)	1.5
05. Intermediate precast shear walls ([1,2]categories *D – F* limited to 40 ft)	4
06. Ordinary precast shear walls ([1]not permitted in categories *C – F*)	3
07. Special reinforced masonry shear walls ([1]categories *D, E* limited to 160 ft; *F* limited to 100 ft)	5
08. Intermediate reinforced masonry shear walls ([1]not permitted in categories *D – F*)	3.5
09. Ordinary reinforced masonry shear walls ([1]not permitted in categories *D – F*; *C* limited to 160 ft)	2
10. Detailed plain masonry shear walls ([1]not permitted in categories *C – F*)	2
11. Ordinary plain masonry shear walls ([1]not permitted in categories *C – F*)	1.5
12. Prestressed masonry shear walls ([1]not permitted in categories *C – F*)	1.5
13. Ordinary reinforced AAC [Autoclaved Aerated Concrete] masonry shear walls ([1]category *C* limited to 35 ft; not permitted in categories *D – F*)	2
14. Ordinary plain AAC [Autoclaved Aerated Concrete] masonry shear walls ([1]not permitted in categories *C – F*)	1.5
15. Light-frame (wood) walls sheathed with wood structural panels rated for shear resistance, or steel sheets ([1]categories *D – F* limited to 65 ft)	6.5
16. Light-frame (cold-formed steel) walls sheathed with wood structural panels rated for shear resistance, or steel sheets ([1]categories *D – F* limited to 65 ft)	6.5
17. Light-frame walls with shear panels of all other materials ([1]category *D* limited to 35 ft; not permitted in categories *E, F*)	2
18. Light-frame (cold-formed steel) wall systems using flat strap bracing ([1]categories *D – F* limited to 65 ft)	4
Building frame systems	
01. Steel eccentrically braced frames ([1,2]categories *D, E* limited to 160 ft; *F* limited to 100 ft)	8
02. Steel special concentrically braced frames ([1,2]categories *D, E* limited to 160 ft; *F* limited to 100 ft)	6
03. Steel ordinary concentrically braced frames ([1]categories *D, E* limited to 35 ft; category *F* not permitted)	3.25
04. Special reinforced concrete shear walls ([1,2]categories *D, E* limited to 160 ft; *F* limited to 100 ft)	6
05. Ordinary reinforced concrete shear walls ([1]not permitted in categories *D – F*)	5
06. Detailed plain concrete shear walls ([1]not permitted in categories *C – F*)	2
07. Ordinary plain concrete shear walls ([1]not permitted in categories *C – F*)	1.5
08. Intermediate precast shear walls ([1,2]categories *D – F* limited to 40 ft)	5
09. Ordinary precast shear walls ([1]not permitted in categories *C – F*)	4
10. Composite steel and concrete eccentrically braced frames ([1]categories *D, E* limited to 160 ft; *F* limited to 100 ft)	8
11. Steel and concrete composite special concentrically braced frames ([1]categories *D, E* limited to 160 ft; *F* limited to 100 ft)	5

(continued)

Table A-2.6 continued (Part *D*)

D. Response modification coefficient, *R* (including height and other limitations based on seismic design category[1])	
12. Ordinary composite steel and concrete braced frames ([1]not permitted in categories *D* – *F*)	3
13. Steel and concrete composite plate shear walls ([1]categories *D*, *E* limited to 160 ft; *F* limited to 100 ft)	6.5
14. Steel and concrete composite special shear walls ([1]categories *D*, *E* limited to 160 ft; *F* limited to 100 ft)	6
15. Steel and concrete composite ordinary shear walls ([1]not permitted in categories *D* – *F*)	5
16. Special reinforced masonry shear walls ([1]categories *D*, *E* limited to 160 ft; *F* limited to 100 ft)	5.5
17. Intermediate reinforced masonry shear walls ([1]not permitted in categories *D* – *F*)	4
18. Ordinary reinforced masonry shear walls ([1]category *C* limited to 160 ft; not permitted in categories *D* – *F*)	2
19. Detailed plain masonry shear walls ([1]not permitted in categories *C* – *F*)	2
20. Ordinary plain masonry shear walls ([1]not permitted in categories *C* – *F*)	1.5
21. Prestressed masonry shear walls ([1]not permitted in categories *C* – *F*)	1.5
22. Light-frame (wood) walls sheathed with wood structural panels rated for shear resistance ([1]categories *D* – *F* limited to 65 ft)	7
23. Light-frame (cold-formed steel) walls sheathed with wood structural panels rated for shear resistance, or steel sheets ([1]categories *D* – *F* limited to 65 ft)	7
24. Light framed walls with shear panels — all other materials ([1]not permitted in categories *E*– *F*; *D* limited to 35 ft)	2.5
25. Buckling-restrained braced frames ([1,2]categories *D*, *E* limited to 160 ft; *F* limited to 100 ft)	8
26. Steel special plate shear walls ([1,2]categories *D*, *E* limited to 160 ft; *F* limited to 100 ft)	7
Moment-resisting frame systems	
01. Special steel moment frames (no limits)	8
02. Special steel truss moment frames ([1]category *D* limited to 160 ft; *E* limited to 100 ft; not permitted in category *F*)	7
03. Intermediate steel moment frames ([1,2]category *D* limited to 35 ft; not permitted in categories *E* – *F*)	4.5
04. Ordinary steel moment frames ([1,2]not permitted in categories *D* – *F*)	3.5
05. Special reinforced concrete moment frames (no limits)	8
06. Intermediate reinforced concrete moment frames ([1]not permitted in categories *D* – *F*)	5
07. Ordinary reinforced concrete moment frames ([1]not permitted in categories *C* – *F*)	3
08. Special composite steel and concrete moment frames (no limits)	8
09. Steel and concrete composite intermediate moment frames ([1]not permitted in categories *D* – *F*)	5
10. Steel and concrete composite partially restrained moment frames ([1]categories *B*, *C* limited to 160 ft; *D* limited to 100 ft; not permitted in categories *E*, *F*)	6
11. Steel and concrete composite ordinary moment frames ([1]not permitted in categories *C* – *F*)	3
12. Cold-formed steel – special bolted moment frame ([1]limited to 35 ft in all categories)	3.5

(continued)

Table A-2.6 continued (Part *D*)

D. Response modification coefficient, *R* (including height and other limitations based on seismic design category[1])	
Dual systems with special moment frames that resist at least 25% of seismic forces	
01. Steel eccentrically braced frames (no limits)	8
02. Special steel concentrically braced frames (no limits)	7
03. Special reinforced concrete shear walls (no limits)	7
04. Ordinary reinforced concrete shear walls ([1]not permitted in categories *D – F*)	6
05. Composite steel and concrete eccentrically braced frames (no limits)	8
06. Composite steel and concrete special concentrically braced frames (no limits)	6
07. Steel and concrete composite plate shear walls (no limits)	7.5
08. Steel and concrete composite special shear walls with steel elements (no limits)	7
09. Steel and concrete composite ordinary shear walls with steel elements ([1]not permitted in categories *D – F*)	6
10. Special reinforced masonry shear walls (no limits)	5.5
11. Intermediate reinforced masonry shear walls ([1]not permitted in categories *D – F*)	4
12. Buckling-restrained braced frame (no limits)	8
13. Special steel plate shear walls (no limits)	8
Dual systems with intermediate moment frames that resist at least 25% of seismic forces	
01. Special steel concentrically braced frames ([1]not permitted in categories *E – F*; *D* limited to 35 ft)	6
02. Special reinforced concrete shear walls ([1]category *D* limited to 160 ft; *E – F* limited to 100 ft)	6.5
03. Ordinary reinforced masonry shear walls ([1]category *C* limited to 160 ft; not permitted in categories *D - F*)	3
04. Intermediate reinforced masonry shear walls ([1]not permitted in categories *D – F*)	3.5
05. Steel and concrete composite special concentrically braced frames ([1]not permitted in category *F*; *D* limited to 160 ft; *E* limited to 100 ft)	5.5
06. Steel and concrete composite ordinary braced frames ([1]not permitted in categories *D – F*)	3.5
07. Steel and concrete composite ordinary shear walls ([1]not permitted in categories *D – F*)	5
08. Ordinary reinforced concrete shear walls ([1]not permitted in categories *D – F*)	5.5
Cantilevered column systems detailed to conform with:	
01. Steel special cantilever column systems ([1]categories *B – F* limited to 35 ft)	2.5
02. Steel ordinary cantilever column systems ([1]not permitted in categories *D – F*; *B,C* limited to 35 ft)	1.25
03. Special reinforced concrete moment frames ([1]categories *B – F* limited to 35 ft)	2.5
04. Intermediate concrete moment frames ([1]categories *B, C* limited to 35 ft; not permitted in categories *D – F*)	1.5
05. Ordinary concrete moment frames ([1]category *B* limited to 35 ft; not permitted in categories *C – F*)	1
06. Timber frames ([1]categories *B – D* limited to 35 ft; not permitted in categories *E, F*)	1.5

(continued)

Table A-2.6 continued (Part *D*)

D. Response modification coefficient, *R* (including height and other limitations based on seismic design category[1])	
Miscellaneous other systems	
Steel systems not specifically detailed for seismic resistance, excluding cantilevered column systems ([1]not permitted in categories *D – F*)	3
Shear wall-frame interactive system with ordinary reinforced concrete moment frames and ordinary reinforced concrete shear walls ([1]not permitted in categories *C – F*)	4.5

Notes for Part *D*:

1. Seismic design categories are described in Table A-2.6 Part *G*, and range from *A* (least severe) to *F* (most severe).

2. Height limits may be increased in certain cases, and buildings may be permitted in certain cases for this seismic force-resisting system (refer to building codes).

E. Fundamental period of vibration, *T* (seconds) — approximate value, and exponent[2], *k*			
[1]*T*	Structure	C_T	*x*
$T = C_T h_n^x$	Steel moment-resisting frame	0.028	0.8
	Concrete moment-resisting frame	0.016	0.9
	Steel eccentrically-braced frame and buckling-restrained braced frames	0.030	0.75
	All other structural types	0.020	0.75

Notes for Part *E*:

1. h_n is the building height (ft).

2. *k* accounts for the more complex effect of longer periods of vibration on the distribution of story forces, and equals 1 for periods ≤ 0.5 seconds; and 2 for periods ≥ 2.5 seconds (with linear interpolation permitted for periods between 0.5 and 2.5 seconds)

F. Importance factor, I_e		
Occupancy category	Description	Factor
I	Low hazard (minor storage, etc.)	1.0
II	Regular (ordinary buildings)	1.0
III	Substantial risk to human life or major economic impact, with or without significant disruption of daily life	1.25
IV	Essential facilities (hospitals, fire stations, etc.)	1.50

(continued)

Table A-2.6 continued (Part *G*)

G. Seismic design category[1]				
Occu-pancy cat-egory	[2]$0 \leq S_{DS} < 0.167$ or $0 \leq S_{D1} < 0.067$	[2]$0.167 \leq S_{DS} < 0.33$ or $0.067 \leq S_{D1} < 0.133$	[2]$0.33 \leq S_{DS} < 0.50$ or $1.33 \leq S_{D1} < 0.02$	[2]$0.50 \leq S_{DS}$ or $0.20 \leq S_{D1}$	$S_1 \geq 0.75$
I	A	B	C	D	E
II	A	B	C	D	E
III	A	B	C	D	E
IV	A	C	D	D	F

Notes for Part *G*:

1. Where more than one category applies, use the more severe category (i.e., *B* before *A*; *C* before *B*, etc.)

2. For buildings with $S_1 < 0.75$, it is permissible to use only the S_{DS} criteria (i.e., one need not consider the criteria involving S_{D1}), but only where all of the following apply:

a) $T < 0.8 S_{D1}/S_{DS}$ where the period *T* is found in Table A-2.5 Part *E*; and S_{D1} and S_{DS} are found in Table A-2.6 Part *C*.

b) Floor-roof systems (acting as structural "diaphragms") are concrete slabs or metal decks with concrete infill; or lateral-force-resisting vertical elements (such as shear walls or trusses) are no more than 40 ft apart.

H. Seismic response coefficient, C_s[1]			
T	Upper limit for C_s	Lower limit for C_s	[2]Provisional C_s
$T \leq T_L$	$\dfrac{S_{D1}}{(TR/I_e)}$	Use the greater value of $0.044 S_{DS} I_e$ or 0.01 or, for $S_1 \geq 0.6$, $0.5 S_1/(R/I_e)$	$\dfrac{S_{DS}}{(R/I_e)}$
$T > T_L$	$\dfrac{S_{D1} T_L}{(T^2 R/I_e)}$		

Notes for Part *H*:

1. Values for S_1 and T_L for selected cities can be found in Table A-2.3; values for S_{DS} and S_{D1} are found in Table A-2.6 Part *C*; values for *R* are found in Table A-2.6 Part *D*; approximate values for *T* are found in Table A-2.6 Part *E*; and values for I_e are found in Table A-2.6 Part *F*.

2. Use the "provisional" value for C_s when it falls between the lower and upper limits; otherwise use the lower limit (when the provisional value is below the lower limit) or the upper limit (when the provisional value is above the upper limit).

Table A-2.7: Combined load factors[1]

A. Strength Design	
Load Combinations	**Combined Loads and Factors**
Dead load	$1.4D$
Dead, live, and roof or snow	$1.2D + 1.6L + 0.5(L_r \text{ or } S)$
Dead, roof or snow, and live[2] or wind	$1.2D + 1.6(L_r \text{ or } S) + (L \text{ or } 0.5W)$
Dead, wind, live,[2] and roof or snow	$1.2D + 1.0W + L + 0.5(L_r \text{ or } S)$
Dead, earthquake, live,[2] and snow	$1.2D + 1.0E + L + 0.2S$
Dead and wind	$0.9D + 1.0W$
Dead and earthquake	$0.9D + 1.0E$

B. Allowable stress design	
Load Combinations	**Combined Loads and Factors**
Dead load	D
Dead and live	$D + L$
Dead and roof or snow	$D + (L_r \text{ or } S)$
Dead, live, and roof or snow	$D + 0.75L + 0.75(L_r \text{ or } S)$
Dead and wind or earthquake	$D + (0.6W \text{ or } 0.7E)$
Dead, live, wind, and roof or snow	$D + 0.75L + 0.75(0.6W) + 0.75(L_r \text{ or } S)$
Dead, live, earthquake, and snow	$D + 0.75L + 0.75(0.7E) + 0.75S$
Dead and wind	$0.6D + 0.6W$
Dead and earthquake	$0.6D + 0.7E$
Where only D, L, S, and L_r are present the allowable stress load combinations are commonly reduced to the following:	
Dead and live	$D + L$
Dead and roof or snow	$D + (L_r \text{ or } S)$
Dead, live, and roof or snow	$D + 0.75L + 0.75(L_r \text{ or } S)$

Notes:

1. Only the following loads are considered in this table:

D = dead load; L = live load; L_r = roof live load (construction, maintenance); W = wind load; S = snow load; E = earthquake load (omitted are fluid, flood, lateral earth pressure, rain, and self-straining forces).

2. The load factor for L in these three cases only can be taken as 0.5 when $L \le 100$ psf (except for garages or places of public assembly).

CHAPTER 3

Wood

Wood is the stuff inside trees; *timber* is wood suitable for (or prepared for) use in structures; *lumber* is timber cut into standard-sized planks. Since we build with lumber (which is also timber, which is also wood), all three of these terms are used, depending on the context.

MATERIAL PROPERTIES

The basic structure of wood can be understood by examining its situation within the tree: the trunk consists of a bundle of cellulose tubes, or fibers, that serve the dual purpose of carrying water and nutrients from the ground to the leaves while providing a cellular geometry ("structure") capable of supporting those leaves and the necessary infrastructure of branches.

Trees have a more-or-less circular cross section, shown schematically in Figure 3.1. The primary structural element of the wood consists of long strands of cellulose, running longitudinally up the tree: $C_6H_{10}O_5$. These "straw-like" cellular structures are cemented together by *lignin*. Wood is strongest in the direction of these cells (longitudinally), and relatively weak perpendicular to this "grain." The rings evident in the cross section correspond to alternating

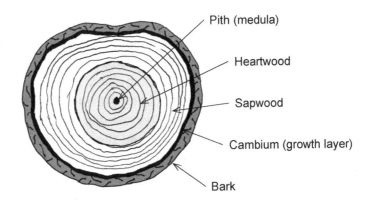

Figure 3.1: Schematic cross section through a tree

periods of rapid (spring) and slower (summer) growth.

Wood is classified into two main types: *softwoods*, or gymnosperms (of which the most important family members are the *conifers*, i.e., cone bearing trees like pine, fir, and spruce but also including *yews*, i.e., fleshy fruit trees such as cherry) and *hardwoods*, or angiosperms, which are deciduous (having broad leaves which turn color in the fall — elm, maple, and oak are examples). In the U.S., softwoods are most commonly used as structural lumber. Common species include Douglas Fir, Southern Pine, or combinations with similar structural properties such as Spruce-Pine-Fir.

Various loads stress the tree trunk in axial compression (dead load and snow load) and in bending (wind load, eccentric dead and snow load). When we cut lumber from the tree, we do so in a way that allows it to be stressed within building structures in the same manner that it was stressed while in the tree. Thus, saw cuts are made parallel to the longitudinal fibers of the wood, since it is the continuity of these fibers that give the wood strength.

Cutting

Lumber cut from a tree immediately has three structural defects, compared to wood in the tree itself: First, it is virtually impossible to cut every piece of lumber so that the orientation of the fibers, or grain, is exactly parallel to the edges of the wood planks. This means that the full potential of the wood's strength is rarely achieved.

Second, the continuous path of those fibers leading from trunk to branch — a functional and structural necessity within the tree — becomes a liability when the tree is cut, as it results in knots and other imperfections which weaken the boards. Wood is graded to account for these and other imperfections.

Third, the shear strength of the wood — i.e., its ability to resist sliding of the cellular fibers relative to each other — is much lower than its strength in tension or compression parallel to those fibers. While a low shear strength is perfectly adapted to a tree's circular cross section, it is not necessarily appropriate for the rectangular cross sections characteristic of lumber. Why this is so can be seen by comparing the two cross-sectional shapes: with a circle, a great deal of material is available at the neutral axis (where shear stresses are highest) so the "glue" or lignin holding the fibers together can be relatively weak; but when the tree is cut into rectangular cross sections, relatively less material is present at the neutral axis, and shear stresses are therefore higher. For this reason, the structural efficiency of lumber with a rectangular cross section, i.e., all lumber, is compromised by a disproportionate weakness in shear.

Seasoning

A dead tree begins losing its internal water until its moisture content reaches equilibrium with the surrounding air. Two things then happen: the wood shrinks, especially perpendicular to the grain, and the wood gets stronger. As atmospheric humidity changes, the wood responds by gaining or losing moisture, expanding or shrinking, and becoming weaker or stronger. Moisture content (MC) is defined as the weight of water in the wood divided by the dry weight of the wood and is expressed as a percentage. Anything less than MC = 19% constitutes "dry" lumber, i.e., lumber that has been *seasoned* through air- or kiln-drying. Air drying takes several months (and results in an MC of 15-18%) versus kiln drying which only takes several days (and results in an MC of 8-11%). Moisture is often added during kiln drying to control the rate of evaporation, in order to reduce the splitting, checking, etc. that would otherwise occur under rapid, uncontrolled drying. Moisture content greater or equal to 19% constitutes "green" lumber. In ordinary applications, it is unwise to use green lumber, as it will shrink, and possibly warp, as it accommodates itself to the ambient humidity characteristic of normal occupancies. For most modern construction, kiln-dried lumber is used.

For structural design, the issue of strength versus moisture content is handled by assuming one of two conditions: either the wood is indoors, where the humidity is controlled and the moisture content of the wood is expected not to exceed 19% (for glued-laminated timber, this condition is met when the moisture content is less than 16%); or outdoors, where the potential exists for the wood to take on added moisture and lose some strength. The wood's moisture content at the time of fabrication also has an impact on its in-service performance, especially for the design of connections between structural elements.

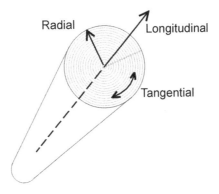

Figure 3.2: Longitudinal, tangential, and radial axes

Shrinkage and Warping

Wood is most stable parallel to grain, i.e., along the *longitudinal* axis corresponding to the vertical orientation of the living tree trunk. It is least dimensionally stable along its so-called *tangential* axis, i.e., parallel to the circular growth rings. *Radial* shrinkage is about half that of shrinkage in the tangential direction. These three axes are shown in Figure 3.2. All such shrinkage (and expansion) corresponds to the loss (or gain) of moisture. Rectangular cross sections are likely to to warp, or "cup," when ambient humidity levels change if, and to the extent that, two opposite faces have different orientations with respect to the *tangential* direction. As a board loses moisture, for example, the face of the board that is more closely aligned with the growth ring, and therefore more oriented along the tangential axis, will shrink more than the opposite face — in such cases, the side of the board that cups will be closer to the bark (Figure 3.3, cross section *a*). Warping in cross sections with similar orientations to the tangential axis (Figure 3.3, cross section *b*) will be much less.

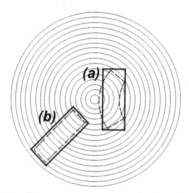

Figure 3.3: Warping, or "cupping," is more pronounced when (*a*) the two wide faces of a board are oriented differently with respect to the tangential axis; such warping is minimized when (*b*) the two wide faces are parallel to the radial axis

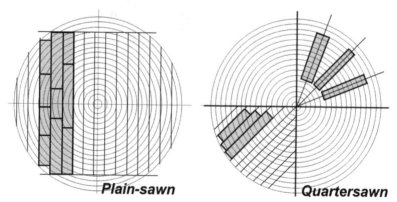

Figure 3.4: Plain-sawn or flat-sawn lumber (left) is less expensive to produce, and is used for most structural applications; quartersawn lumber (right) is more difficult to cut and therefore more expensive

Lumber can be cut in such a way to reduce this warping tendency by orienting its long faces along the radial, rather than the tangential, axis. Such *quartersawn* lumber is used primarily for fine cabinetry, since it is more expensive to produce than *plain-sawn*, or *flat-sawn* lumber (Figure 3.4).

Because wood shrinks or expands more perpendicular to its grain, wooden buildings should be configured so that all lines of structure have more-or-less equal amounts of shrinkage (i.e., equal dimensions of wood perpendicular to grain). In Figure 3.5, the mezzanine intersects one line of structure with elements (joists, plates, and sills) oriented perpendicular to the vertical lines of force. This side of the building would be expected to shrink, or expand, more than the other side, resulting in an unintended slope to the floor or roof above.

Volume

Lumber contains both hidden and visible pockets of low strength, due to imperfections within or between the cellular fibers of the material and larger cracks or knots often visible on the surface. It is impossible to know where all these defects might be in any particular piece of lumber, but one can safely surmise that there will be more of them as the volume of the piece increases.

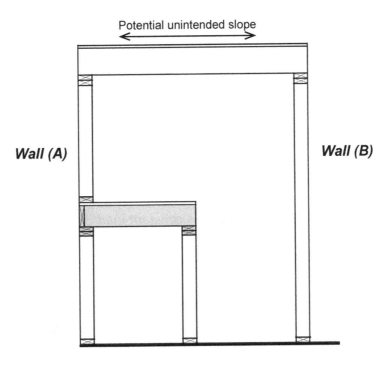

Figure 3.5: Section through a wooden building with the potential for unequal shrinkage, or expansion, in the two enclosing walls (*A* and *B*) due to the joists, plates, and sills — shown shaded — that interrupt wall (*A*)

As the number of defects increases, the probability that larger, or more damaging, defects will exist within critical regions of the structural element also increases. Since these regions of low strength can trigger brittle failure (wood is brittle when stressed in tension), large pieces of lumber will statistically fail at lower levels of stress than small pieces. This does not mean that large beams hold less load than small beams; it simply means that the average stress causing failure will be lower in larger beams.

Interestingly, the theory is validated by test results for all categories of beams and tension elements, with one exception: increases in cross-sectional width seem to make beams stronger (but not tension members), opposite to what the theory of brittle failure predicts. The reason for this anomaly remains unclear, but may have to do with the fact that local failures at regions of low strength are more likely to cascade across the entire width of relatively thin cross sections, and more likely to be contained as cross-sectional width increases. A horizontal break corresponding to a complete discontinuity between the lower and upper parts of a cross section drastically reduces the cross section's ability to resist bending moments, but has no effect on the section's ability to resist axial tension. This would explain why beams, but not tension members, seem to get stronger with increased width. On the other hand, increasing the depth of a structural element has no such beneficial effect, since even a complete vertical break within a cross section neither increases nor decreases a member's bending or tensile strength. Because wide beams seem to be relatively stronger than narrow ones, the allowable stress in beams used flat (stressed about their *weak* axes) is higher than when they are used in their normal orientation, even though their total volume hasn't changed.

Duration of load

Wood fails at a lower stress the longer it is loaded. This phenomenon is similar to the "fatigue" of metals, except that where metal fatigue is brought on by repeated cycling or reversals of stress, loss of strength in wood is purely time dependent and will occur even under a constant load. Thus, wood can sustain a higher stress caused by a short-duration impact load then by a longer-duration wind, snow or live load.

Species and grade

Many species of wood can be used as lumber. Within each species, different grades are identified, depending on such things as overall density, knots, checks and other imperfections. Grading can be done by visual inspection (for "visually graded lumber") or with the aid of machines (for "machine stress rated lumber"). Since each species of wood is subdivided into numerous grades, the result is a multitude of possible material types, each with different structural properties. Practically speaking, the choices in any given geographical region are limited to what is locally available. For that reason, the material properties assumed when designing in timber are not arbitrarily selected from the lists produced by wood industry organizations, but are selected from the much shorter list of regionally-available species and grades. Several common species and grades of wood are listed in Appendix Tables A-3.1, A-3-3, A-3.5, A-3.7, and A-3.9 along with their "allowable stresses" in tension, compression, bending, and shear, and their modulus of elasticity. Adjustments to these values, accounting for the effects of such things as moisture, volume, and duration of load, are listed in Appendix Tables A-3.2, A-3.4, A-3.6, A-3.8, and A-3.10.

Decay

Wood may decay in the presence of wood-eating organisms (fungi) which require the following things in order to operate: water, air (actually oxygen), suitable temperature, and food (i.e., the wood itself). Of course, it is also necessary that the fungi be present, but given their incredible ability to multiply and to disperse through the medium of air, or to be present within soil, it is a rather safe bet that this condition will be met.

It is also possible to use species of wood that are more resistant to fungal attack, but no wood is entirely safe. Pressure-treated wood, like the more naturally decay-resistant species, contains substances that are toxic to fungi.

Water is necessary; however, the low moisture content of wood used indoors (anything below about 20% MC) is unsuitable for fungal growth. The issue, then, is restricted to wood subjected to outside conditions, or to unintended water intrusion that raises its moisture content. Paradoxically, wood submerged entirely in water, like some wooden piles, is not subject to fungal decay, as the water deprives the fungus of oxygen.

A typical fungus's notion of "suitable temperature" pretty much coincides with human preferences — somewhere between about 65°F and 95°F.

Given the difficulty of altering prevailing temperatures, or eliminating oxygen, it is usually easiest to remove the water from the wood, and thereby protect it from decay. This is done primarily through good detailing practice (e.g., sloping all nearly-horizontal surfaces, using *washes* and *drips*, so the water doesn't remain in contact with the wood as shown schematically in Figure 3.6; sloping the grade away from the building on all sides; covering soil under crawl spaces with a moisture barrier; using pressure-treated (PT) lumber where it is within about 18 in. of the soil; and protecting the surface of the wood with coatings such as paint.

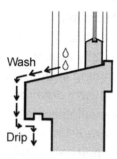

Figure 3.6: Schematic wash and drip

Fire

Wood elements are combustible and are therefore not permitted to be used as structure in certain types of construction. Specifically, it is the combination of building height and number of stories above grade, combined with the nature of the building's occupancy, that determine when wood structural elements are, or are not, allowed. Building codes establish a matrix of construction types (some of which exclude wooden structural elements) and occupancy classifications — Table 503 in the *International Building Code* is the primary U.S. example — which sets limits not only on the structural material, building height, and number of stories, but also on floor area.

Fire-retardant chemicals can be injected into the wood, allowing it to be used in certain structural and nonstructural applications, even in some construction types which otherwise exclude wood. Heavy timber construction, studied and developed in the 19th century for factories and mill buildings, but still viable today, has a greater resistance to fire damage because of the thickness of individual members: a "char" layer forms on the outside of such heavy wooden cross sections when exposed to fire; this layer then protects the inner part of the wooden elements from further damage.

Mass timber buildings, a new form of "heavy timber" not yet officially sanctioned by U.S. building codes (but being built or proposed in Europe, Canada, and the U.S.) use thick wall and floor panels of cross laminated timber (along with laminated strand lumber and laminated veneer lumber plus some steel and reinforced concrete) to reach potential heights of 30 or even 40 stories — see the following section on "related products."

Related products

Several wood-based products have been developed with structural applications:

Glued-laminated (glulam) lumber is made by gluing together flat boards, typically 1⅜ or 1½ in. thick (half that for curved members) to create large cross sections of virtually unlimited length. Material properties can be controlled to some extent within the cross section — poorer-quality grades may be placed near the neutral axis, while higher-strength boards are reserved for the extreme fibers. A typical cross section is shown in Figure 3.7.

Cross laminated timber (CLT) is similar to glulam lumber, except that it is typically configured into wide panels used as floor "slabs" or walls, with each layer of flat boards oriented perpendicular to the next, improving dimensional stability.

Laminated veneer lumber (LVL) is similar to glulam except that the laminations are much thinner, being sliced off a log like paper pulled off a roll, rather than being sawn; and the glued joints between laminations are vertical, rather than horizontal. The grain in each lamination is oriented along the longitudinal axis of the member so that, like glulam, it mimics the aniso-tropic fibrous structure of an ordinary piece of lumber. LVL is used for beams and girders only, and is manufactured in standard sizes consistent with the sizes of sawn lumber; while glulam can be custom-fabricated in an unlimited variety of sizes and geometries. A typical LVL cross section is shown in Figure 3.8.

Parallel strand lumber (PSL) is similar to LVL, except that strips of veneer are used instead of whole veneers.

Figure 3.7: Glulam beam cross section

Figure 3.8: LVL beam cross section

Laminated strand lumber (LSL) is similar to PSL, except that somewhat more random strips of veneer, similar to those used in OSB (and still parallel to the longitudinal axis of the member,) are used instead of rectangular veneer strips.

Plywood is similar to LVL except that alternate laminations (plies) are oriented perpendicular to each other, creating a dimensionally-stable structural membrane, used typically as a substrate (sheathing) for roofs and exterior walls; and as a subfloor over joists in wood-frame construction. Plywood typically contains an odd number of plies, except when the middle two plies are "doubled up" as in 4-ply plywood; in either case, the top and bottom fibers point in the same direction (parallel to the long dimension of the plywood sheet). For this reason, plywood is typically oriented so that it spans in the direction of its long dimension (Figure 3.9). Where this doesn't occur, for example, in certain panelized roof systems, the lower bending strength of the plywood spanning in its short direction needs to be considered.

Oriented strand board (OSB) is similar to plywood, except that the various alternating layers consist of strands of wood glued together.

I-joists are manufactured from various combinations of flange and web materials, and can be used in place of sawn lumber beams. Flange material can be ordinary sawn lumber or LVL; web material is typically plywood or

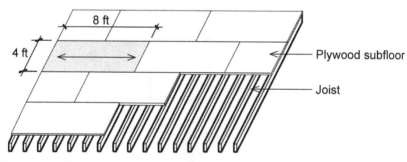

Figure 3.9: Plywood subfloor

Figure 3.10: I-joist

particle board. Cold-formed metal can also be used as a "web" material, creating a composite "truss-joist" consisting of wooden chords and metal diagonals. A typical I-joist cross section is shown in Figure 3.10.

Prefabricated trusses consisting typically of sawn 2 × 4 or 2 × 6 members joined by metal connector plates can be used for both pitched roofs and flat floors. These products can be custom-fabricated, and are often structurally designed (engineered) by the manufacturer.

SECTIONAL PROPERTIES

Within each species, lumber is further classified by its size. Various grades of lumber are then identified for each size classification. The actual ("dressed") sizes of lumber, which are currently ½ in., ¾ in., or 1 in. smaller than their nominal dimensions, are shown in Appendix Table A-3.12, together with some important cross-sectional properties.

Following are the current rules (but be aware that older — even currently available — lumber may follow older rules) that establish the *actual* cross-sectional dimensions of lumber: (1) subtract ½ in. from any nominal dimension of 6 in. or less; (2) subtract ¾ in. from any nominal dimension greater than 6 in. and less than 16 in. (for dimension lumber only, subtract ¾ in. from a nominal dimension of 16 in.); (3) for timbers only, subtract 1 in. from any nominal dimension of 16 in. or greater. Thus, a 2 × 4 is really 1½ in. × 3½ in.; a 4 × 10 is really 3½ in. × 9¼ in.; and a 12 × 20 is really 11¼ in. × 19 in. Because so much older lumber is still in circulation, the prior rules governing lumber sizes may well be encountered: (1) subtract ½ in. from all nominal dimensions except, *for dimension lumber only*, subtract ¾ in. where the nominal dimension is greater than 6 in. It is possible, even likely, that you will encounter even *older* dimensioning rules if you are dealing with renovations of wooden structures from the 1960s or earlier.

Following are the current rules (but be aware that older — even currently available — lumber may follow older rules) that establish the *actual* cross-sectional dimensions of lumber: (1) subtract ½ in. from any nominal dimension of 6 in. or less; (2) subtract ¾ in. from any nominal dimension greater than 6 in. and less than 16 in.; (3) subtract 1 in. from any nominal dimension of 16 in. or greater. Thus, a 2 × 4 is really 1½ in. × 3½ in.; a 4 × 10 is really 3½ in. × 9¼ in.; and a 12 × 20 is really 11¼ in. × 19 in. Because so much older lumber is still in circulation, the prior rules governing lumber sizes may well be encountered: (1) subtract ½ in. from all nominal dimensions except, *for dimension lumber only*, subtract ¾ in. where the nominal dimension is greater than 6 in. It is possible, even likely, that you will encounter even *older* dimensioning rules if you are dealing with renovations of wooden structures from the 1960s or earlier.

When describing wooden elements, the standard nomenclature used in timber design can be quite confusing: the smaller dimension, or *thickness*, is what we ordinarily call "width"; the longer dimension, or *width*, is what we usually call depth. Thus, the section modulus of a timber beam, described later in this chapter, is not "width" times "depth" squared, divided by 6 (as it would be in a strength of materials text); but is thickness times width squared, divided by 6. Got that?

Standard glulam posts and beams come in depths that are multiples of the lamination size; and in an assortment of widths whose finished dimensions are different from those of dimension lumber. Some typical cross-sectional dimensions are shown in Appendix Table A-3.13.

DESIGN APPROACHES

The simplest way to model loads and their supporting elements is to simply add the loads together and make sure that the stresses in the elements that support them are less than the stresses that would cause the elements to fail. These stresses that are *allowed* to be present within a given structural element — *allowable stresses* — are simply the stresses that would cause failure multiplied by a factor of safety that is less than 1 (or divided by a factor of safety that is greater than 1). More sophisticated design methods have been developed (see Chapter 2), but there are still two reasons for continuing to use allowable stress design (ASD) for wood structures.

First, much of the engineering profession in the U.S. still uses this method, in spite of the fact that both ASD and LRFD (*Load and Resistance Factor Design* was described in Chapter 2) are available and sanctioned by industry groups such as the American Wood Council (AWC) and the American Forest & Paper Association (AFPA). The second reason has more relevance to an academic text than to practical applications in the field: even though ASD does not provide the same nuanced approach to risk as does LRFD, it has the great advantage of utilizing section properties that are part of the canonical repertoire derived within strength of materials texts. In particular, ASD uses the *moment of inertia* or *section modulus* (see Chapter 1) in the computation of bending stresses, since all "working" stresses within the wood cross section are assumed to be linear.

Even though the section modulus is retained within LRFD for wood beams (unlike LRFD in steel or strength design in reinforced concrete, where *nonlinear* stress-strain relationships at the limit state are made explicit and therefore preclude the use of the section modulus), much of the naive elegance of the ASD method is lost, especially since allowable stress design values, already tabulated and widely distributed, are retained within the wood LRFD procedures by multiplying them by a "format conversion factor" rather than explicitly tabulating limit state stresses as is done in steel and reinforced concrete.

CONSTRUCTION SYSTEMS

Timber framing systems using large wooden cross sections were prevalent in both Western and Eastern cultures up until the invention of balloon framing (subsequently modified into "platform framing") in the mid-nineteenth century. A typical timber framing joint characteristic of such traditional framing involved a high degree of skill and craftsmanship; today, connections of large, or even small, cross sections often rely on metal fasteners (Figure 3.11).

Balloon framing was invented in the U.S. in the mid-nineteenth century and consists of wood elements with small cross sections (what we now call "dimension lumber") configured in the wall as *plates* (horizontal) and *studs* (vertical); and in the floors and roofs and *joists* and *rafters* respectively. The strength and stiffness of such systems relies on diaphragm action in the walls and floors, created by nailing sheathing (walls) and subfloors (floors) to the studs and joists. In traditional balloon framing, diagonal wood members were "let into" the walls to provide lateral stability; in modern construction, plywood (or OSB) sheathing creates so-called "shear walls" without any diagonal elements required.

Platform framing is a modification of balloon framing and is the prevalent mode of light wood framing today. The main difference between the two systems is that in balloon framing, vertical studs are continuous from foundation to roof, whereas in platform framing, studs are interrupted at each floor level by the floor construction. Platform framing has two advantages over balloon framing: studs are only one story high, so long pieces of lumber are not required, and wall sections can be fabricated on the floor platforms in a horizontal position, and then easily lifted (or tilted) in place.

The main disadvantage of platform framing compared to balloon framing is that platform framing interrupts the continuity of vertical studs with joists and plates oriented with their grain perpendicular to the direction of loads, so

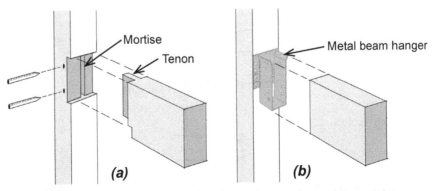

(a)   *(b)*

Figure 3.11: Traditional timber framing (*a*) utilized complex mortise and tenon joints; modern timber framing (*b*) tends to rely on metal fastening devices

that expansion or contraction along the exterior wall surface may be greater at those points. This issue was discussed earlier (see Figure 3.5) in relation to unintended sloping of floor joists; it also should be considered when relatively rigid siding materials, such as brick veneer, are fastened to exterior studs. In such cases, the differential movement where floors intersect the vertical studs should be accommodated with "soft" joints in the brick veneer.

U.S. building with dimension lumber is based on a 4-foot (48-in.) structural module, subdivided either into 16-in. or 24-in. on-center (o.c.) spacing of studs, joists, and rafters. So-called *advanced framing*, actually developed in the 1970s as *optimum value engineering* (OVE) framing, uses the minimum amount of lumber consistent with structural strength and stability: studs,

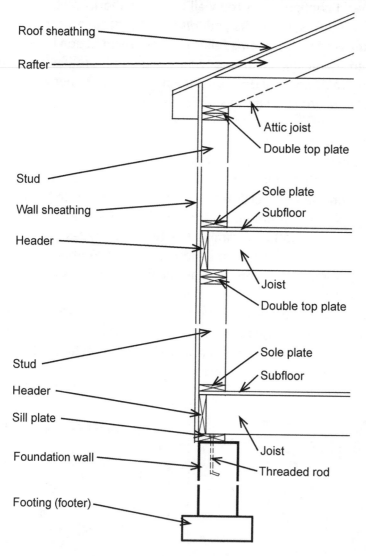

Figure 3.12: Classic platform framing in a two-story structure (showing only the main structural elements, and not including basement slabs)

joists, and rafters are spaced at 24-in. o.c.; double plates are eliminated, with discontinuities in single plates bridged with metal straps or overlapping, but short, wooden plates; 2 × 6 studs replace 2 × 4 studs; all joists, rafters, and studs align vertically, so that loads find consistent paths down to the foundation; windows and doors are framed with single, rather than double, studs, and so on. The contemporary interest in such optimized framing is driven by energy concerns: all of the wood that has been eliminated from the exterior walls is replaced with insulation, minimizing thermal bridging through the wood. The use of 2 × 6 exterior wall studs increases space for insulation and still results in a net savings of wood, compared with traditional 2 × 4 studs with double plates at 16 in. o.c. Traditional platform framing is illustrated in Figure 3.12, with only the basic structrural elements shown. An advanced framing section would appear almost the same, except that single instead of double top plates would be used under the joists. However, many of the "reforms" embodied in advanced framing — including the elimination of numerous studs at corners, doors or windows, and the increased spacing and alignment of studs, joists, and rafters at 24 in. o.c. — do not appear in this type of drawing.

TENSION ELEMENTS

Basic tabular values of allowable stresses in tension are shown in Appendix Table A-3.1 for some common species and grades of visually-graded lumber. The allowable stress in tension (parallel to the grain) for timber elements needs to be modified, or adjusted, to account for the variations in material properties discussed earlier in this chapter. The three most important adjustment factors, corresponding to these material properties, are as follows: C_M for wood structural elements exposed to wet service conditions; C_F for certain cross sections larger or smaller than 2 × 12; and C_D for timber elements exposed to a total cumulative "duration of load" different from the time period associated with normal "occupancy" live loads. This adjusted stress, F_t' is computed by multiplying the basic tabular value, F_t, by the appropriate adjustment factors, C_D, C_M, and C_F (see Appendix Table A-3.2). For an explanation of how the duration of load factor, C_D, is used, see Appendix Table A-3.10.

The actual tension stress within the structural element is computed by dividing the internal tension force by the cross-sectional area available to resist that force. Where bolt holes are present, the gross area, A_g, of the cross section is reduced by the nominal hole area, as shown in Figure 1.53a. The resulting net area, A_n, is therefore:

$$A_n = A_g - (\text{no. of holes})(D_h \times t) \qquad (3.1)$$

where D_h is the bolt hole diameter, taken somewhat larger than the bolt diameter; and t is the thickness of the cross section. Timber industry specifications recommend that the bolt hole diameter be $\frac{1}{32}$ in. to $\frac{1}{16}$ in. larger than the bolt diameter; in the examples that follow, a $\frac{1}{16}$ in. increase will be assumed. The actual stress, f_t, is therefore:

$$f_t = P/A_g \tag{3.2}$$

where no bolt holes are used; and

$$f_t = P/A_n \tag{3.3}$$

where bolt holes are present. These equations can be rewritten to solve for the capacity (allowable load), using the adjusted allowable stress, F_t', instead of the actual stress. Where tension elements are nailed rather than bolted, no reduction for nail holes is made; the full gross area is assumed to be available to resist the internal forces:

$$P_{allow} = F_t' \times A_g \tag{3.4}$$

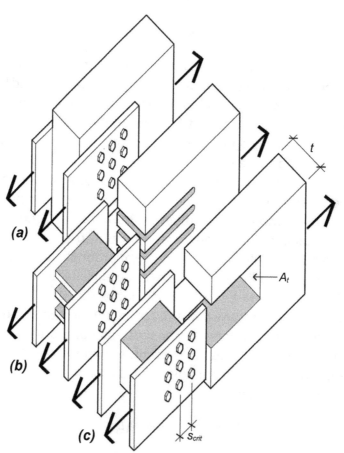

Figure 3.13: Forces on a wood member (a) loaded parallel to grain can cause (b) row tear-out or (c) group tear-out.

Where bolt holes are used:

$$P_{allow} = F_t' \times A_n \qquad (3.5)$$

Where wood elements are loaded in tension parallel to grain, another potential mode of failure must be checked where closely-spaced groups of bolts (or lag screws that fully penetrate the main member) are used as fasteners — this phenomenon does not apply to small-diameter nailed connections. As shown in Figure 3.13, the forces transmitted through a fastener group could cause entire "slots" of wood — either within each row of fasteners or for the entire fastener group taken as a whole — to tear out under the load. To prevent failure in the first case ("row tear-out," Figure 3.13b), and in spite of the fact that the forces acting on the element itself are *tensile*, the external force acting on the connection must be no greater than the total allowable *shear* force that can be developed on all the potential failure planes along the rows of fasteners. In the second case ("group tear-out," Figure 3.13c), the external force must be no greater than the allowable shear and tension forces that can be safely resisted by the three surfaces forming the boundary failure planes for the group of fasteners as a whole. Of these three surfaces, the resistance of the top and bottom parallel planes, stressed in shear, is equivalent to a single row subjected to row tear-out; the third surface, labeled A_t in Figure 3.13c, is stressed in tension.

In calculating row and group tear-out, adjusted allowable stresses for shear and tension are used that correspond to the species and grade of the wood elements being checked. The total length of the surface assumed to be resisting shear stress along a given row of fasteners is taken as the smallest distance between fasteners (or between the end of the wood member and the first fastener) multiplied by the number of fasteners in that row. This accounts for the fact that shear stress along the potential failure planes defined by fastener rows is not uniform, but is higher where the area between fasteners along the shear plane is smallest. Additionally, this shear stress is not uniformly distributed between fasteners, but is assumed to step up and down in a triangular pattern, from maximum to zero, so that the *average* value of shear stress is actually half of its maximum value (corresponding to the average height of such a triangle).

Taking all these caveats into consideration, the allowable maximum force at a connection using bolts or lag screws — where the load is parallel to grain — is limited by the smaller of the following values for row and group tear-out:

a. *For row tear-out:* multiply the force safely resisted by the two shear planes at each row of fasteners by the number of rows (or, if not all rows of fasteners are the same, add the values for each row computed separately). The force resisted by a single row (arbitrarily called *row* 1) is equal to:

$$Z'_{RT-1} = 2n_1(F'_v/2)s_{crit}(t) = n_1(F'_v)s_{crit}(t) \tag{3.6}$$

where n_1 = the number of fasteners in *row* 1; F'_v = the adjusted allowable shear stress for the wood element; s_{crit} = the minimum spacing between fasteners in *row* 1 (or the distance of the first fastener to the end of the member, if smaller); and t = the member thickness.

The force resisted by all fasteners, assuming that all rows are identical, is therefore the force resisted by a single row multiplied by the number of rows, r_n, or:

$$Z'_{RT} = r_n(Z'_{RT-1}) = r_n n_1(F'_v)s_{crit}(t) \tag{3.7}$$

b. *For group tear-out:* add the shear force resisted at the parallel planes defined by the top and bottom fastener rows (in typical cases where the top and bottom fastener rows have the same geometry, this is equal to the value of Z'_{RT-1} computed above for single row tear-out; otherwise, add $Z'_{RT-1}/2$ for the top and bottom rows) plus the tension force resisted by the plane surface joining, and perpendicular to, these shear planes. For A_t representing the area subjected to tension stress between the top and bottom rows of fasteners (see Figure 3.13c), and F'_t being the adjusted allowable tensile stress for the wood, the force resisted, in terms of group tear-out, is:

$$Z'_{GT} = Z'_{RT-1} + F'_t A_t \tag{3.8}$$

These limitations based on row and group tear-out are summarized in Appendix Table A-3.14.

Example 3.1 Analyze wood tension element

Problem definition. Find the maximum load that can be applied to a 2 × 8 tension element connected with six ½ in. diameter bolts. The wood used is Hem-Fir No. 1. Assume live, dead, and wind loads only, dry conditions, and spacing as shown in Figure 3.14.

Problem overview. Find gross area and net area; compute adjusted allowable stress; find capacity, $P = F'_t A_n$, with the net area as shown in Figure 3.15a. Check row tear-out, based on the shear failure planes shown in Figure 3.15b, and group tear-out, based on the shear and tension failure planes shown in

Figure 3.15c. Adjust capacity based on tear-out calculations if necessary.

Problem solution
1. From Appendix Table A-3.12 the cross-sectional area, A_g = 10.875 in².
2. Use Equation 3.1 to find the net area, A_n: Notice that even though there are six bolt holes, only two of them are subtracted from the gross area in calculating the net area, since the "failure plane" passes through only two holes. The hole diameter is taken as $\frac{1}{16}$ in. larger than the bolt diameter, so D_h = 9/16 = 0.5625 in. Therefore, $A_n = A_g - $ (no. of holes)$(D_h \times t)$ = 10.875 − 2(0.5625 × 1.5) = 9.19 in².

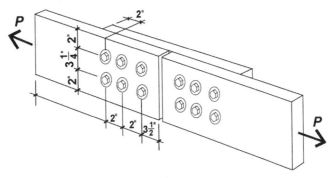

Figure 3.14: Bolted 2 × 8 cross sections for Example 3.1

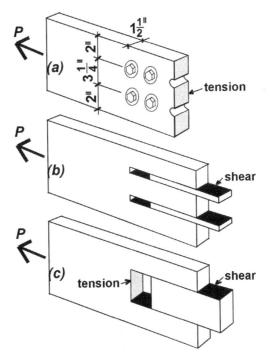

Figure 3.15: Possible failure modes for Example 3.1 include (*a*) tension failure on net area; (*b*) row tear-out; and (*c*) group tear-out

3. From Appendix Table A-3.1 find the tabular value of allowable tension stress, F_t = 625 psi.
4. Compute adjusted allowable tension stress:
   a. From Appendix Table A-3.2, find adjustments to tabular value: C_D = 1.6; C_M = 1.0; C_F = 1.2.
   b. $F_t' = F_t C_D C_M C_F = 625(1.6)(1.0)(1.2) = 1200$ psi.
5. Using Equation 3.5, find capacity (allowable load) based on failure through the net area: $P = F_t' A_n = 1200 \times 9.19 = 11{,}028$ lb.
6. From Appendix Table A-3.14, check capacity based on row and group tear-out, since the orientation of the load is parallel to grain and the member is in tension. The adjusted allowable stress in shear is found from Appendix Tables A-3.7 and A-3.8: F_v = 150 psi and the relevant adjustments are for wet service (C_M = 1.0) and duration of load (C_D = 1.6), so F_v' = 150(1.0)(1.6) = 240 psi. The adjusted allowable tension stress is as found above: F_t' = 1,200 psi. Other parameters needed for this step are as follows: the number of rows, r_n = 2; the number of fasteners in a typical row, n_1 = 3; the area subjected to tension stress (measured between the top and bottom rows of fasteners), A_t = (3.25)(1.5) = 4.875 in²; the minimum spacing between fasteners (or the end distance, if smaller), s_{crit} = 2 in.; and the member thickness, t = 1.5 in.

   The capacities based on row and group tear-out can now be determined:
   a. $Z'_{RT} = r_n n_1 (F_v') s_{crit}(t) = (2)(3)(240)(2)(1.5) = 4320$ lb.
   b. $Z'_{GT} = n_1 (F_v') s_{crit}(t) + F_t' A_t = (3)(240)(2)(1.5) + (1200)(4.875) = 8010$ lb.
   Because the smaller of these two values (4320 lb) is smaller than the capacity found in step 4, row tear-out governs the connection design, and the total adjusted connection capacity, P = 4320 lb.
7. *Conclusion:* the capacity of the 2 × 8 tension element, P = 4320 lb. The capacity of the bolts themselves has not been checked; the design and analysis of such fasteners is discussed later in this chapter.

Example 3.2 Design wood tension element

Problem definition. Find an appropriate 2× cross section (Hem-Fir No. 2) to support a tensile load of 5 kips consisting only of live and dead loads in normal proportions. Use two lines of three ⅜ in. diameter bolts, as shown in Figure 3.16, to connect the wood element to another part of the structure. The bolt hole diameter = bolt diameter + ⅟₁₆ in. = ⁷⁄₁₆ in. = 0.4375 in.

Solution overview. Compute provisional adjusted allowable stress; find required net area; find required gross area; select provisional cross section; check cross section by finding adjusted allowable stress, required net area, and required gross area. Check row and group tear-out.

Problem solution

1. From Appendix Table 3.1, find the tabular value of the allowable tension stress, F_t = 525 psi (use "dimension lumber" for 2× element).
2. Compute provisional adjusted allowable tension stress:
   a. From Appendix Table A-3.2 find adjustments to tabular value: C_D = 1.0; C_M = 1.0; assume C_F = 1.0 (the actual value is unknown at this time).
   b. $F_t' = F_t C_D C_M C_F = 525(1.0)(1.0)(1.0) = 525$ psi.
3. Find required net area, A_n = load/stress = 5000/525 = 9.52 in².
4. Using Equation 3.1 (but solving for A_g), and referring to Figure 3.16, find the required gross area, $A_g = A_n + $ (no. of holes)$(D_h \times t) = 9.52 + 2(0.4375 \times 1.5) = $ 10.83 in².
5. We need a provisional 2× cross section with $A_g \geq$ 10.83 in²; from Appendix Table A-3.12, select a 2 × 8 with A_g = 10.88 in². Not only must *this* cross section be analyzed (using the actual value of C_F) but also the next smaller section (since it has a larger value of C_F).

Trial 1: 2x8

Because the actual value of the size factor for a 2 × 8, C_F = 1.2, is larger than the value initially assumed, the adjusted allowable stress will be higher than assumed, and therefore a 2 × 8 cross section will certainly work. However, it is necessary to analyze (check) the next smaller cross section, since this cross section has an even larger size factor than does the 2 × 8, and so has an even higher adjusted allowable stress.

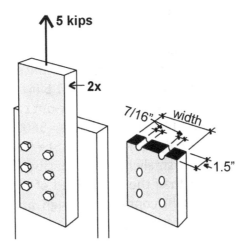

Figure 3.16: Bolted 2× cross section for Example 3.2

Trial 2: 2x6

1. From Appendix Table A-3.12 the cross-sectional area of a 2×6, A_g = 8.25 in^2.
2. Use Equation 3.1 to find the net area, $A_n = A_g -$ (no. of holes)$(D_h \times t)$ = $8.25 - 2(0.4375 \times 1.5) = 6.94$ in^2.
3. As before, find the tabular value of allowable tension stress, $F_t = 525$ psi.
4. Compute adjusted allowable tension stress:
   a. From Appendix Table A-3.2, find adjustments to tabular value: C_D = 1.0; $C_M = 1.0$; $C_F = 1.3$.
   b. $F_t' = F_t C_D C_M C_F = 525(1.0)(1.0)(1.3) = 682.5$ psi.
5. Using Equation 3.5, find capacity (allowable load), $P = F_t' A_n = 682.5 \times 6.94 =$ 4737 lb. This is insufficient capacity to support a load of 5000 lb: the 2×6 is too small. Therefore, the 2×8 must be provisionally selected, pending a check of row and group tear-out.

Check row and group tear-out

1. From Appendix Table A-3.14, check capacity based on row and group tear-out, since the orientation of the load is parallel to grain and the member is in tension. The adjusted allowable stress in shear is found from Appendix Tables A-3.7 and A-3.8: F_v = 150 psi and the relevant adjustments are for wet service (C_M = 1.0) and duration of load (C_D = 1.0), so F_v' = 150(1.0)(1.0) = 150 psi. The adjusted allowable tension stress for the 2×8 was never actually determined above; with a size factor, C_F = 1.2, it is: F_t' = 525(1.2) = 630 psi. Other parameters needed for this step are as follows: the number of rows, r_n = 2; the number of fasteners in a typical row, n_1 = 3. Based on the provisional selection of a 2×8, let the spacing between bolts in a row, and the distance from the last bolt to the end of the wood element, equal 4 in., and the distance between rows of bolts equal 3½ in. Then, the area subjected to tension stress (measured between the left and right rows of fasteners), A_t = (3.5)(1.5) = 5.25 in^2; the minimum spacing between fasteners (or the end distance, if smaller), s_{crit} = 4 in.; and the member thickness, t = 1.5 in.
   The capacities based on row and group tear-out can now be determined:
   a. $Z'_{RT} = r_n n_1 (F_v') s_{crit}(t) = (2)(3)(150)(4)(1.5) = 5400$ lb.
   b. $Z'_{GT} = n_1 (F_v') s_{crit}(t) + F_t' A_t = (3)(150)(4)(1.5) + (630)(5.25) = 6007$ lb.
2. *Conclusion:* Because the smaller of the capacities for row and group tear-out (5400 lb) is larger than the actual load of 5000 lb, neither row nor group tear-out governs the connection design, and the 2×8 provisionally selected above may be used.

COLUMNS

The reduction in allowable compressive stress, F_c, to account for buckling is accomplished by multiplying F_c^* by the column stability factor, C_p. The value, F_c^*, is the tabular value of compressive stress found in Appendix Table A-3.3, F_c, modified by all of the adjustment factors found in Appendix Table A-3.4 *except* C_p. If all columns behaved according to the idealized model analyzed by Euler, the stability factor would be unnecessary, and σ_{cr} modified by some factor of safety would simply replace F_c as the allowable stress. That is, we would have:

$$\text{"Idealized } C_p\text{"} = \sigma_{cr} \text{ (safety factor)}/F_c \tag{3.9}$$

In practice, given the pattern of column failure represented in Figure 1.56, the Euler equation must be modified to account for crushing and non-elastic behavior, especially at low slenderness ratios. The column stability factor, C_p, does just that and more, replacing σ_{cr} with F_{cE} (basically Euler's formula with a safety factor); adding a coefficient, c, to account for the non-ideal condition of various wood materials; and using statistical curve-fitting methods to match the empirical data. The slenderness ratio is simplified for a rectangular section, as only one cross-sectional dimension remains when values of $I_{min} = HB^3/12$ (see Equation 1.9) and $A = BH$ are inserted into the equation for radius of gyration (see Equation 1.13): $r = \sqrt{I_{min}/A} = \sqrt{(HB^3/12)/(BH)} = \sqrt{B^2/12} = 0.289B$. Replacing the generic width term, B, with the wood industry's d, one can still see the Euler buckling equation struggling to assert itself within $F_{cE} = 0.822E'_{min}/(l_e/d)^2$, which appears in both of the terms A and B within this opaque formulation for the column stability factor:

$$C_p = A - \sqrt{A^2 - B} \tag{3.10}$$

In Equation 3.10, $A = [1 + (F_{cE}/F_c^*)]/(2c)$ and $B = (F_{cE}/F_c^*)/c$.

A full description of C_p can be found in Appendix Table A-3.4, along with other adjustments to the allowable compressive stress.

For non-pin-ended columns, the unbraced length, l_e, is multiplied by an effective length coefficient (Appendix Table A-1.2) to account for the change in critical buckling stress resulting from more or less restraint at the column ends.

Example 3.3 Analyze wood column

Problem definition. Check the capacity (allowable load) of a 10 × 10 Douglas Fir-Larch Select Structural column 8.5 ft high, used indoors, supporting live load (L), roof live load (i.e., construction live load, L_r), dead load (D) and snow load (S) as follows:

$$L = 40 \text{ kips}; \quad L_r = 20 \text{ kips}; \quad D = 50 \text{ kips}; \text{ and } S = 20 \text{ kips}.$$

Solution overview. Find relevant material properties and adjustment factors; compute adjusted allowable stress; find capacity by multiplying cross-sectional area by adjusted allowable stress; compare capacity to governing load combination.

Problem solution

1. From Tables A-3.3 and A-3.9, find material properties F_c and E_{min}; the tabular (unadjusted) values are: F_c = 1150 psi, and E_{min} = 580,000 psi. These values are taken from "posts and timbers" since the cross section being analyzed is larger than 5 × 5 and the larger of the two cross-sectional dimensions is less than 4 in. greater than the smaller dimension.

2. Find adjustment factors for F_c:
   a. From Table A-3.4, C_M = 1.0.
   b. From Table A-3.4, C_F = 1.0.
   c. Find load duration factor, C_D, and the governing load combination: Two load combinations from Appendix Table A-2.7 (for allowable stress design) should be considered: $D + L$; and also $D + 0.75L + 0.75(L_r \text{ or } S)$. Wind and earthquake forces are not included, as they do not appear in the problem definition. The other listed load combinations in Appendix Table A-2.7 need not be considered, since it is evident that their effect will not be as severe. For the two selections, we divide each possible load combination by the load duration factor corresponding to the shortest load duration within that combination, as explained in Appendix Table A-3.10. The roof construction live load and snow load are not considered to act simultaneously. Starting with $D + L$, we get:

$$(D + L)/C_D = (50 + 40)/1.0 = 90.0.$$

Then, looking at $D + 0.75L + 0.75(L_r \text{ or } S)$, we get either:

$$D + 0.75L + 0.75(S)/C_D = (50 + 30 + 15)/1.15 = 82.61$$
or
$$D + 0.75L + 0.75(L_r)/C_D = (50 + 30 + 15)/1.25 = 76.0$$

Dead plus live load ($D + L$) governs, so C_D = 1.00, and the load used to design (or analyze) the column is ($D + L$) = (50 + 40) = 90 kips. The duration of load factor, used to determine the governing condition, does not appear in the governing load itself. Rather, it will be applied to the allowable stress. It was not necessary to include the load combination consisting only of dead plus roof construction live load ($D + L_r$) since not only is the sum of these loads less than the combination of dead plus live load, but the duration of load factor ($C_D = 1.25$) effectively makes the wood stronger for this combination.

    d. From Appendix Table A-3.4, find the column stability factor, C_P (to account for buckling):

From Table A-3.9, find $E'_{min} = E_{min} \times C_M$. Since $C_M = 1.0$ for timbers (do not confuse this adjustment with the value for C_M applied to the allowable compressive stress, F_c), we get:

$E_{min} = 580,000$ psi; $E'_{min} = 580,000 \times 1.0 = 580,000$ psi.
$l_e = 8.5$ ft $= 102$ in.
$d = 9.25$ in.
$F_{cE} = 0.822E'_{min} / (l_e / d)^2 = 0.822\,(580,000)/(102/9.25)^2 = 3920.9$ psi.
$F_c^* = F_c C_D C_M C_F = 1150(1.00)(1.0)(1.0) = 1150$ psi.
$c = 0.8$ for sawn lumber.
$A = [1 + (F_{cE}/F_c^*)]/(2c) = [1 + (3920.9/1150)]/1.6 = 2.76.$
$B = (F_{cE}/F_c^*)/c = (3920.9/1150)/0.8 = 4.26.$
$C_P = A - \sqrt{A^2 - B} = 2.76 - \sqrt{2.76^2 - 4.26} = 0.928.$

3. Compute adjusted allowable stress in compression: from step 2, $F_c^* = 1150$ psi and $C_P = 0.928$; so $F_c' = F_c^*(C_P) = 1150(0.928) = 1067$ psi.
4. Find capacity, $P = F_c' \times A$: From Appendix Table A-3.12 the cross-sectional area for a 10 × 10, $A = 85.56$ in^2; therefore, $P = 1067(85.56) = 91,293$ lb $= 91.3$ kips.
5. Check capacity: since the capacity of 91.3 kips ≥ governing load combination of 90 kips, the column is OK.

The value of $C_P = 0.928$ indicates that buckling has reduced the column's allowable compressive stress to 92.8% of its "crushing" strength.

Example 3.4 Design wood column

Problem definition. Find the lightest cross section for a wood column (Douglas Fir-Larch Select Structural) that is 8.5 ft high, used indoors, on the second floor of the 3-story building shown in Figure 3.17, supporting live load (L), roof live load (i.e., construction live load, L_r), dead load (D) and snow load (S) as follows:

$L = 40$ psf; $L_r = 20$ psf; $D = 25$ psf; and $S = 30$ psf.

Solution overview. Find relevant material properties and adjustment factors (assuming a provisional value for C_p); compute adjusted allowable stress; find cross-sectional area by dividing load by adjusted allowable stress; select pro- visional cross section and analyze; repeat this step by selecting new cross sec- tion until capacity is just larger than load.

Problem solution

1. Using Appendix Tables A-3.3 and A-3.9, find material properties F_c and E_{min}; as in the last example, the tabular (unadjusted) value of F_c is 1150 psi, and the minimum modulus of elasticity, E_{min} = 580,000 psi. The value of F_c assumes a "post and timber" size.

2. Find adjustment factors for F_c, except for C_p:
   a. From Appendix Table A-3.4, C_M = 1.0.
   b. From Appendix Table A-3.4, C_F = 1.0 (assuming that "dimension lum- ber" will not be used).
   c. From Appendix Tables A-3.10 and A-2.7, C_D depends on which load combination proves to be critical. To find C_D, divide each possible load combination by the load duration factor corresponding to the short- est load duration within each combination. The roof construction live load and snow load are not considered to act simultaneously. The tributary area for the typical column is 15 × 20 = 300 ft² per floor for both the third floor live and dead load, and for the roof construc- tion live load (or snow load) and dead load. Referring to Appendix Table A-2.2, part *B*, live load reduction for the third floor live load is appropriate since K_{LL} times its tributary area of 300 ft², or 1200 ft², is greater than 400 ft². For such an "influence area," the live load reduc- tion coefficient is 0.25 + 15/√4 × 300 = 0.68, so the reduced live load is 0.68(40) = 27.2 psf. Roof construction/maintenance live loads are not reduced. The duration of load factor, C_D, is found by dividing the various load combinations by the appropriate load duration factors (where loads are computed by multiplying each square foot value by

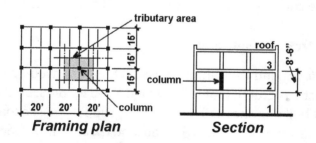

Framing plan　　　　**Section**

Figure 3.17: Framing plan and building section for Example 3.4

the corresponding tributary area). Only two load combinations from Appendix Table A-2.7 need be considered, since the others evidently will not produce effects as severe. These combinations are: $D + L$ and also $D + 0.75L + 0.75(L_r$ or $S)$. In the latter combination, wind and earthquake forces are not included, as they do not appear in the problem definition. We divide each possible load combination by the load duration factor corresponding to the shortest load duration within that combination, as explained in Appendix Table A-3.10. The roof construction live load and snow load are not considered to act simultaneously. Starting with $D + L$, we get:

$$(D + L)/C_D = [25(600) + 27.2(300)]/1.0 = 23,160 \text{ lb}$$

Then, looking at $D + 0.75L + 0.75(L_r$ or $S)$, we get:

$$(D + .75L + .75S)/C_D = [25(600) + .75(27.2)(300) + .75(30)(300)]/1.15 =$$
$$24,235 \text{ lb}$$

or

$$(D + .75L + .75L_r)/C_D = [25(600) + .75(27.2)(300) + .75(20)(300)]/1.25 =$$
$$20,496 \text{ lb.}$$

The first case of the *second* load combination governs (using dead, live, and snow load), so $C_D = 1.15$, and the load used to design the column is $(D + .75L + .75S)$, or:

$$25(600) + 0.75(27.2)(300) + 0.75(30)(300) = 27,870 \text{ lb.}$$

3. Select cross section by trial. The stability factor, C_p, cannot be determined directly, since it depends upon the cross-sectional dimensions of the column which haven't yet been found. Design therefore turns into an iterative process, repeatedly making and testing assumptions about the column's stability until the tests (i.e., column analyses) confirm the assumptions. To begin the iterative process:
   a. Assume a value for C_p, for example, $C_p = 0.8$.
   b. Compute $F_c^* = F_c C_D C_M C_F = 1150(1.15)(1.0)(1.0) = 1322.5$ psi.
   c. Compute $F_c' = F_c^* \times C_p = 1322.5(0.80) = 1058$ psi.
   d. Compute the provisional required cross-sectional area, A_{req}:

   $$A_{req} = \text{axial load / stress} = 27,870/1058 = 26.3 \text{ in}^2.$$

Trial 1:

1. From Appendix Table A-3.12, select trial cross section based on provisional required area of 26.3 in²: A 6 × 6 has an area of 30.25 in², but since the provisional required area of 26.3 in² was based on an assumption about the column's stability ($C_P = 0.8$), it is not immediately clear whether the choice is correct: what we must enter into at this point is the first step of an iterative process. We start by checking the 6 × 6 for its actual capacity and comparing this capacity to the applied load. This process is identical to the timber column analysis method illustrated in Example 3.3.

2. From Appendix Table A-3.4, find the actual column stability factor, C_P, for the 6 × 6 column:

   From Appendix Table A-3.9, find E'_{min} = the adjusted minimum modulus of elasticity = $E_{min} \times C_M$; since $C_M = 1.0$ for timbers, $E'_{min} = 580{,}000$ psi.

   $l_e = 8.5$ ft $= 102$ in.
   $d = 5.5$ in.
   $F_{cE} = 0.822E'_{min}/(l_e / d)^2 = 0.822(580{,}000)/(102/5.5)^2 = 1386.2$ psi.
   $F_c^* = F_c\, C_D\, C_M\, C_F = 1150(1.15)(1.0)(1.0) = 1322.5$ psi (unchanged from above).
   $c = 0.8$ for sawn lumber.
   $A = [1 + (F_{cE}/F_c^*)]/(2c) = [1 + (1386.2/1322.5)]/1.6 = 1.28.$
   $B = (F_{cE}/F_c^*)/c = (1386.2/1322.5)/0.8 = 1.31.$
   $C_P = A - \sqrt{A^2 - B} = 1.28 - \sqrt{1.28^2 - 1.31} = 0.71.$

3. Compute the adjusted allowable stress in compression:

   $F_c' = F_c^* \times C_P = 1322.5(0.71) = 939.0$ psi.

4. Find capacity, $P = F_c' \times A$: From Appendix Table A-3.12, find cross-sectional area for 6 × 6: $A = 30.25$ in²; then, $P = 939.0(30.25) = 28{,}405$ lb.

5. Check capacity: the capacity of 28,405 lb is greater than the actual load of 27,870 lb. In other words, analysis shows that the 6 × 6 column is acceptable. If the capacity of a 6 × 6 column were insufficient, we would try the next largest size, i.e., a 6 × 8; and then an 8 × 8, etc. until a cross section was found with adequate capacity. In this case, however, even though the 6 × 6 is acceptable, it is possible that a *smaller* column size will also work, for two reasons: first, the next smaller size (a 4 × 6) falls under the dimension lumber size classification, which has a higher allowable compressive stress than what was assumed for posts and timbers.

Second, allowable stresses for dimension lumber generally increase as the cross-sectional area gets smaller, due to the size factor adjustment. For these reasons, we now check a 4 × 6 column.

Trial 2:

1. From Appendix Table A-3.12, a 4 × 6 has an area of 19.25 in².
2. From Appendix Table A-3.4, find the actual column stability factor, C_P, for the 4 × 6 column:

   From Appendix Table A-3.9, find E'_{min} = the adjusted minimum modulus of elasticity = $E_{min} \times C_M$; since $C_M = 1.0$ for any dry service condition, $E'_{min} = 690,000$ psi.

   $l_e = 8.5$ ft = 102 in.
   $d = 3.5$ in.;
   $F_{cE} = 0.822E'_{min}/(l_e / d)^2 = 0.822(690,000)/(102/3.5)^2 = 667.8$ psi;
   $F_c^* = F_c\, C_D\, C_M\, C_F = 1700(1.15)(1.0)(1.0) = 1955$ psi (with the allowable stress, F_c, taken for dimension lumber).
   $c = 0.8$ for sawn lumber.
   $A = [1 + (F_{cE}/F_c^*)]/(2c) = [1 + (667.8/1955)]/1.6 = 0.84.$
   $B = (F_{cE}/F_c^*)/c = (667.8/1955)/0.8 = 0.43.$
   $C_P = A - \sqrt{A^2 - B} = 0.84 - \sqrt{0.84^2 - 0.43} = 0.32.$

3. Compute the adjusted allowable stress in compression:

   $F_c' = F_c^* \times C_P = 1955(0.32) = 615.9$ psi.

4. Find capacity, $P = F_c' \times A$: From Appendix Table A-3.12, find cross-sectional area for 4 × 6: $A = 19.25$ in²; then, $P = 615.9(19.25) = 11,856$ lb.
5. Check capacity: the capacity of 11,856 lb is less than the actual load of 27,870 lb. Therefore, the 4 × 6 column is *not* OK: select the 6 × 6 column from Trial 1.

BEAMS

Wood beams are generally designed for bending stress and then checked for shear and deflection. Using allowable stress design, the required section modulus is found by dividing the maximum bending moment by the adjusted allowable bending stress, F_b', as shown in Equation 1.24. This adjusted value is found by multiplying the tabular value, F_b (Appendix Table A-3.5), by various adjustment factors. In addition to factors for load duration, wet service conditions, and size, three new adjustment factors are introduced for bending: a flat use factor, a repetitive member factor, and a beam stability factor (Appendix Table A-3.6).

The flat use factor, C_{fu}, accounts for the apparent increase in bending strength when beams are stressed about their weak axes. The repetitive member factor, C_r, accounts for the increased safety of joists and rafters made from dimension lumber when they are joined by floor or roof decks and spaced not more than 24 in. on center. Wood beams acting individually must be designed according to the most conservative assumptions regarding their actual strength; whereas closely-spaced joists or rafters enjoy an additional margin of safety — particularly heavy concentrated loads (or unusually weak joists or rafters) are "helped out" by the adjacent members. The beam stability factor, C_L, accounts for the possibility of lateral-torsional buckling when the compression edge of a beam is not adequately braced. For beams continuously braced by roof or floor decks, as is often the case with dimension lumber, $C_L = 1.0$. Otherwise, an effective length is found by multiplying the distance between lateral braces (often determined by the location of concentrated loads) by a coefficient and applying the formulas found in Appendix Table A-3.6.

For glued-laminated (glulam) beams only, the size factor is replaced by a "volume" factor, C_V. Like the size factor, the volume factor is designed to account for the increased probability of brittle tensile failure in larger structural elements. Because the beam stability factor, C_L, accounts for compressive buckling, while the volume factor accounts for tensile failure, it is not necessary to combine both of these factors when adjusting the allowable bending stress. Instead, only the smaller value of C_V or C_L is used for glulam beams.

Because some adjustment factors cannot be determined until the cross-sectional dimensions of the beam are known, the design process may become an iterative one, based on the analysis of trial sections. In this process, tabular values of allowable bending stress and modulus of elasticity are found in Appendix Tables A-3.5 and A-3.9; values for allowable shear stress, F_v, are found in Table A-3.7. Shear stress is only adjusted for duration of load and wet service conditions (Table A-3.8). When computing deflections, the only adjustment to modulus of elasticity, E, is for wet service conditions (Appendix Table A-3.9). The average modulus of elasticity (E), and not the minimum modulus of elasticity (E_{min}), is used in deflection calculations.

In the examples that follow, the maximum shear force, V, could have been reduced by considering the value at a distance, d, from the face of the supports, as illustrated in Figure 1.67. Where shear does not appear to be a critical factor in the design of the beam, this reduction is usually unnecessary; however, if shear appears to govern the beam design, it may be beneficial to use the reduced value of V in the calculation of actual shear stress.

Example 3.5 Analyze wood beam, dimension lumber

Problem definition. Can a 2 × 8 Hem-Fir No. 2 joist, spaced 16 in. on center, be used in a residential application, spanning 12 ft? Assume a dead load corresponding to that listed in Appendix Table A-2.1 for wood floor systems with 2 × 10 joists.

Solution overview. Find loads; check bending stress (or required section modulus); check shear stress (or required cross-sectional area); check deflection.

Problem solution
1. Find loads:
    a. From Appendix Table A-2.2, the live load, L = 40 psf; the live load distributed on 1 linear foot of the joist is L = 40($^{16}\!/_{12}$) = 53.33 lb/ft. Live load reduction does not apply since $A_T K_{LL}$ (the tributary area multiplied by the live load element factor — see Appendix Table A-2.2, part B — is less than 400 ft².
    b. From Appendix Table A-2.1, the dead load, D = 10.5 psf; the dead load distributed on 1 linear foot of the joist is D = 10.5 ($^{16}\!/_{12}$) = 14 lb/ft.
    c. The total distributed load, w = 53.33 + 14.0 = 67.33 lb/ft.
2. Create load, shear and moment diagrams as shown in Figure 3.18 to determine critical (i.e., maximum) shear force and bending moment.
3. Find adjusted allowable bending stress:
    a. From Appendix Table A-3.5, find the tabular allowable bending stress: F_b = 850 psi.
    b. From Appendix Table A-3.6, find all relevant adjustments: C_F = 1.2; C_r = 1.15; $C_M = C_D$ = 1.0.
    c. Multiply the tabular stress value by the adjustments to get the adjusted allowable stress: F_b' = 850(1.2)(1.15) = 1173 psi.
4. From Equation 1.24, compute the required section modulus: $S_{req} = M/F_b'$ = 14,543/1173 = 12.4 in³.

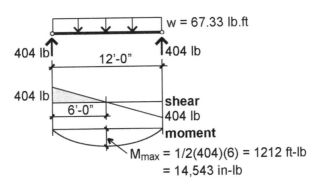

Figure 3.18: Load, shear, and moment diagrams for Example 3.5

5. From Appendix Table A-3.12, check the actual section modulus for a 2 × 8, bent about its strong (x) axis: $S_x = 13.14$ in³; since actual $S_x = 13.14$ in³ ≥ required $S_x = 12.4$ in³, the 2 × 8 section is OK for bending.

6. Find adjusted allowable shear stress:
   a. From Appendix Table A-3.7, the tabular allowable shear stress, $F_v = 150$ psi.
   b. From Appendix Table A-3.8, find all relevant adjustments: $C_M = 1.0$; $C_D = 1.0$.
   c. Multiply the tabular stress value by the adjustments to get the adjusted allowable stress: $F_v' = 150(1.0)(1.0) = 150$ psi.

7. From Equation 1.29, compute the required area, $A_{req} = 1.5V/F_v' = 1.5(404)/150 = 4.04$ in².

8. From Appendix Table A-3.12, check the actual area of the cross section: $A_{act} = 10.88$ in²; since $A_{act} = 10.88$ in² ≥ $A_{req} = 4.04$ in², the 2 × 8 section is OK for shear.

9. From Appendix Table A-1.3, find the allowable total-load deflection for a floor joist: $\Delta_{allow}^T = $ span/240 = (12 × 12)/240 = 0.6 in.; and the allowable live-load deflection for a floor joist: $\Delta_{allow}^L = $ span/360 = (12 × 12)/360 = 0.4 in.

10. Using Appendix Table A-3.15, check the actual total-load deflection. $\Delta_{act}^T = CP(L/12)^3/(EI)$ where:
    $C = 22.46$.
    $L = 12 \times 12 = 144$ in. (We are using the same symbol, L, for span and "live load"; the meaning should be clear from the context).
    $P = w(L/12) = 67.33(144/12) = 808$ lb.
    $E = 1{,}300{,}000$ psi (Appendix Table A-3.9).
    $I_x = 47.63$ in⁴ (Appendix Table A-3.12).

    $\Delta_{act}^T = 22.46(808)(144/12)^3/(1{,}300{,}000 \times 47.63) = 0.5$ in.
    Since $\Delta_{act}^T = 0.5$ in. ≤ $\Delta_{allow}^T = 0.6$ in., the beam is OK for total-load deflection.

11. Using Appendix Table A-3.15, check the actual live-load deflection. $\Delta_{act}^L = CP(L/12)^3/(EI)$ where:
    $C = 22.46$.
    $L = 12 \times 12 = 144$ in. (We are using the same symbol, L, for span and "live load"; the meaning should be clear from context).
    $P = w(L/12) = 53.33(144/12) = 640$ lb (Use live load only!).
    $E = 1{,}300{,}000$ psi (Appendix Table A-3.9).
    $I_x = 47.63$ in⁴ (Appendix Table A-3.12).

    $\Delta_{act}^L = 22.46(640)(144/12)^3/(1{,}300{,}000 \times 47.63) = 0.4$ in.
    Since $\Delta_{act}^L = 0.4$ in. ≤ $\Delta_{allow}^L = 0.4$ in., the beam is OK for live-load deflection.

12. *Conclusion:* The 2 × 8 is OK for bending, shear and deflection. Therefore it is acceptable.

Example 3.6 Analyze wood beam, timbers

Problem definition. Can a 14 × 20 Hem-Fir No. 2 girder be used in a "heavy timber" office building application, as shown in Figure 3.19? Assume that beams framing into the girder provide lateral bracing at the third points. Assume a total dead load of 18 psf and a live load corresponding to office occupancy.

Solution overview. Find loads; check bending stress (or required section modulus); check shear stress (or required cross-sectional area); check deflection.

Problem solution
1. Find loads:
   a. From Appendix Table A-2.2, the live load for office occupancy, L = 50 psf; with live load reduction, we get: $L = 50(0.25 + 15/\sqrt{2} \times 24 \times 10) = 50(0.935) = 46.7$ psf.
   b. The dead load, D = 18 psf (given).
   c. A total concentrated load, P, acts on a tributary area of $10 \times 8 = 80$ ft², so $P = (D + L)(80) = (18 + 46.7)(80) = 5176$ lb.
2. Create load, shear and moment diagrams as shown in Figure 3.20 to determine critical (i.e., maximum) shear force and bending moment.
3. From Appendix Table A-3.5, the tabular value is F_b = 850 psi.

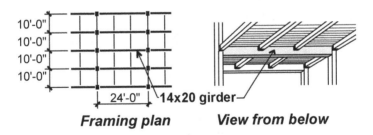

Figure 3.19: Framing plan and view of girder for Example 3.6

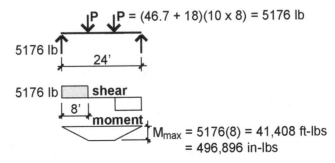

Figure 3.20: Load, shear, and moment diagrams for Example 3.6

4. Find the adjustments to the allowable bending stress:
   a. From Appendix Table A-3.6: $C_F = (12/19.5)^{1/9} = 0.95$.
   b. From Appendix Table A-3.6: $C_r = 1.0$.
   c. From Appendix Table A-3.6: $C_M = 1.0$.
   d. From Appendix Table A-3.6: $C_D = 1.0$.
   e. In addition, the beam stability factor must be computed:
   $C_L = A - \sqrt{A^2 - B}$ where:

   $l_e = 1.68 l_u = (1.68)(8 \times 12) = 161$ in. (for point loads providing lateral support at the third points)
   $E'_{min} = 400{,}000$ psi (from Appendix Table A-3.9)
   $b = 13.25$ in.; $d = 19.0$ in. (actual dimensions of a 14 × 20 from Appendix Table A-3.12)
   $F_b^* = F_b C_M C_D C_F = 675(1.0)(1.0)(0.95) = 640$ psi
   $F_{bE} = 1.20(13.25^2)(400{,}000)/(161 \times 19.0) = 27{,}548$
   $A = (1 + 27{,}548/640)/1.9 = 23.18$
   $B = (27{,}548/640)/0.95 = 45.31$

   f. $C_L = A - \sqrt{A^2 - B} = 23.18 - \sqrt{23.18^2 - 45.31} = 0.999$.
5. The adjusted allowable stress, $F_B' = F_b^* C_L = 640(0.999) = 639$ psi.
6. From Equation 1.24, compute the required section modulus: $S_{req} = M/F_b' = 496{,}896/639 = 778$ in^3.
7. From Appendix Table A-3.12, check the actual section modulus about the strong (x) axis: $S_x = 797.2$ in^3; since the actual $S_x = 797.2$ in$^3 \geq$ the required $S_x = 778$ in^3, the section is OK for bending.
8. Find the adjusted allowable shear stress:
   a. From Appendix Table A-3.7, the tabular allowable shear stress, $F_v = 140$ psi.
   b. From Appendix Table A-3.8, find all relevant adjustments: $C_M = 1.0$; $C_D = 1.0$.
   c. The adjusted allowable shear stress, $F_v' = 140(1.0)(1.0) = 140$ psi.
9. From Equation 1.29, compute the required area, $A_{req} = 1.5V/F_v' = 1.5(5176)/140 = 55.5$ in^2.
10. From Appendix Table A-3.12, check the actual area of a 14 × 20 cross section: $A_{act} = 251.8$ in^2. Since $A_{act} = 251.8$ in$^2 \geq A_{req} = 55.5$ in^2, the section is OK for shear.
11. From Appendix Table A-1.3, find the allowable total-load deflection for a floor beam: $\Delta^T_{allow} = $ span/240 $= (24 \times 12)/240 = 1.2$ in.; and the allowable live-load deflection for a floor joist: $\Delta^L_{allow} = $ span/360 $= (24 \times 12)/360 = 0.8$ in.
12. From Appendix Table A-1.3, check the actual total-load deflection: $\Delta^T_{act} = CP(L/12)^3/(EI)$ where:

$C = 61.34$.

$L = 24 \times 12 = 288$ in.

$P = (46.7 + 18)(10 \times 8) = 5176$ lb.

$E = 1,100,000$ psi (from Appendix Table A-3.9).

$I = 7573$ in^4 (from Appendix Table A-3.12).

$\Delta^T_{act} = 61.34(5176)(288/12)^3/(1,100,000 \times 7573) = 0.53$ in.

Since $\Delta^T_{act} = 0.53$ in. $\leq \Delta^T_{allow} = 1.2$ in., the girder is OK for total-load deflection.

13. From Appendix Table A-3.15, check the actual live-load deflection: $\Delta^L_{act} = CP(L/12)^3/(EI)$ where:

    $C = 61.34$.

    $L = 24 \times 12 = 288$ in.

    $P = 46.7(10 \times 8) = 3736$ lb (Use live load only!)

    $E = 1,100,000$ psi (from Appendix Table A-3.9).

    $I = 7573$ in^4 (from Appendix Table A-3.12).

    $\Delta^L_{act} = 61.34(3736)(288/12)^3/(1,100,000 \times 7573) = 0.38$ in.

    Since $\Delta^L_{act} = 0.38$ in. $\leq \Delta^L_{allow} = 0.8$ in., the girder is OK for live-load deflection.

14. *Conclusion:* The 14 × 20 is OK for bending, shear and deflection. Therefore it is acceptable.

Example 3.7 Design wood beam, glulam

Problem definition. Design a 32 ft-long glulam roof girder of stress class 20F-1.5E for the one-story industrial building shown in the framing plan (Figure 3.21). Assume a snow load, $S = 30$ psf and a dead load, $D = 20$ psf. Use a beam width of 8¾ in., with 1½ in. laminations (i.e., assume that "Western Species" will be used). Beams framing into the girder provide lateral bracing at the quarter points. Use snow load only in computing "live load" deflection, and assume that the deflection criteria will be based on a roof structure with no ceiling.

Solution overview. Find loads; begin iterative design process by assuming unknown adjustments to allowable stresses; then check bending stress (required section modulus), shear stress (required cross-sectional area) and deflection,

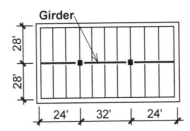

Figure 3.21: Framing plan for Example 3.7

as in analysis examples. Recompute if necessary with bigger (or smaller) cross section until bending, shear and deflection are OK.

Problem solution

1. Find loads:
   $S = 30$ psf (given).
   $D = 20$ psf (given).
   From Appendix Table A-2.7, it can be seen by examining the various load combinations that the most severe effects occur with the combination: dead load plus snow load, or $D + S$.
   Using $D + S$, the total concentrated load, P, acts on tributary area of $28 \times 8 = 224$ ft², so: $P = (D + S) \times$ (tributary area) $= (20 + 30)(224) = 11,200$ lb.

2. Create load, shear and moment diagrams as shown in Figure 3.22 to determine critical (i.e., maximum) shear force and bending moment.

3. Find provisional adjusted allowable bending stress:
   a. From Appendix Table A-3.5 part D, the design (tabular) value for bending is: $F_b = 2000$ psi.
   b. From Appendix Table A-3.6, the relevant adjustments are as follows: $C_r = 1.0$; $C_M = 1.0$; $C_D = 1.15$; C_L and C_V cannot yet be determined, since they depend on the actual cross section size; for now, choose any reasonable value for the smaller of C_L or C_V; for example, assume that the smaller of C_L or $C_V = 0.9$.
   c. The adjusted value for allowable bending stress, $F_b' = 2000(1.15)(0.9) = 2070$ psi.

4. From Equation 1.24, compute the required section modulus: $S_{req} = M/F_b' = 2,150,400/2070 = 1039$ in³.

5. Compute the required depth, d, based on the section modulus for a rectangular cross section, $S = bd^2/6 = 1039$ in³ and $b = 8.75$ in. (given). In this case, $8.75d^2/6 = 1039$, from which $d = 26.7$ in. Rounding up to the first multiple of 1.5 in. (the depth of an individual lamination), we get: $d = 27$ in.

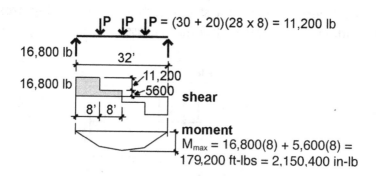

Figure 3.22: Load, shear, and moment diagrams for Example 3.7

Trial 1: 8-3/4 in. x 27 in. cross section

1. Find allowable bending stress: as before, F_b = 2000 psi.
2. Find adjustments to allowable bending stress (Appendix Table A-3.6):
   C_r = 1.0.
   C_M = 1.0.
   C_D = 1.15.
   C_L or C_V (the smaller value still needs to be determined).
   $C_V = (21/32)^{1/10}(12/27)^{1/10}(5.125/8.75)^{1/10}$ = 0.84.
   $C_L = A - \sqrt{A^2 - B}$ where:
      $l_e = 1.54\,l_u = (1.54)(8 \times 12)$ = 148 in.
      E'_{min} = 780,000 psi, from Appendix Table A-3.9 parts B and C.
      b = 8.75 in.; d = 27 in.
      $F_b^* = F_b C_D = 2000(1.15)$ = 2300 psi.
      $F_{bE} = 1.20(8.75^2)(780,000)/(148 \times 27)$ = 17,934.
      $A = (1 + 17,934/2300)/1.9$ = 4.63.
      $B = (17,934/2300)/0.95$ = 8.21.
      $C_L = A - \sqrt{A^2 - B} = 4.63 - \sqrt{4.63^2 - 8.21}$ = 0.99.
      Since C_V = 0.84 < C_L = 0.99, use C_V only.
3. The adjusted design value for bending is $F_b' = F_b^* C_V = 2300(0.84)$ = 1932 psi.
4. From Equation 1.24, compute the required section modulus: $S_{req} = M/F_b'$ = 2,150,400/1932 = 1113 in³.
5. Check that actual section modulus is greater or equal to required section modulus: actual $S_x = bd^2/6 = 8.75(27^2)/6$ = 1063 in³; since actual S_x = 1063 in³ < required S_x = 1113 in³, the section is *not* OK for bending. Try next larger section (increase depth, not width!).

Trial 2: 8-3/4 in. x 28-1/2 in. cross section (Figure 3.23)

1. Find allowable bending stress: as before, F_b = 2000 psi.
2. Find adjustments to allowable bending stress (Appendix Table A-3.6):
   C_r = 1.0.
   C_M = 1.0.
   C_D = 1.15.

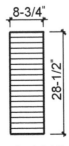

8-3/4"

28-1/2"

Figure 3.23: Glued laminated cross section for trial 2, Example 3.7

C_L or C_V (the smaller value still needs to be determined).
$C_V = (21/32)^{1/10}(12/28.5)^{1/10}(5.125/8.75)^{1/10} = 0.83$.
$C_L = A - \sqrt{A^2 - B}$ where:

    $l_e = 1.54 l_u = (1.54)(8 \times 12) = 148$ in.
    $E'_{min} = 780,000$ psi, from Appendix Table A-3.9 parts B and C.
    $b = 8.75$ in.; $d = 28.5$ in.
$F_b^* = F_b C_D = 2000(1.15) = 2300$ psi.
$F_{bE} = 1.20(8.75^2)(780,000)/(148 \times 28.5) = 16,990$.
$A = (1 + 16,990/2300)/1.9 = 4.41$.
$B = (16,990/2300)/0.95 = 7.78$.
$C_L = A - \sqrt{A^2 - B} = 4.41 - \sqrt{4.41^2 - 7.78} = 0.99$.
Since $C_V = 0.83 < C_L = 0.99$, use C_V only.

3. The adjusted design value for bending is $F_b' = F_b^* C_V = 2300(0.83) = 1909$ psi.
4. From Equation 1.24, compute the required section modulus: $S_{req} = M/F_b' = 2,150,400/1909 = 1126$ in^3.
5. Check that actual section modulus is greater or equal to required section modulus: actual $S_x = bd^2/6 = 8.75(28.5^2)/6 = 1185$ in^3; since actual $S_x = 1185$ in$^3 \geq$ required $S_x = 1126$ in^3, the section is OK for bending.
6. Find adjusted allowable shear stress:
   a. From Appendix Table A-3.7 part C, the design value for shear, $F_v = 195$ psi.
   b. From Appendix Table A-3.8, the relevant adjustments are as follows: $C_M = 1.0$; $C_D = 1.15$.
   c. The adjusted allowable stress for shear, $F_v' = 195(1.15) = 224.25$ psi.
7. Based on Equation 1.29, the required cross-sectional area to resist shear, $A_{req} = 1.5V/F_v' = 1.5(16,800)/224.25 = 112.4$ in^2.
8. Check actual cross-sectional area $= 8.75 \times 28.5 = 249.4$ in^2; since the actual area, $A_{act} = 249.4$ in$^2 \geq A_{req} = 112.4$ in^2, section is OK for shear.
9. From Appendix Table A-1.3, the allowable total load deflection for a roof with no ceiling, $\Delta_{allow}^T = $ span$/120 = 32(12)/120 = 3.20$ in.; and the allowable live load (actually *snow load* in this case) deflection for a roof with no ceiling, $\Delta_{allow}^L = $ span$/180 = 32(12)/180 = 2.13$ in.
10. From Appendix Table A-3.15, the actual total load deflection is $\Delta_{act}^T = CP(L/12)^3/(EI)$ where:
    $C = 85.54$.
    $P = (S + D)$(tributary area) $= (30 + 20)(28 \times 8) = 11,200$ lb.
    $L = 32 \times 12 = 384$ in.
    $E' = 1,500,000$ psi, from Table A-3.9 parts A and C. The "average" adjusted modulus of elasticity, E', is used for deflection calculations, whereas the adjusted *minimum* modulus of elasticity, E'_{min}, is used in buckling or stability calculations.
    $I = bd^3/12 = (8.75)(28.5^3)/12 = 16,879.6$ in^4 (Equation 1.8).

Δ^T_{act} = 85.54(11,200)(384/12)^3/(1,500,000 × 16,880) = 1.24 in. Since Δ^T_{act} = 1.24 in. ≤ Δ^T_{allow} = 3.20 in., the beam is OK for total-load deflection.

11. From Appendix Table A-3.15, the actual live (snow) load deflection is
Δ^L_{act} = $CP(L/12)^3/(EI)$ where:
C = 85.54.
P = (S)(tributary area) = (30)(28 × 8) = 6720 lb (Use snow load only!).
L = 32 × 12 = 384 in.
E' = 1,500,000 psi, from Table A-3.9 parts A and C. The "average" adjusted modulus of elasticity, E', is used for deflection calculations, whereas the adjusted *minimum* modulus of elasticity, E'_{min}, is used in buckling or stability calculations.
I = $bd^3/12$ = (8.75)(28.5^3)/12 = 16,879.6 in^4.
Δ^L_{act} = 85.54(6720)(384/12)^3/(1,500,000 × 16,880) = 0.74 in. Since Δ^L_{act} = 0.74 in. ≤ Δ^L_{allow} = 2.13 in., the beam is OK for live load (snow load) deflection.

12. *Conclusion:* The 8¾ in. × 28½ in. section is OK for bending, shear and deflection. Therefore it is acceptable.

Example 3.8 Design wood beam, dimension lumber

Problem definition. Design a Douglas Fir-Larch (North) No.1/No.2 girder using 4× lumber to support a residential live load as shown in Figure 3.24. Assume 10.5 psf for dead load. Loads on the girder can be modeled as being *uniformly distributed* since joists are spaced closely together.

Solution overview. Find loads; find known adjustments to allowable bending stress; use Appendix Table A-3.16 to directly compute lightest cross section for bending; check for shear and deflection. Alternatively, begin iterative design process by assuming unknown adjustments to allowable stresses; then check bending stress (required section modulus), shear stress (required cross-sectional area) and deflection, as in analysis examples. Recompute if necessary with bigger (or smaller) cross section until bending, shear and deflection are OK.

Problem solution
1. Find loads:
   a. From Appendix Table A-2.2, the live load for a residential occupancy, L = 40 psf.
   b. The dead load, D = 10.5 psf (given).
   c. The total distributed load, w = (D + L)(tributary area) = (10.5 + 40)(6) = 303 lb/ft. Live load reduction does not apply since K_{LL} times the tributary area is less than 400 ft^2. The tributary area for w is measured

along one linear foot of the girder, in the direction of its span, as shown in the framing plan (Figure 3.24).

2. Create load, shear and moment diagrams as shown in Figure 3.25 to determine critical (i.e., maximum) shear force and bending moment.

3. Find partially-adjusted allowable bending stress:
   a. From Appendix Table A-3.5, the design (tabular) value for bending stress, F_b = 850 psi.
   b. From Appendix Table A-3.6, the following adjustments can be determined: C_r = 1.0; C_M = 1.0; C_D = 1.0; C_L = 1.0 (assume continuous bracing by floor deck). The size factor, C_F, need not, and cannot, be determined at this point.
   c. The adjusted value for bending stress, with all adjustments known except for C_F, is F_b'' = $850C_F$ psi (the double "prime" distinguishes this value from the fully adjusted value, F_b').

4. From Equation 1.24, compute the required section modulus: S_{req} = M/F_b' = $M/(850C_F)$ = $25,566/(850C_F)$. This can be rewritten as $C_F S_{req}$ = $M/(850)$ = $25,566/(850)$ = 30.08 in³.

5. Rather than doing several "trial" designs, it is possible to find the correct cross section for bending directly, by using a table of combined size factors (C_F) and section moduli (S_x) with the lightest values highlighted.

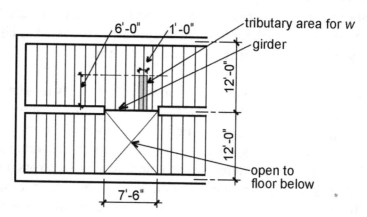

Figure 3.24: Framing plan for Example 3.8

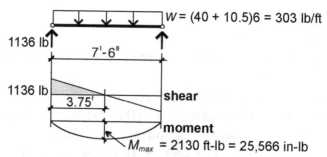

Figure 3.25: Load, shear, and moment diagrams for Example 3.8

In this method, the adjusted allowable stress is computed *without* the size factor, since C_F is combined with the section modulus in the table. Appendix Table A-3.16 indicates directly that the lightest 4× section for bending is a 4 × 8, based on a combined $C_F S_x$ value of 39.86 in^3, which is larger than the required value of $C_F S_{req}$ = 30.08 in^3 found in step 4. Appendix Table A-3.16 also shows that a 2 × 12 is actually the lightest acceptable section for bending, since it is the first bold-faced (highlighted) entry with a value of $C_F S_x$ greater than or equal to 30.08 in^3. However, in this problem, a 4× section was called for, so we provisionally select the 4 × 8 section.

6. Find adjusted allowable shear stress:
   a. From Appendix Table A-3.7, the design (tabular) allowable shear stress F_v = 180 psi.
   b. From Appendix Table A-3.8, there are no adjustments for shear stress; i.e.: C_M = 1.0; C_D = 1.0.
   c. The adjusted value for allowable shear stress, F_v' = 180 psi.
7. Based on Equation 1.29, the required cross-sectional area to resist shear, A_{req} = $1.5V/F_v'$ = 1.5(1136)/180 = 9.47 in^2.
8. From Appendix Table A-3.12, we can check the actual area of the cross section, A_{act} = 25.38 in^2; since A_{act} = 25.38 in^2 ≥ A_{req} = 9.47 in^2, the section is OK for shear.
9. From Appendix Table A-1.3, find the allowable total-load deflection for a floor beam: Δ_{allow}^T = span/240 = (7.5 × 12)/240 = 0.375 in.; and the allowable live-load deflection for a floor joist: Δ_{allow}^L = span/360 = (7.5 × 12)/360 = 0.25 in.
10. From Appendix Table A-3.15, we can check the actual total-load deflection: $\Delta_{act}^T = CP(L/12)^3/(EI)$ where:
    C = 22.46.
    L = 7.5 × 12 = 90 in.
    P = w (L/12) = (40 + 10.5)(6)(90/12) = 2272.5 lb.
    E = E' = 1,600,000 psi (from Appendix Table A-3.9).
    I = 111.1 in^4 (directly from Appendix Table A-3.12, or from the equation, $I = bd^3/12$).
    Δ_{act}^T = 22.46(2272.5)(90/12)^3/(1,600,000 × 111.1) = 0.12 in. Since Δ_{act}^T = 0.12 in. ≤ Δ_{allow}^T = 0.375 in., the beam is OK for total-load deflection.
11. From Appendix Table A-3.15, we can check the actual live-load deflection: $\Delta_{act}^L = CP(L/12)^3/(EI)$ where:
    C = 22.46.
    L = 7.5 × 12 = 90 in.
    P = w (L/12) = (40 × 6)(90/12) = 1800 lb (Use live load only!).
    E = E' = 1,600,000 psi (from Appendix Table A-3.9).
    I = 111.1 in^4 (directly from Appendix Table A-3.12, or from the equation,

$I = bd^3/12$).

$\Delta_{act}^L = 22.46(1800)(90/12)^3/(1,600,000 \times 111.1) = 0.096$ in. Since $\Delta_{act}^L = 0.096$ in. $\leq \Delta_{allow}^L = 0.25$ in., the beam is OK for deflection.

12. *Conclusion:* The 4 × 8 section is OK for bending, shear and deflection. Therefore it is acceptable.

Alternate method

It is also possible to find the lightest 4× section using an iterative design process without Appendix Table A-3.16. Using this method, the size factor, C_F, would need to be assumed, and then checked after a provisional cross section is found, as follows:

1. Assuming a size factor, $C_F = 1.0$, the adjusted allowable bending stress becomes $F_b' = 850(1.0) = 850$ psi. Then, from Equation 1.24, we compute the required section modulus: $S_{req} = M/F_b' = M/850 = 25,566/850 = 30.08$ in^3.

2. From Appendix Table A-3.12, we provisionally select a 4 ×10 with actual $S_x = 32.38$ in^3.

Trial 1: 4 x 10 cross section

1. Find actual adjusted allowable bending stress: The design (tabular) value remains $F_b = 850$ psi; the actual size factor for a 4 ×10 is $C_F = 1.20$, so the adjusted allowable bending stress, $F_b' = 850(1.20) = 1020$ psi. Since this value for a 4 ×10 is greater than the allowable stress initially assumed, the 4 ×10 must be OK for bending. But is it the lightest acceptable choice? Because the size factor actually increases for smaller sections, we must try the next smaller size.

Trial 2: 4 x 8 cross section

1. Find actual adjusted allowable bending stress for the 4 × 8: The size factor, $C_F = 1.3$, so the adjusted allowable bending stress, $F_b' = 850(1.3) = 1105$ psi.

2. From Equation 1.24, compute the required section modulus: $S_{req} = M/F_b' = 25,566/1105 = 23.14$ in^3.

3. From Appendix Table A-3.12, the actual section modulus for a 4 × 8, $S_x = 30.66$ in^3; since actual $S_x = 30.66$ in$^3 \geq S_{req} = 23.14$ in^3, the 4 × 8 section is OK for bending.

4. Shear and deflection for the 4 × 8 are checked as shown above, using the first method, and are both OK.

5. *Conclusion:* The 4 × 8 section is OK for bending, shear and deflection. Therefore it is acceptable. But what about a 4 × 6, with a size factor just

as large?

Trial 3: 4 x 6 cross section

1. Find actual adjusted allowable bending stress for the 4 × 6: The size factor, C_F = 1.3, so the adjusted allowable bending stress, F_b' = 850(1.3) = 1105 psi.
2. From Equation 1.24, compute the required section modulus: S_{req} = M/F_b' = 25,566/1105 = 23.14 in³.
3. From Appendix Table A-3.12, the actual section modulus for a 4 × 6, S_x = 17.65 in³; since actual S_x = 17.65 in³ < S_{req} = 23.14 in³, the 4 × 6 section is *not* OK for bending.
4. *Conclusion:* Since the 4 × 6 is not OK, select the 4 × 8 section.

CONNECTIONS

Were it only the force of gravity — the resistance to live and dead loads — that wood structures encountered, it would be possible to assemble structural elements by literally resting one upon the other: i.e., by stacking them so that the ends of beams or the bottom of posts *bear* upon plates, beams, or posts positioned below them, with the surfaces in contact between elements subject only to compressive stress. However, because there are always other loads, including both the horizontal and upward components of wind and earthquake forces, and various impact loads that could dislodge or overturn elements designed exclusively for downward-acting loads, the idealized condition represented by this model must be adjusted by using fasteners that respond to those non-gravity forces as well. That being said, the basic idea of stacking one wood element on top of the other remains an important strategy for assembling many wood structures, as can be seen by examining a typical light wood framing system (Figure 3.26): in such cases, the necessary resistance to lateral and upward loads, from foundation to roof, is often accomplished by superimposing metal straps and other fasteners at key joints.

Aside from the use of metal straps, plates, and other more complex hangers and brackets, wood elements are typically connected using nails, bolts, and screws (of the screws, we will be considering only lag screws, sometimes referred to as "lag bolts," here). These fasteners can be used in two distinct ways: primarily as *dowels* inserted perpendicular to the direction of load; but also in *withdrawal*, i.e., subject to tension forces parallel to the direction of load. The designation for the capacity of a dowel-type fastener (i.e., a fastener stressed in shear) is Z; the capacity of a fastener used in withdrawal is designated as W, as shown in Figure 3.27. In both cases, the capacity must be multiplied by adjustment factors; the adjusted capacities are designated Z' and W' respectively.

Where the head of a lag screw or bolt, or the nut of a bolt, comes in contact with a wood member, a circular or square *washer* is inserted between the metal and wood surfaces in order to distribute the load imparted by the metal fastener over a greater surface area of wood. This is a requirement for bolts and lag screws subjected to either shear or tension.

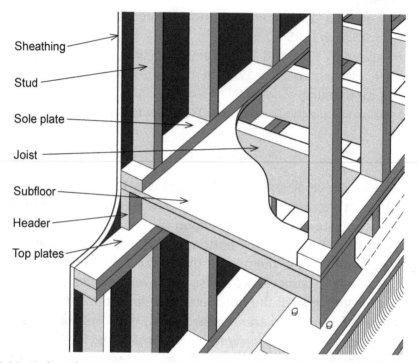

Sheathing
Stud
Sole plate
Joist
Subfloor
Header
Top plates

Figure 3.26: Platform framing showing joists bearing on plates; plates bearing on studs; and studs bearing on plates (siding, building paper, insulation, vapor retarder, and interior finishes not shown)

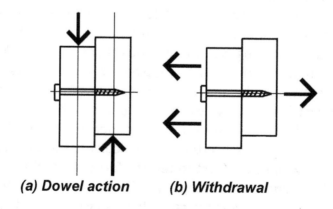

(a) Dowel action   **(b) Withdrawal**

Figure 3.27: Wood fasteners with (*a*) dowel action; or (*b*) in withdrawal

Shear

With respect to dowel-type action, nails and screws typically connect only two members (the *side member* being the piece into which the nail is first hammered or the screw is first inserted; the *main member* being the piece connected behind the side member). Such connections are in "single shear," since there is only a single shear plane between the side and main member (Figure 3.28*a*). Bolts can connect two members in single shear, but also can connect three members in "double shear." In the latter case, the "main member" is in the center, with the two outside members defined as "side members," as shown in Figure 3.28*b*. Where bolts are used in single shear, the main member is defined as the thicker piece (if any), since either side could serve as the point of insertion without altering the behavior of the connection.

Typical idealized diagrams representing the forces on dowel-type fasteners in single shear are often misleading, since neither the structure (Figure 3.29*a*) nor the fasteners themselves (Figure 3.29*b*) would be in rotational equilibrium with only a single force couple.

The actual pattern of forces acting on such fasteners is more complex, since these forces must satisfy all three equations of equilibrium. Several possibilities exist for the arrangement of forces on the fasteners that are consistent with the requirements for equilibrium. For example, as shown in Figure 3.30*a*, the force acting downward on the left-hand member can be "balanced" by two forces in the right-hand member; critical stress patterns applied to the wood by the fasteners are shown schematically in Figure 3.30*b*, assuming that only stresses in the left-hand member have reached critical values. This pattern of stress is designated Mode I.

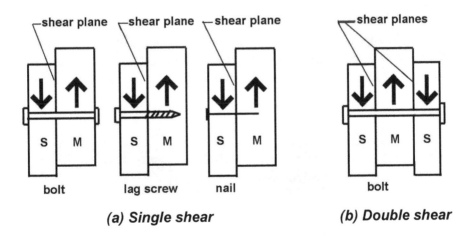

Figure 3.28: Examples of (*a*) single shear and (*b*) double shear. "*S*" indicates side member; "*M*" indicates main member

Several other patterns of force and stress can develop in the wood connection. Figure 3.31 illustrates Mode II, in which critical stresses develop in both members. The inclination of the fastener (Figure 3.31*b*) is exaggerated to show how the pattern of critical stresses develops alternately on opposite sides of the fastener.

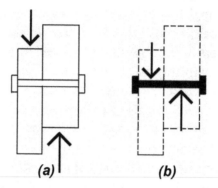

(a)   **(b)**

Figure 3.29: Simple single shear model with two equal and opposite forces, but rotational equilibrium unaccounted for: (*a*) forces acting on wood members; (*b*) forces acting on dowel-type fastener

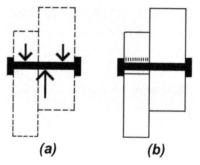

(a)   **(b)**

Figure 3.30: Mode I behavior of fastener in single shear, showing (*a*) pattern of forces on fastener; and (*b*) corresponding critical stresses on wood member

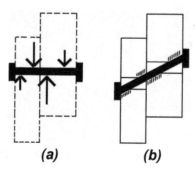

(a)   **(b)**

Figure 3.31: Mode II behavior of fastener in single shear, showing (*a*) pattern of forces on fastener; and (*b*) corresponding critical stresses on wood member

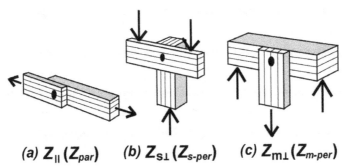

(a) $Z_\parallel$ *(Z_{par})*   *(b)* $Z_{s\perp}$ *($Z_{s\text{-}per}$)*   *(c)* $Z_{m\perp}$ *($Z_{m\text{-}per}$)*

Figure 3.32: For dowel-type fasteners, three orientations of load to wood grain are possible, shown with their commonly-used designations and equivalent keyboard-friendly designations, Z_{par}, $Z_{s\text{-}per}$, and $Z_{m\text{-}per}$. The latter designations are used in this text: *(a)* Z_{par} is the fastener capacity where both the side and main members are loaded parallel to grain; *(b)* $Z_{s\text{-}per}$ is the fastener capacity where the side member is loaded perpendicular to grain while the main member is loaded parallel to grain; and *(c)* $Z_{m\text{-}per}$ is the fastener capacity where the main member is loaded perpendicular to grain while the side member is loaded parallel to grain. The case where both members are loaded perpendicular to grain is uncommon, and is therefore not considered here.

All together, researchers have identified four behavioral modes with dowel-type fasteners. For Modes III and IV (not illustrated), yielding of the fastener itself is presumed to have occurred; in these two latter cases, not only is the resistance of the wood to the pressure exerted by the fastener considered, but also the strength of the steel fastener itself. With these four modes, plus two variations each for Modes I and III (where critical stresses might occur either in the main or side member), there are six possible ways in which stress can develop in a single-shear connection, resulting in six possible values for the force that a single fastener can safely develop. Clearly, it is the smallest of these six allowable forces that governs the connection design. For members connected in double shear, two of the modes are not considered, as they are incompatible with the geometry of elements in double-shear. Thus, only four equations need to be checked for double-shear connections.

Because the equations that have been developed for these six behavioral modes (four for double shear) acknowledge possible yielding of the steel fasteners, they are known as "yield limit" equations. They can be used for bolts, lag screws, or nails — and not only for wood-to-wood connections, but also where steel plates are used for the side member(s). They are really not intended to be solved by hand: instead, three alternative strategies are commonly employed to design wood fasteners: (1) the use of spreadsheets or structural analysis software to solve the equations, (2) the use of tables containing commonly encountered fastener capacities, and (3) the use of "rules of thumb" in the form of tables and figures showing fastener details sanctioned by building codes. In most of the examples that follow, tables are used to find lateral design values. For a more detailed look at the use of yield limit equations, see Example 3.15 and Appendix Table A-3.31.

In general, fasteners should be placed in wood connections in such a way that the lines of force in the members being joined are aligned; a misaligned force is just another word for a force couple, which results in bending at the joint. Single-shear connections, as shown in Figure 3.28a, are inherently subject to such bending; whereas double-shear connections, as shown in Figure 3.28b, are inherently symmetrical, and therefore less likely to be subject to unanticipated bending stresses. On the other hand, many single-shear connections are embedded within, and attached to, a matrix of structural elements — sheathing, transverse members, and so on — that effectively relieve the fasteners themselves of the burden of resisting stresses arising out of the misalignment. In the single-shear examples that follow, it is assumed that such additional structural elements (not shown in the examples) are actually present.

Aside from material properties for wood and steel, two other relationships between fastener and wood member must be accounted for: the *penetration* of lag screws and nails into the main member of the connection, as described in Appendix Table A-3.19; and the *grain orientation* of the various members being connected, with respect to the direction of load, as shown in Figure 3.32. To obtain full lateral design values, lag screw penetration must be at least equal to $8D$, and nail penetration must be at least equal to $10D$ (where D is the fastener diameter).

Just as the allowable stresses for wood structural elements in tension, compression, or bending are adjusted to account for the actual behavioral properties of wood, the design values for wood fasteners are also adjusted in several ways. Two of these adjustments have already been discussed under the heading, *material properties*, although there are subtle differences in their application to fasteners. The duration of load factor (C_D) accounts for changes in the strength of wood connections based on the length of time (duration) that the load is applied. However, because the yield limit equations used to analyze single- and double-shear connections can also be used where steel side members are combined with wood main members, the allowable stress for such steel members has been reduced by a factor of 1.6, corresponding to the maximum duration-of-load adjustment for wood members under wind or seismic loading. In this way, C_D may be applied to the entire connection design (so that the steel stress, already reduced, is increased up to its actual value in cases where the load combination includes wind or seismic forces), simplifying the design process, although making the steel side-member design conservative for load combinations that do not include wind or seismic forces (since in those cases, the steel stress is still initially reduced, but not increased by the same amount).

The wet service factor (C_M) accounts for the increased strength of wood when used "dry." For connection design, it is also important to consider the moisture content of the wood when it was first fabricated, since a change from an initial "wet" fabrication condition to a "dry" service condition can weaken the connection in some cases.

Two additional adjustments apply to dowel-type fasteners only, and only when the fastener diameter is greater or equal to ¼ in. (i.e., for bolts and lag screws). The group action adjustment (C_g) accounts for reductions in strength that may occur when comparing the behavior of a single fastener to that of a group of fasteners; the geometry factor (C_Δ) includes a series of possible reductions that come into play when fasteners are closely spaced, or are placed too close to the edge or end of a wood member, as shown in Figure 3.33. The orientation of the wood grain determines the "edge" and "end" of the members, irrespective of the load direction; whereas "row spacing" parameters are measured with respect to the direction of the load (a "row of fasteners" being parallel to the direction of load).

For nails only, a toe-nail factor adjustment, C_{tn}, is used for lateral or withdrawal design values (see Appendix Table A-3.24) when the side and main members are fastened with nails driven at a 30° angle to the face of the side member.

The general strategy for designing wood connections is to first find the capacity of a single fastener, using one of the strategies discussed (i.e., using yield limit equations, or various tabular design aids), and then to multiply that capacity by the number of fasteners comprising the connection. As already suggested, this total capacity for multiple fasteners is explicitly modified using

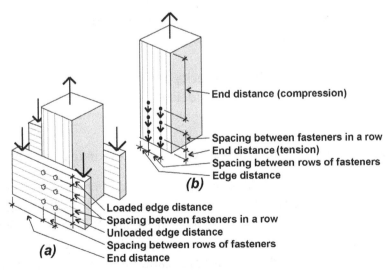

Figure 3.33: Geometry factor parameters: (*a*) a 3-member connection is illustrated, with the grain represented by parallel lines on the surface of the members; (*b*) a free-body diagram shows how the geometry factor parameters are measured on the middle member

the group action adjustment factor C_g; the other adjustments — C_D, C_M, and C_Δ — can be applied to either the entire connection or just a single fastener, but should only be applied once each per connection. A temperature factor, C_t, should be applied to wood elements subjected to sustained high temperatures: see Appendix Table A-3.25.

The complete dowel-type fastener design process for wood elements is summarized below; this summary constitutes the "Solution overview" within the examples that follow (with steps 4 and 5 eliminated where the connection consists of a single fastener only):

1. Find the capacity for a single fastener, Z.

2. For lag screws and nails, check that penetration into the main member is at least $4D$ (for lag screws) or $6D$ (for nails), and adjust capacity, Z, accordingly.

3. Adjust for duration of load, wet service conditions, and geometry.

4. For multiple-fastener connections only, adjust for group action, and then multiply the adjusted single-fastener capacity by the number of fasteners in the connection.

5. Remember that in addition to the fasteners, the element itself must be designed in a manner that accounts for the presence of bolt or lag screw holes (nail holes are not considered in structural element design). For multiple-fastener connections only, and only where forces are parallel to grain and in tension, also check the element for row and group tear-out (discussed earlier under the heading, *tension*).

Tables for computing fastener capacity are included in the appendix tables at the end of this chapter; specific guidelines for the use of these tables are provided in the examples that follow.

Example 3.9 Analyze wood single-shear connection using one bolt

Problem definition. Find the capacity of a connection (single shear) consisting of a 2 × 10 beam connected to a 6 × 6 post using one ¾ in. diameter bolt, as shown in Figure 3.34. The wood used is Hem-Fir, and the bolts are fabricated from ordinary, low-strength, A307 steel, as is typical for wood connections. Assume live and dead loads only, dry fabrication and service conditions, and spacing as shown.

Solution overview

1. Find the capacity for a single fastener, Z.
2. For lag screws and nails, check that penetration into the main member is at least 4D (for lag screws) or 6D (for nails), and reduce capacity, Z, if necessary.
3. Adjust for duration of load, moisture, and geometry.
4. Adjust for group action (not applicable for single fastener connections).
5. Check that the element itself is designed in a manner that accounts for the presence of bolt or lag screw holes (not included in this example).

Problem solution

1. From Appendix Table A-3.26, the lateral design value, Z_{s-per}, is 460 lb. The value of Z chosen corresponds to the following condition: the side member (for bolted connections in single shear, the side member is defined as the thinner of the two members) is oriented so that the load is perpendicular to the direction of grain, while the main member is oriented so that the load is parallel to the direction of grain. This corresponds to Z_{s-per}, as defined in Figure 3.32.
2. From Appendix Table A-3.19 (Note 4), penetration is only an issue with lag screws and nails, since bolts must always fully penetrate the members being connected. Therefore, no reduction of the tabular lateral design value is necessary, and it remains equal to Z_{s-per} = 460 lb.
3. Adjustments are as follows:
   C_D for typical values of live and dead load is 1.0 (Appendix Table A-3.20).
   C_M for members fabricated and used "dry" is 1.0 (Appendix Table A-3.21).
   C_g does not apply to single-fastener connections.
   C_Δ is found by testing four separate criteria (Appendix Table A-3.23): spacing between fasteners in a row (not applicable where only one fastener is

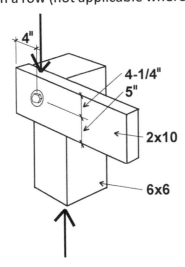

Figure 3.34: Single-shear bolted connection with a single fastener, for Example 3.9

used); spacing between rows of fasteners (not applicable where only one fastener is used); end distance; and edge distance. It is sometimes useful to sketch the members separately, showing dimensions for the relevant geometry factor parameters (Figure 3.35). In the calculations that follow, the fastener diameter is: D = ¾ in. = 0.75 in.

Spacing criteria: For a single fastener connection, the spacing criteria (for spacing between rows and spacing of fasteners within a row) do not apply.

End distance: Adjustment criteria for end distance appear in Appendix Table A-3.23, part *C*. For the horizontal member, the loading direction is perpendicular to grain, so the minimum end distance for full value (i.e., for C_Δ = 1.0) is $4D$ = 4 × 0.75 = 3 in. Since the actual end distance of 4 in. exceeds this value (and the other, unspecified, end distance is clearly larger), the geometry factor, C_Δ = 1.0 for horizontal member end distance. For the vertical member, the loading direction is parallel to grain and the specified wood is a "softwood," so the minimum end distance for full value for "tension" (i.e., for C_Δ = 1.0) is $7D$ = 7 × 0.75 = 5.25 in. Since the actual end distance, although unspecified, clearly exceeds this, the geometry factor, C_Δ = 1.0 for vertical member end distance (tension). For the full value in "compression," we need a minimum end distance of $4D$ = 4 × 0.75 = 3 in., which the actual end distance of 4¼ in. exceeds. The geometry factor therefore is also C_Δ = 1.0 for vertical member end distance (compression).

Edge distance: Adjustment criteria for edge distance appear in Appendix Table A-3.23, part *D*. For the horizontal member, the loading direction is perpendicular to grain, so the loaded and unloaded edges must be determined separately. The minimum distance for the loaded edge (i.e., the edge towards which the fastener itself is bearing) is $4D$ = 4 × 0.75 = 3 in.,

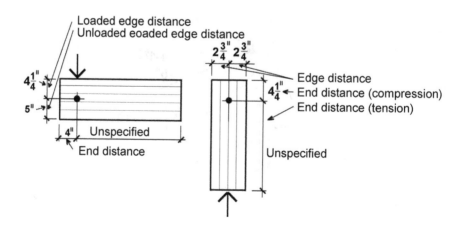

Figure 3.35: Geometry factor parameters for Example 3.9

which the actual loaded edge distance of 4¼ in. exceeds. The minimum distance for the unloaded edge (i.e., the opposite edge away from which the fastener itself is bearing) is $1.5D = 1.5 \times 0.75 = 1.125$ in., which the actual unloaded edge distance of 5 in. exceeds. For the vertical member, the loading direction is parallel to grain, so the minimum edge distance is determined from the so-called slenderness ratio of the fastener, l/D. The length of the fastener, l, within the main member is 5½ in., so $l/D = 5.5/0.75 = 7.33$. Since this value is greater than 6, the minimum edge distance is $1.5D = 1.5 \times 0.75 = 1.125$ in., which the actual edge distance of 2.75 in. exceeds. Since all the criteria for full value are met, the geometry factor for edge distance is $C_\Delta = 1.0$.

The geometry factor for the entire connection is found by using the smallest of the geometry factors found for any of the four conditions tested above (end, edge, and the two spacing conditions where applicable): therefore, we use $C_\Delta = 1.0$.

The adjusted lateral design value for the single fastener in the connection is found by multiplying the lateral design value from step 2 by the various adjustment factors determined in step 3: $Z' = Z(C_D)(C_M)(C_\Delta) = 460(1.0)(1.0)(1.0) = 460$ lb.

4. The group action factor, C_g, is 1.0 for all single-fastener connections (since only multiple fastener connections can have "group action"). Therefore, the connection capacity is equal to $Z'(C_g) = 460(1.0) = 460$ lb.

5. We are not considering the design of the structural elements themselves in this example.

6. *Conclusion:* The total capacity of the connection (consisting of a single ¾ in. diameter bolt) is 460 lb.

Example 3.10 Analyze wood single-shear connection using multiple bolts

Problem definition. Find the capacity of a connection (single shear) consisting of two 2 × 8 tension elements connected by a 2 × 8 member using six ½ in. diameter bolts in each member. The wood used is Hem-Fir No. 1, and the bolts are fabricated from ordinary, low-strength, A307 steel, as is typical for wood connections. Assume live, dead, and wind loads only, dry fabrication and service conditions, and spacing as shown in Figure 3.36.

Solution overview
1. Find the capacity for a single fastener, Z.
2. For lag screws and nails, check that penetration into the main member is at least $4D$ (for lag screws) or $6D$ (for nails), and reduce capacity, Z, if necessary.
3. Adjust for duration of load, moisture, and geometry.

4. Adjust for group action, and then multiply the adjusted single-fastener capacity by the number of fasteners in the connection.
5. Check that the element itself is designed in a manner that accounts for the presence of bolt or lag screw holes (not included in this example).

Problem solution

1. From Appendix Table A-3.26, the lateral design value, Z_{par}, is 410 lb. The value of Z chosen corresponds to the following condition: both the side and main member are oriented so that the load is parallel to the direction of grain, as defined in Figure 3.32.
2. From Appendix Table A-3.19 (Note 4), penetration is only an issue with lag screws and nails, since bolts must always fully penetrate the members being connected. Therefore, no reduction of the tabular lateral design value is necessary, and it remains equal to Z_{par} = 410 lb.
3. Adjustments are as follows:
   C_D for live, dead, and wind load is 1.6 (Appendix Table A-3.20);
   C_M for members fabricated and used "dry" is 1.0 (Appendix Table A-3.21);
   C_Δ is found by testing four separate criteria (Appendix Table A-3.23): spacing between fasteners in a row; spacing between rows of fasteners; end distance; and edge distance. It is sometimes useful to sketch the members separately, showing dimensions for the relevant geometry factor parameters (Figure 3.37):
   In the calculations that follow, D is the fastener diameter of ½ in.
   Spacing criteria: Adjustment criteria for spacing appear in Appendix Table A-3.23, parts A and B. For spacing between fasteners in a row, where the loading direction is parallel to grain, the minimum spacing for full value is $4D = 4 \times 0.5 = 2$ in. Since the actual spacing is 2 in., the full value applies, and C_Δ = 1.0 for spacing between fasteners in a row. For spacing between rows of fasteners, again with the loading direction parallel to

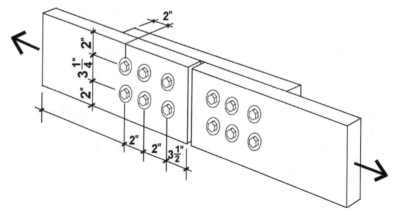

Figure 3.36: Single-shear bolted connection with multiple fasteners, for Example 3.10

grain, the minimum required spacing is $1.5D = 1.5 \times 0.5 = 0.75$ in. Since the actual spacing (between rows) of 3.25 in. exceeds this value, and is no greater than 5 in. (the maximum distance allowed between the outer rows of fasteners), the geometry factor is $C_\Delta = 1.0$ for spacing between rows of fasteners.

End distance: Adjustment criteria for end distance appear in Appendix Table A-3.23, part *C*. For all the members, the loading direction is parallel to grain. Where the fasteners are bearing towards the member end (in "tension") and where the wood is "softwood," the minimum end distance for full value (i.e., for $C_\Delta = 1.0$) is $7D = 7 \times 0.5 = 3.5$ in. For the primary members, the actual end distance of 3.5 in. is no less than this, so the geometry factor, $C_\Delta = 1.0$. However, for the connecting member, shown to the right in Figure 3.37, the actual distance of 2 in. is between the absolute minimum ($3.5D = 1.75$ in.) and the required distance for full value ($7D = 3.5$ in.); therefore the geometry factor is taken as the actual end distance divided by the minimum distance for full value, or $C_\Delta = 2/3.5 = 0.571$.

Edge distance: Adjustment criteria for edge distance appear in Appendix Table A-3.23, part *D*. For all the members, the loading direction is parallel to grain, so the minimum edge distance is determined from the so-called slenderness ratio of the fastener, l/D. The length of the fastener, l, within all members is 1½ in., so $l/D = 1.5/0.5 = 3.0$. Since this value is less than or equal to 6, the minimum edge distance is $1.5D = 1.5 \times 0.5 = 0.75$ in., which the actual edge distance of 2.0 in. exceeds. The geometry factor for edge distance is therefore $C_\Delta = 1.0$.

The geometry factor for the entire connection is found by using the smallest of the geometry factors found for any of the four conditions tested above (end, edge, and the two spacing conditions where applicable): therefore, we use $C_\Delta = 0.571$, which was computed for the end distance of the connecting member.

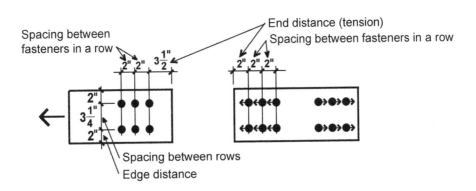

Figure 3.37: Geometry factor parameters for Example 3.10

The adjusted lateral design value for a single bolt in the connection is found by multiplying the lateral design value from step 2 by the various adjustment factors determined in step 3: $Z' = Z(C_D)(C_M)(C_\Delta) =$ 410(1.6)(1.0)(0.571) = 374.6 lb.

4. From Appendix Table A-3.22, the group action factor, C_g, is 0.993, a conservative value based on 2 × 8 main and side members ($A_m = A_s =$ approximately 11 in²), with three fasteners in a single row. The actual modulus of elasticity (Appendix Table A-3.9) for Hem-Fir No.1 is E = 1,500,000 psi, which is larger than the nominal value of 1,400,000 psi assumed in Appendix Table A-3.22; the actual fastener spacing, s = 2 in., is smaller than the value, s = 3 in., assumed in the table, and the actual fastener diameter, D = ½ in., is smaller than the value, D = ¾ in., assumed in the table. Therefore, the tabular value, C_g = 0.993, is conservative and can be used. Alternatively, a more accurate value for C_g can be found, based on the method described in Note 3 of Appendix Table A-3.22, and illustrated in Example 3.15.

   Adjusting for group action and multiplying the single-fastener value for Z' found in step 3 by the number of fasteners in the connection, we get a total adjusted connection capacity equal to 374.6(0.993)(6) = 2232 lb.

5. We are not considering the design of the structural elements themselves in this example. Tension, row and group tear-out are considered in Example 3.1.

6. *Conclusion:* The total capacity of the connection (consisting of a six ½ in. diameter bolts) is 2232 lb.

Example 3.11 Analyze wood double-shear connection using multiple bolts

Problem definition. Find the capacity of a connection (double shear) consisting of two 2 × 8 tension elements connected by two shorter 2 × 8 members, using six ½ in. diameter bolts in each member. The wood used is Hem-Fir No.1, and the bolts are fabricated from ordinary, low-strength, A307 steel, as is typical for wood connections. Assume live, dead, and wind loads only, dry fabrication and service conditions, and spacing as shown in Figure 3.38.

Solution overview
1. Find the capacity for a single fastener, Z.
2. For lag screws and nails, check that penetration into the main member is at least 4D (for lag screws) or 6D (for nails), and reduce capacity, Z, if necessary.
3. Adjust for duration of load, moisture, and geometry.
4. Adjust for group action, and then multiply the adjusted single-fastener capacity by the number of fasteners in the connection.

5. Not included in this example (check that the element itself is designed in a manner that accounts for the presence of bolt or lag screw holes).

Problem solution

1. From Appendix Table A-3.27, the lateral design value, Z_{par}, is 900 lb. The value of Z chosen corresponds to the following condition: both the side and main member are oriented so that the load is parallel to the direction of grain, as defined in Figure 3.32.
2. From Appendix Table A-3.19 (Note 4), penetration is only an issue with lag screws and nails, since bolts must always fully penetrate the members being connected. Therefore, no reduction of the tabular lateral design value is necessary, and it remains equal to Z_{par} = 900 lb.
3. Adjustments are as follows:
   C_D for live, dead, and wind load is 1.6 (Appendix Table A-3.20);
   C_M for members fabricated and used "dry" is 1.0 (Appendix Table A-3.21);
   C_Δ is found by testing four separate criteria (Appendix Table A-3.23): spacing between fasteners in a row; spacing between rows of fasteners; end distance; and edge distance. It is sometimes useful to sketch the members separately, showing dimensions for the relevant geometry factor parameters (Figure 3.39).

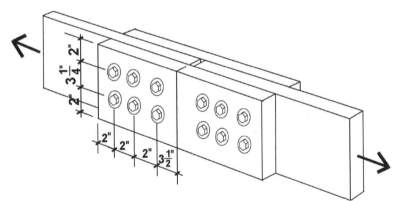

Figure 3.38: Double-shear bolted connection with multiple fasteners, for Example 3.11

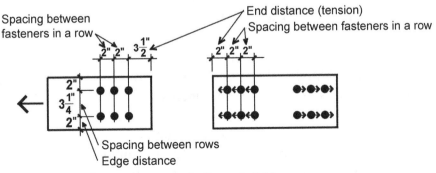

Figure 3.39: Geometry factor parameters for Example 3.11

In the calculations that follow, D is the fastener diameter of ½ in.

Spacing criteria: Adjustment criteria for spacing appear in Appendix Table A-3.23, parts *A* and *B*. For spacing between fasteners in a row, where the loading direction is parallel to grain, the minimum spacing for full value is $4D = 4 \times 0.5 = 2$ in. Since the actual spacing is 2 in., the full value applies, and $C_\Delta = 1.0$. For spacing between rows of fasteners, again with the loading direction parallel to grain, the minimum required spacing is $1.5D = 1.5 \times 0.5 = 0.75$ in. Since the actual spacing (between rows) of 3.25 in. exceeds this value, and is no greater than 5 in. (the maximum distance allowed between the outer rows of fasteners), the geometry factor is $C_\Delta = 1.0$.

End distance: Adjustment criteria for end distance appear in Appendix Table A-3.23, part *C*. For all the members, the loading direction is parallel to grain. Where the fasteners are bearing towards the member end, i.e., in "tension" and for "softwood," the minimum end distance for full value (i.e., for $C_\Delta = 1.0$) is $7D = 7 \times 0.5 = 3.5$ in. For the main members, the actual end distance of 3.5 in. is no less than this, so the geometry factor, $C_\Delta = 1.0$. However, for the connecting member, shown to the right in Figure 3.39, the actual distance of 2 in. is between the absolute minimum ($3.5D = 1.75$ in.) and the required distance for full value ($7D = 3.5$ in.); therefore the geometry factor is taken as the actual end distance divided by the minimum distance for full value, or $C_\Delta = 2/3.5 = 0.571$.

Edge distance: Adjustment criteria for edge distance appear in Appendix Table A-3.23, part *D*. For all the members, the loading direction is parallel to grain, so the minimum edge distance is determined from the so-called slenderness ratio of the fastener, l/D. The fastener length, l, within all members is 1½ in., so $l/D = 1.5/0.5 = 3.0$. Since this value is less than or equal to 6, the minimum edge distance is $1.5D = 1.5 \times 0.5 = 0.75$ in., which the actual edge distance of 2.0 in. exceeds. The geometry factor therefore is $C_\Delta = 1.0$.

The geometry factor for the entire connection is found by using the smallest of the geometry factors found for any of the four conditions tested above (end, edge, and the two spacing conditions where applicable): therefore, we use $C_\Delta = 0.571$, which was computed for the end distance of the connecting member.

The adjusted lateral design value for a single bolt in the connection is found by multiplying the lateral design value from step 2 by the various adjustment factors determined in step 3: $Z' = Z(C_D)(C_M)(C_\Delta) = 900(1.6)(1.0)(0.571) = 822.2$ lb.

4. From Appendix Table A-3.22, the group action factor, C_g, is 0.983, a conservative value based on a single 2 × 8 main member and two 2 × 8 side members (A_m = approximately 11 in²; A_s = approximately 17 in²), with

three fasteners in a single row. The actual modulus of elasticity (Appendix Table A-3.9) for Hem-Fir No.1 is $E = 1,500,000$ psi, which is larger than the nominal value of 1,400,000 psi assumed in the table; the actual fastener spacing, $s = 2$ in., is smaller than the value, $s = 3$ in., assumed in the table, and the actual fastener diameter, $D = \frac{1}{2}$ in., is smaller than the value, $D = \frac{3}{4}$ in., assumed in the table; therefore, the tabular value, $C_g = 0.983$, is conservative and can be used. Alternatively, a more accurate value for C_g can be found, based on the method described in Note 3 of Appendix Table A-3.22, and illustrated in Example 3.15.

Adjusting for group action and multiplying the single-fastener value for Z' found in step 3 by the number of fasteners in the connection, we get a total adjusted connection capacity equal to $822.2(0.983)(6) = 4849$ lb.

5. We are not considering the design of the structural elements themselves in this example. Tension, row and group tear-out are considered in Example 3.1.

6. *Conclusion:* The total capacity of the connection (consisting of a six ½ in. diameter bolts) is 4849 lb.

Example 3.12 Analyze wood double-shear connection using multiple bolts and steel side plates

Problem definition. Find the capacity of a connection (double shear) consisting of a 6 × 6 tension member connected by two ¼ in. steel side plates, using four ⅝ in. diameter bolts. The wood used is Douglas Fir-Larch (North) No. 1, the steel plates are ASTM A36 steel, and the bolts are fabricated from ordinary, low-strength, A307 steel, as is typical for wood connections. Assume live and dead loads only, dry fabrication and service conditions, and spacing as shown in Figure 3.40.

Solution overview
1. Find the capacity for a single fastener, Z.
2. For lag screws and nails, check that penetration into the main member is at least $4D$ (for lag screws) or $6D$ (for nails), and reduce capacity, Z, if necessary.
3. Adjust for duration of load, moisture, and geometry.
4. Adjust for group action, and then multiply the adjusted single-fastener capacity by the number of fasteners in the connection.
5. Not included in this example (check that the element itself is designed in a manner that accounts for the presence of bolt or lag screw holes).

Problem solution
1. From Appendix Table A-3.28, the lateral design value, Z_{par}, is 2390 lb.

The value of Z chosen corresponds to the following condition: the main member is oriented so that the load is parallel to the direction of grain, as defined in Figure 3.32. The orientation of the steel side plates to the direction of load is not relevant, since there is no "grain" in the steel plates that influences its strength.

2. From Appendix Table A-3.19 (Note 4), penetration is only an issue with lag screws and nails, since bolts must always fully penetrate the members being connected. Therefore, no reduction of the tabular lateral design value is necessary, and it remains equal to $Z_{par} = 2390$ lb.

3. Adjustments are as follows:

C_D for typical values of live and dead load is 1.0 (Appendix Table A-3.20); C_M for members fabricated and used "dry" is 1.0 (Appendix Table A-3.21); C_Δ is found by testing four separate criteria (Appendix Table A-3.23): spacing between fasteners in a row; spacing between rows of fasteners; end distance; and edge distance. It is sometimes useful to sketch the members separately, showing dimensions for the relevant geometry factor parameters (Figure 3.41). Only the wood main member is considered here; the tension capacity and bolt spacing in the steel plate must be considered separately (see Chapter 4 for discussion of steel subjected to tension and for discussion of bolt spacing).

In the calculations that follow, D is the fastener diameter of ⅝ in. = 0.625 in.

Spacing criteria: Adjustment criteria for spacing appear in Appendix Table A-3.23, parts A and B. For spacing between fasteners in a row, where the loading direction is parallel to grain, the minimum spacing for full value is $4D = 4 \times 0.625 = 2.5$ in. Since the actual spacing is 2.5 in., the full value applies, and $C_\Delta = 1.0$. For spacing between rows of fasteners, again

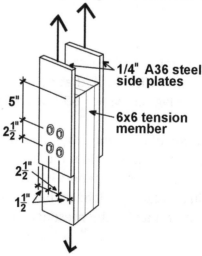

Figure 3.40: Double-shear bolted connection with multiple fasteners and steel side plates, for Example 3.12

with the loading direction parallel to grain, the minimum required spacing is $1.5D = 1.5 \times 0.625 = 0.9375$ in. Since the actual spacing (between rows) of 2.5 in. exceeds this value, and is no greater than 5 in. (the maximum distance allowed between the outer rows of fasteners), the geometry factor is $C_\Delta = 1.0$.

End distance: Adjustment criteria for end distance appear in Appendix Table A-3.23, part *C*. For the main member, the loading direction is parallel to grain. Where the fasteners are bearing towards the member end (in "tension") and where the wood is "softwood," the minimum end distance for full value (i.e., for $C_\Delta = 1.0$) is $7D = 7 \times 0.625 = 4.375$ in. The actual end distance of 5 in. is greater than this, so the geometry factor, $C_\Delta = 1.0$.

Edge distance: Adjustment criteria for edge distance appear in Appendix Table A-3.23, part *D*. For the main member, the loading direction is parallel to grain, so the minimum edge distance is determined from the so-called slenderness ratio of the fastener, l/D. The fastener length, l, within the main member is 5½ in., so $l/D = 5.5/0.625 = 8.8$. Since this value is greater than 6, the minimum edge distance is either $1.5D = 1.5 \times 0.625 = 0.9375$ in., or one half of the spacing between rows $= 0.5 \times 2.5 = 1.25$ in., whichever is greater: the minimum edge distance is therefore 1.25 in., which the actual edge distance of 1.5 in. exceeds. The geometry factor therefore is $C_\Delta = 1.0$.

The geometry factor for the entire connection is found by using the smallest of the geometry factors found for any of the four conditions tested above (end, edge, and the two spacing conditions where applicable): therefore, we use $C_\Delta = 1.0$.

The adjusted lateral design value for a single bolt in the connection is found by multiplying the lateral design value from step 2 by the various adjustment factors determined in step 3: $Z' = Z(C_D)(C_M)(C_\Delta) = 2390(1.0)(1.0)(1.0) = 2390$ lb.

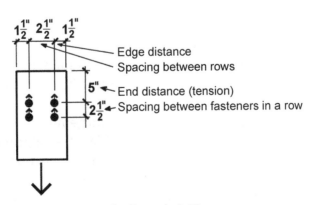

Figure 3.41: Geometry factor parameters for Example 3.12

4. From Appendix Table A-3.22 (part *B* for steel side members) the group action factor, C_g, is 0.997, a conservative value based on a 6 × 6 main member and two ¼ in. steel side plates (A_m = approximately 30 in²; A_s = approximately 3 in²), with two fasteners in a single row. The actual modulus of elasticity (Appendix Table A-3.9) for Douglas Fir-Larch (North) No.1 is E = 1,600,000 psi (for "posts and timbers"), which is larger than the nominal value of 1,400,000 psi assumed in the table; the actual fastener spacing, s = 2.5 in., is smaller than the value, s = 3 in., assumed in the table, and the actual fastener diameter, D = ⅝ in., is smaller than the value, D = ¾ in., assumed in the table; therefore, the tabular value, C_g = 0.997, is conservative and can be used. Alternatively, a more accurate value for C_g can be found, based on the method described in Note 3 of Appendix Table A-3.22, and illustrated in Example 3.15.

   Adjusting for group action and multiplying the single-fastener value for Z' found in step 3 by the number of fasteners in the connection, we get a total adjusted connection capacity equal to 2390(0.997)(4) = 9531 lb.

5. We are not considering the design of the structural elements themselves in this example. Tension, row and group tear-out are considered in Example 3.1.

6. *Conclusion:* The total capacity of the connection (consisting of a four ⅝ in. diameter bolts) is 9531 lb.

Example 3.13 Analyze wood single-shear connection using multiple lag screws

Problem definition. Find the capacity of a connection (single shear) consisting of a 4 × 10 beam connected to an 8 × 8 post using six 6-in.-long, ½-in.-diameter lag screws. The wood used is Douglas Fir-Larch No.2, and the lag screws are fabricated from ordinary, low-strength, A307 steel. Assume live and dead loads only, dry fabrication and service conditions, and spacing as shown in Figure 3.42.

Solution overview
1. Find the capacity for a single fastener, Z.
2. For lag screws and nails, check that penetration into the main member is at least 4D (for lag screws) or 6D (for nails), and reduce capacity, Z, if necessary.
3. Adjust for duration of load, moisture, and geometry.
4. Adjust for group action, and then multiply the adjusted single-fastener capacity by the number of fasteners in the connection.
5. Not included in this example (check that the element itself is designed in a manner that accounts for the presence of bolt or lag screw holes).

Problem solution

1. From Appendix Table A-3.29, the lateral design value, $Z_{s\text{-}per}$, is 270 lb. The value of Z chosen corresponds to the following condition: the side member is oriented so that the load is perpendicular to the direction of grain, while the main member is oriented so that the load is parallel to its grain, as defined in Figure 3.32.

2. Penetration must be checked for lag screws (see Appendix Table A-3.19 for notes on penetration; lag screw dimensions can be found in Appendix Table A-3.17). The actual penetration, $p = 2.1875$ in., can be found by first subtracting the side member thickness of 3.5 in. from the lag screw length, $L = 6$ in., to get 2.5 in.; and then subtracting the length of the tapered tip, $E = 0.3125$ in., from the 2.5 in. length within the main member, as illustrated in Figure 3.43.

   This actual penetration is then compared to the minimum lengths for lag screw penetration in Appendix Table A-3.19: the absolute minimum is $4D = 4 \times 0.5 = 2$ in.; the minimum penetration to obtain the full value of Z is $8D = 8 \times 0.5 = 4$ in. Since the actual penetration is between these two values, the lateral design value, Z, is reduced by multiplying it by $p/(8D) = 2.1875/4 = 0.547$. Therefore, we use a lateral design value of $270 \times 0.547 = 148$ lb.

3. Adjustments are as follows:

   C_D for typical values of live and dead load is 1.0 (Appendix Table A-3.20);
   C_M for members fabricated and used "dry" is 1.0 (Appendix Table A-3.21);

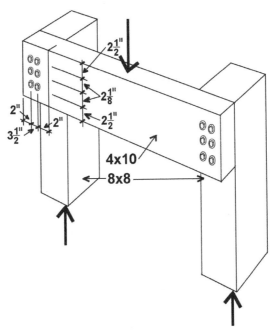

Figure 3.42: Single-shear lag screw connection with multiple fasteners, for Example 3.13

C_Δ is found by testing four separate criteria (Appendix Table A-3.23): spacing between fasteners in a row; spacing between rows of fasteners; end distance; and edge distance. It is sometimes useful to sketch the members separately, showing dimensions for the relevant geometry factor parameters (Figure 3.44):

In the calculations that follow, D is the fastener diameter of ½ in. (however, for lag screws, the so-called reduced body diameter, $D_r = 0.371$ in., is used to calculate lateral design values).

Spacing criteria: Adjustment criteria for spacing appear in Appendix Table A-3.23, parts *A* and *B*. For spacing between fasteners in a row for the horizontal member, where the loading direction is perpendicular to grain, the minimum spacing for full value is determined by the required values for the attached member (i.e., for the vertical member with loading parallel to grain). For spacing between rows of fasteners, again with the loading direction perpendicular to grain, the minimum required spacing is determined from the so-called slenderness ratio of the fastener, l/D. For lag screws, the dowel bearing length equals the penetration within the main member found in step 2, as noted in Appendix Table A.3.19. Therefore, the dowel bearing length, l, equals 2.1875 in., and $l/D = 2.1875/0.5 = 4.375$. Since this value is between 2 and 6, the minimum spacing between rows of fasteners is $(5l + 10D)/8 = (5 \times 2.1875 + 10 \times 0.5)/8 = 1.992$ in., which the actual spacing between rows of 3.5 in. exceeds. Therefore, the geometry factor is $C_\Delta = 1.0$.

For spacing between fasteners in a row, where the loading direction is parallel to grain, the minimum spacing for full value is $4D = 4 \times 0.5 = 2$ in. Since the actual spacing is 2⅛ in., the full value applies here (and also to the horizontal member), and $C_\Delta = 1.0$. For spacing between rows of fasteners, again with the loading direction parallel to grain, the minimum required spacing is $1.5D = 1.5 \times 0.5 = 0.75$ in. Since the actual spacing (between rows) of 3.5 in. exceeds this value, and is no greater than 5 in. (the

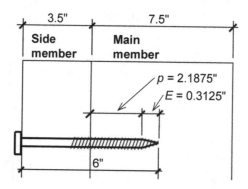

Figure 3.43: Penetration of lag screw into main member, for Example 3.13

maximum distance allowed between the outer rows of fasteners), the geometry factor is $C_\Delta = 1.0$.

End distance: Adjustment criteria for end distance appear in Appendix Table A-3.23, part *C*. For the horizontal member, the loading direction is perpendicular to grain, so the minimum end distance for full value (i.e., for $C_\Delta = 1.0$) is $4D = 4 \times 0.5 = 2$ in. Since the actual end distance of 2 in. equals this value (and the other, unspecified, end distance is clearly larger), the geometry factor, $C_\Delta = 1.0$. For the vertical member, the loading direction is parallel to grain and the specified wood is a "softwood," so the minimum end distance for full value for "tension" (i.e., for $C_\Delta = 1.0$) is $7D = 7 \times 0.5 = 3.5$ in. Since the actual end distance, although unspecified, clearly exceeds this, the geometry factor, $C_\Delta = 1.0$. For the full value in "compression," we need a minimum end distance of $4D = 4 \times 0.5 = 2$ in., which the actual end distance of 2½ in. exceeds. The geometry factor therefore is also $C_\Delta = 1.0$.

Edge distance: Adjustment criteria for edge distance appear in Appendix Table A-3.23, part *D*. For the horizontal member, the loading direction is perpendicular to grain, so the loaded and unloaded edges must be determined separately. The minimum distance for the loaded edge (i.e., the edge towards which the fastener itself is bearing) is $4D = 4 \times 0.5 = 2$ in., which the actual loaded edge distance of 2½ in. exceeds. The minimum distance for the unloaded edge (i.e., the opposite edge away from which the fastener itself is bearing) is $1.5D = 1.5 \times 0.5 = 0.75$ in., which the actual unloaded edge distance of 2½ in. exceeds. For the vertical member, the loading direction is parallel to grain, so the minimum edge distance is determined from the so-called slenderness ratio of the fastener, l/D. The dowel bearing length, l, within the main member is 2.1875 in., so $l/D = 2.1875/0.5 = 4.375$. Since this value is less than or equal to 6, the minimum edge distance is $1.5D = 1.5 \times 0.5 = 0.75$ in., which the actual edge

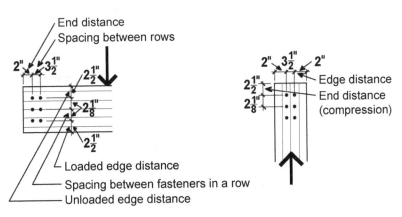

Figure 3.44: Geometry factor parameters for Example 3.13

distance of 2.0 in. exceeds. The geometry factor therefore is $C_\Delta = 1.0$.

The geometry factor for the entire connection is found by using the smallest of the geometry factors found for any of the four conditions tested above (end, edge, and the two spacing conditions where applicable): therefore, we use $C_\Delta = 1.0$.

The adjusted lateral design value for a single lag screw in the connection is found by multiplying the lateral design value from step 2 by the various adjustment factors determined in step 3: $Z' = Z(C_D)(C_M)(C_\Delta) = 148(1.0)(1.0)(1.0) = 148$ lb.

4. From Appendix Table A-3.22, the group action factor, C_g, is 0.970, a conservative value based on an 8 × 8 main member and a side member with an effective area of 12.25 in^2 (because the side member is loaded perpendicular to grain, its effective area is taken as its thickness of 3.5 in. multiplied by the distance between the outer rows of fasteners, also 3.5 in.). For use in Appendix Table A-3.22, these areas are rounded as follows: $A_m = 56$ in^2 and $A_s = 11$ in^2. The actual modulus of elasticity (Appendix Table A-3.9) for Hem-Fir No.1 is $E = 1,500,000$ psi, which is larger than the nominal value of 1,400,000 psi assumed in the table; the actual fastener spacing, $s = 2$ in., is smaller than the value, $s = 3$ in., assumed in the table, and the actual fastener diameter, $D = \frac{1}{2}$ in., is smaller than the value, $D = \frac{3}{4}$ in., assumed in the table; therefore, the tabular value, $C_g = 0.970$, is conservative and can be used. Alternatively, a more accurate value for C_g can be found, based on the method described in Note 3 of Appendix Table A-3.22, and illustrated in Example 3.15.

Adjusting for group action (using $C_g = 0.970$), and multiplying the single-fastener value for Z' found in step 3 by the number of fasteners in the connection, we get a total adjusted connection capacity equal to $148(0.970)(6) = 861$ lb.

5. We are not considering the design of the structural elements themselves in this example.

6. *Conclusion:* The total capacity of the connection (consisting of a six ½ × 6 in. lag screws) is 861 lb.

Example 3.14 Design wood single-shear connection using common nails

Problem definition. Determine the number of 10d common nails needed to connect a typical 2 × 10 floor joist, spanning 11.5 ft and spaced at 16 in. on center, to a 2 × 6 stud, as shown in Figure 3.45. The wood used is Spruce-Pine-Fir No.1/No.2, the distributed loads on the floor consist of 40 psf live load and 10.5 psf dead load, and the wood is fabricated and used "dry."

Solution overview

1. Find the capacity for a single fastener, Z.
2. For lag screws and nails, check that penetration into the main member is at least 4D (for lag screws) or 6D (for nails), and reduce capacity, Z, if necessary.
3. Adjust for duration of load, moisture, and geometry.
4. Group action does not apply to nailed connections.
5. Check that the element itself is designed in a manner that accounts for the presence of bolt or lag screw holes (not applicable).
6. Find the total force acting on the connection and divide by the adjusted capacity for a single fastener to find the number of fasteners required.

Problem solution

1. From Appendix Table A-3.30, the lateral design value, Z, is 100 lb, for a 10d nail and a 1½ in. side member.
2. In general, penetration must be checked for nails (see Appendix Table A-3.19): however, tabular values in Appendix Table A-3.30 already include reductions for penetration, so this step is only necessary when lateral design values are computed using other means. We can confirm that a penetration reduction is not necessary by computing the actual penetration, p = 1½ in., as shown in Figure 3.46. First, subtract the side member thickness of 1½ in. from the nail length of 3 in., to get 1½ in. (nail dimensions can be found in Appendix Table A-3.18).

   Next, the actual penetration is compared to the minimum requirements for nail penetration in Appendix Table A-3.19. Since p = 1.5 in. ≥ $10D$ = 10 × 0.148 = 1.48 in., we can use the full lateral design value. For values of $p < 10D$, lateral capacity would need to be reduced by $p/(10d)$. In all cases where yield limit equations are used for nails, the dowel bearing

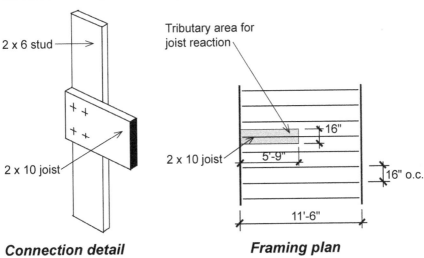

Connection detail   **Framing plan**

Figure 3.45: Single-shear nailed connection for Example 3.14

length in the main member, l_m, is taken as the penetration minus half the length of the tapered tip, so that tabular lateral design values, which do not consider this reduced dowel bearing length, may be slightly noncon-servative in some cases (specifically, they may differ in cases where the governing yield limit equation includes the dowel bearing length param-eter).

The lateral design value, Z, remains 100 lb.

3. Adjustments are as follows:

C_D for live and dead load is 1.0 (Appendix Table A-3.20);

C_M for members fabricated and used "dry" is 1.0 (Appendix Table A-3.21);

$C_\Delta = 1.0$ for dowel-type fasteners with $D < \frac{1}{4}$ in. This applies to virtually all nails, certainly for 10d nails with $D = 0.148$ in. (see Appendix Table A-3.18). While no specific numerical requirements are given for nail spacing, and edge or end distances, nails should be configured so that splitting of the wood members does not occur.

The adjusted lateral design value for the connection is found by mul-tiplying the lateral design value from step 2 by the various adjustment factors determined in step 3: $Z' = Z(C_D)(C_M)(C_\Delta) = 100(1.0)(1.0)(1.0) = 100$ lb.

4. The group action factor, $C_g = 1.0$, for fasteners with diameter, $D < \frac{1}{4}$ in., i.e., for most nailed connections.

5. We are not considering the design of the structural elements themselves in this example.

6. To determine the number of nails needed, we first find the total force acting at the connection, i.e., the reaction of a typical joist, by multi-plying the floor loads by the tributary area for half of a single joist: $(40 + 10.5)(5.75 \times 1.33) = 387.2$ lb. Dividing this total force by 100 lb (the capacity of a single fastener), we get the required number of fasteners, $n = 387.2/100 = 3.87$; i.e., we need four 10d nails.

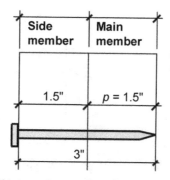

Figure 3.46: Penetration of nail into main member, for Example 3.14

Example 3.15 Analyze wood double-shear bolted connection using yield limit and group action equations

Problem definition. Find the capacity of a connection (double shear) consisting of a 6 × 6 tension member connected by two ¼ in. steel side plates, using four ⅝ in. diameter bolts. The wood used is Douglas Fir-Larch (North) No. 1, the side plates are ASTM A36 steel, and the bolts are fabricated from ordinary, low-strength, A307 steel, as is typical for wood connections. Assume live and dead loads only, dry fabrication and service conditions, and spacing as shown in Figure 3.47. Use yield limit and group action equations, rather than tabular values (see Example 3.12 for solution using tabular values).

Solution overview
1. Find the capacity for a single fastener, Z, using yield limit equations.
2. For lag screws and nails, check that penetration into the main member is at least $4D$ (for lag screws) or $6D$ (for nails), and reduce capacity, Z, if necessary.
3. Adjust for duration of load, moisture, and geometry.
4. Adjust for group action using group action factor equations, and then multiply the adjusted single-fastener capacity by the number of fasteners in the connection.
5. Check that the element itself is designed in a manner that accounts for the presence of bolt or lag screw holes (not included in this example).

Problem solution
1. To find the lateral design value, Z, for a single fastener using yield limit equations, follow the step-by-step method outlined in Appendix Table A-3.31. The main member is oriented so that the load is parallel to the direction of grain, as defined in Figure 3.32. The orientation of the steel side plates to the direction of load is not relevant, since there is no "grain" in a steel plate that influences its strength.
   a. From Appendix Table A-3.11, $G = 0.49$ for Douglas Fir-Larch (North).
   b. $D = ⅝$ in. $= 0.625$ in.
   c. Main member ($D > 0.25$ in., wood, loaded parallel to grain): $F_{em} = 11,200G = 11,200 × 0.49 = 5488$ psi. Side member (A36 steel): $F_{es} = 87,000$ psi. It is common to round these values to the nearest 50 psi, so we will use $F_{em} = 5500$ psi.
   d. $F_{yb} = 45,000$ psi for bolts.
   e. Dowel bearing lengths are $l_m = 5.5$ in. and $l_s = 0.25$ in.
   f. Compute the terms $R_e = F_{em}/F_{es} = 5500/87,000 = 0.06322$; and $R_t = l_m/l_s = 5.5/0.25 = 22.0$.

g. $R_d = 4K_\theta = 4(1.0) = 4$ (for yield modes I_m and I_s); $R_d = 3.6K_\theta = 3.6(1.0) = 3.6$ (for yield mode II); and $R_d = 3.2K_\theta = 3.2(1.0) = 3.2$ (for yield modes III_m, III_s, IV). In these equations, $K_\theta = 1 + 0.25(\theta/90) = 1.0$, since $\theta = 0°$.

h. Compute the following coefficients:

$$k_1 = \frac{\sqrt{R_e + 2R_e^2(1 + R_t + R_t^2) + R_t^2 R_e^3} - R_e(1 + R_t)}{(1 + R_e)}$$

$$= \frac{\sqrt{0.06322 + 2(0.06322)^2(1 + 22 + 22^2) + 22^2(0.06322)^3} - 0.06322(1 + 22)}{(1 + 0.06322)}$$

$$= 0.5687$$

$$k_2 = -1 + \sqrt{2(1 + R_e) + \frac{2F_{yb}(1 + 2R_e)D^2}{3F_{em}l_m^2}}$$

$$= -1 + \sqrt{2(1 + 0.06322) + \frac{2(45{,}000)(1 + 2 \times 0.06322)(0.625)^2}{3(5500)(5.5)^2}} = 0.4852$$

$$k_3 = -1 + \sqrt{\frac{2(1 + R_e)}{R_e} + \frac{2F_{yb}(2 + R_e)D^2}{3F_{em}l_s^2}}$$

$$= \sqrt{\frac{2(1 + 0.06322)}{0.06322} + \frac{2(45{,}000)(2 + 0.06322)(0.625)^2}{3(5500)(0.25)^2}} = 9.1967$$

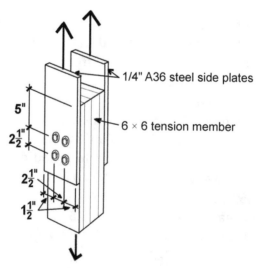

Figure 3.47: Double-shear bolted connection with multiple fasteners and steel side plates, for Example 3.15 (same as Figure 3.40 for Example 3.12)

i. Compute Z for all applicable yield modes (four applicable modes for double shear):

For yield mode I_m, $Z = Dl_m F_{em}/R_d = 0.625(5.5)(5500)/4 = 4726.6$ lb.

For yield mode I_s, $Z = 2Dl_s F_{es}/R_d = 2(0.625)(0.25)(87,000)/4 = 6796.9$ lb   for double shear.

Yield mode II does not apply to double shear connections.

Yield mode III_m does not apply to double shear connections.

For Yield Mode III_s, $Z = \dfrac{2k_3 Dl_s F_{em}}{(2 + R_e)R_d} = \dfrac{2(9.1967)(0.625)(0.25)(5500)}{(2 + 0.06322)(3.2)}$

$$= 2394.1 \text{ lb.}$$

For Yield Mode IV, $Z = \dfrac{2D^2}{R_d}\sqrt{\dfrac{2F_{em}F_{yb}}{3(1 + R_e)}} = \dfrac{2(0.625)^2}{3.2}\sqrt{\dfrac{2(5500)(45,000)}{3(1 + 0.06322)}}$

$$= 3041.4 \text{ lb.}$$

The smallest of the various yield mode values is then selected: $Z = 2394.1$ lb based on yield mode III_s.

2. Penetration is only an issue with lag screws and nails, since bolts must always fully penetrate the members being connected. Therefore, no reduction of the lateral design value is necessary, and it remains equal to $Z = 2394.1$ lb.

3. Adjustments are as follows (same as for Example 3.12):

C_D for typical values of live and dead load is 1.0 (Appendix Table A-3.20);

C_M for members fabricated and used "dry" is 1.0 (Appendix Table A-3.21);

C_Δ is found by testing four separate criteria (Appendix Table A-3.23): spacing between fasteners in a row; spacing between rows of fasteners; end distance; and edge distance. It is sometimes useful to sketch the members separately, showing dimensions for the relevant geometry factor parameters (Figure 3.48). Only the wood main member is considered here; the tension capacity and bolt spacing in the steel plate must be considered separately (see Chapter 4 for discussion of tension and bolt spacing in steel):

In the calculations that follow, D is the fastener diameter of ⅝ in. = 0.625 in.

Spacing criteria: Adjustment criteria for spacing appear in Appendix Table A-3.23, parts A and B. For spacing between fasteners in a row, where the loading direction is parallel to grain, the minimum spacing for full value is $4D = 4 \times 0.625 = 2.5$ in. Since the actual spacing is 2.5 in., the full value applies, and $C_\Delta = 1.0$. For spacing between rows of fasteners, again with the loading direction parallel to grain, the minimum required spacing is $1.5D = 1.5 \times 0.625 = 0.9375$ in. Since the actual spacing (between rows) of 2.5 in. exceeds this value, and is no greater than 5 in. (the maximum distance allowed between the outer rows of fasteners), the geometry factor is $C_\Delta = 1.0$.

End distance: Adjustment criteria for end distance appear in Appendix Table A-3.23, part C. For the main member, the loading direction is parallel to grain. Where the fasteners are bearing towards the member end (in "tension") and for "softwood," the minimum end distance for full value (i.e., for $C_\Delta = 1.0$) is $7D = 7 \times 0.625 = 4.375$ in. The actual end distance of 5 in. is greater than this, so the geometry factor, $C_\Delta = 1.0$.

Edge distance: Adjustment criteria for edge distance appear in Appendix Table A-3.23, part D. For the main member, the loading direction is parallel to grain, so the minimum edge distance is determined from the so-called slenderness ratio of the fastener, l/D. The fastener length, l, within the main member is 5½ in., so $l/D = 5.5/0.625 = 8.8$. Since this value is greater than 6, the minimum edge distance is either $1.5D = 1.5 \times 0.625 = 0.9375$ in., or one half of the spacing between rows $= 0.5 \times 2.5 = 1.25$ in., whichever is greater: the minimum edge distance is therefore 1.25 in., which the actual edge distance of 1.5 in. exceeds. The geometry factor therefore is $C_\Delta = 1.0$.

The geometry factor for the entire connection is found by using the smallest of the geometry factors found for any of the four conditions tested above (end, edge, and the two spacing conditions where applicable): therefore, we use $C_\Delta = 1.0$.

The adjusted lateral design value for a single bolt in the connection is found by multiplying the lateral design value from step 2 by the various adjustment factors determined in step 3: C_D, C_M, and C_Δ: $Z' = Z(C_D)(C_M)(C_\Delta) = 2394.1(1.0)(1.0)(1.0) = 2394.1$ lb.

4. The group action factor, C_g, can be found based on the method described in Note 3 of Appendix Table A-3.22:

    $D = 0.625$ in.

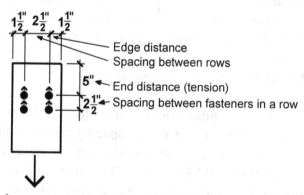

Figure 3.48: Geometry factor parameters for Example 3.15 (same as Figure 3.31 for Example 3.12)

$\gamma = 270,000(D^{1.5}) = 270,000(0.625^{1.5}) = 133,409.$
$s = 2.5$ in.
$E_m = 1,600,000$ psi (see Appendix Table A-3.9).
$E_s = 29,000,000$ psi (see Chapter 4 for the modulus of elasticity of steel).
$A_m = 30.25$ in^2; $A_s = 2(0.25 \times 5.5) = 2.75$ in^2 (Appendix Table A-3.12).

$$u = 1 + (133,409)\frac{2.5}{2}\left[\frac{1}{(1,600.000)(30.25)} + \frac{1}{(29,000,000)(2.75)}\right] = 1.0055$$

$$m = 1.0055 - \sqrt{1.0055^2 - 1} = 0.900.$$

$$R_{EA} = \frac{(1,600,000)(30.25)}{(29,000,000)(2.75)} = 0.607.$$

$n = 2.$

$$C_g = \left[\frac{0.900(1 - 0.900^{2(2)}}{2[(1+0.607 \times 0.900^2)(1+0.900) - 1 + 0.900^{2(2)}]}\right]\frac{1+0.607}{1-0.900} = 0.999.$$

Adjusting for group action and multiplying the single-fastener value for Z' found in step 3 by the number of fasteners in the connection, we get a total adjusted connection capacity equal to 2394.1(0.999)(4) = 9567 lb.

5. We are not considering the design of the structural elements themselves in this example. Tension, row and group tear-out are considered in Example 3.1.
6. *Conclusion:* The total capacity of the connection (consisting of a six ½ in. diameter bolts) is 9567 lb.

Withdrawal

Where a fastener is itself stressed in tension, it is considered to be loaded in "withdrawal," as a failure of the connection would cause it to "withdraw" — pull out — from the member into which it was inserted. For lag screws and nails, selected withdrawal design values, designated W to distinguish them from lateral design values, Z, are tabulated in Appendix Tables A-3.32 and A-3.33. These tabular values increase with higher wood specific gravity, G, and larger shaft diameter, D, and are based on the following empirical equations: for lag screws, $W = 1800G^{3/2}D^{3/4}$; for nails, $W = 1380G^{5/2}D$. In these equations, W is the withdrawal design value per inch of penetration (lb); G is the specific gravity of the wood; and D is the fastener diameter (in.). While it is permitted to use nails in withdrawal, it is advisable to alter the connection geometry, if possible, so that such unthreaded fasteners are stressed in shear, rather than in tension. Unlike the penetration length of lag screws stressed in shear (laterally), the penetration of lag screws in withdrawal only includes that portion of the shank length that is both embedded in the main member, and threaded (excluding the tapered tip).

Lag screw withdrawal values must be reduced by 75% when the lag screws are inserted into the end grain of a wood member; nails are not permitted to be loaded in withdrawal from the end grain of wood members. Aside from computing the capacity of a connection based on computed withdrawal values, W, the tensile strength of lag screws loaded in withdrawal must also be checked, and, where the head (or washer) of the lag screw is in contact with a wood member, the bearing stress of the washer on this member must also be checked. Finally, the adjusted withdrawal capacity per inch of penetration, W', is computed by multiplying W by the appropriate adjustment factors: where in-service temperatures are no more than 100°F, only duration of load and wet service factors apply to fasteners in withdrawal (see Appendix Tables A-3.20 and A-3.21).

For bolted connections, "withdrawal" is not possible; instead, where bolts are placed in tension, the tensile strength of the bolt itself, as well as the bearing of the bolt (or washer) on the surface of the wood member, must be checked.

Example 3.16 Design wood connection in withdrawal, using lag screws

Problem definition. Determine the number of 3-in.-long, ½-in.-diameter, lag screws needed to connect a ¼ in. steel plate holding a 2800 lb load to a 4 × 10 wood beam, as shown in Figure 3.49. The wood used is Spruce-Pine-Fir No.1/No.2, the loads are dead and live only (so that $C_D = 1.0$), and the wood is fabricated and used dry. Assume that the steel plate capacity is adequate.

Solution overview. Find the capacity of a single lag screw in withdrawal; divide the total load by this value to determine the required number of lag screws.

Problem solution
1. From Appendix Table A-3.32, the withdrawal design value, W, per inch of penetration, is 291 lb, for a 3-in.-long, ½-in.-diameter lag screw. The adjusted value, $W' = W(C_D)(C_M) = 291(1.0)(1.0) = 291$ lb.
2. From Appendix Table A-3.17, it can be seen that the actual penetration into the main member (i.e., the length of the threaded portion of the lag screw that engages the main member, not including the tapered tip, or $T - E$) = 1.6875 in. Therefore, each lag screw resists $(291)(1.6875) = 491$ lb in withdrawal.
3. Since the total load to be resisted is 2800 lb, the required number of lag screws = 2800/491 = 5.7. Round up and use six 3-in.-long, ½-in.-diameter, lag screws.

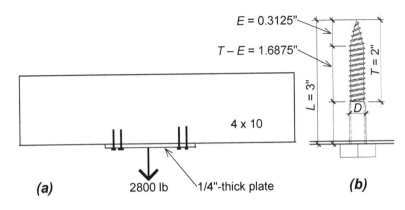

Figure 3.49: Withdrawal load on lag screws for Example 3.16

Example 3.17 Analyze wood connection in withdrawal, using common nails

Problem definition. A steel bracket designed to hold heavy items is fastened to the floor joist above it using four 16d common nails, as shown in Figure 3.50. These nails must go through a ½ in. drywall ceiling, as well as the ⅛ in.-thick steel bracket itself, before reaching the wood joist, fabricated from Douglas Fir-Larch. How much load can the bracket carry, based on the capacity of the fasteners (and assuming that the strength of the bracket itself is adequate)?

Solution overview. Find the capacity of a single nail in withdrawal; multiply the single-nail capacity by the number of nails to find the capacity of the bracket.

Problem solution
1. From Appendix Table A-3.33, the withdrawal design value for a single

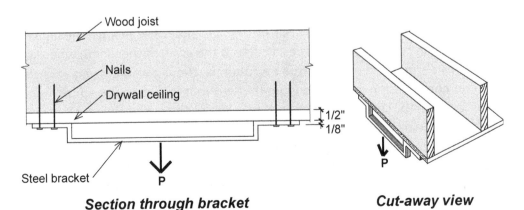

Section through bracket   Cut-away view

Figure 3.50: Withdrawal load on nailed bracket for Example 3.17

16d nail, W, per inch of penetration, is 40 lb. The adjusted value, $W' = W(C_D)(C_M) = 40(0.9)(1.0) = 36$ lb. The decision to use a value of $C_D = 0.9$ is based on an evaluation of the loads, which are essentially of a permanent nature (i.e., dead loads).

2. The actual penetration into the main member is the total nail length minus the drywall and steel thickness; from Appendix Table A-3.18, we see that $p = 3.5 - (\frac{1}{2} + \frac{1}{8}) = 2.875$ in. Therefore, each nail resists $(36)(2.875) = 103.5$ lb in withdrawal.

3. Since there are four nails, the total capacity of the rack, $P = 4(103.5) = 414$ lb. However, it would be wiser to use a threaded connector (such as a screw or lag screw) instead of a nail in this situation.

Bearing

Where a wooden column or beam bears on another structural element, a compressive stress acts on the bearing surfaces. The use of the plural ("surfaces") indicates that bearing always acts in two directions, so that, for example, a joist bearing on a plate implies that the plate is also bearing on the joist. In theory, the bearing stress is the same on both surfaces; in practice, the effective bearing area in some cases may be increased by adding $\frac{3}{8}$ in. in the direction of the bearing length — measured in the direction parallel to the grain of the wood — to account for the ability of the wood grain to distribute the load across a larger area. For the beam and post shown in Figure 3.51, the bearing stress of the post on the beam, or the beam on the post, is equal to the load, P, divided by the bearing area, $W \times T$. Since wood is weaker when stressed perpendicular to its grain, the critical bearing stress will almost always occur acting downward on the surface of the beam, rather than upward on the post. If the distance, D, measured from the edge of the post to the end of the beam, is greater than three inches, and the bearing length, W, of the post is less than six inches, we can reduce the effective bearing stress of the post on the beam by dividing the load, P, by the larger effective bearing area, $T \times (W + \frac{3}{8}$ in.$)$. This stress is then compared to the adjusted allowable compressive stress (perpendicular to grain). For joists and other beams, the allowable stress is in compression, perpendicular to the grain of the wood, whereas when considering the bearing stress on columns, the allowable stress value is taken for compression parallel to grain (but without including the adjustment factor for stability, since buckling is not relevant at the surface where bearing stresses are being measured).

For compressive stresses parallel to grain, a steel plate must be used at the point of bearing to distribute such stresses more evenly across the surfaces in contact, but only in cases when these stresses exceed 75% of F_c^*. See Appendix Table A-3.4 for adjustments to allowable compressive stresses.

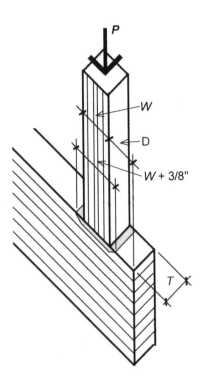

Figure 3.51: Bearing of post on beam: the direction of grain is indicated by the parallel lines on each surface

Example 3.18 Check wood connection in bearing

Problem definition. A 4 × 4 post bears at the midpoint of a 4 × 10 girder. The 5000 lb load transferred to the girder through the post consists of live, dead, and wind loads. Check whether the bearing capacity is adequate, assuming that both members are Hem-Fir No.2.

Solution overview. Find the effective bearing area of the post on the girder; find the actual "effective" bearing stress on the girder; compare this stress to the allowable compressive stress perpendicular to grain.

Problem solution

1. Because the post has a bearing length less than six inches, and is more than three inches from the end of the girder, we can use an effective bearing length ⅜ in. greater than its actual bearing length of 3.5 in. (see Appendix Table A-3.12 for cross-sectional dimensions). The effective bearing area is therefore = $T \times (W + ⅜)$ = 3.5(3.5 + 0.375) = 13.56 in². The actual bearing stress on surface of the girder = 5000/13.56 = 369 psi.

2. This value is compared with the adjusted allowable bearing stress, $F'_{c\text{-}per}$. From Appendix Table A-3.3, the design value for compression perpendicular to grain for the Hem-Fir girder is $F_{c\text{-}per}$ = 405 psi.

3. Assuming that the members are used indoors, the relevant adjustment factor is for wet service only ($C_M = 0.67$ only when the moisture content is greater than 19% for long periods of time — i.e., when used outdoors — but can be taken as 1.0 when used indoors); the size and duration of load factors do not apply to compression perpendicular to grain. Therefore, $F'_{c\text{-}per} = 405(1.0) = 405$ psi, which is greater than the actual effective bearing stress. The connection is satisfactory with respect to bearing.

4. The 4 × 4 post need not be directly checked for bearing stress (since its allowable stress in compression parallel to grain will be greater than the girder's allowable stress perpendicular to grain). However, we check to see whether the actual stress on the post exceeds 75% of F_c^*, the allowable compressive stress parallel to grain with all adjustments except for the column stability factor; if it does, a steel bearing plate should be specified. The actual stress is the load divided by the post area, or $5000/(3.5 \times 3.5) = 408$ psi, where the cross-sectional dimensions can be found in Appendix Table A-3.12. From Appendix Tables A-3.3 and A-3.4, the adjusted allowable stress (without C_p) multiplied by 75% is $(0.75)1300(1.15)(1.0) = 1121$ psi (the size factor, $C_F = 1.15$, for the 4 × 4 post). Since this value is greater than the actual stress, no bearing plates are required between the post and girder.

In the design of such a connection, it must not be assumed that gravity will hold the post firmly against the girder under all conditions; the two members must also be mechanically connected to guard against unintended movement.

CHAPTER 3 APPENDIX

Table A-3.1: Design values for tension, F_t (psi) for visually graded lumber and glued-laminated timber

A. Dimension lumber (2 in. – 4 in. thick)

Species	Select Structural	No. 1	No. 2	No. 3	Miscellaneous
Douglas Fir-Larch	1000	675	575	325	[1]800
Douglas Fir-Larch (North)	825	n/a	n/a	300	[2]500
Douglas Fir-South	900	600	525	300	
Hem-Fir	925	625	525	300	[1]725
Hem-Fir (North)	775	n/a	n/a	325	[2]575
Spruce-Pine-Fir	700	n/a	n/a	250	[2]450
Spruce-Pine-Fir (South)	575	400	350	200	
Southern Pine[3]	1000	650	525	300	

B. Beams and stringers[4]

Species	Select Structural	No. 1	No. 2	No. 3	Miscellaneous
Douglas Fir-Larch	950	675	425	n/a	
Douglas Fir-Larch (North)	950	675	425	n/a	
Douglas Fir-South	900	625	425	n/a	
Hem-Fir	750	525	350	n/a	
Hem-Fir (North)	725	500	325	n/a	
Spruce-Pine-Fir	650	450	300	n/a	
Spruce-Pine-Fir (South)	625	450	300	n/a	
Southern Pine[5]	1000	900	550	n/a	

C. Posts and timbers[6]

Species	Select Structural	No. 1	No. 2	No. 3	Miscellaneous
Douglas Fir-Larch	1000	825	475	n/a	
Douglas Fir-Larch (North)	1000	825	475	n/a	
Douglas Fir-South	950	775	450	n/a	
Hem-Fir	800	650	375	n/a	
Hem-Fir (North)	775	625	375	n/a	
Spruce-Pine-Fir	700	550	325	n/a	
Spruce-Pine-Fir (South)	675	550	325	n/a	
Southern Pine[5]	1000	900	550	n/a	

(continued)

Table A-3.1 continued (Part *D*)

D. Glued-laminated softwood timber				
Species	**Grade (and Identification No.)**			
Douglas Fir-Larch (DF)	**L3 (ID#1)** 950	**L2 (ID#2)** 1250	**L2D (ID#3)** 1450	**L1D L1 (ID#5)** 1650
Softwood Species (SW)	**L3 (ID#22)** 525			
Alaska Cedar (AC)	**L3 (ID#69)** 725	**L2 (ID#70)** 975	**L1D (ID#71)** 1250	**L1S (ID#72)** 1250
Southern Pine (SP)	**N2M14 N2M12 (ID#47)** 1200	**N2D14 N2D12 (ID#48)** 1400	**N1M16 (ID#49)** 1350	**N1D14 (ID#50)** 1550

Notes:

1. No.1 & better

2. No.1/No.2

3. Values for Southern Pine for dimension lumber are approximate: typical published values include the size factor and therefore list different values for each lumber width; whereas the values in this table have been normalized (i.e., do not include the size factor) and have been rounded down to values that may be slightly conservative.

4. Beams and stringers are a subset of the "timbers" size category, 5 in. x 5 in. or larger, where the width is at least 4 in. bigger than the thickness.

5. Southern Pine values for timbers (beams and stringers; and posts and timbers) are for wet service conditions.

6. Posts and timbers are a subset of the "timbers" size category, 5 in. x 5 in. or larger, where the width is equal to, or no more than 2 in. bigger than, the thickness.

Table A-3.2: Adjustments to allowable stress in tension, F_t, for visually-graded lumber and glued-laminated softwood timber

A. Size factor							
Size factor, C_F = 1.0 for tension stress, except for the following sizes of dimension lumber:							
Size	C_F	**Size**	C_F	**Size**	C_F	**Size**	C_F
$^2 2 \times 2$	1.5	$^4 2 \times 8$	1.2	$^{1,4} 2 \times 14, 4 \times 14$	0.9	$^4 4 \times 8$	1.2
$^2 2 \times 4$	1.5	$^4 2 \times 10$	1.1	$^2 4 \times 4$	1.5	$^4 4 \times 10$	1.1
$^3 2 \times 6$	1.3	$^4 2 \times 12$	1.0	$^3 4 \times 6$	1.3	$^4 4 \times 12$	1.0

B. Wet service factor
Wet service factor, C_M = 1.0, except for glulam with a moisture content of at least 16% (e.g., used outdoors), in which case C_M = 0.8. In any dry service condition, C_M = 1.0.

C. Load duration factor					
Load duration factor, C_D, is as follows:					
Load type	**Duration**	C_D	**Load type**	**Duration**	C_D
Dead load, D	Permanent	0.90	Construction load, L_r	1 week	1.25
Live load, L	10 years	1.00	Wind or seismic load, W or E	10 minutes	1.60
Snow load, S	2 months	1.15	Impact load, I	Instant	2.00

(continued)

Table A-3.2 continued (Part *D*)

D. Temperature factor, C_t	
Temperature, T (° F)	**C_t**
$T \leq 100°$ F	1.0
$100°$ F $< T \leq 150°$ F	0.9

Notes:

1. $C_F = 0.9$ for all 2× or 4× dimension lumber having nominal width greater or equal to 14.

2. Exceptions: $C_F = 1.1$ for stud grade 2 × 2, 2 × 4, and 4 × 4 lumber; $C_F = 1.0$ for construction and standard 2 × 2, 2 × 4, and 4 × 4 lumber; and $C_F = 0.4$ for utility grade 2 × 2 lumber

3. Exceptions: $C_F = 1.0$ for stud grade 2 × 6 and 4 × 6 lumber

4. Exceptions: For stud grade lumber with nominal width of 8 or higher, use No.3 grade values for F_t and C_F

Table A-3.3: Design values for compression (psi), parallel to grain (F_c) and perpendicular to grain ($F_{c\text{-}per}$) for visually-graded lumber and glued-laminated softwood timber

A. Dimension lumber (2 in. – 4 in. thick)						
Species	**F_c** (parallel to grain)					**$F_{c\text{-}per}$** (perpendicular to grain)
	Select Struct.	**No. 1**	**No. 2**	**No. 3**	**Misc.**	**All grades[7]**
Douglas Fir-Larch	1700	1500	1350	775	[1]1550	625
Douglas Fir-Larch (North)	1900	n/a	n/a	825	[2]1400	625
Douglas Fir-South	1600	1450	1450	775		520
Hem-Fir	1500	1350	1300	725	[1]1350	405
Hem-Fir (North)	1700	n/a	n/a	850	[2]1450	405
Spruce-Pine-Fir	1400	n/a	n/a	650	[2]1150	425
Spruce-Pine-Fir (South)	1200	1050	1000	575		335
Southern Pine[3]	1800	1575	1425	825		565

B. Beams and stringers[4]						
Species	**F_c** (parallel to grain)					**$F_{c\text{-}per}$** (perpendicular to grain)
	Select Struct.	**No. 1**	**No. 2**	**No. 3**	**Misc.**	**All grades[7]**
Douglas Fir-Larch	1100	925	600	n/a		625
Douglas Fir-Larch (North)	1100	925	600	n/a		625
Douglas Fir-South	1000	850	550	n/a		520
Hem-Fir	925	750	500	n/a		405
Hem-Fir (North)	900	750	475	n/a		405
Spruce-Pine-Fir	775	625	425	n/a		425
Spruce-Pine-Fir (South)	675	550	375	n/a		335
Southern Pine[5]	950	825	525	n/a		375

(continued)

Table A-3.3 continued (Part *C*)

C. Posts and timbers[6]

Species	F_c (parallel to grain)					$F_{c\text{-}per}$ (perpendicular to grain)
	Select Struct.	No. 1	No. 2	No. 3	Misc.	All grades[7]
Douglas Fir-Larch	1150	1000	700	n/a		625
Douglas Fir-Larch (North)	1150	1000	700	n/a		625
Douglas Fir-South	1050	925	650	n/a		520
Hem-Fir	975	850	575	n/a		405
Hem-Fir (North)	950	850	575	n/a		405
Spruce-Pine-Fir	800	700	500	n/a		425
Spruce-Pine-Fir (South)	700	625	425	n/a		335
Southern Pine[5]	950	825	525	n/a		375

D. Glued-laminated softwood timber

Species	Grade (and Identification No.)							
	F_c (parallel to grain)				$F_{c\text{-}per}$ (perpendicular to grain)			
	L3 (ID#1)	L2 (ID#2)	L2D (ID#3)	L1 (ID#5)	L3 (ID#1)	L2 (ID#2)	L2D (ID#3)	L1 (ID#5)
Douglas Fir-Larch[8] (DF)	1550	1950	2300	2400	560	560	650	650
(less than 4 laminations)	1250	1600	1900	2100	560	560	650	650
	L3 (ID#22)				L3 (ID#22)			
Softwood Species[8] (SW)	850				315			
(less than 4 laminations)	525				315			
	L3 (ID#69)	L2 (ID#70)	L1D (ID#71)	L1S (ID#72)	L3 (ID#69)	L2 (ID#70)	L1D (ID#71)	L1S (ID#72)
Alaska Cedar[8] (AC)	1150	1450	1900	1900	470	470	560	560
(less than 4 laminations)	1100	1450	1900	1900	470	470	560	560
	N2M12 (ID#47)	N2D12 (ID#48)	N1M16 (ID#49)	N1D14 (ID#50)	N2M12 (ID#47)	N2D12 (ID#48)	N1M16 (ID#49)	N1D14 (ID#50)
Southern Pine[8] (SP)	1900	2200	2100	2300	650	740	650	740
(less than 4 laminations)	1150	1350	1450	1700	650	740	650	740

Species	Combination Symbol							
	F_c (parallel to grain)				$F_{c\text{-}per}$ (perpendicular to grain)			
Various species[9]	16F-1.3E	20F-1.5E	24F-1.7E	24F-1.8E	16F-1.3E	20F-1.5E	24F-1.7E	24F-1.8E
	925	925	1000	1600	315	425	500	650

Notes:

1. No.1 & better

2. No.1/No.2

3. Values for Southern Pine for dimension lumber are approximate: typical published values include the size factor and therefore list different values for each lumber width; whereas the values in this table have been normalized (i.e., do not include the size factor) and have been rounded down to values that may be slightly conservative.

4. Beams and stringers are a subset of the "timbers" size category, 5 in. × 5 in. or larger, where the width is at least 4 in. bigger than the thickness.

(continued)

Table A-3.3 continued (Notes)

5. Southern Pine values for timbers (beams and stringers; posts and timbers) are for wet service conditions.

6. Posts and timbers are a subset of the "timbers" size category, 5 in. × 5 in. or larger, where the width is equal to, or no more than 2 in. bigger than, the thickness.

7. Values for compression perpendicular to grain apply to all the size categories listed in this table (i.e., listed under compression parallel to grain). However, "dense" variations of Douglas Fir-Larch and Southern Pine, not listed here, have higher values.

8. These species designations are designed primarily for axially-loaded elements (compression and tension).

9. These combination designations are designed primarily for bending elements, although they can be used in axial compression or tension with the values that appear in this table. Values for F_{c-per} (compression perpendicular to grain) are based on loading perpendicular to the wide face of the laminations.

Table A-3.4: Adjustments to allowable stress in compression, F_c, for visually-graded lumber and glued-laminated softwood timber

A. Size factor[3]

Size factor, C_F = 1.0 for compression stress, except for the following sizes of dimension lumber:

Size	C_F	Size	C_F	Size	C_F	Size	C_F
[6]2 × 2	1.15	[8]2 × 8	1.05	[1,8]2 × 14, 4 × 14	0.9	[8]4 × 8	1.05
[6]2 × 4	1.15	[8]2 × 10	1.00	[6]4 × 4	1.15	[8]4 × 10	1.00
[7]2 × 6	1.10	[8]2 × 12	1.00	[7]4 × 6	1.10	[8]4 × 12	1.00

B. Wet service factor

Wet service factor, C_M, is as follows: for dimension lumber[2], C_M = 0.8; for timbers, C_M = 0.91; for glulam, C_M = 0.73. In any dry service condition, C_M = 1.0.

C. Load duration factor[4]

Load duration factor, C_D, is as follows:

Load type	Duration	C_D	Load type	Duration	C_D
Dead load, D	Permanent	0.90	Construction load, L_r	1 week	1.25
Live load, L	10 years	1.00	Wind or seismic load, W or E	10 minutes	1.60
Snow load, S	2 months	1.15	Impact load, I	Instant	2.00

D. Column stability factor[5]

The column stability factor, C_P, is as follows: $C_P = A - \sqrt{A^2 - B}$
where:

$$A = \frac{1 + \dfrac{F_{cE}}{F_c^*}}{2c} \quad \text{and } B = \frac{\dfrac{F_{cE}}{F_c^*}}{c}$$

$$F_{cE} = \frac{0.822E'_{min}}{(l_e/d)^2} \quad \text{and } F_c^* = F_c C_D C_M C_F$$

$E'_{min} = E_{min}C_M$ (see Appendix Table A-3.9 for adjustments to E and E_{min})

    d = cross-sectional dimension (in.) corresponding to the unbraced length, l_e. Where the unbraced length is the same for both axes of the cross section, d should be taken as the smaller cross-sectional dimension; otherwise, use the larger value of l_e/d

l_e = the unbraced length corresponding to the cross-sectional dimension, d

    c = 0.8 for sawn lumber, and 0.9 for glulam

(continued)

Table A-3.4 continued (Part *E*)

E. Temperature factor, C_t		
Temperature, T (° F)	C_t (used dry)	C_t (used wet)
$T \leq 100°$ F	1.0	1.0
$100°$ F $< T \leq 125°$ F	0.8	0.7
$125°$ F $< T \leq 150°$ F	0.7	0.5

Notes:

1. $C_F = 0.9$ for all 2× or 4× dimension lumber having nominal width greater or equal to 14.

2. $C_M = 1.0$ for dimension lumber when $F_c C_F \leq 750$ psi.

3. Size factor adjustments are not used for compression perpendicular to grain.

4. Load duration adjustments are not used for compression perpendicular to grain.

5. Column stability factor adjustments are not used for compression perpendicular to grain.

6. Exceptions: $C_F = 1.05$ for stud grade 2 × 2, 2 × 4, and 4 × 4 lumber; $C_F = 1.0$ for construction and standard 2 × 2, 2 × 4, and 4 × 4 lumber; and $C_F = 0.6$ for utility grade 2 × 2 lumber

7. Exceptions: $C_F = 1.0$ for stud grade 2 × 6 and 4 × 6 lumber

8. Exceptions: For stud grade lumber with nominal width of 8 or higher, use No.3 grade values for F_c and C_F

Table A-3.5: Design values for bending, F_b (psi) for visually-graded lumber and glued-laminated softwood timber

A. Dimension lumber (2 in. – 4 in. thick)					
Species	Select Structural	No. 1	No. 2	No. 3	Miscellaneous
Douglas Fir-Larch	1500	1000	900	525	[1]1200
Douglas Fir-Larch (North)	1350	n/a	n/a	475	[2]850
Douglas Fir-South	1350	925	850	500	
Hem-Fir	1400	975	850	500	[1]1100
Hem-Fir (North)	1300	n/a	n/a	575	[2]1000
Spruce-Pine-Fir	1250	n/a	n/a	500	[2]875
Spruce-Pine-Fir (South)	1300	875	775	450	
Southern Pine[3]	1850	1175	950	550	

B. Beams and stringers[4]					
Species	Select Structural	No. 1	No. 2	No. 3	Miscellaneous
Douglas Fir-Larch	1600	1350	875	n/a	
Douglas Fir-Larch (North)	1600	1300	875	n/a	
Douglas Fir-South	1550	1300	825	n/a	
Hem-Fir	1300	1050	675	n/a	
Hem-Fir (North)	1250	1000	675	n/a	
Spruce-Pine-Fir	1100	900	600	n/a	
Spruce-Pine-Fir (South)	1050	900	575	n/a	
Southern Pine[5]	1500	1350	850	n/a	

(continued)

Table A-3.5 continued (Part *C*)

C. Posts and timbers[6]					
Species	**Select Structural**	**No. 1**	**No. 2**	**No. 3**	**Miscellaneous**
Douglas Fir-Larch	1500	1200	750	n/a	
Douglas Fir-Larch (North)	1500	1200	725	n/a	
Douglas Fir-South	1450	1150	675	n/a	
Hem-Fir	1200	975	575	n/a	
Hem-Fir (North)	1150	925	550	n/a	
Spruce-Pine-Fir	1050	850	500	n/a	
Spruce-Pine-Fir (South)	1000	800	475	n/a	
Southern Pine[5]	1500	1350	850	n/a	

D. Glued-laminated softwood timber								
Species	**Grade (and Identification No.)**							
	F_b (for beams with $d > 15$ in.)				F_b (for beams with $d \leq 15$ in.)			
Douglas Fir-Larch[7] (DF)	L3 (ID#1) 1100	L2 (ID#2) 1496	L2D (ID#3) 1760	L1 (ID#5) 1936	L3 (ID#1) 1250	L2 (ID#2) 1700	L2D (ID#3) 2000	L1 (ID#5) 2200
Softwood Species[7] (SW)	L3 (ID#22) 638				L3 (ID#22) 725			
Alaska Cedar[7] (AC)	L3 (ID#69) 880	L2 (ID#70) 1188	L1D (ID#71) 1540	L1S (ID#72) 1672	L3 (ID#69) 1000	L2 (ID#70) 1350	L1D (ID#71) 1750	L1S (ID#72) 1900
Southern Pine[7] (SP)	N2M12 (ID#47) 1232	N2D12 (ID#48) 1408	N1M16 (ID#49) 1584	N1D14 (ID#50) 1848	N2M12 (ID#47) 1400	N2D12 (ID#48) 1600	N1M16 (ID#49) 1800	N1D14 (ID#50) 2100
Various species[8]	**Combination Symbols for Stress Classes**							
	F_b (for positive bending[9])				F_b (for negative bending[9])			
	16F-1.3E 1600	20F-1.5E 2000	24F-1.7E 2400	24F-1.8E 2400	16F-1.3E 925	20F-1.5E 1100	24F-1.7E 1450	24F-1.8E 1450

(continued)

Table A-3.5 continued (Part *E*)

E. Glued-laminated softwood timber bent about y-axis (loaded parallel to wide face of laminations)								
Species	**Grade (and Identification No.)**							
	F_b (for 4 or more laminations)				F_b (for 3 laminations)			
Douglas Fir-Larch[7] (DF)	L3 (ID#1) 1450	L2 (ID#2) 1800	L2D (ID#3) 2100	L1 (ID#5) 2400	L3 (ID#1) 1250	L2 (ID#2) 1600	L2D (ID#3) 1850	L1 (ID#5) 2100
Softwood Species[7] (SW)	L3 (ID#22) 800				L3 (ID#22) 700			
Alaska Cedar[7] (AC)	L3 (ID#69) 1100	L2 (ID#70) 1400	L1D (ID#71) 1850	L1S (ID#72) 1850	L3 (ID#69) 975	L2 (ID#70) 1250	L1D (ID#71) 1650	L1S (ID#72) 1650
Southern Pine[7] (SP)	N2M12 (ID#47) 1750	N2D12 (ID#48) 2000	N1M16 (ID#49) 1950	N1D14 (ID#50) 2300	N2M12 (ID#47) 1550	N2D12 (ID#48) 1800	N1M16 (ID#49) 1750	N1D14 (ID#50) 2100

Species	**Combination Symbols for Stress Classes**			
	F_b (all cases)			
Various species[8]	16F-1.3E 800	20F-1.5E 800	24F-1.7E 1050	24F-1.8E 1450

Notes:

1. No.1 & better

2. No.1/No.2

3. Values for Southern Pine for dimension lumber are approximate: typical published values include the size factor and therefore list different values for each lumber width; whereas the values in this table have been normalized (i.e., do not include the size factor) and have been rounded down to values that may be slightly conservative.

4. Beams and stringers are a subset of the "timbers" size category, 5 in. × 5 in. or larger, where the width is at least 4 in. bigger than the thickness.

5. Southern Pine values for timbers (beams and stringers; and posts and timbers) are for wet service conditions.

6. Posts and timbers are a subset of the "timbers" size category, 5 in. × 5 in. or larger, where the width is equal to, or no more than 2 in. bigger than, the thickness.

7. These species designations are designed primarily for axially-loaded elements (compression and tension), although they can be used for bending with the values that appear in this table. For bending about the x-axis only, these elements are assumed to have no special tension laminations; such special tension laminations would increase the bending design values (for all cross-section sizes bent about the x-axis) to the values shown for d ≤ 15 in. multiplied by a factor of 1.18.

8. These combination designations are designed primarily for simply-supported bending elements (i.e., for beams with only positive bending moments), and are manufactured with higher strength grades of wood used in the extreme fibers (for bending about the x-axis) where bending stresses are greatest.

9. The combination symbols in this table refer to cross sections that are "unbalanced"; i.e., they are manufactured to optimize the behavior of simply-supported beams with only positive curvature. Where such unbalanced combinations are used for beams subjected to negative bending moments — i.e., for continuous or cantilevered beams — lower values for F_b must be used at those cross sections with negative moment. For beams subjected to reversals of curvature (and therefore both positive and negative bending), "balanced" (symmetrical) combinations can be specified where F_b is the same for both positive and negative bending, for example: combination symbols 16F-V6 with F_b = 1600 psi; 20F-V7 with F_b = 2000 psi; and 24F-V8 with F_b = 2400 psi.

Table A-3.6: Adjustments to allowable stress in bending, F_b, for visually-graded lumber and glued-laminated softwood timber

A. Size factor[3]

Size factor, C_F. (1) For glulam, size factor does not apply (use smaller of C_V and C_L — see Table A-3.6 Parts C and F below). (2) For timbers (beams and stringers; posts and timbers): when d > 12 in., C_F = $(12/d)^{1/9} \leq 1$; when loaded on the wide face, C_F = 0.86 (select structural), 0.74 (No.1), or 1.00 (No.2); otherwise, C_F = 1.00. (3) For dimension lumber, C_F is as shown here:

Size	C_F	Size	C_F	Size	C_F	Size	C_F
[3]2 × 2	1.5	[5]2 × 8	1.2	[1,5]2 × 14	0.9	[5]4 × 8	1.3
[3]2 × 4	1.5	[5]2 × 10	1.1	[3]4 × 4	1.5	[5]4 × 10	1.2
[4]2 × 6	1.3	[1,5]2 × 12, 4 × 14	1.0	[4]4 × 6	1.3	[1,5]4 × 12	1.1

B. Flat use factor

Flat use factor, C_{fu}, is used only when dimension lumber (or glulam) is oriented about its weak axis:

(1) For dimension lumber:

Size	C_{fu}	Size	C_{fu}	Size	C_{fu}	Size	C_{fu}
2 × 4	1.10	2 × 10	1.20	4 × 6	1.05	4 × 12	1.10
2 × 6	1.15	2 × 12	1.20	4 × 8	1.05	4 × 14	1.10
2 × 8	1.15	2 × 14	1.20	4 × 10	1.10	4 × 16	1.10

(2) For glulam:
For glulam beams bent about their weak (y) axis, and where the depth, d < 12 in.:

$$C_{fu} = (12/d)^{1/9}$$

Load direction on beam

The approximate values shown below can be used as an alternative:

Depth, d (in.)	C_{fu}	Depth, d (in.)	C_{fu}
2½	1.19	6¾	1.07
3 or 3⅛	1.16	8½ or 8¾	1.04
5 or 5⅛	1.10	10½ or 10¾	1.01

C. Volume factor

The volume factor, C_V, is used only for glulam beams loaded about their strong axes, and only if smaller than C_L (see below). For these conditions:

$$C_V = \left[\frac{21}{L}\right]^{1/x} \left[\frac{12}{d}\right]^{1/x} \left[\frac{5.125}{b}\right]^{1/x} \leq 1.0$$

where

L = the length of the simply-supported beam, or, for other beam types the distance between points of zero moment (ft)

d = beam depth (in.)

b = beam width (in.)

x = 10 (except x = 20 for Southern Pine only)

(continued)

Table A-3.6 continued (Part *D*)

D. Wet service factor

Wet service factor, C_M is as follows: for [2]dimension lumber, $C_M = 0.85$; for timbers, $C_M = 1.0$; for glulam, $C_M = 0.8$. In any dry service condition, $C_M = 1.0$.

E. Repetitive member factor

Repetitive member factor, $C_r = 1.15$, is used only for dimension lumber spaced 24 in. on center or less (typically the case with joists and rafters).

F. Beam stability factor

The beam stability factor, C_L, may apply to glulam and timber beams, but not ordinarily to dimension lumber, and only when the compression edge of the beam is unbraced by a roof or floor deck. For continuously braced beams, i.e., when $l_e = 0$, $C_L = 0$. For glulam, use only the smaller value of C_L or C_V. For timbers, combine C_L with the size factor, C_F. Use only when the beam depth is greater than its width. For these conditions, the beam stability factor, C_L, is as follows: $C_L = A - \sqrt{A^2 - B}$ where:

$$A = \frac{\left[1 + \dfrac{F_{bE}}{F_b^*}\right]}{1.9} \quad \text{and} \quad B = \frac{\left[\dfrac{F_{bE}}{F_b^*}\right]}{0.95}$$

$$F_{cE} = \frac{1.20b^2 E'_{min}}{(l_e d)}$$

$E'_{min} = E_{min}C_M$ (see Appendix Table A-3.9 for adjustments to E and E_{min})
   d = beam depth (in.) and b = beam width (in.)
   l_u = the unsupported (unbraced) length (in.), i.e., the greatest distance between lateral braces, including bridging or blocking, along the length of the beam
   l_e = the effective unsupported length (in.) where continuous lateral support is not provided as shown in these selected loading patterns:

Load arrangement	Effective length, l_e
Uniform load: no lateral support except at ends.	$l_e = 2.06l_u$ for $l_u/d < 7$ $l_e = 1.63l_u + 3d$ for $l_u/d \geq 7$
Single point load at midspan: no lateral support except at ends.	$l_e = 1.80l_u$ for $l_u/d < 7$ $l_e = 1.37l_u + 3d$ for $l_u/d \geq 7$
Single point load at midspan: lateral support under load and ends only.	$l_e = 1.11l_u$
Point loads at third points: lateral support under loads and ends only.	$l_e = 1.68l_u$
Point loads at quarter points: lateral support under loads and ends only.	$l_e = 1.54l_u$

(continued)

Table A-3.6 continued (Part *G*)

G. Load duration factor					
Load duration factor, C_D, is as follows:					
Load type	**Duration**	C_D	**Load type**	**Duration**	C_D
Dead load, *D*	Permanent	0.90	Construction load, L_r	1 week	1.25
Live load, *L*	10 years	1.00	Wind or seismic load, *W* or *E*	10 minutes	1.60
Snow load, *S*	2 months	1.15	Impact load, *I*	Instant	2.00

H. Temperature factor, C_t		
Temperature, T (° F)	C_t **(used dry)**	C_t **(used wet)**
$T \le 100°$ F	1.0	1.0
$100°$ F $< T \le 125°$ F	0.8	0.7
$125°$ F $< T \le 150°$ F	0.7	0.5

Notes:

1. $C_F = 0.9$ for all 2× dimension lumber having nominal width greater or equal to 14. $C_F = 1.0$ for all 4× dimension lumber having nominal width greater or equal to 14.

2. $C_M = 1.0$ for dimension lumber when $F_b C_F \le 1150$ psi.

3. Exceptions: $C_F = 1.1$ for stud grade 2 × 2, 2 × 4, and 4 × 4 lumber; $C_F = 1.0$ for construction and standard 2 × 2, 2 × 4, and 4 × 4 lumber; and $C_F = 0.4$ for utility grade 2 × 2 lumber

4. Exceptions: $C_F = 1.0$ for stud grade 2 × 6 and 4 × 6 lumber

5. Exceptions: For stud grade lumber with nominal width of 8 in. or higher, use No.3 grade values for F_b and C_F

Table A-3.7: Design values for shear, F_v (psi) for visually-graded lumber and glued-laminated softwood timber

A. Dimension lumber (2 in. – 4 in. thick)					
Species	**Select Structural**	**No. 1**	**No. 2**	**No. 3**	**Miscellaneous**
Douglas Fir-Larch	180	180	180	180	[1]180
Douglas Fir-Larch (North)	180	n/a	n/a	180	[2]180
Douglas Fir-South	180	180	180	180	
Hem-Fir	150	150	150	150	[1]150
Hem-Fir (North)	145	n/a	n/a	145	[2]145
Spruce-Pine-Fir	135	n/a	n/a	135	[2]135
Spruce-Pine-Fir (South)	135	135	135	135	
Southern Pine[3]	175	175	175	175	

(continued)

Table A-3.7 continued (Part *B*)

B. Timbers[3]

Species	Select Structural	No. 1	No. 2	No. 3	Miscellaneous
Douglas Fir-Larch	170	170	170	n/a	
Douglas Fir-Larch (North)	170	170	170	n/a	
Douglas Fir-South	165	165	165	n/a	
Hem-Fir	140	140	140	n/a	
Hem-Fir (North)	135	135	135	n/a	
Spruce-Pine-Fir	125	125	125	n/a	
Spruce-Pine-Fir (South)	125	125	125	n/a	
Southern Pine[5]	165	165	165	n/a	

C. Glued-laminated softwood timber bent about *x*-axis (loaded perpendicular to wide face of laminations)

Species	Grade (and Identification No.) F_v (for bending about *x*-axis[7])			
Douglas Fir-Larch[5] (DF)	L3 (ID#1) 265	L2 (ID#2) 265	L2D (ID#3) 265	L1D L1 (ID#5) 265
Softwood Species[5, 8] (SW)	L3 (ID#22) 195			
Alaska Cedar[5] (AC)	L3 (ID#69) 265	L2 (ID#70) 265	L1D (ID#71) 265	L1S (ID#72) 265
Southern Pine[5] (SP)	N2M14 N2M12 (ID#47) 300	N2D14 N2D12 (ID#48) 300	N1M16 (ID#49) 300	N1D14 (ID#50) 300
Species	Combination Symbols for Stress Classes F_v (for bending about *x*-axis[7])			
Various species[6]	16F-1.3E 195	20F-1.5E 195	24F-1.7E 210	24F-1.8E 265

D. Glued-laminated softwood timber bent about *y*-axis (loaded parallel to wide face of laminations)

Species	Grade (and Identification No.) F_v (for bending about *x*-axis[7])			
Douglas Fir-Larch[5] (DF)	L3 (ID#1) 230	L2 (ID#2) 230	L2D (ID#3) 230	L1D L1 (ID#5) 230
Softwood Species[5, 8] (SW)	L3 (ID#22) 170			
Alaska Cedar[5] (AC)	L3 (ID#69) 230	L2 (ID#70) 230	L1D (ID#71) 230	L1S (ID#72) 230
Southern Pine[5] (SP)	N2M14 N2M12 (ID#47) 260	N2D14 N2D12 (ID#48) 260	N1M16 (ID#49) 260	N1D14 (ID#50) 260
Species	Combination Symbols for Stress Classes F_v (for bending about *x*-axis[7])			
Various species[6]	16F-1.3E 170	20F-1.5E 170	24F-1.7E 185	24F-1.8E 230

(continued)

Table A-3.7 continued (Notes)

Notes:

1. No.1 & better

2. No.1/No.2

3. Timbers include "beams and stringers" and "posts and timbers," i.e., all cross sections 5 in. × 5 in. or larger.

4. Southern Pine values for timbers (beams and stringers; and posts and timbers) are for wet service conditions.

5. These species designations are designed primarily for axially-loaded elements (compression and tension), although they can be used for bending with the shear values that appear in this table.

6. These combination designations are designed primarily for bending elements, and are manufactured with higher strength grades of wood used in the extreme fibers where bending stresses are greatest when bent about the x-axis.

7. These values for horizontal shear must be reduced by a factor of 0.72 when used in the design of mechanical connections.

8. The design values for F_v shown for "softwood species" must be reduced by 10 psi (before adjustments are considered) when the following species are used in combination: Coast Sitka Spruce, Coast Species, Western White Pine, and Eastern White Pine.

Table A-3.8: Adjustments to allowable stress in shear, F_v, for visually-graded lumber and glued-laminated softwood timber

A. Wet service factor
Wet service factor, C_M, is as follows: for dimension lumber, $C_M = 0.97$; for timbers, $C_M = 1.0$; for glulam, $C_M = 0.875$. In any dry service condition, $C_M = 1.0$.

B. Load duration factor					
Load duration factor, C_D, is as follows:					
Load type	Duration	C_D	Load type	Duration	C_D
Dead load, D	Permanent	0.90	Construction load, L_r	1 week	1.25
Live load, L	10 years	1.00	Wind or seismic load, W or E	10 minutes	1.60
Snow load, S	2 months	1.15	Impact load, I	Instant	2.00

C. Temperature factor, C_t		
Temperature, T (° F)	C_t (used dry)	C_t (used wet)
$T \le 100°$ F	1.0	1.0
$100°$ F $< T \le 125°$ F	0.8	0.7
$125°$ F $< T \le 150°$ F	0.7	0.5

Table A-3.9: Design values for modulus of elasticity, E and E_{min} (psi) for visually-graded lumber and glued-laminated softwood timber (values and adjustments)

A. Modulus of elasticity, E (psi)[5]					
Dimension lumber (2 in. - 4 in. thick)	**Select Structural**	**No. 1**	**No. 2**	**No. 3**	**Miscellaneous**
Douglas Fir-Larch	1,900,000	1,700,000	1,600,000	1,400,000	[1]1,800,000
Douglas Fir-Larch (North)	1,900,000	n/a	n/a	1,400,000	[2]1,600,000
Douglas Fir-South	1,400,000	1,300,000	1,200,000	1,100,000	
Hem-Fir	1,600,000	1,500,000	1,300,000	1,200,000	[1]1,500,000
Hem-Fir (North)	1,700,000	n/a	n/a	1,400,000	[2]1,600,000
Spruce-Pine-Fir	1,500,000	n/a	n/a	1,200,000	[2]1,400,000
Spruce-Pine-Fir (South)	1,300,000	1,200,000	1,100,000	1,000,000	
Southern Pine	1,800,000	1,700,000	1,600,000	1,400,000	
Timbers[3]	**Select Structural**	**No. 1**	**No. 2**	**No. 3**	**Miscellaneous**
Douglas Fir-Larch	1,600,000	1,600,000	1,300,000	n/a	
Douglas Fir-Larch (North)	1,600,000	1,600,000	1,300,000	n/a	
Douglas Fir-South	1,200,000	1,200,000	1,000,000	n/a	
Hem-Fir	1,300,000	1,300,000	1,100,000	n/a	
Hem-Fir (North)	1,300,000	1,300,000	1,100,000	n/a	
Spruce-Pine-Fir	1,300,000	1,300,000	1,100,000	n/a	
Spruce-Pine-Fir (South)	1,200,000	1,200,000	1,000,000	n/a	
Southern Pine[4]	1,500,000	1,500,000	1,200,000	n/a	
Glued-Laminated Software Timber	**Grade (and Identification No.)**				
Douglas Fir-Larch[7] (DF)	**L3 (ID#1)** 1,500,000	**L2 (ID#2)** 1,600,000	**L2D (ID#3)** 1,900,000	**L1 (ID#5)** 2,000,000	
Softwood Species[7,9] (SW)	**L3 (ID#22)** 1,000,000				
Alaska Cedar[7] (AC)	**L3 (ID#69)** 1,200,000	**L2 (ID#70)** 1,300,000	**L1D (ID#71)** 1,600,000	**L1S (ID#72)** 1,600,000	
Southern Pine[7] (SP)	**N2M12 (ID#47)** 1,400,000	**N2D12 (ID#48)** 1,700,000	**N1M16 (ID#49)** 1,700,000	**N1D14 (ID#50)** 1,900,000	
Combination Symbols for Stress Classes					
Various species (bending about x-axis)[8]	**16F-1.3E** 1,300,000	**20F-1.5E** 1,500,000	**24F-1.7E** 1,700,000	**24F-1.8E** 1,800,000	
Various species (bending about y-axis)[8]	**16F-1.3E** 1,100,000	**20F-1.5E** 1,200,000	**24F-1.7E** 1,300,000	**24F-1.8E** 1,600,000	

(continued)

Table A-3.9 continued (Part *B*)

B. Minimum modulus of elasticity, E_{min} (psi)[6]					
Dimension lumber (2 in. - 4 in. thick)	Select Structural	No. 1	No. 2	No. 3	Miscella-neous
Douglas Fir-Larch	690,000	620,000	580,000	510,000	[1]660,000
Douglas Fir-Larch (North)	690,000	n/a	n/a	510,000	[2]580,000
Douglas Fir-South	510,000	470,000	440,000	400,000	
Hem-Fir	580,000	550,000	470,000	440,000	[1]550,000
Hem-Fir (North)	620,000	n/a	n/a	510,000	[2]580,000
Spruce-Pine-Fir	550,000	n/a	n/a	440,000	[2]510,000
Spruce-Pine-Fir (South)	470,000	440,000	400,000	370,000	
Southern Pine	660,000	620,000	580,000	510,000	
Timbers[3]	Select Structural	No. 1	No. 2	No. 3	Miscella-neous
Douglas Fir-Larch	580,000	580,000	470,000	n/a	
Douglas Fir-Larch (North)	580,000	580,000	470,000	n/a	
Douglas Fir-South	440,000	440,000	370,000	n/a	
Hem-Fir	470,000	470,000	400,000	n/a	
Hem-Fir (North)	470,000	470,000	400,000	n/a	
Spruce-Pine-Fir	470,000	470,000	370,000	n/a	
Spruce-Pine-Fir (South)	440,000	440,000	370,000	n/a	
Southern Pine[4]	550,000	550,000	440,000	n/a	
Glued-Laminated Software Timber	Grade (and Identification No.)				
Douglas Fir-Larch[7] (DF)	L3 (ID#1) 790,000	L2 (ID#2) 850,000	L2D (ID#3) 1,000,000	L1 (ID#5) 1,060,000	
Softwood Species[7,10] (SW)	L3 (ID#22) 530,000				
Alaska Cedar[7] (AC)	L3 (ID#69) 630,000	L2 (ID#70) 690,000	L1D (ID#71) 850,000	L1S (ID#72) 850,000	
Southern Pine[7] (SP)	N2M12 (ID#47) 740,000	N2D12 (ID#48) 900,000	N1M16 (ID#49) 900,000	N1D14 (ID#50) 1,000,000	
	Combination Symbols for Stress Classes				
Various species (bending about x-axis)[8]	16F-1.3E 690,000	20F-1.5E 790,000	24F-1.7E 900,000	24F-1.8E 1,000,000	
Various species (bending about y-axis)[8]	16F-1.3E 580,000	20F-1.5E 630,000	24F-1.7E 690,000	24F-1.8E 850,000	

C. Wet service adjustment (C_M) to E and E_{min}
Wet service factor, where applicable, is as follows: for dimension lumber, C_M = 0.9; for glulam, C_M = 0.833; for any other condition, C_M = 1.0. In any dry service condition, C_M = 1.0.

(continued)

Table A-3.9 continued (Part D)

D. Temperature factor adjustment (C_t) to E and E_{min}	
Temperature, T (° F)	C_t
$T \leq 100°$ F	1.0
$100°$ F $< T \leq 150°$ F	0.9

Notes:

1. No.1 & better

2. No.1/No.2

3. Timbers include "beams and stringers" and "posts and timbers," i.e., all cross sections 5 in. × 5 in. or larger.

4. Southern Pine values for timbers (beams and stringers; and posts and timbers) are for wet service conditions.

5. The modulus of elasticity, E, is an average value, used in the calculation of beam deflections, but not for column or beam stability calculations.

6. The minimum modulus of elasticity, E_{min}, is a conservative (low) value, based on statistical analyses of moduli for tested samples, and is used in calculations of column buckling (C_P) and beam stability (C_L).

7. These species designations are designed primarily for axially-loaded elements (compression and tension), although they can be used in any context with the values that appear in this table.

8. These combination designations are designed primarily for bending elements, although they can be used in any context with the values that appear in this table.

9. The design values for E shown for "softwood species" must be reduced from 1,000,000 psi to 900,000 psi when the following species are used in combination: Western Cedars, Western Cedars (North), Western Woods, and Redwood (open grain).

10. The design values for E_{min} shown for "softwood species" must be reduced from 530,000 psi to 477,200 psi when the following species are used in combination: Western Cedars, Western Cedars (North), Western Woods, and Redwood (open grain).

Table A-3.10: Use of load duration factor, C_D, for wood elements

Where more than one load type acts on a wood structural element, C_D corresponds to the load of shortest duration. Values of C_D for tension, compression, bending, and shear can be found in Appendix Tables A-3.2, A-3.4, A-3.6, and A-3.8 respectively. It is sometimes necessary to check various combinations of loads (where the corresponding value of C_D changes) to determine the critical loading condition. Since the strength of lumber depends on the duration of loading, it is possible that a smaller load, with a longer duration, will be more critical than a larger load that acts on the element for less time.

For example, consider a wooden column supporting the following loads:

• a "construction" or roof live load, L_r = 6000 lb.
• a live load, L = 20,000 lb.
• a dead load, D = 15,000 lb.
• a snow load, S = 16,000 lb.

L_r and S are not considered simultaneously since it is unlikely that roof maintenance or construction will occur during a major snow storm.

Several load combinations should be analyzed, per Chapter 2 Appendix Table A-2.7 (using Allowable Stress Design for wood):

1. $D + L$ with C_D = 1.0 (corresponding to the live load).
2. $D + S$ with C_D = 1.15 (corresponding to the snow load).
3. $D + 0.75L + 0.75S$ with C_D = 1.15 (corresponding to the snow load).

It is usually unnecessary to go through the entire design procedure for each load combination; instead, divide the loads in each case by the corresponding load duration factor to get a measure of the relative "load effects;" that is:

1. (15,000 + 20,000)/1.00 = 35,000/1.0 = 35,000 lb;
2. (15,000 + 8,000)/1.15 = 23,000/1.15 = 20,000 lb;
3. (15,000 + 0.75 x 20,000 + 0.75 x 16,000)/1.15 = **42,000**/1.15 = <u>36,522</u> lb.

The third load combination is the critical one in this case, based on the underlined value being largest of the three choices. However, the structural element should be designed for the bold-faced value of 42,000 lb, and not the underlined value of 36,522 lb which is used only to determine the governing load value. The governing duration of load factor, C_D = 1.15, will then be applied, not to the loads, but to the allowable stress.

Where only "occupancy" live loads and dead loads are present, C_D can almost always be taken as 1.0 (corresponding to the load duration factor for live loads). The case of dead load acting alone, with C_D = 0.9, is critical only when more than 90% of the total load is dead load.

Table A-3.11: Specific gravity for selected wood species ((based on oven-dry weight and volume)

Species or Species Combination	Specific Gravity	Species or Species Combination	Specific Gravity
Douglas Fir-Larch	0.50	Hem-Fir (North)	0.46
Douglas Fir-Larch (North)	0.49	Spruce-Pine-Fir	0.42
Douglas Fir-South	0.46	Spruce-Pine-Fir (South)	0.36
Hem-Fir	0.43	Southern Pine	0.55

Table A-3.12: Dimensions and properties of lumber

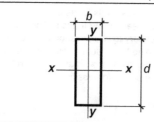

Properties of rectangular cross sections:
Cross-sectional area, $A = bd$
Section modulus, $S_x = bd^2/6$
Moment of inertia, $I_x = bd^3/12$
Moment of inertia, $I_y = db^3/12$

A. Dimension lumber

Dimension lumber nominal size	Actual size, $b \times d$ (in.)	Area (in²)	S_x (in³)	I_x (in⁴)	I_y (in⁴)
2 × 3	1.5 × 2.5	3.75	1.563	1.953	0.703
2 × 4	1.5 × 3.5	5.25	3.063	5.359	0.984
2 × 6	1.5 × 5.5	8.25	7.563	20.80	1.547
2 × 8	1.5 × 7.25	10.88	13.14	47.63	2.039
2 × 10	1.5 × 9.25	13.88	21.39	98.93	2.602
2 × 12	1.5 × 11.25	16.88	31.64	178.0	3.164
2 × 14	1.5 × 13.25	19.88	43.89	290.8	3.727
4 × 4	3.5 × 3.5	12.25	7.146	12.51	12.51
4 × 6	3.5 × 5.5	19.25	17.65	48.53	19.65
4 × 8	3.5 × 7.25	25.38	30.66	111.1	25.90
4 × 10	3.5 × 9.25	32.38	49.91	230.8	33.05
4 × 12	3.5 × 11.25	39.38	73.83	415.3	40.20
4 × 14	3.5 × 13.25	46.38	102.4	678.5	47.34
4 × 16	3.5 × 15.25	53.38	135.7	1034.4	54.49

B. Beams and stringers

Dimension lumber nominal size	Actual size, $b \times d$ (in.)	Area (in²)	S_x (in³)	I_x (in⁴)	I_y (in⁴)
6 × 10	5.5 × 9.25	50.88	78.43	362.7	128.2
6 × 12	5.5 × 11.25	61.88	116.0	652.6	156.0
6 × 14	5.5 × 13.25	72.88	160.9	1066	183.7
6 × 16	5.5 × 15	82.50	206.3	1547	208.0
6 × 18	5.5 × 17	93.50	264.9	2252	235.7
6 × 20	5.5 × 19	104.5	330.9	3144	263.4
6 × 22	5.5 × 21	115.5	404.3	4245	291.2
8 × 12	7.25 × 11.25	81.56	152.9	860.2	357.3
8 × 14	7.25 × 13.25	96.06	212.1	1405	420.8
8 × 16	7.25 × 15	108.8	271.9	2039	476.3
8 × 18	7.25 × 17	123.3	349.2	2968	539.9
8 × 20	7.25 × 19	137.8	436.2	4144	603.4
8 × 22	7.25 × 21	152.3	532.9	5595	666.9
8 × 24	7.25 × 23	166.8	639.2	7351	730.4
10 × 14	9.25 × 13.25	122.6	270.7	1793	873.9
10 × 16	9.25 × 15	138.8	346.9	2602	989.3
10 × 18	9.25 × 17	157.3	455.5	3787	1121
10 × 20	9.25 × 19	175.8	556.5	5287	1253
10 × 22	9.25 × 21	194.3	679.9	7139	1385
10 × 24	9.25 × 23	212.8	815.5	9379	1517
12 × 16	11.25 × 15	168.8	421.9	3164	1780
12 × 18	11.25 × 17	191.3	541.9	4606	2017
12 × 20	11.25 × 19	213.8	676.9	6430	2254
12 × 22	11.25 × 21	236.3	826.9	8682	2492
12 × 24	11.25 × 23	258.8	991.9	11407	2729

(continued)

Table A-3.12 continued (Part *B*)

B. Beams and stringers					
Dimension lumber nominal size	Actual size, $b \times d$ (in.)	Area (in²)	S_x (in³)	I_x (in⁴)	I_y (in⁴)
14 × 18	13.25 × 17	225.3	638.2	5425	3295
14 × 20	13.25 × 19	251.8	797.2	7573	3683
14 × 22	13.25 × 21	278.3	793.9	10226	4041
14 × 24	13.25 × 23	304.8	1168	13434	4459
16 × 20	15 × 19	285.0	902.5	8574	5344
16 × 22	15 × 21	315.0	1103	11576	5906
16 × 24	15 × 23	345.0	1323	15209	6469

C. Posts and timbers					
Dimension lumber nominal size	Actual size, $b \times d$ (in.)	Area (in²)	S_x (in³)	I_x (in⁴)	I_y (in⁴)
6 × 6	5.5 × 5.5	30.25	27.73	76.26	76.26
6 × 8	5.5 × 7.25	39.88	48.18	174.7	100.5
8 × 8	7.25 × 7.25	52.56	63.51	230.2	230.2
8 × 10	7.25 × 9.25	67.06	103.4	478.2	293.7
10 × 10	9.25 × 9.25	85.56	131.9	610.1	610.1
10 × 12	9.25 × 11.25	104.1	195.1	1098	742.0
12 × 12	11.25 × 11.25	126.6	237.3	1335	1335
12 × 14	11.25 × 13.25	149.1	329.2	2181	1572
14 × 14	13.25 × 13.25	175.6	387.7	2569	2569
14 × 16	13.25 × 15	198.8	496.9	3727	2908
16 × 16	15 × 15	225.0	562.5	4219	4219
16 × 18	15 × 17	255.0	722.5	6141	4781
18 × 18	17 × 17	289.0	818.8	6960	6960
18 × 20	17 × 19	323.0	1023	9717	7779

Table A-3.13: Dimensions of typical glulam posts and beams[1] (in.)

Southern Pine (1⅜ in. laminations)		Western Species[2] (1½ in. laminations)	
Width (in.)	Depth (in.)	Width (in.)	Depth (in.)
2⅛	5½ to 24¾	2⅛	6 to 27
3 or 3⅛	5½ to 24¾	3⅛	6 to 27
5 or 5⅛	5½ to 35¾	5⅛	6 to 36
6¾	6⅞ to 48⅛	6¾	7½ to 48
8½	8¼ to 63¼	8¾	9 to 63
10½	9⅝ to 77	10¾	10½ to 81
12	11 to 86⅝	12¼	12 to 88½
14	13¾ to 100⅜	14¼	13½ to 102

Notes:

1. Values are for premium, architectural, and industrial appearance grades; framing appearance grades are generally surfaced less so that they match standard lumber widths, e.g., 2½ in., 3½ in., 5½ in., and 7¼ in.

2. Western Species (WS) consists of numerous species groups, not all of which are produced in the western US, including: Alaska Cedar (AC); Douglas Fir-Larch (DF) and Douglas Fir South (DFS); Eastern Spruce (ES), Hem-Fir (HF); Softwood Species (SW); and Spruce Pine Fir (SPF).

Table A-3.14: Allowable force (lb) based on row and group tear-out[1,2]

Row tear-out	Group tear-out
$Z'_{RT} = r_n n_1 (F_v') s_{crit}(t)$	$Z'_{GT} = n_1 (F_v') s_{crit}(t) + F_t' A_t$

Notes:

1. The terms in the equations for Z'_{RT} and Z'_{GT} are defined as follows:

Z'_{RT} = the maximum force that can be safely resisted by all fasteners subjected to row tear-out (lb)

Z'_{GT} = the maximum force that can be safely resisted by all fasteners subjected to group tear-out (lb)

r_n = the number of rows of fasteners

n_1 = the number of fasteners in a typical row

F_v' = the adjusted allowable shear stress for the wood element (psi)

F_t' = the adjusted allowable tension stress for the wood element (psi)

A_t = the area subjected to tension stress between the top and bottom rows of fasteners (in²)

s_{crit} = the minimum spacing between fasteners, or the distance of the first fastener to the end of the member,   if smaller (inches)

t = the member thickness (inches).

2. Row and group tear-out apply to wood tension members when the following conditions are met: (a) the direction of the tension force is parallel to the grain of the tension element; (b) the fasteners consist of bolts or lag screws; and (c) the connection consists of multiple fasteners in a row for row tear-out; and multiple rows of fasteners for group tear-out.

Table A-3.15: Maximum (actual) deflection in a beam[1,2,3]

Deflection coefficient, C, for maximum (actual) deflection, Δ (in.), where $\Delta = \dfrac{CP(L/12)^3}{EI_x}$				
$P = w(L/12)$	22.46	9.33	4.49	216
P	35.94	16.07	8.99	n/a
$P \quad P$	61.34	26.27	13.31	n/a
$P \ P \ P$	85.54	36.12	17.97	n/a
P	n/a	n/a	n/a	576

Notes:

1. Beam diagram symbols in top row of tables represent the following conditions (from left to right): simply-supported; one end pinned and one end continuous; both ends continuous; and cantilever.

2. Units for the maximum (actual) deflection equation are as follows:

Δ = maximum (actual) deflection (in.)

C = deflection coefficient

L = span (in.): The quantity ($L/12$) that appears in the deflection equation is therefore the span in feet

E = modulus of elasticity (psi when load is in lb; or ksi when load is in kips)

I_x = moment of inertia about axis of bending (in⁴)

(continued)

Table A-3.15 continued (Notes)

P = concentrated load or resultant of uniformly-distributed load (lb or kips)

w = uniformly-distributed load (lb/ft or kips/ft)

3. Allowable deflections (from Appendix Table A-1.3) are as follows:

For live load only (or snow or wind only), the typical basic floor beam limit is L/360 while typical roof beam limits are L/180, L/240, or L/360 (for no ceiling, nonplaster ceiling, or plaster ceiling respectively).

For total loads (combined live and dead), the typical basic floor beam limit is L/240 while typical roof beam limits are L/120, L/180, or L/240 (for no ceiling, nonplaster ceiling, or plaster ceiling respectively).

Table A-3.16: "Adjusted" section modulus ($C_F S_x$) values for wood sections in bending (lightest shown in bold face)[1,2]

Shape	$C_F S_x$ (in³)	Shape	$C_F S_x$ (in³)	Shape	$C_F S_x$ (in³)
2 × 4	**4.594**	**4 × 12**	**81.21**	**8 × 22**	**500.8**
Double 2 × 4	9.188	Triple 2 × 12	94.92	12 × 18	521.3
2 × 6	**9.831**	**4 × 14**	**102.4**	10 × 20	528.8
Triple 2 × 4	13.78	6 × 12	116.0	**8 × 24**	**594.6**
2 × 8	**15.77**	Triple 2 × 14	118.5	14 × 18	614.0
Double 2 × 6	19.66	**4 × 16**	**135.7**	**10 × 22**	**638.9**
4 × 6	22.94	**8 × 12**	**152.9**	12 × 20	643.2
2 × 10	**25.53**	**6 × 14**	**159.2**	14 × 20	757.5
Triple 2 × 6	29.49	**6 × 16**	**201.2**	**10 × 24**	**758.7**
Double 2 × 8	31.54	8 × 14	209.8	**12 × 22**	**777.0**
2 × 12	**31.64**	**6 × 18**	**254.9**	16 × 20	857.6
2 × 14	**39.50**	8 × 16	265.2	14 × 22	915.2
4 × 8	**39.86**	10 × 14	267.7	**12 × 24**	**922.7**
Double 2 × 10	**47.06**	**6 × 20**	**314.4**	16 × 22	1036
Triple 2 × 8	47.31	8 × 18	336.0	**14 × 24**	**1087**
4 × 10	**59.89**	10 × 16	338.4	18 × 22	1174
Double 2 × 12	**63.28**	**6 × 22**	**379.9**	**16 × 24**	**1230**
Triple 2 × 10	70.59	12 × 16	411.5	20 × 22	1312
6 × 10	78.43	**8 × 20**	**414.5**	**18 × 24**	**1394**
Double 2 × 14	79.00	10 × 18	428.6	**20 × 24**	**1558**

Notes:

1. "Double" or "triple" indicates that two or three sections, respectively, are nailed together to create a single bending element.

2. The "adjusted" section modulus consists of the size factor, C_F, multiplied by the section modulus, S_x.

Table A-3.17: Selected lag screw (lag bolt) dimensions

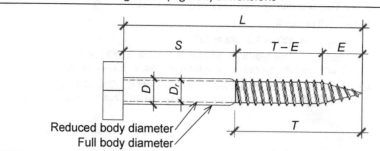

L (in.)	D (in.)	D_r (in.)	T (in.)	T − E (in.)	E (in.)
3	0.250	0.173	2.0	0.1562	0.1562
3	0.375	0.265	2.0	0.2187	0.2187
3	0.500	0.371	2.0	0.3125	0.3125
3	0.625	0.471	2.0	0.4062	0.4062
4	0.250	0.173	2.5	0.1562	0.1562
4	0.375	0.265	2.5	0.2187	0.2187
4	0.500	0.371	2.5	0.3125	0.3125
4	0.625	0.471	2.5	0.4062	0.4062
5	0.250	0.173	3.0	0.1562	0.1562
5	0.375	0.265	3.0	0.2187	0.2187
5	0.500	0.371	3.0	0.3125	0.3125
5	0.625	0.471	3.0	0.4062	0.4062
6	0.250	0.173	3.5	0.1562	0.1562
6	0.375	0.265	3.5	0.2187	0.2187
6	0.500	0.371	3.5	0.3125	0.3125
6	0.625	0.471	3.5	0.4062	0.4062

Table A-3.18: Selected common wire nail dimensions

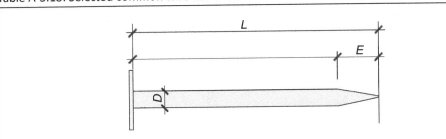

Designation[1]	L (in.)	D (in.)	[2]E (in.)
6d	2.00	0.113	0.226
8d	2.50	0.131	0.262
10d	3.00	0.148	0.296
12d	3.25	0.148	0.296
16d	3.50	0.162	0.324
20d	4.00	0.192	0.384
30d	4.50	0.207	0.414
40d	5.00	0.225	0.450
50d	5.50	0.244	0.488

Notes:

1. The designation for nails once had some relation to the cost of 100 nails; it now refers only to the nail's size. The letter "d" in the designation refers to the pennyweight of the nails and is said to be derived from the biblical use of *denarius* (hence "d") as the historical equivalent of the modern penny (hence "penny-weight"). We continue to use the abbreviation "d" to stand for "penny" and we say "10-penny nail" when reading "10d nail."

2. E = approximate length of tapered tip, assumed to be equal to $2D$.

Table A-3.19: Penetration and dowel bearing length[1]

Type of fastener		Required penetration distance, p	
		Absolute minimum	Minimum for full value of Z
Lag screw[2]		$4D$	$8D$
Nail[3]		$6D$	$10D$
Bolt[4]		n/a	n/a

Notes:

1. The dowel bearing length in the main member (l_m), used in yield limit calculations, may be different from the penetration as defined in the illustrations above: for lag screws, the dowel bearing length in the main member equals the penetration (which excludes the tapered tip); however, for nailed connections, the dowel bearing length in the main member equals the penetration (which includes the tapered tip) minus half the length of the tapered tip.

2. For lag screws where the penetration, p, falls between the two values shown in the table, the lateral design value, Z, is multiplied by $p/(8D)$. Therefore, where the penetration equals the absolute minimum value of $4D$, the lateral design value is taken as one half the tabular (or computed) value of Z.

3. For nails where the penetration, p, falls between the two values shown in the table, the lateral design value, Z, is multiplied by $p/(10D)$. Therefore, where the penetration equals the absolute minimum value of $6D$, the lateral design value is taken as 0.6 times the tabular (or computed) value of Z.

4. For bolts, "penetration" is always, by definition, 100% through both the main member and side member(s), so there is no need to calculate its effect on the lateral design value, Z.

Table A-3.20: Duration of load adjustment factor, C_D, for wood connectors[1]

Load type	Duration	C_D	Load type	Duration	C_D
Dead load, D	Permanent	0.90	Construction load, L_r	1 week	1.25
Live load, L	10 years	1.00	Wind load, W	10 minutes	1.60
Snow load, S	2 months	1.15	Seismic load, E	10 minutes	1.60

Note:

1. Applies to both dowel-type connectors and connectors subject to withdrawal loads

Table A-3.21: Wet service adjustment factor, C_M, for wood connectors[1,2]

Fastener type with lateral load	C_M
"Dowel-type," wet when made, dry in-service:	varies as follows:
• 1 fastener only	1.00
• 2 or more fasteners in single row parallel to grain	1.00
• Multiple rows of fasteners parallel to grain, separate splice plate each row	1.00
• Fastener with diameter < ¼ in.	0.70
• Multiple rows of fasteners with diameter ≥ ¼ in., without separate splice plates	0.40
"Dowel-type," wet when used (in-service)	0.70
Fastener type with withdrawal load	C_M
Nails, wet when made, dry in-service	0.25
Nails, dry when made, wet in-service	0.25
Nails, wet when made, wet in-service	1.00
Lag screws and wood screws, wet in-service	0.70

Notes:

1. Applies to both dowel-type connectors and connectors subject to withdrawal loads.

2. C_M = 1.0 for fasteners that are dry when fabricated and when used (in-service).

Table A-3.22: Group action adjustment factor, C_g, for wood connectors[1,2,3,4]

A. C_g, bolt (or lag screw) connections, wood members with same properties: E = 1,400,000 psi; bolt or lag screw diameter, D = 3/4 in.; spacing between fasteners in a row, s = 3 in.

A_m = Area of main member, in²	number fasteners in row	A_s = Area of side member(s), in²								
		5	8	11	14	17	30	40	56	64
5	2	1.000	0.991	0.987	0.985	0.983	0.980	0.979	0.978	0.978
	3	0.984	0.962	0.952	0.947	0.943	0.936	0.933	0.931	0.931
	4	0.954	0.918	0.902	0.893	0.887	0.875	0.871	0.868	0.867
	5	0.914	0.866	0.844	0.831	0.823	0.807	0.802	0.798	0.796
	6	0.867	0.809	0.783	0.768	0.758	0.739	0.733	0.728	0.726
	7	0.817	0.752	0.723	0.707	0.696	0.675	0.688	0.662	0.660
	8	0.766	0.698	0.667	0.650	0.638	0.616	0.608	0.602	0.600
	9	0.716	0.647	0.616	0.598	0.587	0.563	0.556	0.549	0.547
	10	0.669	0.601	0.570	0.552	0.540	0.517	0.510	0.503	0.501
8	2	0.991	1.000	0.996	0.993	0.992	0.989	0.988	0.987	0.987
	3	0.962	0.990	0.979	0.973	0.970	0.962	0.959	0.957	0.956
	4	0.918	0.971	0.953	0.942	0.936	0.922	0.918	0.914	0.913
	5	0.866	0.943	0.918	0.903	0.894	0.875	0.869	0.863	0.862
	6	0.809	0.910	0.877	0.859	0.847	0.823	0.815	0.809	0.806
	7	0.752	0.873	0.834	0.812	0.798	0.770	0.761	0.753	0.751
	8	0.698	0.833	0.790	0.766	0.750	0.719	0.708	0.700	0.697
	9	0.647	0.792	0.746	0.720	0.703	0.670	0.659	0.650	0.647
	10	0.601	0.751	0.704	0.677	0.659	0.624	0.613	0.603	0.600

(continued)

Table A-3.22 continued (Part *A*)

A. C_g, bolt (or lag screw) connections, wood members with same properties: E = 1,400,000 psi; bolt or lag screw diameter, D = 3/4 in.; spacing between fasteners in a row, s = 3 in.

A_m = Area of main member, in²	number fasteners in row	A_s = Area of side member(s), in²								
		5	8	11	14	17	30	40	56	64
11	2	0.987	0.996	1.000	0.998	0.996	0.993	0.992	0.991	0.991
	3	0.952	0.979	0.993	0.986	0.983	0.975	0.972	0.970	0.969
	4	0.902	0.953	0.978	0.967	0.961	0.947	0.942	0.938	0.937
	5	0.844	0.918	0.958	0.942	0.932	0.911	0.905	0.899	0.897
	6	0.783	0.877	0.932	0.911	0.898	0.871	0.862	0.855	0.853
	7	0.723	0.834	0.903	0.877	0.861	0.828	0.818	0.809	0.806
	8	0.667	0.790	0.870	0.841	0.822	0.785	0.772	0.762	0.759
	9	0.616	0.746	0.836	0.804	0.783	0.741	0.728	0.717	0.713
	10	0.570	0.704	0.801	0.766	0.744	0.700	0.685	0.673	0.669
14	2	0.985	0.993	0.998	1.000	0.998	0.995	0.994	0.993	0.993
	3	0.947	0.973	0.986	0.994	0.990	0.982	0.979	0.977	0.976
	4	0.893	0.942	0.967	0.983	0.976	0.961	0.956	0.952	0.951
	5	0.831	0.903	0.942	0.966	0.956	0.934	0.927	0.921	0.919
	6	0.768	0.859	0.911	0.945	0.931	0.902	0.893	0.885	0.883
	7	0.707	0.812	0.877	0.921	0.903	0.867	0.856	0.846	0.843
	8	0.650	0.766	0.841	0.894	0.873	0.831	0.817	0.805	0.802
	9	0.598	0.720	0.804	0.864	0.841	0.793	0.778	0.765	0.761
	10	0.552	0.677	0.766	0.834	0.808	0.756	0.739	0.725	0.721
17	2	0.983	0.992	0.996	0.998	1.000	0.997	0.996	0.995	0.995
	3	0.943	0.970	0.983	0.990	0.995	0.987	0.984	0.982	0.981
	4	0.887	0.936	0.961	0.976	0.986	0.971	0.966	0.962	0.961
	5	0.823	0.894	0.932	0.956	0.972	0.950	0.943	0.936	0.934
	6	0.758	0.847	0.898	0.931	0.954	0.924	0.914	0.906	0.904
	7	0.696	0.798	0.861	0.903	0.934	0.895	0.883	0.873	0.869
	8	0.638	0.750	0.822	0.873	0.910	0.864	0.850	0.837	0.833
	9	0.587	0.703	0.783	0.841	0.885	0.832	0.815	0.801	0.797
	10	0.540	0.659	0.744	0.808	0.858	0.799	0.781	0.765	0.760
30	2	0.980	0.989	0.993	0.995	0.997	1.000	0.999	0.998	0.998
	3	0.936	0.962	0.975	0.982	0.987	0.997	0.995	0.992	0.991
	4	0.875	0.922	0.947	0.961	0.971	0.992	0.987	0.983	0.981
	5	0.807	0.875	0.911	0.934	0.950	0.984	0.976	0.969	0.967
	6	0.739	0.823	0.871	0.902	0.924	0.973	0.963	0.953	0.950
	7	0.675	0.770	0.828	0.867	0.895	0.961	0.947	0.935	0.931
	8	0.616	0.719	0.785	0.831	0.864	0.946	0.929	0.914	0.909
	9	0.563	0.670	0.741	0.793	0.832	0.930	0.909	0.891	0.886
	10	0.517	0.624	0.700	0.756	0.799	0.912	0.888	0.867	0.861
40	2	0.979	0.988	0.992	0.994	0.996	0.999	1.000	0.999	0.999
	3	0.933	0.959	0.972	0.979	0.984	0.995	0.998	0.996	0.995
	4	0.871	0.918	0.942	0.956	0.966	0.987	0.994	0.989	0.988
	5	0.802	0.869	0.905	0.927	0.943	0.976	0.988	0.981	0.979
	6	0.733	0.815	0.862	0.893	0.914	0.963	0.980	0.970	0.967
	7	0.668	0.761	0.818	0.856	0.883	0.947	0.970	0.957	0.954
	8	0.608	0.708	0.772	0.817	0.850	0.929	0.959	0.943	0.938
	9	0.556	0.659	0.728	0.778	0.815	0.909	0.946	0.927	0.921
	10	0.510	0.613	0.685	0.739	0.781	0.888	0.932	0.909	0.902

(continued)

Table A-3.22 continued (Part *A*)

A. C_g, bolt (or lag screw) connections, wood members with same properties: $E = 1{,}400{,}000$ psi; bolt or lag screw diameter, $D = 3/4$ in.; spacing between fasteners in a row, $s = 3$ in.

A_m = Area of main member, in²	number fasteners in row	A_s = Area of side member(s), in²								
		5	8	11	14	17	30	40	56	64
56	2	0.978	0.987	0.991	0.993	0.995	0.998	0.999	1.000	1.000
	3	0.931	0.957	0.970	0.977	0.982	0.992	0.996	0.999	0.998
	4	0.868	0.914	0.938	0.952	0.962	0.983	0.989	0.996	0.994
	5	0.798	0.863	0.899	0.921	0.936	0.969	0.981	0.991	0.989
	6	0.728	0.809	0.855	0.885	0.906	0.953	0.970	0.985	0.982
	7	0.662	0.753	0.809	0.846	0.873	0.935	0.957	0.978	0.974
	8	0.602	0.700	0.762	0.805	0.837	0.914	0.943	0.970	0.965
	9	0.549	0.650	0.717	0.765	0.801	0.891	0.927	0.961	0.954
	10	0.503	0.603	0.673	0.725	0.765	0.867	0.909	0.950	0.942
64	2	0.978	0.987	0.991	0.993	0.995	0.998	0.999	1.000	1.000
	3	0.931	0.956	0.969	0.976	0.981	0.991	0.995	0.998	0.999
	4	0.867	0.913	0.937	0.951	0.961	0.981	0.988	0.994	0.996
	5	0.796	0.862	0.897	0.919	0.934	0.967	0.979	0.989	0.992
	6	0.726	0.806	0.853	0.883	0.904	0.950	0.967	0.982	0.987
	7	0.660	0.751	0.806	0.843	0.869	0.931	0.954	0.974	0.981
	8	0.600	0.697	0.759	0.802	0.833	0.909	0.938	0.965	0.974
	9	0.547	0.647	0.713	0.761	0.797	0.886	0.921	0.954	0.965
	10	0.501	0.600	0.669	0.721	0.760	0.861	0.902	0.942	0.956

B. C_g, bolt (or lag screw) connections, wood main member with $E = 1{,}400{,}000$ psi; steel side member(s) with $E = 29{,}000{,}000$ psi; bolt or lag screw diameter, $D = 3/4$ in.; spacing between fasteners in a row, $s = 3$ in.

A_m = Area of main member, in²	number fasteners in row	A_s = Area of steel side member(s), in²								
		1	2	3	4	5	7	10	12	15
5	2	0.973	0.969	0.968	0.967	0.967	0.966	0.966	0.966	0.966
	3	0.915	0.905	0.902	0.900	0.899	0.898	0.897	0.897	0.896
	4	0.838	0.824	0.819	0.816	0.815	0.813	0.812	0.811	0.811
	5	0.758	0.739	0.733	0.73	0.728	0.726	0.724	0.724	0.723
	6	0.682	0.660	0.653	0.650	0.648	0.645	0.643	0.643	0.642
	7	0.613	0.591	0.583	0.579	0.577	0.575	0.573	0.572	0.571
	8	0.554	0.531	0.523	0.519	0.517	0.514	0.512	0.512	0.511
	9	0.502	0.480	0.472	0.468	0.466	0.463	0.461	0.461	0.460
	10	0.458	0.436	0.429	0.425	0.423	0.420	0.419	0.418	0.417
8	2	0.986	0.982	0.980	0.980	0.979	0.979	0.978	0.978	0.978
	3	0.951	0.941	0.937	0.935	0.934	0.933	0.932	0.932	0.932
	4	0.901	0.884	0.878	0.875	0.874	0.872	0.870	0.870	0.869
	5	0.843	0.819	0.812	0.808	0.806	0.803	0.801	0.800	0.799
	6	0.782	0.754	0.744	0.740	0.737	0.734	0.731	0.730	0.729
	7	0.722	0.691	0.680	0.675	0.672	0.668	0.666	0.664	0.663
	8	0.666	0.633	0.621	0.616	0.612	0.609	0.606	0.605	0.604
	9	0.615	0.580	0.569	0.563	0.560	0.556	0.553	0.552	0.550
	10	0.569	0.534	0.522	0.517	0.513	0.509	0.506	0.505	0.504

(continued)

Table A-3.22 continued (Part *B*)

B. C_g, bolt (or lag screw) connections, wood main member with E = 1,400,000 psi; steel side member(s) with E = 29,000,000 psi; bolt or lag screw diameter, D = 3/4 in.; spacing between fasteners in a row, s = 3 in.

| A_m = Area of main member, in² | number fasteners in row | A_s = Area of steel side member(s), in² | | | | | | | | |
		1	2	3	4	5	7	10	12	15
11	2	0.992	0.988	0.986	0.986	0.985	0.985	0.984	0.984	0.984
	3	0.970	0.959	0.955	0.953	0.952	0.951	0.950	0.950	0.949
	4	0.935	0.916	0.910	0.907	0.905	0.903	0.902	0.901	0.900
	5	0.892	0.866	0.857	0.853	0.850	0.847	0.845	0.844	0.843
	6	0.844	0.811	0.800	0.795	0.792	0.788	0.785	0.784	0.783
	7	0.794	0.756	0.743	0.737	0.733	0.729	0.726	0.725	0.723
	8	0.745	0.703	0.689	0.682	0.678	0.673	0.670	0.668	0.667
	9	0.698	0.653	0.639	0.631	0.627	0.622	0.618	0.616	0.615
	10	0.654	0.608	0.592	0.585	0.580	0.575	0.571	0.569	0.568
14	2	0.996	0.991	0.990	0.989	0.989	0.988	0.988	0.988	0.988
	3	0.981	0.969	0.966	0.964	0.963	0.961	0.960	0.960	0.960
	4	0.956	0.936	0.930	0.927	0.925	0.923	0.921	0.920	0.920
	5	0.924	0.896	0.886	0.882	0.879	0.876	0.873	0.873	0.872
	6	0.886	0.850	0.838	0.832	0.829	0.825	0.822	0.820	0.819
	7	0.846	0.802	0.788	0.781	0.777	0.772	0.768	0.767	0.766
	8	0.804	0.755	0.739	0.731	0.726	0.721	0.716	0.715	0.713
	9	0.762	0.709	0.691	0.683	0.677	0.671	0.667	0.665	0.664
	10	0.721	0.665	0.647	0.638	0.632	0.626	0.621	0.619	0.617
17	2	0.998	0.994	0.992	0.991	0.991	0.990	0.990	0.990	0.990
	3	0.988	0.976	0.973	0.971	0.970	0.968	0.967	0.967	0.967
	4	0.970	0.950	0.943	0.940	0.938	0.936	0.934	0.934	0.933
	5	0.946	0.917	0.907	0.902	0.899	0.896	0.893	0.892	0.892
	6	0.917	0.878	0.865	0.859	0.855	0.851	0.848	0.847	0.845
	7	0.884	0.837	0.822	0.814	0.809	0.804	0.800	0.799	0.797
	8	0.849	0.795	0.777	0.768	0.763	0.757	0.752	0.750	0.749
	9	0.813	0.753	0.733	0.723	0.717	0.711	0.706	0.704	0.702
	10	0.777	0.712	0.691	0.680	0.674	0.667	0.661	0.659	0.657
30	2	0.997	0.998	0.997	0.996	0.996	0.995	0.995	0.995	0.994
	3	0.987	0.991	0.988	0.986	0.984	0.983	0.982	0.982	0.981
	4	0.970	0.980	0.973	0.969	0.967	0.965	0.963	0.962	0.962
	5	0.947	0.964	0.953	0.948	0.945	0.941	0.938	0.937	0.936
	6	0.919	9.944	0.929	0.922	0.918	0.913	0.909	0.908	0.906
	7	0.888	0.921	0.902	0.893	0.888	0.881	0.877	0.875	0.873
	8	0.855	0.896	0.873	0.862	0.856	0.848	0.842	0.840	0.838
	9	0.821	0.869	0.843	0.830	0.822	0.813	0.807	0.804	0.802
	10	0.786	0.841	0.812	0.797	0.788	0.779	0.771	0.768	0.765
40	2	0.996	1.000	0.998	0.998	0.997	0.997	0.996	0.996	0.996
	3	0.983	0.996	0.993	0.991	0.989	0.988	0.987	0.987	0.986
	4	0.963	0.990	0.983	0.979	0.977	0.975	0.973	0.972	0.971
	5	0.936	0.981	0.970	0.964	0.961	0.957	0.954	0.953	0.952
	6	0.905	0.968	0.953	0.945	0.941	0.936	0.932	0.930	0.929
	7	0.871	0.954	0.934	0.924	0.918	0.911	0.906	0.904	0.902
	8	0.835	0.937	0.913	0.900	0.893	0.885	0.879	0.876	0.874
	9	0.798	0.919	0.890	0.875	0.867	0.857	0.849	0.847	0.844
	10	0.761	0.899	0.865	0.849	0.839	0.828	0.819	0.816	0.813

(continued)

Table A-3.22 continued (Part B)

B. C_g, bolt (or lag screw) connections, wood main member with E = 1,400,000 psi; steel side member(s) with E = 29,000,000 psi; bolt or lag screw diameter, D = 3/4 in.; spacing between fasteners in a row, s = 3 in.

A_m = Area of main member, in²	number fasteners in row	A_s = Area of steel side member(s), in²								
		1	2	3	4	5	7	10	12	15
56	2	0.994	0.999	1.000	0.999	0.998	0.998	0.998	0.997	0.997
	3	0.980	0.994	0.997	0.995	0.994	0.992	0.991	0.991	0.991
	4	0.957	0.985	0.992	0.988	0.986	0.983	0.982	0.981	0.980
	5	0.927	0.974	0.984	0.979	0.975	0.971	0.969	0.967	0.966
	6	0.893	0.959	0.975	0.967	0.962	0.957	0.953	0.951	0.949
	7	0.856	0.942	0.963	0.953	0.947	0.939	0.934	0.932	0.930
	8	0.817	0.922	0.950	0.937	0.929	0.920	0.914	0.911	0.908
	9	0.778	0.901	0.935	0.919	0.910	0.899	0.891	0.888	0.885
	10	0.740	0.879	0.919	0.901	0.890	0.877	0.868	0.864	0.860
64	2	0.994	0.998	1.000	0.999	0.999	0.998	0.998	0.998	0.998
	3	0.979	0.993	0.998	0.996	0.995	0.994	0.993	0.992	0.992
	4	0.955	0.983	0.994	0.991	0.989	0.986	0.984	0.984	0.983
	5	0.925	0.971	0.987	0.983	0.980	0.976	0.973	0.972	0.971
	6	0.890	0.955	0.980	0.974	0.969	0.963	0.959	0.958	0.956
	7	0.852	0.936	0.970	0.962	0.956	0.949	0.943	0.941	0.939
	8	0.812	0.916	0.959	0.949	0.941	0.932	0.925	0.922	0.920
	9	0.772	0.893	0.946	0.935	0.925	0.914	0.905	0.902	0.899
	10	0.733	0.869	0.932	0.919	0.907	0.894	0.884	0.881	0.877

Notes:

1. Values in this table are conservative when using smaller fastener diameter, smaller fastener spacing, and greater modulus of elasticity.

2. For both the table and the exact method shown below, cross-sectional areas are used for A_m and A_s when the member is loaded parallel to grain; when loaded perpendicular to grain, an equivalent area is used for A_m or A_s, based on the member thickness (measured in a direction parallel to the fastener) multiplied by an equivalent member width. This equivalent width is taken as the distance between the outer rows of fasteners or, where there is only one row of fasteners, as the minimum spacing between rows that would be computed if there were multiple rows of fasteners.

3. C_g = 1.0 for dowel-type fasteners with diameter, D < 0.25 in. Other values for C_g can be determined exactly (for fastener diameters greater than 0.25 in. and less than or equal to 1.0 in.) based on the following method:

   a. Find the bolt or lag screw diameter, D;

   b. Find the so-called load/slip modulus, γ, as follows:

   γ = 180,000($D^{1.5}$) for dowel-type fasteners in wood-wood connections

   γ = 270,000($D^{1.5}$) for dowel-type fasteners in wood-metal connection

   c. Find s, the spacing (center-to-center) between fasteners in a row;

   d. Find E_m and E_s, the moduli of elasticity (psi) for the main and secondary members, respectively;

(continued)

Table A-3.22 continued (Notes)

e. Find A_m and A_s, the cross-sectional areas (in²) for the main member and for the side member (or the sum of the areas of the side members, if there are more than one), respectively;

f. Find $u = 1 + \gamma \dfrac{s}{2} \left[\dfrac{1}{E_m A_m} + \dfrac{1}{E_s A_s} \right]$ and $m = u - \sqrt{u^2 - 1}$

g. Find $R_{EA} = \dfrac{E_s A_s}{E_m A_m}$ or $\dfrac{E_m A_m}{E_s A_s}$, whichever is smaller.

h. Find n = the number of fasteners in a row.

i. Find $C_g = \dfrac{m(1 - m^{2n})}{n[(1 + R_{EA}m^n)(1 + m) - 1 + m^{2n}]} \times \dfrac{1 + R_{EA}}{1 - m}$

4. Applies to dowel-type connectors only.

Table A-3.23: Geometry adjustment factor, C_Δ, for wood connectors (bolts and lag screws)

A. Spacing (in.) between fasteners in a row[a,b,d]		
Loading direction	**Absolute minimum**	**Minimum for full value**
Parallel to grain	3D	4D
Perpendicular to grain	3D	Whatever is required for attached members[c]

Notes for Part A:

a. Required spacing (in.) is a multiple of the fastener diameter, D (in.).

b. A distance below the absolute minimum is, of course, not permitted — in that case, the geometry factor, C_Δ = 0. For any distance equal to or greater than the "minimum for full value," the geometry factor, C_Δ = 1.0. For spacing between the two values shown in the table, the geometry factor, C_Δ, is taken as the actual spacing divided by the minimum spacing for full value. For example, if the actual spacing between fasteners in a row, where the load was parallel to grain, is 3.5D, the geometry factor, C_Δ = 3.5D/(4D) = 0.875. If the spacing in this case equaled the absolute minimum of 3D, the geometry factor, C_Δ = 3D/(4D) = 0.75.

c. For fasteners in a row, where the loading is perpendicular to grain, the minimum spacing necessary to obtain the full value of the geometry factor, i.e., C_Δ = 1.0, is based on meeting the requirements for the member to which it is attached — i.e., the member whose load is parallel to grain — as long as this distance is no less than the absolute minimum value of 3D (assuming that both members in the connection are not oriented so that the load is perpendicular to grain).

d. See general notes below.

(continued)

Table A-3.23 continued (Part *B*)

B. Spacing (in.) between rows of fasteners[a,b,d]		
Loading direction	**Condition**	**Minimum spacing**
Parallel to grain	All conditions	1.5*D*
Perpendicular to grain[c]	$l/D \leq 2$ $2 < l/D < 6$ $l/D \geq 6$	2.5*D* (5*l* + 10*D*) / 8 5*D*

Notes for Part *B*:

a. Required spacing (in.) is a multiple of the fastener diameter, *D* (in.).

b. Where the minimum spacing between rows of fasteners is met, the geometry factor, $C_\Delta = 1.0$. Otherwise, where the spacing is below the minimum allowed, the connection is not permitted — i.e., $C_\Delta = 0$. Interestingly, the maximum spacing between rows of fasteners is also limited in the following way: a 5 in. maximum limit is placed on the spacing between the outer rows of fasteners, in cases where the rows are parallel to the grain of the wood. This reduces the possibility of splitting as the wood member shrinks or expands (due to changes in its moisture content) perpendicular to the grain, while the bolts are fixed in place by a connecting member.

c. The fastener length, *l* (in.), is defined as the length of the fastener that is actually embedded within either the main member (the dowel bearing length — see Appendix Table A-3.27), or the total length within one or more secondary members, whichever is smaller. *D* is the fastener diameter (in.).

d. See general notes below.

C. End distance (in.)[a,b,c]		
Loading direction	**Absolute minimum**	**Minimum for full value**
Parallel to grain: Compression Tension – softwood Tension – hardwood	2*D* 3.5*D* 2.5*D*	4*D* 7*D* 5*D*
Perpendicular to grain	2*D*	4*D*

Notes for Part *C*:

a. Required end distance (in.) is a multiple of the fastener diameter, *D* (in.).

b. A distance below the absolute minimum is, of course, not permitted — in that case, the geometry factor, $C_\Delta = 0$; for any distance equal to or greater than the "minimum for full value," the geometry factor, $C_\Delta = 1.0$. For end distances between the two values shown in the table, the geometry factor, C_Δ, is taken as the actual end distance divided by the minimum distance for full value. For example, if the end distance of a fastener loaded parallel to grain in compression is 3*D*, the geometry factor, $C_\Delta = 3D/(4D) = 0.75$. If the end distance in this case equaled the absolute minimum of 2*D*, the geometry factor, $C_\Delta = 2D/(4D) = 0.50$.

c. See general notes below.

(continued)

Table A-3.23 continued (Part *D*)

D. Edge distance (in.)[a,b,d,e]		
Loading direction	**Condition[1]**	**Minimum Edge Distance**
Parallel to grain	$l/D \leq 6$ $l/D > 6$	1.5D the greater of 1.5D or ½ spacing between rows
Perpendicular to grain[c]	loaded edge unloaded edge	4D 1.5D

Notes for Part *D*:

a. Required edge distance (in.) is a multiple of the fastener diameter, *D* (in.).

b. Where the loading direction is parallel to grain, let *l* be the fastener length that is actually embedded within either the main member (the dowel bearing length — see Appendix Table A-3.19), or the total length within one or more secondary members, whichever is smaller. *D* is the bolt or lag screw diameter.

c. Loads should not be suspended in such a way that fasteners are stressing the wood members perpendicular to grain where such fasteners are inserted below the neutral axis (that is, in the tension region) of a single beam.

d. Where the minimum edge distance is met, the geometry factor, $C_\Delta = 1.0$. Otherwise, the connection is not permitted — i.e., $C_\Delta = 0$.

e. See general notes below.

E. Spacing and end-edge distances for loading parallel and perpendicular to grain	
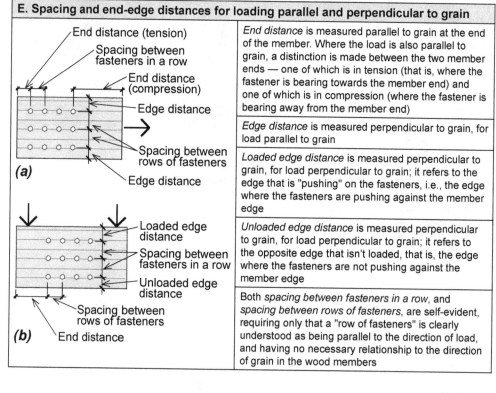	*End distance* is measured parallel to grain at the end of the member. Where the load is also parallel to grain, a distinction is made between the two member ends — one of which is in tension (that is, where the fastener is bearing towards the member end) and one of which is in compression (where the fastener is bearing away from the member end)
	Edge distance is measured perpendicular to grain, for load parallel to grain
	Loaded edge distance is measured perpendicular to grain, for load perpendicular to grain; it refers to the edge that is "pushing" on the fasteners, i.e., the edge where the fasteners are pushing against the member edge
	Unloaded edge distance is measured perpendicular to grain, for load perpendicular to grain; it refers to the opposite edge that isn't loaded, that is, the edge where the fasteners are not pushing against the member edge
	Both *spacing between fasteners in a row*, and *spacing between rows of fasteners*, are self-evident, requiring only that a "row of fasteners" is clearly understood as being parallel to the direction of load, and having no necessary relationship to the direction of grain in the wood members

(continued)

Table A-3.23 continued (Notes)

General notes for Table A-3.23:

1. The geometry factor for any connection is taken as the smallest single value computed for any fastener in the connection, based on any of the criteria listed in Appendix Table A-3.23 parts *A*, *B*, *C*, or *D*, i.e., for both spacing requirements as well as for end and edge distance. All such required spacing and distances are computed as multiples of the fastener diameter, *D*, for all wood fasteners comprising the connection; but only the smallest geometry factor found within the entire connection is applied to the connection design.

2. C_Δ = 1.0 for "end distance" and "spacing between fasteners in a row" when minimum conditions for the full value are met. There are also smaller allowable lengths for these parameters (although subject to an absolute minimum) which, while permitted, reduce the geometry factor to a value less than 1.0.

3. A fastener row refers to a minimum of two fasteners in a line parallel to the direction of the load, whether or not it is parallel or perpendicular to the direction of the grain of wood. On the other hand, end and edge distance are measured parallel and perpendicular, respectively, to the direction of grain, not load, as shown in Appendix Table A-3.23, part *E*.

4. Applies to dowel-type connectors only, and only when the fastener diameter, $D \geq \frac{1}{4}$ in. Otherwise, C_Δ = 1.0.

Table A-3.24: Toe-nail adjustment factor, C_{tn}, for nails[1]

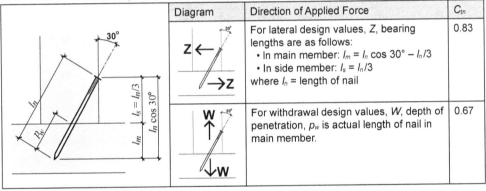

	Diagram	Direction of Applied Force	C_{tn}
	Z← →Z	For lateral design values, *Z*, bearing lengths are as follows: • In main member: $l_m = l_n \cos 30° - l_n/3$ • In side member: $l_s = l_n/3$ where l_n = length of nail	0.83
	W↑ ↓W	For withdrawal design values, *W*, depth of penetration, p_w is actual length of nail in main member.	0.67

Note:

1. Toe-nailing values are based on two assumptions:

   a. That the nail is driven at an angle of approximately 30° to the face of the side member.

   b. That the nail insertion point is ⅓ of the nail length ($l_n/3$) above the end of the side member

Table A-3.25: Temperature factor, C_t, for wood fasteners

Temperature, *T* (° F)	C_t (used dry)	C_t (used wet)
$T \leq 100°$ F	1.0	1.0
$100°$ F $< T \leq 125°$ F	0.8	0.7
$125°$ F $< T \leq 150°$ F	0.7	0.5

Table A-3.26: Lateral design value, Z (lb) for bolts: single-shear connections, with 1½ in. side member thickness, both members same species (or same specific gravity)[1]

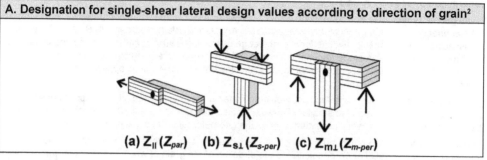

A. Designation for single-shear lateral design values according to direction of grain[2]

(a) $Z_{\parallel}$ (Z_{par})   (b) $Z_{s\perp}$ ($Z_{s\text{-}per}$)   (c) $Z_{m\perp}$ ($Z_{m\text{-}per}$)

B. 1½ in. main member thickness

Species or Species Combination	½ in. diameter Bolts			¾ in. diameter Bolts			1 in. diameter Bolts		
	Z_{par}	$Z_{s\text{-}per}$	$Z_{m\text{-}per}$	Z_{par}	$Z_{s\text{-}per}$	$Z_{m\text{-}per}$	Z_{par}	$Z_{s\text{-}per}$	$Z_{m\text{-}per}$
Douglas Fir-Larch	480	300	300	720	420	420	970	530	530
Douglas Fir-Larch (North)	470	290	290	710	400	400	950	510	510
Douglas Fir-South	440	270	270	670	380	380	890	480	480
Hem-Fir	410	250	250	620	350	350	830	440	440
Hem-Fir (North)	440	270	270	670	380	380	890	480	480
Spruce-Pine-Fir	410	240	240	610	340	340	810	430	430
Spruce-Pine-Fir (South)	350	200	200	520	280	280	700	360	360
Southern Pine	530	330	330	800	460	460	1060	580	580

C. 3½ in. main member thickness

Species or Species Combination	½ in. diameter Bolts			¾ in. diameter Bolts			1 in. diameter Bolts		
	Z_{par}	$Z_{s\text{-}per}$	$Z_{m\text{-}per}$	Z_{par}	$Z_{s\text{-}per}$	$Z_{m\text{-}per}$	Z_{par}	$Z_{s\text{-}per}$	$Z_{m\text{-}per}$
Douglas Fir-Larch	610	370	430	1200	590	610	1830	680	740
Douglas Fir-Larch (North)	610	360	420	1190	560	490	1790	650	710
Douglas Fir-South	580	340	400	1140	520	550	1680	600	660
Hem-Fir	550	320	380	1100	460	500	1570	540	600
Hem-Fir (North)	580	340	400	1140	520	550	1680	600	660
Spruce-Pine-Fir	540	320	370	1080	450	480	1530	530	590
Spruce-Pine-Fir (South)	490	280	300	990	360	400	1320	420	480
Southern Pine	660	400	470	1270	660	690	2010	770	830

(continued)

Table A-3.26 continued (Part *D*)

D. 5½ in. main member thickness									
Species or Species Combination	⅝ in. diameter Bolts			¾ in. diameter Bolts			1 in. diameter Bolts		
	Z_{par}	$Z_{s\text{-}per}$	$Z_{m\text{-}per}$	Z_{par}	$Z_{s\text{-}per}$	$Z_{m\text{-}per}$	Z_{par}	$Z_{s\text{-}per}$	$Z_{m\text{-}per}$
Douglas Fir-Larch	610	370	430	1200	590	790	2050	680	1060
Douglas Fir-Larch (North)	610	360	420	1190	560	780	2030	650	1010
Douglas Fir-South	580	340	400	1140	520	740	1930	600	940
Hem-Fir	550	320	380	1100	460	700	1800	540	860
Hem-Fir (North)	580	340	400	1140	520	740	1930	600	940
Spruce-Pine-Fir	540	320	370	1080	450	690	1760	530	830
Spruce-Pine-Fir (South)	490	280	330	990	360	570	1520	420	680
Southern Pine	660	400	470	1270	660	850	2150	770	1190

Notes:

1. Member thickness is measured parallel to the axis of the fastener.

2. Designations for lateral design values are as illustrated: (a) Z_{par} for both members with direction of grain parallel to load; (b) $Z_{s\text{-}per}$ for side member with grain perpendicular to load and main member with grain parallel to load; and (c) $Z_{m\text{-}per}$ for main member with grain perpendicular to load and side member with grain parallel to load. A fourth possibility, with both members having grain perpendicular to the direction of load, is rarely encountered and not included here. The official designations also shown below the illustrations contain "parallel" and "perpendicular" symbols instead of the abbreviations, "par" and "per" used in these tables and text.

Table A-3.27: Lateral design value, Z (lb) for bolts: double-shear connections, with 1½ in. side member thickness, both members same species (or same specific gravity)[1]

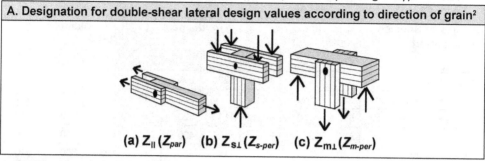

A. Designation for double-shear lateral design values according to direction of grain[2]

(a) $Z_{\parallel}$ (Z_{par})   (b) $Z_{s\perp}$ ($Z_{s\text{-}per}$)   (c) $Z_{m\perp}$ ($Z_{m\text{-}per}$)

B. 1½ in. main member thickness

Species or Species Combination	½ in. diameter Bolts			¾ in. diameter Bolts			1 in. diameter Bolts		
	Z_{par}	$Z_{s\text{-}per}$	$Z_{m\text{-}per}$	Z_{par}	$Z_{s\text{-}per}$	$Z_{m\text{-}per}$	Z_{par}	$Z_{s\text{-}per}$	$Z_{m\text{-}per}$
Douglas Fir-Larch	1050	730	470	1580	1170	590	2100	1350	680
Douglas Fir-Larch (North)	1030	720	460	1550	1130	560	2060	1290	650
Douglas Fir-South	970	680	420	1450	1040	520	1930	1200	600
Hem-Fir	900	650	380	1350	920	460	1800	1080	540
Hem-Fir (North)	970	680	420	1450	1040	520	1930	1200	600
Spruce-Pine-Fir	880	640	370	1320	900	450	1760	1050	530
Spruce-Pine-Fir (South)	760	560	290	1140	720	360	1520	840	420
Southern Pine	1150	800	550	1730	1330	660	2310	1530	770

C. 3½ in. main member thickness

Species or Species Combination	½ in. diameter Bolts			¾ in. diameter Bolts			1 in. diameter Bolts		
	Z_{par}	$Z_{s\text{-}per}$	$Z_{m\text{-}per}$	Z_{par}	$Z_{s\text{-}per}$	$Z_{m\text{-}per}$	Z_{par}	$Z_{s\text{-}per}$	$Z_{m\text{-}per}$
Douglas Fir-Larch	1230	730	860	2400	1170	1370	4090	1350	1580
Douglas Fir-Larch (North)	1210	720	850	2380	1130	1310	4050	1290	1510
Douglas Fir-South	1160	680	810	2280	1040	1210	3860	1200	1400
Hem-Fir	1100	650	760	2190	920	1080	3600	1080	1260
Hem-Fir (North)	1160	680	810	2280	1040	1210	3860	1200	1400
Spruce-Pine-Fir	1080	640	740	2160	900	1050	3530	1050	1230
Spruce-Pine-Fir (South)	980	560	660	1990	720	840	3040	840	980
Southern Pine	1320	800	940	2550	1330	1550	4310	1530	1790

(continued)

Table A-3.27 continued (Part *D*)

D. 5½ in. main member thickness									
Species or Species Combination	⅝ in. diameter Bolts			¾ in. diameter Bolts			1 in. diameter Bolts		
	Z_{par}	$Z_{s\text{-}per}$	$Z_{m\text{-}per}$	Z_{par}	$Z_{s\text{-}per}$	$Z_{m\text{-}per}$	Z_{par}	$Z_{s\text{-}per}$	$Z_{m\text{-}per}$
Douglas Fir-Larch	1760	1040	1190	2400	1170	1580	4090	1350	2480
Douglas Fir-Larch (North)	1740	1030	1170	2380	1130	1550	4050	1290	2370
Douglas Fir-South	1660	940	1110	2280	1040	1480	3860	1200	2200
Hem-Fir	1590	840	1050	2190	920	1400	3600	1080	1980
Hem-Fir (North)	1660	940	1110	2280	1040	1480	3860	1200	2200
Spruce-Pine-Fir	1570	830	1040	2160	900	1380	3530	1050	1930
Spruce-Pine-Fir (South)	1430	660	920	1990	720	1230	3040	840	1540
Southern Pine	1870	1130	1290	2550	1330	1690	4310	1530	2700

Notes:

1. Member thickness is measured parallel to the axis of the fastener.

2. Designations for lateral design values are as illustrated: (a) Z_{par} for both members with direction of grain parallel to load; (b) $Z_{s\text{-}per}$ for side member with grain perpendicular to load and main member with grain parallel to load; and (c) $Z_{m\text{-}per}$ for main member with grain perpendicular to load and side member with grain parallel to load. A fourth possibility, with both members having grain perpendicular to the direction of load, is rarely encountered and not included here. The official designations also shown below the illustrations contain "parallel" and "perpendicular" symbols instead of the abbreviations, "par" and "per" used in these tables and text.

Table A-3.28: Lateral design value, Z (lb) for bolts: double-shear connections, with two ¼ in. A36 steel side plates[1]

A. Designation for double-shear lateral design values according to direction of grain[2]

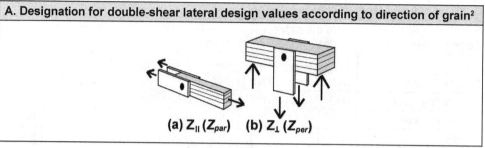

(a) $Z_{||}$ (Z_{par})   **(b) $Z_{\perp}$ (Z_{per})**

B. 1½ in. main member thickness

Species or Species Combination	½ in. diameter Bolts		¾ in. diameter Bolts		1 in. diameter Bolts	
	Z_{par}	Z_{per}	Z_{par}	Z_{per}	Z_{par}	Z_{per}
Douglas Fir-Larch	1050	470	1580	590	2100	680
Douglas Fir-Larch (North)	1030	460	1550	560	2060	650
Douglas Fir-South	970	420	1450	520	1930	600
Hem-Fir	900	380	1350	460	1800	540
Hem-Fir (North)	970	420	1450	520	1930	600
Spruce-Pine-Fir	880	370	1320	450	1760	530
Spruce-Pine-Fir (South)	760	290	1140	360	1520	420
Southern Pine	1150	550	1730	660	2310	770

C. 3½ in. main member thickness

Species or Species Combination	½ in. diameter Bolts		¾ in. diameter Bolts		1 in. diameter Bolts	
	Z_{par}	Z_{per}	Z_{par}	Z_{per}	Z_{par}	Z_{per}
Douglas Fir-Larch	1650	1030	3340	1370	4090	1580
Douglas Fir-Larch (North)	1640	1010	3320	1310	4810	1510
Douglas Fir-South	1590	970	3220	1210	4510	1400
Hem-Fir	1540	890	3120	1080	4200	1260
Hem-Fir (North)	1590	970	3220	1210	4510	1400
Spruce-Pine-Fir	1530	860	3080	1050	4110	1230
Spruce-Pine-Fir (South)	1430	680	2660	840	3540	980
Southern Pine	1720	1100	3480	1550	5380	1790

(continued)

Table A-3.28 continued (Part *D*)

D. 5½ in. main member thickness						
Species or Species Combination	**⅝ in. diameter Bolts**		**¾ in. diameter Bolts**		**1 in. diameter Bolts**	
	Z_{par}	Z_{per}	Z_{par}	Z_{per}	Z_{par}	Z_{per}
Douglas Fir-Larch	2410	1420	3340	1890	5720	2480
Douglas Fir-Larch (North)	2390	1400	3320	1850	5670	2370
Douglas Fir-South	2330	1340	3220	1780	5510	2200
Hem-Fir	2260	1280	3120	1690	5330	1980
Hem-Fir (North)	2330	1340	3220	1780	5510	2200
Spruce-Pine-Fir	2230	1270	3090	1650	5280	1930
Spruce-Pine-Fir (South)	2090	1140	2890	1320	4930	1540
Southern Pine	2510	1510	3480	2000	5960	2810

Notes:

1. Member thickness is measured parallel to the axis of the fastener.

2. Designations for lateral design values are as illustrated: (a) Z_{par} for main member with direction of grain parallel to load; and (b) Z_{per} for main member with grain perpendicular to load. The official designations also shown below the illustrations contain "parallel" and "perpendicular" symbols instead of the abbreviations, "par" and "per" used in these tables and text.

Table A-3.29: Lateral design value, Z (lb) for lag screws: single-shear connections, both members same species (or same specific gravity)[1,2,3,4]

A. Designation for single-shear lateral design values according to direction of grain[2]

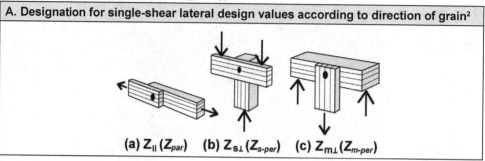

(a) $Z_{\parallel}$ (Z_{par}) (b) $Z_{s\perp}$ ($Z_{s\text{-}per}$) (c) $Z_{m\perp}$ ($Z_{m\text{-}per}$)

B. 1½ in. side member thickness

Species or Species Combination	½ in. diameter Lag Screws			¾ in. diameter Lag Screws			1 in. diameter Lag Screws		
	Z_{par}	$Z_{s\text{-}per}$	$Z_{m\text{-}per}$	Z_{par}	$Z_{s\text{-}per}$	$Z_{m\text{-}per}$	Z_{par}	$Z_{s\text{-}per}$	$Z_{m\text{-}per}$
Douglas Fir-Larch	390	220	270	770	440	510	1290	530	810
Douglas Fir-Larch (North)	390	220	260	760	430	510	1280	500	790
Douglas Fir-South	370	210	250	730	400	480	1230	470	760
Hem-Fir	350	190	240	700	360	450	1180	420	720
Hem-Fir (North)	370	210	250	730	400	480	1230	470	760
Spruce-Pine-Fir	350	190	240	690	350	440	1160	410	710
Spruce-Pine-Fir (South)	310	160	210	620	280	390	1070	330	630
Southern Pine	410	250	290	830	470	560	1360	600	870

C. 3½ in. side member thickness

Species or Species Combination	½ in. diameter Lag Screws			¾ in. diameter Lag Screws			1 in. diameter Lag Screws		
	Z_{par}	$Z_{s\text{-}per}$	$Z_{m\text{-}per}$	Z_{par}	$Z_{s\text{-}per}$	$Z_{m\text{-}per}$	Z_{par}	$Z_{s\text{-}per}$	$Z_{m\text{-}per}$
Douglas Fir-Larch	390	270	270	960	600	610	1740	850	1060
Douglas Fir-Larch (North)	390	260	260	950	580	600	1730	830	1040
Douglas Fir-South	380	250	250	920	550	580	1670	790	1000
Hem-Fir	360	240	240	890	500	550	1610	740	950
Hem-Fir (North)	380	250	250	920	550	580	1670	790	1000
Spruce-Pine-Fir	360	240	240	880	490	540	1600	720	940
Spruce-Pine-Fir (South)	340	220	220	820	420	490	1450	630	850
Southern Pine	410	290	290	1010	650	650	1830	930	1120

Notes:

1. Member thickness is measured parallel to the axis of the fastener.

2. Designations for lateral design values are as illustrated: (a) Z_{par} for both members with direction of grain parallel to load; (b) $Z_{s\text{-}per}$ for side member with grain perpendicular to load and main member with grain parallel to load; and (c) $Z_{m\text{-}per}$ for main member with grain perpendicular to load and side member with grain parallel to load. A fourth possibility, with both members having grain perpendicular to the direction of load, is rarely encountered and not included here. The official designations also shown below the illustrations contain "parallel" and "perpendicular" symbols instead of the abbreviations, "par" and "per" used in these tables and text.

(continued)

Table A-3.29 continued (Notes)

3. Tabular values are based on full value minimum penetration, p, into main member. For penetration into main member between $4D$ and $8D$, multiply tabular values by $p/8D$.

4. The reduced body diameter, D_r, is used in yield limit calculations for these lag screw lateral design values, except in the calculation of the dowel bearing strength for loading perpendicular to grain, $F_{e\text{-}perp}$, in which case the nominal diameter, D, is used.

Table A-3.30: Lateral design value, Z (lb) for common nails: single-shear connections, both members same species (or same specific gravity)[1,2,4]

A. ¾ in. side member thickness

Species or Species Combination	Nail Size (pennyweight)								
	6d	8d	10d	12d	16d	20d	30d	40d	50d
Douglas Fir-Larch	72	90	105	105	121	138	147	158	162
Douglas Fir-Larch (North)	71	87	102	102	117	134	143	154	158
Douglas Fir-South	65	80	94	94	108	125	133	144	147
Hem-Fir	58	73	85	85	99	114	122	132	136
Hem-Fir (North)	65	80	94	94	108	125	133	144	147
Spruce-Pine-Fir	57	70	83	83	96	111	119	129	132
Spruce-Pine-Fir (South)	46	58	69	69	80	93	101	110	113
Southern Pine	79	104	121	121	138	157	166	178	182

B. 1½ in. side member thickness

Species or Species Combination	Nail Size (pennyweight)								
	6d	8d	10d	12d	16d	20d	30d	40d	50d
Douglas Fir-Larch	—	[3]97	118	118	141	170	186	205	211
Douglas Fir-Larch (North)	—	[3]95	115	115	138	166	182	201	206
Douglas Fir-South	—	[3]90	109	109	131	157	172	190	196
Hem-Fir	—	[3]84	102	102	122	147	161	178	181
Hem-Fir (North)	—	[3]90	109	109	131	157	172	190	196
Spruce-Pine-Fir	—	[3]82	100	100	120	144	158	172	175
Spruce-Pine-Fir (South)	—	[3]72	87	87	104	126	131	138	141
Southern Pine	—	[3]106	128	128	154	185	203	224	230

Notes:

1. Member thickness is measured parallel to the axis of the fastener.

2. Where values are not indicated, nail penetration into main member does not satisfy minimum requirements. Otherwise, except as indicated in Note 3, it is assumed that the minimum penetration of the nail into the main member is equal to $10D$ (see Appendix Table A-3.19 for notes on penetration).

3. These values must be reduced according to Note 3 in Appendix Table A-3.19, since the penetration falls below the minimum for full value. Nail dimensions can be found in Appendix Table A-3.18.

4. In all cases where yield limit equations are used to compute lateral design values for nails, the dowel bearing length in the main member, l_m, is taken as the penetration minus half the length of the tapered tip. Because these tabular lateral design values do not consider this reduced dowel bearing length, they may be slightly non-conservative in some cases (specifically, they may differ in cases where the governing yield limit equation includes the dowel bearing length parameter).

Table A-3.31: Method for determining lateral design value, Z, based on yield limit equations

For wood-wood or wood-metal connections that do not correspond to the parameters listed in the various Appendix tables, lateral design values may be determined using yield limit equations.

1. Using Appendix Table A-3.11 (specific gravity for wood members), find the specific gravity (G) for wood main and side member(s).
2. Find fastener diameter: use diameter, D, for bolts and nails (unthreaded shanks in contact with members) and reduced body diameter, D_r, for lag screws (in either case, designated as "D" in what follows);
3. Find dowel bearing strength, F_e, for main (F_{em}) and side (F_{es}) member(s), in psi units, using the appropriate specific gravity value for each wood member:
   a. For D > 0.25 in. and wood members loaded parallel to grain, $F_e = 11,200G$.

   b. For D > 0.25 in. and wood members loaded perpendicular to grain, $F_e = \dfrac{6100G^{1.45}}{\sqrt{D}}$.

   c. For D ≤ 0.25 in. and wood members, $F_e = 16,600G^{1.84}$.
   d. For A36 steel, $F_e = 87,000$.
   e. For A653 GR33 steel (used in certain die-formed galvanized connector plates), $F_e = 61,850$.
4. Find the dowel bending yield strength, F_{yb}, in psi units:
   a. For bolts, use $F_{yb} = 45,000$.
   b. For lag screws with D = ¼ in., use $F_{yb} = 70,000$; with D = 5/16 in., use $F_{yb} = 60,000$; for D ≥ ⅜ in., use $F_{yb} = 45,000$.
   c. For nails with 0.099 in. ≤ D ≤ 0.142 in., use $F_{yb} = 100,000$; with 0.142 in. < D ≤ 0.177 in., use $F_{yb} = 90,000$; with 0.177 in. < D ≤ 0.236 in., use $F_{yb} = 80,000$; with 0.236 in. < D ≤ 0.273 in., use $F_{yb} = 70,000$;
5. Find the main member and side member dowel bearing lengths, l_m and l_s, in inches (see Appendix Table A-3.19 for guidance). Even where there are two side members, the side member bearing length only includes the bearing length in a single side member.

6. Compute the terms $R_e = \dfrac{F_{em}}{F_{es}}$; and $R_t = \dfrac{l_m}{l_s}$.

7. Compute the "reduction term," R_d, which varies according to yield mode and fastener diameter, as follows:
   a. For D ≤ 0.17 in. (i.e., for nails 16d or smaller), $R_d = 2.2$.
   b. For 0.17 in. < D < 0.25 in. (i.e., for most nails larger than 16d), $R_d = 10D + 0.5$.
   c. For 0.25 in. ≤ D ≤ 1 in. (i.e., for most bolts and lag screws), $R_d = 4K_\theta$ (for yield modes I_m and I_s); $R_d = 3.6K_\theta$ (for yield mode II); and $R_d = 3.2K_\theta$ (for yield modes III_m, III_s, and IV). In these equations, $K_\theta = 1 + 0.25(\theta/90)$, where θ = the maximum angle (degrees) between the load and the direction of grain for either member: for example, where the load is parallel to the direction of grain in all members, θ = 0 degrees, and $K_{\theta w} = 1.0$; where one or more member's grain is perpendicular to the load, θ = 90°, and $K_\theta = 1.25$. For angles other than 0 or 90°, θ is always measured in such a way that it falls between 0 and 90 (i.e., instead of using θ = 120°, or θ = –45°, use θ = 60° or θ = 45°, respectively).
8. Compute the coefficients k_1, k_2, and k_3, as follows:

   a. $k_1 = \dfrac{\sqrt{R_e + 2R_e^2(1 + R_t + R_t^2) + R_t^2 R_e^3} - R_e(1 + R_t)}{1 + R_e}$

   b. $k_2 = -1 + \sqrt{2(1 + R_e) + \dfrac{2F_{yb}(1 + 2R_e)D^2}{3F_{em}l_m^2}}$

   c. $k_3 = -1 + \sqrt{\dfrac{2(1 + R_e)}{R_e} + \dfrac{2F_{yb}(2 + R_e)D^2}{3F_{em}l_s^2}}$

(continued)

Table A-3.31 continued

9. Compute the lateral design value, Z, for all applicable yield modes (i.e., for all six modes in single shear, and for all modes except II and III$_m$ in double shear), and select the smallest value:

a. For Yield Mode I$_m$, $Z = \dfrac{Dl_m F_{em}}{R_d}$

b. For Yield Mode I$_s$, $Z = \dfrac{Dl_s F_{es}}{R_d}$ for single shear and $Z = \dfrac{2Dl_s F_{es}}{R_d}$ for double shear.

c. For Yield Mode II (single shear only), $Z = \dfrac{k_1 Dl_s F_{es}}{R_d}$

d. For Yield Mode III$_m$ (single shear only), $Z = \dfrac{k_2 Dl_m F_{em}}{(1 + 2R_e)R_d}$

e. For Yield Mode III$_s$, $Z = \dfrac{k_3 Dl_s F_{em}}{(2 + R_e)R_d}$ for single shear and $Z = \dfrac{2k_3 Dl_s F_{em}}{(2 + R_e)R_d}$ for double shear.

f. For Yield Mode IV, $Z = \dfrac{D^2}{R_d}\sqrt{\dfrac{2F_{em}F_{yb}}{3(1 + R_e)}}$ for single shear and $Z = \dfrac{2D^2}{R_d}\sqrt{\dfrac{2F_{em}F_{yb}}{3(1 + R_e)}}$ for double shear.

Table A-3.32: Withdrawal design value, W, per inch of penetration (lb) for lag screws[1,2]

Species or Species Combination	Unthreaded shank diameter, D (in.)								
	1/4	5/16	3/8	7/16	1/2	5/8	3/4	7/8	1
Douglas Fir-Larch	225	266	305	342	378	447	513	576	636
Douglas Fir-Larch (North)	218	258	296	332	367	434	498	559	617
Douglas Fir-South	199	235	269	302	334	395	453	508	562
Hem-Fir	179	212	243	273	302	357	409	459	508
Hem-Fir (North)	199	235	269	302	334	395	453	508	562
Spruce-Pine-Fir	173	205	235	264	291	344	395	443	490
Spruce-Pine-Fir (South)	137	163	186	209	231	273	313	352	389
Southern Pine	260	307	352	395	437	516	592	664	734

Notes:

1. Penetration length for lag screws excludes tapered tip; see Appendix Table A-3.17 for dimensions, and Appendix Table A-3.19 for notes on penetration.

2. Withdrawal design values assume penetration into side grain of wood member, and must be reduced by 75% when inserted into end grain.

Table A-3.33: Withdrawal design value, *W*, per inch of penetration (lb) for nails[1,2]

Species or Species Combination	Nail size (pennyweight)								
	6d	8d	10d	12d	16d	20d	30d	40d	50d
Douglas Fir-Larch	28	32	36	36	40	47	50	55	60
Douglas Fir-Larch (North)	26	30	34	34	38	45	48	52	57
Douglas Fir-South	22	26	29	29	32	38	41	45	48
Hem-Fir	19	22	25	25	27	32	35	38	41
Hem-Fir (North)	22	26	29	29	32	38	41	45	48
Spruce-Pine-Fir	18	21	23	23	26	30	33	35	38
Spruce-Pine-Fir (South)	12	14	16	16	17	21	22	24	26
Southern Pine	35	41	46	46	50	59	64	70	76

Notes:

1. Penetration length for nails includes tapered tip; see Appendix Table A-3.18 for dimensions, and Appendix Table A-3.19 for notes on penetration.

2. Withdrawal design values assume penetration into side grain of wood member. Nails subject to withdrawal are not permitted to be inserted into end grain of wood member.

CHAPTER 4

Steel

Steel is one of several products derived from iron ore, traditionally made in a blast furnace by combining the iron ore with carbon (originally in the form of charcoal, then refined coal or *coke*), which acts as a "reducing agent" by drawing off oxygen from the iron oxides of the ore; and limestone, which removes impurities by forming a slag of lighter density which can be scraped off the top as the ingredients are heated to a molten mix.

The product of such a process is *pig iron* which contains quite a large percentage of carbon, and can be reheated and formed directly into *cast iron*. But cast iron, while strong in compression, is hard and brittle, especially in tension, and therefore not suitable for use as a modern structural material. *Wrought iron* is made by driving virtually all the carbon from the iron mix, which results in a material that is more ductile than cast iron, and can be safely stressed in tension. However, it is softer, more malleable, and less strong, making it also less suitable for structural use, especially when an alternative (*mild carbon steel*) became available at or about the beginning of the twentieth century which combined some of the hardness and compressive strength of cast iron with the ductility and tensile strength of wrought iron. While all three of these materials — cast iron, wrought iron, and steel — were still in use in 1900, mild carbon steel soon became the de facto standard and is now the only iron-based (*ferrous*) structural material in use (the other two remain in use primarily as ornamental materials and railings, or as pipes in the case of cast iron). A summary of the three iron-based (ferrous) metals follows:

1. Wrought iron contains 0.05-0.1% carbon. It is soft, malleable, and resists corrosion.
2. Plain carbon steel contains less than 2% carbon (while mild carbon steel contains less than 0.3% carbon); it is strong, stiff, and ductile in both compression and tension.
3. Cast iron contains more than 1.71% carbon. It is hard, brittle, strong in compression, but weak in tension. It is used in pipes and for ornamental metal applications.

Note that carbon is the most important ingredient in terms of the structural properties that result. Alloys of steel can be made by adding other ingredients into the mix; two examples are weathering steel (*Cor-ten* is one proprietary brand name) and stainless steel (which contains chromium and/or nickel).

In the U.S., wide-flange (W) shapes are no longer commonly manufactured from iron ore in a "basic oxygen" process, but are made almost entirely from recycled cars in an "electric arc" furnace, a continuous casting process that takes approximately three hours from car to W-shape.

MATERIAL PROPERTIES

Steel is subject to corrosion if not protected, and loss of strength and stiffness at high temperatures if not fireproofed (except that, as noted above, weathering and stainless steels resist corrosion). While these are extremely important material properties, the structural design of steel elements presupposes that these issues have been addressed within the architectural design process.

Stress-strain

Steel has a distinct elastic region in which stresses are proportional to strains, and a plastic region that begins with the yielding of the material and continues until a so-called strain-hardening region is reached (Figure 4.1). The yield

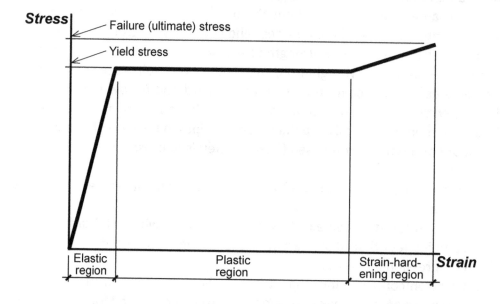

Figure 4.1: Schematic representation of a stress-strain curve for steel showing elastic, plastic, and strain hardening regions

stress defines the limit of elastic behavior, and can be taken as 36 ksi for ASTM A36, or 50 ksi for what is becoming the de facto standard, at least for wide-flange (W) shapes: ASTM A992.

Within the plastic range, yielded material strains considerably under constant stress (the yield stress), but does not rupture. In fact, rupture only occurs at the end of the strain-hardening region, at an ultimate or failure stress (strength) much higher than the yield stress. Bending cold-formed steel to create structural shapes out of flat sheet steel stretches the material at the outer edges of these bends beyond both the elastic and plastic regions, and into the strain-hardening region. This actually increases the strength of these structural elements, even though the direction of stretching is perpendicular to the longitudinal axis of the element.

High-strength steels (with yield stresses up to 100 ksi) are available, but their utility is limited in the following two ways: First, the modulus of elasticity of steel does not increase as strength increases, but is virtually the same for all steel (29,000 ksi). Reducing the size of structural elements because they are stronger makes it more likely that problems with serviceability (i.e., deflections and vibrations) will surface since these effects are related, not to strength, but to the modulus of elasticity.

Second, increased strength is correlated with decreased ductility, and a greater susceptibility to fatigue failure. Therefore, where dynamic and cyclic loading is expected, high-strength steel is not recommended; where dead load dominates, and the load history of the structural element is expected to be relatively stable, high-strength steel may be appropriate, as long as the first criteria relating to stiffness (modulus of elasticity) is met. The most commonly used steels, along with their yield and ultimate stresses, are listed in Appendix Table A-4.1. Alowable stresses and available strengths are found in Appendix Table A-4.2.

Residual stress

Hot-rolled steel shapes contain residual stresses even before they are loaded. These are caused by the uneven cooling of the shapes after they are rolled at temperatures of about 2000° F. The exposed flanges and webs cool and contract sooner than the web-flange intersections; the contraction of these junction points is then inhibited by the adjacent areas which have already cooled, so they are forced into tension as they simultaneously compress the areas that cooled first. The typical pattern of residual stresses within a wide-flange cross section is shown in Figure 4.2. Residual stresses have an impact on the inelastic buckling of steel columns, since partial yielding of the cross section occurs at a lower compressive stress than would be the case if the residual compressive stresses "locked" into the column were not present.

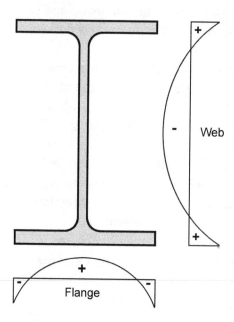

Figure 4.2: Residual stresses in steel rolled section, with "+" indicating tension and "-" indicating compression

Related products

Aside from standard rolled structural shapes, several other structural applications of steel should be noted:

Cold-formed steel is made by bending steel sheet (typically with 90° bends) into various cross-sectional shapes, used primarily as studs (closely-spaced vertical compression elements), joists (closely-spaced beams), or elements comprising light-weight trusses. Manufacturers provide tables for these products containing section properties and allowable loads, or stresses.

Hollow structural sections (HSS) are closed tubular steel shapes that can be formed and welded in various ways from flat sheets or plates; these shapes can be circular, square, or rectangular. Circular *pipes* are similar to round HSS, except that they are fabricated with a different grade of steel.

Open-web steel joists (OWSJ) are lightweight prefabricated trusses made from steel angles and rods. Spans of up to 144 feet are possible with "deep longspan" or DLH-series joists; regular "longspan" (LH-series) joists span up to 96 feet, while ordinary H-series joists span up to 60 feet. These products are relatively flexible, subject to vibration, and are most often used to support roof structures in large one-story commercial or industrial buildings.

Space-frame (actually "space-truss") systems consist of linear elements and connecting nodes based on various geometries, most commonly tetrahedral or pyramid shaped.

Corrugated steel decks constitute the floor and roof system for almost all steel-framed buildings. For floor systems, they are often designed compositely with concrete fill, effectively creating a reinforced concrete floor system in which the reinforcement (and formwork) consists of the steel deck itself.

Cables and rods can be used as structural elements where the only expected stresses are tension, or where the element is prestressed into tension: the flexibility of these elements prevents them from sustaining any compressive or bending stresses. Applications include elements within trusses, bridges, and membrane structures.

SECTION PROPERTIES

Wide-flange shapes are commonly used for both beams and columns within steel-framed structures. They are designated by a capital W, followed by the cross section's nominal depth (in.) and weight per linear foot (lb). For example, a W14 × 38 has a nominal depth of 14 in. and weighs 38 lb per linear foot (see Figure 4.3). Unlike standard "I-beam" (S) sections, whose flange surfaces

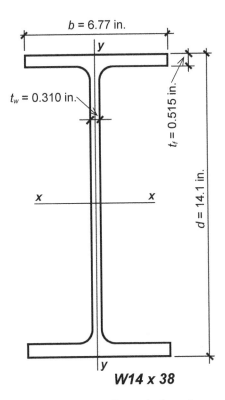

Figure 4.3: Cross-section of a typical steel wide-flange (W) section

are not parallel — the inner surface slopes about 16% relative to the outer surface — wide-flange (W) sections have parallel flange surfaces, making it somewhat easier to make connections to other structural elements. Wide-flange sections are manufactured in groups with a common set of inner rollers. Within each of these groups, the dimensions and properties are varied by increasing the overall depth of the section (thereby increasing the flange thickness) and letting the web thickness increase as well. For this reason, actual depths may differ considerably from the nominal depths given to each group of shapes. On the other hand, traditional standard I-beam (S) sections are still manufactured with fixed outer rollers and variable inner rollers, so that actual depths are fixed for each group, and can therefore be configured with exact integer dimensions ranging from 3 to 24 inches (whereas wide-flange *nominal* depths range from 4 to 44 inches). A schematic illustration of roller positions for wide-flange shapes within a group is shown in Figure 4.4.

Dimensions of commonly available W shapes are listed in Appendix Table A-4.3. Other shapes, such as channels (C or MC), angles (L), pipes, and hollow structural sections (HSS) also have many structural applications; standard dimensions for some of these shapes are listed in Appendix Tables A-4.4 through A-4.8. The designation for channels (C and MC) follows that for wide-flange sections, with the nominal depth in inches followed by the weight in pounds per linear foot. For angles, three numbers are given after the symbol, L: the first two are the overall lengths of the two legs; the third is the leg thickness (always the same for both legs). Hollow structural sections (HSS) are designated with either two or three numbers corresponding to the diameter and nominal thickness (for round sections), or the two outside dimensions and nominal thickness (for rectangular sections). Steel pipe, similar in shape to round HSS, is designated by nominal outside diameter in three "weights": standard, extra strong, and double-extra strong.

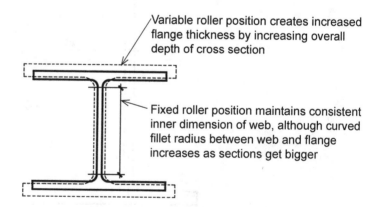

Variable roller position creates increased flange thickness by increasing overall depth of cross section

Fixed roller position maintains consistent inner dimension of web, although curved fillet radius between web and flange increases as sections get bigger

Figure 4.4: Schematic illustration of a wide-flange cross section (solid line) and another member of its "family" or group (dotted line) manufactured with the same set of rollers

Design Approaches

Earlier versions of the *Steel Construction Manual* published by the American Institute of Steel Construction (AISC) contained design procedures based on the allowable stress design (ASD) method. In 1986, the first edition of a "Load & Resistance Factor Design" (LRFD) *Steel Construction Manual* became available as an alternative to the traditional ASD Manual. More recent AISC Manuals have discarded the Allowable Stress Design concept in favor of an Allowable *Strength* Design method (still ASD); in both cases (allowable stress and allowable strength), determination of loads and load combinations is the same (see Appendix Table A-2.7 Part *B*). What changes are the limit states and factors of safety: whereas the allowable stress method defines the limit state as the moment when any part of the cross section yields, the newer allowable strength method defines the limit state as the point where all *available* strength is exhausted — i.e., the moment when the *entire* cross section has yielded.

Of course, the LRFD method is still published as an alternative to ASD, but one that will not be used in this text. In fact, the two methods (ASD and LRFD) yield identical results for structural elements for which the magnitude of live loads is exactly three times that of dead loads — safety factors for ASD and LRDF have been calibrated to achieve that result. However, because the LRFD safety factor for live load is greater than that for dead load, structural elements designed with the ASD method and with a live-to-dead load ratio greater than three will be slightly conservative compared with the same elements designed with LRDF; conversely, elements designed with the ASD method and with a live-to-dead load ratio less than three will end up smaller (and therefore slightly less strong) than elements designed with LRFD. For most structures, these differences are small and will not compromise the safety of buildings designed using either method.

Construction Systems

Steel-framed structures often consist of columns, girders, beams, and corrugated steel decks (with concrete fill when used for floors and for some roofs), stabilized with some sort of lateral-force-resisting system. In fact, it is common for all major steel elements in a building structure to consist of a single cross-sectional type: the wide-flange (W) shape. These shapes are remarkably versatile and efficient, especially for bending (beams), but also for columns. Such "open" cross sections facilitate making connections with clip angles, bolts, and welds. "Closed" sections, such as round or rectangular hollow structural sections (HSS), cannot be as easily bolted together, since their insides are inaccessible — how would you tighten the nut on a bolt, or even get the nut inside such a cross section? On the other hand, it is fairly easy to overcome this problem by welding small plates to the closed sections in the steel fabrication shop; these plates, being open, can be easily bolted to adjacent elements. Alternatively, but with somewhat more difficulty and expense, closed structural elements can be directly welded to each other in the field, as can open cross sections.

There really are no limits to the ways in which steel can be configured as structure; numerous examples can be found that illustrate creative and unusual applications utilizing assemblages of cables, rods, and plates, along with standard rolled sections and even one-of-a-kind steel castings (while not particularly common, steel can be cast as well as hot-rolled). Sections can be bent and curved; plates can be cut; and all sorts of composite elements can be configured by welding or bolting the various pieces together. Yet, in spite of this potential, most steel-framed buildings are far more conventional in their choices of elements and connections. Even buildings whose "architectural" qualities are highly idiosyncratic may hide rather conventional skeletal structures beneath their expressive outer forms; the Statue of Liberty, while not exactly a "building," nevertheless illustrates this strategy (Figure 4.5*a*). On the other hand, as demonstrated in the Guggenheim Museum Bilbao, it is possible to twist and distort the structure itself so that it directly follows the contours of the architectural form (Figure 4.5*b*).

Most steel-framed buildings are neither defined by complex doubly curved forms nor supported by inventive or unusual structural systems. Instead, they most often have "skeletal" steel frames consisting of wide-flange columns, girders, and beams. This hierarchical pattern of steel structural elements really hasn't changed much since the late nineteenth century (Figure 4.6), except that spans have increased as steel as gotten stronger, floor systems no longer rely on short masonry arches spanning between closely-spaced beams to provide fire protection, and riveted connections have been superseded by bolts and welds. Columns are still typically aligned on an orthogonal grid with girders spanning between columns in one direction only and beams spanning between girders (but with some beams aligning with — and therefore supported by — the columns) approximately 10 feet apart, more or less. This spacing between beams, which is actually quite variable, corresponds to the allowable span of corrugated steel decks (often designed to act compositely with concrete fill, in which case they really behave more like reinforced concrete slabs than steel decks).

Span tables are provided by steel deck manufacturers and are easily found online. Variables in these span tables include the gauge (thickness) of the sheet steel used to fabricate the corrugated deck, the centerline spacing of

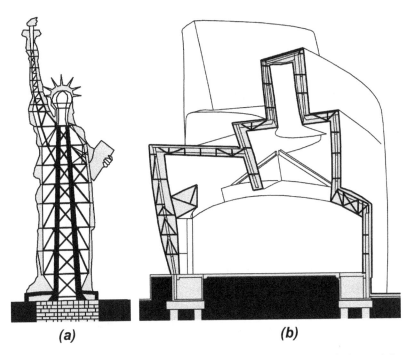

(a) *(b)*

Figure 4.5: Alexandre-Gustave Eiffel's structural design for the Statue of Liberty (*a*), completed in 1883, consists of a wrought iron skeletal framework in stark contrast to the more famous and sculptural copper skin, designed by Frédéric-Auguste Bartholdi, that it supports; the Chicago office of Skidmore Owings & Merrill's structural design for the Guggenheim Museum Bilbao (*b*), designed by Frank Gehry, consists of a complex and idiosyncratic steel framework that closely follows the doubly-curved surface of the titanium skin, leaving the interior spaces largely free of conventional columns and beams.

Figure 4.6: The Fair Store in Chicago, designed by Jenney & Mundie in 1892, has one of the first all-steel skeletal frames (prior "iron" buildings often employed combinations of cast iron columns and wrought iron beams), and illustrates the hierarchical pattern of column-girder-beam that remains typical for modern steel-framed buildings.

beams between which the deck is spanning, the thickness of the deck (or the deck "type"), the total thickness of the composite deck (including the concrete fill), and the weight of the concrete (normalweight concrete is stronger than lightweight concrete). Concrete fill is always used in corrugated deck *floor* systems, at a minimum to provide a horizontal surface to support human occupation directly, or to support a so-called finish floor — carpet, tile, wood, etc. — but often also to provide the compressive resistance which, together with the steel deck acting in tension composite with the concrete, comprises the structural spanning element between beams. Such fill is often omitted in *roof* systems, since loads acting on the roof may be smaller, and rigid insulation, placed directly over the corrugated steel deck, can be used as the necessary horizontal substrate for various single-ply roofing systems.

In plan, the typical pattern of columns, girders, and beams appears as shown in Figure 4.7, with the distance between columns often in the range of 30–40 ft, or even more (the spacing of such columns in late 19th-century or early 20th-century buildings is typically closer to 15 ft). At the edge, or spandrel, girder, some sort of curtain wall system is "hung" from the steel frame, and various mechanical/electrical/plumbing systems are inserted between the bottom of the floor structure and the top of a suspended ceiling (unless some or all of these systems are placed *above* the floor structure, under a raised access floor system). The connection of enclosure system to structure, along with other elements typically found in this type of steel-framed construction, is represented schematically in Figure 4.8. In order that the top flanges of the

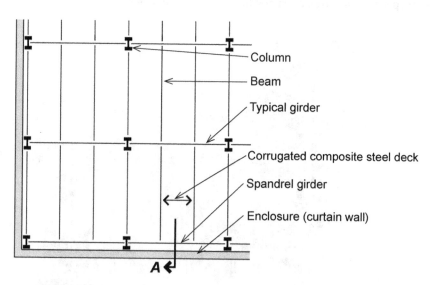

Figure 4.7: Typical framing plan for steel-framed building consisting of a grid of columns with girders spanning between columns in one direction, beams spanning between girders in the perpendicular direction, and a composite corrugated deck (steel with concrete fill) spanning between beams, as shown; the section through the spandrel girder (marked *A*) is illustrated in Figure 4.8.

beams and girders align (so that the corrugated steel deck can be placed on a consistently level grid of structural elements), the ends of beams framing into girders are *coped*, or cut. In this way, as shown in Figure 4.8, the beam's web can be fastened to the girder's web without having the beam's top flange collide with the top flange of the girder.

Other strategies for attaching enclosure systems to steel framing systems are represented in Figure 4.9. From left to right, the strategies show (*a*) vertical

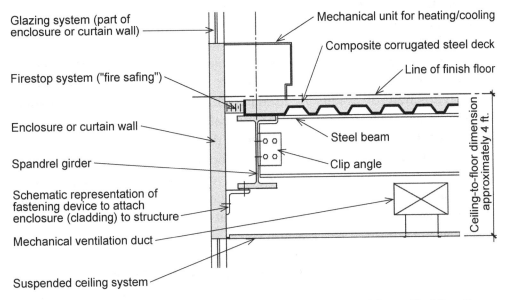

Glazing system (part of enclosure or curtain wall)

Mechanical unit for heating/cooling

Composite corrugated steel deck

Line of finish floor

Firestop system ("fire safing")

Enclosure or curtain wall

Steel beam

Spandrel girder

Clip angle

Schematic representation of fastening device to attach enclosure (cladding) to structure

Mechanical ventilation duct

Suspended ceiling system

Ceiling-to-floor dimension, approximately 4 ft.

Figure 4.8: Schematic section through spandrel (edge) girder in steel-framed building; the mechanical unit at the building perimeter is increasingly omitted as glazing systems become more efficient, thereby reducing heat loss or heat gain through the curtain wall

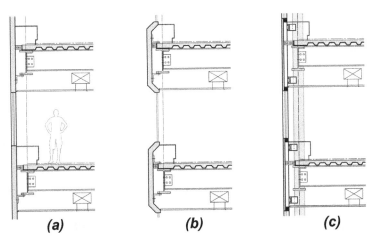

(a)   *(b)*   *(c)*

Figure 4.9: Schematic sections showing three strategies for attaching enclosure systems to steel structural framing using (*a*) vertical elements spanning from floor to floor, (*b*) two points of support at each floor, leaving a structure-free space for glazing, and (*c*) trusses supporting cladding panels, fabricated off-site, spanning horizontally from column to column.

supports for the enclosure system spanning from floor to floor, (b) enclosure system elements supported entirely from a single floor, and (c) truss-support-ed enclosure systems spanning horizontally from column to column — the black squares in this last image represent the top and bottom chords of the trusses. Of the three systems, the first is commonly associated with aluminum and glass curtain walls but can also be adapted to various other systems (e.g., metal panels, precast panels, EIFS, stone veneer, brick veneer with steel stud support, etc.); the second can be used with precast concrete or other clad-ding panels where a continuous band of horizontal glazing is desired, and the third — less commonly encountered than the other strategies — can be used where off-site fabrication of large enclosure panels is desired.

Columns in multi-story steel-framed buildings must be spliced together from smaller lengths. In general, the largest lengths compatible with trans-port and erection constraints are used in order to minimize the work needed on-site to make such connections. This typically results in two- or three-story column lengths that are connected above the finish floor levels, as shown in Figure 4.10a. Small inefficiencies come about from this strategy, since the upper part of a typical two- or three-story section is stronger than it would otherwise need to be (its strength being governed by the heavier loads sup-ported on the lower part of the section), but such inefficiencies are justified by savings in fabrication and erection costs. Steel cap and base plates may or may not be used where steel column sections are joined together; the sim-plest connections omit such plates in favor of "filler" or "packing" plates that account for misalignment of flange and web surfaces (where adjacent col-umns are not the same size) so that *splice plates* can tie the separate ele-ments together (Figure 4.10b).

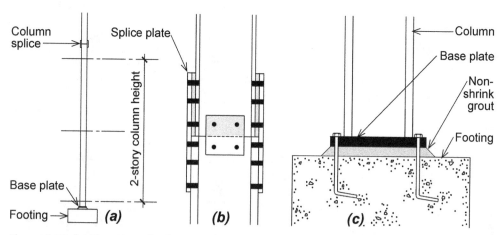

Figure 4.10: (a) Elevation of column in multi-story building spliced at 2-story increments; (b) detail at column splice, with gray tones representing locations of filler, or packing, plates behind splice plates; and (c) detail at column base plate with non-shrink grout filling space between base plate and footing subsequent to alignment of column.

Where columns meet the foundation, and therefore must be connected to the building's reinforced concrete substructure, base plates are always used. These plates, which are typically shop-welded or bolted to the bottom of the *lowest* steel columns, do not actually touch the top surface of the concrete substructure, but are designed to be "suspended" about an inch or less above the top surface of the concrete. Such tolerances are always required, since as-built conditions of both steel and concrete systems cannot be assumed to have the precision of, for example, factory-made components like windows or doors. The vertical alignment of steel columns is then carefully adjusted in the field, using shims or leveling bolts under the base plate, and the space betweeen base plate and footing is filled with *non-shrink grout* so that compressive loads may be transfered from the column to the foundation (Figure 4.10c). Threaded rods, already positioned in the concrete substructure so that they align with bolt holes in the column base plate, are designed to prevent both lateral and vertical movement of the column when *nuts* are screwed onto the rods and tightened against the top of the base plates.

TENSION ELEMENTS

Unlike tension elements designed in timber, two modes of failure are considered when designing tension members in steel. First, the element might become functionally useless if yielding occurs across its gross area, at the yield stress, F_y. Since internal tensile forces are generally uniform throughout the entire length of the element, yielding would result in extremely large deformations. On the other hand, if yielding commenced on the net area (where bolt holes reduce the gross area), the part of the element subjected to yield strains would be limited to the local area around the bolts, and excessive deformations would not occur. However, a second mode of failure might occur at these bolt holes: rupture of the element could occur if, after yielding, the stresses across the net area reached the ultimate stress, F_u. As in wood design, typical bolt hole diameters are ¹⁄₁₆ in. larger than the actual bolt diameter. However, because a small amount of material surrounding the bolt hole is damaged as the hole is punched, an additional ¹⁄₁₆ in. is added to the hole diameter for the purpose of calculating net area, resulting in a bolt hole diameter taken as ⅛ in. larger than the nominal bolt diameter for steel elements.

Another difference in the design of wood and steel tension elements occurs because nonrectangular cross sections are often used in steel. If connections are made through only certain parts of the cross section, as illustrated in Figure 4.11, the net area in the vicinity of the connection will be effectively reduced, depending on the geometry of the elements being joined, and the number of bolts being used. This *effective* net area, A_e, is obtained by multiplying the net area, A_n, by a coefficient, U, defined in Appendix Table A-4.9.

Where all parts (i.e., flanges, webs, etc.) of a cross section are connected, and the so-called *shear lag* effect described above cannot occur, the coefficient U is taken as 1.0, and the effective net area equals the net area, just as in timber design. For short connection fittings like splice plates and gusset plates, U is also taken as 1.0, but $A_e = A_n$ cannot exceed 0.85 times the gross area. These short connecting elements may have an effective width less than their actual width to account for the shear lag effect, based on what is known as the "Whitmore section," shown in Figure 4.12. For a length, L, of the fastener group measured in the direction of load, and a distance, W, between the outer rows of bolts or welds, the effective width is computed by extending a 30° line out from both sides of the fastener group; it can be seen that the effective width, l_w, is equal to $2L\tan 30° + W$.

Finally, the lengths of tension members, other than rods and cables, are limited to a slenderness ratio — defined as the ratio of effective length to least radius of gyration — of 300, to prevent excessive vibrations and protect against damage during transportation and erection. The radius of gyration, a property of the cross section, is equal to $\sqrt{I/A}$, where I is the moment of inertia and A is the cross-sectional area of the element.

From the preceeding discussion, it can be seen that two values for available strength, or allowable stress, in tension need to be determined: one for yielding of the gross area and one for failure (rupture) of the effective net area. These two values are:

$$F_t^{gross} = 0.6F_y \tag{4.1}$$

and

$$F_t^{net} = 0.5F_u \tag{4.2}$$

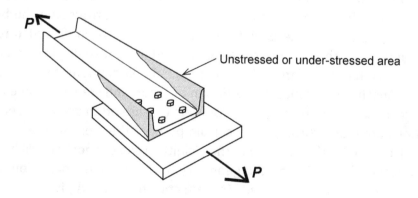

Figure 4.11: Shear lag in steel tension element showing unstressed or under-stressed areas

where F_t^{gross} and F_t^{net} are the allowable tensile stresses for steel corresponding to the two modes of failure, or limit states: F_y is the yield stress and F_u is the ultimate stress for steel (Appendix Table A-4.1). The tensile stress is computed on the gross area in the same manner as for wood (see Equation 3.2). Rupture on a failure surface through bolted or welded connections, however, is determined using the effective net area rather than the net area, so Equation 3.3 must be modified for steel connections as follows:

$$f_t = P/A_e \qquad (4.3)$$

When computing the capacity based on yielding, the full gross area is available to resist the internal forces:

$$P_{allow} = F_t^{gross} \times A_g \qquad (4.4)$$

When computing the capacity on the effective net area:

$$P_{allow} = F_t^{net} \times A_e \qquad (4.5)$$

The "available strength" limit states listed in Appendix Table A-4.2 are equivalent to these formulations based on allowable stress.

The following example illustrates the application of these principles to a steel tension problem. Different procedures are used for cables, eyebars, threaded rods, and pin-connected plates.

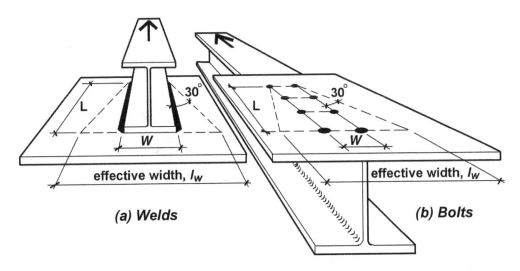

Figure 4.12: The Whitmore section for connecting plates limits the effective width of the plate to $2L \tan 30° + W$ for both (a) welded connections; and (b) bolted connections

Example 4.1 Analyze steel tension element

Problem definition. Find the maximum tension load, *P*, that can be applied to a
W8 × 24 element connected to gusset plates within a truss with ¾-in.-diameter
bolts, as shown in Figure 4.13. Use A36 steel. Find the required thickness of
the gusset plates so that their capacity is no smaller than that of the W8 × 24
tension element. The bolt hole diameter = bolt diameter + ⅛ in. = ⅞ in. =
0.875 in.

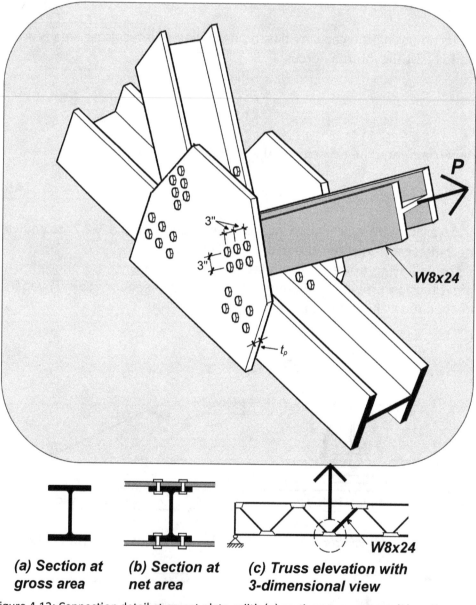

(a) Section at gross area   **(b) Section at net area**   **(c) Truss elevation with 3-dimensional view**

Figure 4.13: Connection detail at gusset plate, wiith (*a*) section at gross area, (*b*) section at
net area, and (*c*) truss elevation with 3-dimensional view for Example 4.1

Solution overview. Find cross-sectional dimensions and material properties; find gross area capacity; find effective net area capacity; the governing capacity is the lower of these two values. For gusset plate thickness, find effective width based on Whitmore section; apply equations for gross and net area capacity to determine required plate thickness.

Problem solution

1. From Appendix Table A-4.3, find cross-sectional dimensions (Figure 4.14):

    $A_g = 7.08$ in^2

    $d = 7.93$ in.

    $b_f = 6.50$ in.

    $t_f = 0.400$ in.

2. From Appendix Table A-4.1, find $F_y = 36$ ksi and $F_u = 58$ ksi.
3. Gross area: find capacity, P:
    a. Using Equation 4.1 (or Appendix Table A-4.2) find $F_t^{gross} = 0.6F_y = 0.6(36) = 22$ ksi.
    b. Using Equation 4.4, $P = F_t^{gross} \times A_g = 22(7.08) = 156$ kips.
4. Effective net area: find capacity, P:
    a. From Appendix Table A-4.9, find the shear lag coefficient, U:
        $U = 0.90$ since the following criteria are met:
        - Bolts connect wide-flange (W) shape? Yes.
        - Flange width, b_f is no less than $0.67d$? In other words,
          $6.5 \geq 0.67(7.93) = 5.3$? Yes.
        - Flange is connected with at least 3 bolts per line? Yes.
    b. Using Equation 3.1, find the net area, A_n. As shown in Figure 4.15:

        $A_n = A_g - $ (number of holes)$(D_h \times t) = 7.08 - 4(0.875 \times 0.400) = 5.68$ in^2.

    c. $A_e = U(A_n) = 0.9(5.68) = 5.11$ in^2.
    d. Using Equation 4.2, find $F_t^{net} = 0.5F_u = 0.5(58) = 29$ ksi.
    e. Using Equation 4.5, find $P = F_t^{net} \times A_e = 29(5.11) = 148$ kips.

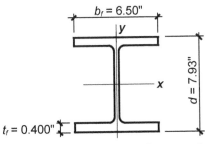

Figure 4.14: Cross-sectional dimensions of W8 × 24 for Example 4.1

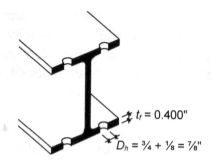

$t_f = 0.400"$

$D_h = ¾ + ⅛ = ⅞"$

Figure 4.15: Net area diagram for Example 4.1

5. *Conclusion*: failure on the effective net area governs since 148 kips < 156 kips. The capacity (allowable load) is 148 kips.
6. We now can determine the thickness of the gusset plate, stressed in tension, with two lines of bolt holes per plate, using the Whitmore section to determine the effective width of the plate. As can be seen in Figure 4.12, the effective width, l_w = 2(6)(tan 30°) + 3 = 9.9 in. The tensile capacity of the gusset plates may be based on either yielding of the gross area or rupture of the net area. First, the capacity based on yielding of the gross area of both plates is $F_t A_g$ = 0.6(36)(2)(9.9t_p) = 428t_p kips. Next, the effective net area A_e = (2)(9.9 − 2 × ⅞)t_p = 16.3t_p in², which cannot exceed 85% of the gross area for small gusset plates; i.e., it must be no larger than 0.85(2)(9.9t_p) = 16.8t_p in². Therefore, the capacity based on rupture is 0.5(58)(16.3t_p) = 473t_p. Yielding governs, so the required thickness of the plate can be found by setting the required tensile capacity, 428t_p equal to the governing load of 148 kips, from which t_p = 0.35 in. Rounding up, we select a ⅜-in. thick gusset plate with t_p = 0.375 in.

Example 4.2 Design steel tension element

Problem definition. Select a W section bolted as shown in Figure 4.16 with ⅝ in. diameter bolts, and 3 bolts per line, to resist a tension force of 100 kips. Assume A36 steel. The effective bolt hole diameter = bolt diameter + ⅛ in. = ⅝ + ⅛ = ¾ in. = 0.75 in.

Solution overview. Find the required area based on net area capacity, assuming values for shear lag coefficient, U, and flange thickness, t_f; find required area based on gross area capacity; use the larger of the two area values to provisionally select a W section; check using "analysis" method if either U is smaller or t_f is larger than assumed values. The area of the selected W section can be somewhat smaller than the "required" area if either U is larger or t_f is smaller than assumed values — check using "analysis" method.

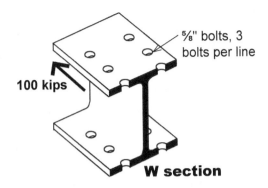

Figure 4.16: Net area diagram for Example 4.2

Problem solution

1. *Gross area:* find required gross area based on yielding. From Equation 4.4, the required gross area, $A_g = P/F_t^{gross} = 100/(0.6 \times 36) = 4.63$ in^2.

2. *Effective net area:* find required gross area after determining effective net area based on rupture through failure surface (assume $U = 0.9$ and $t_f = 0.4$ in.):

   a. From Equation 4.5, the required effective net area, $A_e = P/F_t^{net} = 100/(0.5 \times 58) = 3.45$ in^2.

   b. Working backwards, the required net area, $A_n = A_e/U = 3.45/0.9 = 3.83$ in^2.

   c. Finally, the required gross area can be computed: $A_g = A_n + $ (bolt hole area) $= 3.83 + 4(0.75 \times 0.4) = 5.03$ in^2.

3. Since 5.03 in^2 > 4.63 in^2, the calculation based on effective net area governs, and a W section must be selected with $A_g \geq 5.03$ in^2. Many wide-flange shapes could be selected. From Appendix Table A-4.3, the following candidates are among those that could be considered:

   a. Check a W8 × 18 with $A_g = 5.26$ in^2. Two assumptions need to be tested: that $U = 0.9$, and that $t_f \leq 0.4$ in. From Appendix Table A-4.3, $b_f = 5.25$ in., $d = 8.14$ in. and $t_f = 0.330$ in. From Appendix Table A-4.9, the criteria for $U = 0.9$ requires that $b_f = 5.25 \geq 0.67d = 0.67(8.14) = 5.45$ in. Since this condition is not met, we must use $U = 0.85$. Additionally, the flange thickness is different from our assumed value of 0.40 in., so that the calculation of net and effective area will change: $A_n = A_g - $ (bolt hole area) $= 5.26 - 4(0.75 \times 0.330) = 4.27$ in^2 and $A_e = U \times A_n = 0.85(4.27) = 3.63$ in^2. The capacity based on rupture through the effective net area is $P = F_t^{net} \times A_e = (0.5 \times 58)(3.63) = 105$ k. The capacity based on yielding on the gross area has already been found satisfactory (since the gross area of the W8 × 18 is greater or equal to the required gross area computed above). Therefore, the W8 × 18 is acceptable.

b. Check a W6 × 20 with A_g = 5.87 in². The same two assumptions need to be tested: that U = 0.9, and that t_f ≤ 0.4. From Appendix Table A-4.3, b_f = 6.02 in., d = 6.20 in. and t_f = 0.365 in. From Appendix Table A-4.9, the criteria for U = 0.9 requires that b_f = 6.02 ≥ 0.67d = 0.67(6.20) = 4.15 in. Since this condition is met, and since its net area is greater than assumed (this is so because its flange thickness, t_f, is *less* that the value assumed, so that the bolt hole area is less than assumed, and therefore the net area is greater than assumed), the W6 × 20 is acceptable.

Both the W8 ×18 and the W6 × 20 would work, as would many other wide-flange shapes. Of the two sections considered, the W8 × 18 is lighter (based on the second number in the W-designation that refers to beam weight in pounds per linear foot), and therefore would be less expensive.

Steel threaded rods

Threaded rods are designed using an allowable tensile stress, F_t = 0.375F_u, which is assumed to be resisted by the gross area of the unthreaded part of the rod. This value for the allowable stress is found by dividing the nominal rod tensile strength of 0.75F_u by a safety factor, Ω = 2.00. While there are no limits on slenderness, diameters are normally at least 1/500 of the length, and the minimum diameter rod for structural applications is usually set at ⅝ in. Assuming A36 steel, with F_u = 58 ksi (Appendix Table A-4.1), the smallest acceptable rod with area, $A = \pi(\frac{5}{16})^2$ can support a tensile load, $P = F_t \times A = 0.375F_u \times \pi(\frac{5}{16})^2 = 21.75 \times 0.3068 = 6.67$ kips.

Pin-connected plates

Where plates are connected with a single pin, as shown in Figure 4.17, the net area, A_n, is defined, not by the length, b, on either side of the pin hole, but rather by an effective length, $b_e = 2t + 0.63 \le b$, where t is the thickness of the plate (Figure 4.17b):

$$A_n = 2t \times b_e \qquad (4.6)$$

The plate capacity in tension is governed by either yielding on the gross area or rupture on the net area, whichever is smaller (there is no *effective* net area in this case), with $P_{gross} = 0.6F_y \times A_g$ and $P_{net} = 0.5F_u \times A_n$ as before. It is possible to cut the plate at a 45° angle as shown in Figure 4.17, as long as length c is greater or equal to length a, which in turn must be greater or equal to 1.33b_e.

Aside from failure in tensile rupture or yielding, a third limit state for pin-connected plates is *shear failure*, or the relative *sliding* of areas A_{sf} as illustrated in Figure 4.17c. In this case, the allowable shear stress is taken as $0.3F_u$ so that $P_{shear} = 0.3F_u \times A_{sf}$.

A fourth limit state for pin-connected plates is *bearing*, or compressive stress caused by the pin itself in direct contact with the adjacent plate. Here, the allowable stress on the projected area (A_{pb}) of the pin that bears on the plate is $0.9F_y$ so that the allowable bearing strength is $0.9F_y A_{pb}$.

All four limit states must be checked, with the capacity of the pin-connected plate determined by the *lowest* of the four limits. Values for yield and ultimate stress used in these calculations, F_y and F_u, are listed in Appendix Table A-4.1.

For such pin-connected plates, as well as for all other bolted connections, the fasteners themselves, and not only the stresses they produce on the elements being joined, must also be checked. This aspect of structural element design is discussed more thoroughly in the section of this chapter dealing with steel connections.

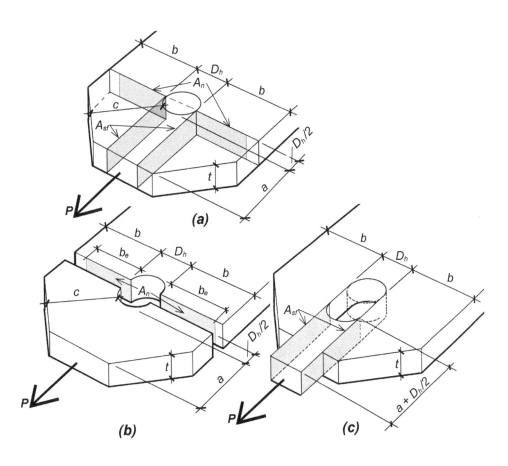

Figure 4.17: (*a*) Overview of pin-connected plates; (*b*) rupture on net area and (*c*) shear failure

COLUMNS

Steel columns with high slenderness ratios are designed using the Euler buckling equation, while "fatter" columns, which buckle inelastically or crush without buckling, are designed according to formulas corresponding to test results. Residual compressive stresses within hot-rolled steel sections precipitate this inelastic buckling, as they cause local yielding to occur sooner than might otherwise be expected. Unlike timber column design, the two design equations corresponding to elastic and inelastic buckling have not been integrated into a single unified formula, so the underlying rationale remains more apparent. The slenderness ratio dividing elastic from inelastic buckling is set, somewhat arbitrarily, at the point where the Euler critical buckling stress equals 0.44 times the yield stress; i.e., at the stress:

$$\sigma_{cr} = \frac{\pi^2 E}{(KL/r)^2} = 0.44 F_y \tag{4.7}$$

This particular slenderness ratio separating elastic from inelastic buckling is found by solving for (KL/r) in Equation 4.7:

$$KL/r = \sqrt{\frac{\pi^2 E}{0.44 F_y}} \tag{4.8}$$

For $F_y = 50$ ksi, the value of KL/r is 113; for $F_y = 36$ ksi, the value is 134. For a slender column with a slenderness ratio greater than this separating value, elastic buckling is assumed, and the allowable ("available") axial compressive stress, based on Euler's equation (multiplied by a factor of 0.877, and divided by a safety factor, $\Omega = 1.67$), is:

$$F_c = \frac{0.877}{1.67} \frac{\pi^2 E}{(KL/r)^2} = 0.525 \frac{\pi^2 E}{(KL/r)^2} \tag{4.9}$$

The coefficient, 0.525, in Equation 4.9 corresponds to the safety factor of 12/23 previously used for elastic buckling of steel columns.

Where KL/r is less than the value separating elastic from inelastic buckling, inelastic buckling governs, and the allowable ("available") axial compressive stress is found by dividing the critical stress for inelastic buckling by the same factor of safety, $\Omega = 1.67$:

$$F_c = \frac{0.658^{(F_y/F_e)} F_y}{1.67} \tag{4.10}$$

In this equation, F_e is the elastic buckling stress shown in Equation 1.19; that is:

$$F_e = \frac{\pi^2 E}{(KL/r)^2} \tag{4.11}$$

The slenderness ratio, KL/r, should not exceed 200 for steel axial compression elements. Values for K are shown in Appendix Table A-1.2. We are also assuming that compression elements are proportioned so that local buckling of their flanges or web does not occur; this requires that the compression element (typically a column) is not defined as *slender*. Wide-flange elements that are determined to be slender for compression are noted in Appendix Table A-4.3. Their design, involving calculations that effectively reduce the load they can safely carry, is beyond the scope of this discussion.

The two curves representing allowable stresses for elastic and inelastic buckling make a smooth transition at the slenderness ratio separating them, as shown in Figure 4.18. Rather than apply these equations to the solution

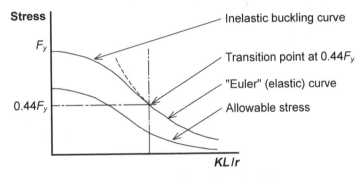

Figure 4.18: Inelastic and elastic critical stress curves for column buckling

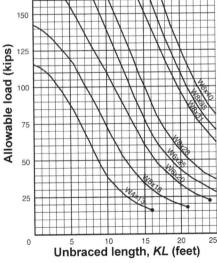

Figure 4.19: Allowable axial column load plotted against unbraced length

of axial compression problems in steel, allowable stress tables (for *analysis*, Appendix Tables A-4.11 through A-4.14) or allowable load tables (for *design*, Appendix Table A-4.10) are more often used. If values for allowable load are plotted instead of tabulated, the curves have the same pattern schematically represented in Figure 4.18. Examples of these axial column load curves are shown in Figure 4.19.

Example 4.3 Analyze steel column

Problem definition. Find the capacity (allowable load) of a W14 × 61 pin-ended column with an unbraced length of 10 ft. Assume A36 steel.

Solution overview. Find relevant section properties; compute slenderness ratio; find allowable stress and capacity.

Problem solution
1. From Appendix Table A-4.3, r_{min} = 2.45 in.
2. Compute slenderness ratio:
   a. From Appendix Table A-1.2, the effective length coefficient, K = 1.0.
   b. The unbraced length, L = 10.0 × 12 = 120 in.
   c. KL/r_{min} = (1.0)(120)/2.45 = 48.98. Round up to 49.
3. From Appendix Table A-4.14, the allowable stress: F_c = 19.0 ksi.
4. Find capacity: From Appendix Table A-4.3, the area of the steel column, A = 17.9 in². The capacity, $P = F_c × A$ = 19.0(17.9) = 340 kips.

From Equation 4.8, the slenderness ratio separating elastic and inelastic column behavior is 134 for A36 steel. The column analyzed in Example 4.3 has a slenderness ratio of 48.98, which is less than this separating value; therefore, it fails inelastically. Using Equation 4.10 to determine the "inelastic" allowable stress, we get the same result as was obtained in the example. The calculations are as follows, using F_y = 36 ksi:
From Equation 4.11, $F_e = \pi^2(29,000)/(48.98^2)$ = 119.3. Then, from Equation 4.10:

$$F_c = \frac{0.658^{(F_y/F_e)}F_y}{1.67} = \frac{0.658^{(36/119.3)}36}{1.67} = 19.0 \text{ ksi}$$

It can be seen that this is the same allowable stress as was obtained in Example 4.3.

Example 4.4 Design steel column

Problem definition. Select the lightest (most economical) wide-flange section for the first-floor column shown in Figure 4.20. Assume office occupancy;

a roof (construction) live load of 20 psf; a typical steel floor system; and an allowance for steel stud partitions. Assume pin-ended (simple) connections. Use A992 steel.

Solution overview. Find total load on column; find effective length; select lightest section.

Problem solution
1. Find total column load:
    a. From Appendix Table 2.2, the live load (L) for office occupancy = 50 psf.
    b. From Appendix Table 2.1, the typical dead load (D) = 47 psf (steel floor system, etc.) + 8 psf (steel stud partition allowance) = 55 psf.
    c. The roof live load (L_r) = 20 psf, according to the Problem Definition.
    d. Find tributary area (see Figure 1.5): The column's tributary area is 25 ft × 40 ft = 1000 ft^2 per floor, or 5000 ft^2 for the five levels on which occupancy live loads are computed (excluding the roof).
    e. Using Appendix Table A-2.2, compute the reduced live load; the live load reduction factor is: $0.25 + 15/\sqrt{4 \times 5000} = 0.36$, but no reduction less than 0.40 is permitted. Therefore, the live load can be reduced to 0.40 × 50 = 20 psf for the first-floor column under consideration.
    f. Using Appendix Table A-2.7 for allowable stress design, find the total column load, accounting for reductions due to load combinations:

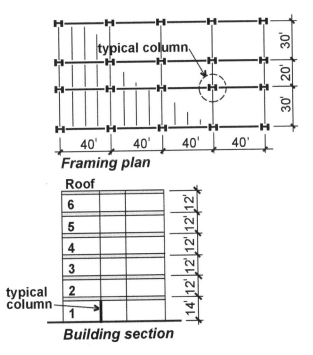

Figure 4.20: Framing plan and building section for Example 4.4

$L = (25 \text{ ft} \times 40 \text{ ft}) \times (20 \text{ psf}) \times 5 \text{ floors} = 100{,}000 \text{ lb}$

$D = (25 \text{ft} \times 40 \text{ ft}) \times (55 \text{ psf}) \times 6 \text{ floors} = 330{,}000 \text{ lb}$

$L_r = (25 \text{ft} \times 40 \text{ ft}) \times (20 \text{ psf}) \times 1 \text{ floor} = 20{,}000 \text{ lb}$

For the three loads potentially present, only two load combinations need be considered (the others listed will produce less severe effects). For the second load combination, wind or seismic effects on the column may also be considered. However, in this example, we assume that the column is not part of the lateral force-resisting system for wind or seismic, and that any negative (uplift) wind load on the roof can be conservatively ignored. The two relevant load combinations to consider are as follows:

$$D + L = 330{,}000 + 100{,}000 = 430{,}000 \text{ lb}$$

$$D + 0.75L + 0.75L_r = 330{,}000 + 0.75(100{,}000) + 0.75(20{,}000)$$

$$= 330{,}000 + 75{,}000 + 15{,}000 = 420{,}000 \text{ lb.}$$

The first case governs; therefore the total column load = 430,000 lb = 430 kips.

2. Using Appendix Table A-1.2, find the unbraced effective length: $KL = (1.0)(14) = 14 \text{ ft.}$
3. Select the most economical section:
   a. Using Appendix Table A-4.10, pick the lightest acceptable section from each "nominal depth" group (i.e., one W8, one W10, one W12, and so on), to assemble a group of "likely candidates." Some columns are clearly either to small or too large; the three possible candidates for a load of 430 kips and an effective length of 14 ft. are:

   - W10 × 68 can support 440 kips
   - W12 × 65 can support 456 kips
   - W14 × 74 can support 466 kips

   b. Choose lightest section: The W12 × 65 is the most economical since its weight per linear foot (65 pounds) is smallest.

To check the result in Example 4.4, first determine the slenderness ratio of the W12 × 65, finding the minimum (y-axis) radius of gyration, $r = 3.02$ in., from Appendix Table A-4.3. Then, $KL/r = (1.0)(14 \times 12)/3.02 = 55.63$. From Equation 4.8, the slenderness ratio separating elastic from inelastic behavior for A992 steel is 113, so the column fails inelastically. Using Equation 4.10 to determine the "inelastic" allowable stress, we get the same result as was obtained in the example. The calculations are as follows, using $F_y = 50$ ksi:

From Equation 4.11, $F_e = \pi^2(29,000)/(55.63^2) = 92.5$. Then, from Equation 4.10:

$$F_c = \frac{0.658^{(F_y/F_e)}F_y}{1.67} = \frac{0.658^{(50/92.5)}50}{1.67} = 23.9 \text{ ksi}$$

From Appendix Table A-4.3, the area of the W12 × 65, A = 19.1 in². Therefore, the capacity, $P = F_c \times A = 23.9 \times 19.1 = 456$ kips, the same value found in Example 4.4.

BEAMS

The design of steel wide-flange beams using the "allowable strength design" method is quite similar to the procedures used to design timber beams (see Chapter 3). Cross sections are selected based on their strength in bending, and then checked for shear and deflection.

Bending of laterally-braced and compact beams

Unlike wood beams, however, steel beams are designed based on their "available" strength, rather than on the more convention notion of an "allowable" stress. Whereas the strength of a wood beam corresponds to its outer fibers reaching a failure stress, steel beams do not fail when their outer fibers first begin to yield at the stress, F_y. A steel cross section is able to carry increased loads beyond the so-called elastic moment, shown in Figure 4.21a, up until the entire cross section has yielded, as shown in Figure 4.21b. The plastic section modulus corresponds to this so-called plastic moment, reached when the strain at a cross section is of sufficient magnitude so that virtually the entire section has yielded.

Previously, steel used an "allowable stress" method based on a limit state corresponding to the elastic moment; and if the plastic moment were always stronger than the elastic moment to the same extent for all cross sections, one could simply adjust the factor of safety for allowable *strength* (plastic moment) design so that the method corresponded precisely to allowable *stress* (elastic moment) design. However, it can be shown that the extra margin of safety gained by moving beyond the elastic, to the plastic moment (i.e., from the condition of Figure 4.21a to Figure 4.21b), is not the same for all cross sections, so that allowable stress design for steel does not provide a consistent margin of safety against the limit state of complete yielding.

For wide-flange (I-shaped) sections, the extremes can be represented by a hypothetical section with no web (i.e., consisting entirely of flanges of infinite density, or no thickness, as shown in Figures 4.21c and 4.21d); and, at the other extreme, a section whose flanges merge together at the neutral axis (i.e., a rectangular section, as shown in Figures 4.21g and 4.21h). In the first case, it is clear that the elastic moment and plastic moment coincide, and the so-called "shape factor" defining the ratio of plastic to elastic section modulus, Z_x/S_x, equals 1.0. In the second case, the elastic section modulus can be computed by examining the rotational equilibrium of the force resultants shown in Figure 4.21g. Since the moment arm between them equals $(\frac{2}{3})h$, and the resultant force, C, equals $(\frac{1}{2})(h/2)(b)(F_y)$, the moment, M, equals $(\frac{2}{3})(h)(\frac{1}{2})(h/2)(b)(F_y)$ and, solving for the section modulus, $S_x = M/F_y$, we get

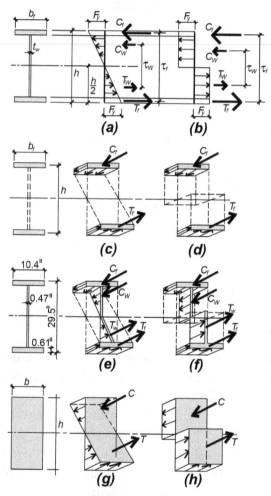

Figure 4.21: Bending stresses acting on steel wide-flange (I-shaped) cross section corresponding to the (a) elastic moment and (b) plastic moment, with three examples: (c) and (d) illustrate elastic and plastic moments for a hypothetical section with all its area at the extreme fibers; (e) and (f) illustrate elastic and plastic moments for a typical W30 × 90 section; while (g) and (h) illustrate elastic and plastic moments for a rectangular section

$S_x = bh^2/6$. Performing the same equilibrium calculation on Figure 4.21*h* (with a moment arm equal to $h/2$), and solving for the plastic section modulus, $Z_x = M/F_y$, we get $Z_x = bh^2/4$. The shape factor in this case is $Z_x/S_x = 1.5$.

Clearly, all I-shaped sections must have a shape factor between these two extremes, i.e., between 1.0 and 1.5. The shape factor for a typical W-shape (W30 × 90), shown in Figures 4.21*e* and 4.21*f*, can be determined in the same manner, abstracting from the complexities of the actual shape by considering only perfectly rectangular flange and web areas. Using the dimensions shown, and performing the same equilibrium calculations as in the cases above, we get $S_x = 240$ in^3 and $Z_x = 277$ in^3, so the shape factor, $Z_x/S_x = 277/240 = 1.15$. The actual values for elastic and plastic section modulus are found in Appendix Table A-4.3, and it can be seen that the approximate calculations are both conservative and reasonably accurate: the correct values are actually $S_x = 245$ in^3 and $Z_x = 283$ in^3, so the real shape factor, $Z_x/S_x = 283/245 = 1.16$.

The equation for plastic section modulus, $Z_x = M/F_y$, presumes that the cross section is able to reach a state of complete yielding before one of two types of buckling occurs: either *lateral-torsional buckling* within any unbraced segment along the length of the span or *local flange or web buckling*. Therefore, to use this equation in design, based on the maximum moment encountered, the beam must be protected from both of these buckling modes, in the first case by limiting the unbraced length and, in the second case, by regulating the proportions of the beam flange and web (i.e., using a so-called *compact section*). Then, rewriting this equation in the form most useful for steel design, we get:

$$Z_{req} = \Omega M_{max}/F_y \tag{4.12}$$

where M_{max} = the maximum bending moment (in-kips), F_y is the yield stress of the steel, and Ω is a safety factor equal to 1.67 for bending.

We found earlier that the shape factor for a W30 × 90 section equals 1.16. By looking at the ratio of plastic to elastic section modulus for all wide-flange shapes, it can be seen that these shape factors fall between 1.098 (for a W14 × 90), and 1.297 (for a W14 × 730). One could therefore conservatively create a safety factor for elastic allowable stress design by assuming a shape factor of 1.10, and by multiplying this value by the safety factor for allowable *strength* design, $1/\Omega = 1/1.67 = 0.60$ (inverted to be consistent with the conventions for allowable stress safety factors). Equation 4.12 would then become $S_{req} = M_{max}/(1.1 \times 0.6 \times F_y) = M_{max}/(0.66F_y)$. This, in fact, is the design equation for what used to be called "allowable stress design" in steel. It may still be used, but will give slightly conservative values compared with the available stress method using the plastic section modulus, Z_x.

Choosing the lightest (i.e., most economical) laterally-braced, compact section is facilitated by the use of tables in which steel cross sections are ranked, first in terms of plastic section modulus, and then by least weight. Appendix Table A-4.15 is an example of such a list, in which only the lightest sections appear. Thus, a W30 × 191 (with a plastic section modulus of 675 in³) is not listed, since a *lighter* section, W40 × 167, has a higher plastic section modulus (693 in³).

Bending of laterally-unsupported or noncompact beams

When the compression flange of a beam is not continuously braced, lateral-torsional buckling can reduce the available bending moment below the value of M_p/Ω assumed earlier for laterally braced beams. How much this stress is reduced depends on whether the beam buckles before or after the cross section begins to yield, and how bending stresses vary over the beam's un-braced length. Figure 1.64 shows several possible stress stages for a cross-sectional shape as the bending moment increases. At Figure 1.64c, the outer fibers begin to yield, and the elastic moment, M_y, is reached. At Figure 1.64d and Figure 1.64e, yielding progresses further into the cross section, as the moment increases. Finally, at Figure 1.64f, the entire cross section has yielded at the maximum plastic moment that the section can sustain.

Being able to resist the full plastic moment represents an extra margin of safety: if a beam can develop this plastic moment without buckling, the maximum available bending moment of M_p/Ω is used, as shown in Equation 4.12. In addition to lateral-torsional buckling (Figure 4.22a), various types of local flange and web buckling must also be prevented from occurring before the plastic moment is reached (Figure 4.22b). Local buckling is prevented by limiting the ratio of flange width to flange thickness, as well as web width

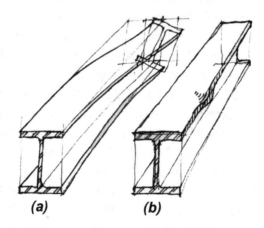

(a)   *(b)*

Figure 4.22: Two modes of buckling limiting the strength of a wide-flange (I-shaped) beam: (a) lateral-torsional buckling; and (b) local flange buckling

to web thickness. Sections proportioned so that local buckling will not occur are called compact sections; these sections must be used to qualify for the full available moment of M_p/Ω. As it turns out, all but one of the wide-flange shapes listed in Appendix Table A-4.3 are compact sections when made from A36 steel (the exception being W6 × 15). For 50 ksi steel, all but ten (W6 × 8.5, W6 × 9, W6 × 15, W8 × 10, W8 × 31, W10 × 12, W12 × 65, W14 × 90, W14 × 99, and W21 × 48) are compact.

For sections that are compact and laterally braced, Equation 4.12 applies, and the full strength of the beam is utilized. However, as shown in Figure 4.23, this available strength must be reduced if either local flange buckling (where the section is not compact) or lateral-torsional buckling (where the section is not adequately braced) occurs before the plastic moment is reached.

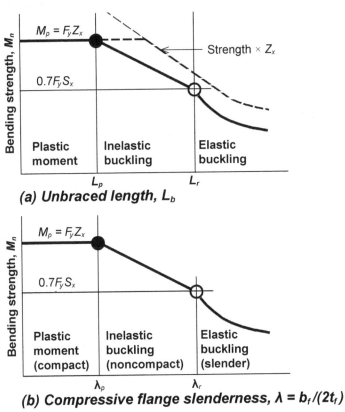

Figure 4.23: Influence of lateral-torsional buckling and flange slenderness on available moment: three zones are defined for (*a*) lateral torsional buckling, with the boundaries established by the unbraced length, L_p (the greatest unbraced length where the section can reach a plastic moment without lateral torsional buckling) and L_r (the greatest unbraced length where the section will buckle inelastically before reaching the plastic moment); and for (*b*) flange slenderness, with the boundaries established by the ratio of half the flange width to flange thickness, $\lambda = b_f/(2t_f)$, set equal to λ_p (the greatest flange slenderness where the section can reach a plastic moment without local flange buckling) and λ_r (the greatest flange slenderness where the flange will buckle locally in an inelastic manner before reaching the plastic moment)

Lateral-torsional buckling

For beams with an unbraced length, L_b, that falls within the "middle zone" illustrated in Figure 4.23a (i.e., where the onset of buckling occurs before a full plastic moment, but after the elastic moment, is reached), the nominal bending strength is linearly reduced from the full plastic moment, $M_p = F_y Z_x$, to 70% of the elastic moment, or $0.7F_y S_x$. The two boundaries (unbraced lengths) that bracket this condition of inelastic lateral-torsional buckling are called L_p and L_r. For an unbraced length, L_b, less than L_p, lateral-torsional buckling is not an issue, as the full plastic moment can be reached. For an unbraced length greater than L_r, the onset of lateral-torsional buckling is characterized entirely by elastic behavior, and the nominal bending strength must be reduced even further. These boundaries are defined as follows: L_p is set at $1.76r_y\sqrt{E/F_y}$, where E is the modulus of elasticity (29,000 ksi for all steel), F_y is the yield stress (50 ksi for A992 steel, and 36 ksi for A36 steel), and r_y is the minimum radius of gyration about the y-axis (see Table A-4.3 for wide-flange shapes). The other boundary, L_r, can be conservatively approximated as $\pi r_{ts}\sqrt{E/(0.7F_y)}$, where r_{ts} may itself be approximated as the radius of gyration for the compression flange and part of the web; i.e., $r_{ts} = b_f/\sqrt{12 + 2ht_w/(b_f/t_f)}$. In this equation, b_f and t_f are the flange width and thickness, respectively, and h is the length of the "straight" part of the web (i.e., the clear distance between flanges, minus the radii at the web-flange intersections).

However, all these equations are based on the assumption that the beam is subject to a uniform bending moment along its entire length; where the moment varies, as is almost always the case, this assumption is overly conservative, since lateral-torsional buckling is less likely to be triggered where bending stresses are not entirely at their maximum value along the whole length of an unbraced segment. For this reason, a coefficient, C_b, should be applied to the available strength of each unbraced segment of the beam, based on the distribution and magnitude of bending moments along that segment's length. This "lateral-torsional buckling modifier" is defined as follows for doubly-symmetric bending elements such as wide-flange beams:

$$C_b = \frac{12.5M_{max}}{2.5M_{max} + 3M_A + 4M_B + 3M_C} \tag{4.13}$$

where M_{max} is the greatest moment within the unbraced segment; and M_A, M_B, and M_C are the bending moments at the quarter point, midpoint, and three-quarters point, respectively, along the segment. Where a segment is not braced at its endpoint (for example, where the end of a cantilevered beam is not braced), C_b should be taken as 1.0. Of course, C_b is not used where a beam is laterally braced and, in any case, can never increase the nominal bending strength beyond the plastic moment, M_p, as shown in Figure 4.23a.

Local flange buckling

Compact sections are proportioned so that neither the flange nor the web will buckle locally before the onset of a plastic moment. Since all wide-flange *webs* meet the standards for compact sections, only the flange slenderness, defined as $\lambda = b_f/(2t_f)$, is at issue (where b_f and t_f are the flange width and thickness, respectively). In much the same way that boundaries are established for unbraced length that define the reduction in the bending strength due to lateral-torsional buckling (Figure 4.23a), similar boundaries are established for flange slenderness, with similar consequences for beam strength (Figure 4.23b). The limit for compact behavior — i.e., the maximum flange slenderness for which beams are still able to reach the plastic moment without local flange buckling — is defined by $\lambda_p = 0.38\sqrt{E/F_y}$. The other boundary (i.e., the maximum flange slenderness for which inelastic behavior characterizes the onset of local flange buckling) is defined by $\lambda_r = 1.0\sqrt{E/F_y}$. In these equations, E is the modulus of elasticity of steel (29,000 ksi) and F_y is the material's yield stress (50 ksi for A992 steel, and 36 ksi for A36 steel).

As with reductions for lateral-torsional buckling, the nominal bending strength begins with the plastic moment, $M_p = F_yZ_x$, for compact sections, and is linearly reduced to 70% of the elastic moment, or $0.7F_yS_x$, between λ_p and λ_r, with further reductions beyond λ_r.

Where a beam is both noncompact and laterally unbraced, both criteria illustrated in Figure 4.23 are tested, and the smaller capacity governs. For beams that are both compact and laterally braced, Appendix Table A-4.15 can be used to select the lightest W-shape for bending. For A992 wide-flange beams that are not adequately braced laterally (i.e, where $L_b > L_p$), Appendix Table A-4.16 can be used to select the lightest beam. Of course, by setting the unbraced length to zero, Appendix Table A-4.16 can be used for laterally-braced beams as well.

Shear

Once a selection is made based on bending stress, the section is then checked for shear and deflection. The nominal shear strength, V_n, equals $0.6F_yA_w$, where F_y is the yield stress of the steel and A_w is the web area (equal to the beam depth times the web thickness, $d \times t_w$). For most cross sections, the safety factor can be taken as $\Omega = 1.5$, so that the available strength is $V_n/\Omega = 0.6/\Omega(F_yA_w) = 0.4F_yA_w$. This can be converted into an "allowable stress" equation by defining the allowable shear stress, $F_v = 0.4F_y$, and solving for the required web area for a given shear force, V:

$$\text{required } A_w = V/F_v \tag{4.14}$$

For a small group of wide-flange beams with slender webs, the safety factor for shear is increased from 1.5 to 1.67, and so the allowable shear stress becomes $F_v = (0.6/1.67)F_y = 0.36F_y$. These sections are listed in Appendix Table A-4.3 (see Note 3).

Block shear

Where the top flange of a steel beam is coped (so that it may be fastened to the web of a girder while keeping the top surfaces of girder and beam flanges aligned), a mode of failure combining both shear and tension stresses in the beam web must be checked, with the shear and tension failure planes assumed to occur at the surface defined by the bolt centerline, as shown in Figure 4.24.

The nominal capacity of such a connection is found by adding the capacity of the net shear area subject to rupture (or the gross shear area subject to yielding) to the capacity of the net tension area subject to rupture. Where both net areas are subject to rupture, the capacity is defined as: $R_n = 0.6F_u A_{nv} + U_{bs} F_u A_{nt}$. Where yielding governs the failure of the shear area, the capacity is defined as: $R_n = 0.6F_y A_{gv} + U_{bs} F_u A_{nt}$. The smaller of these two values determines the capacity of the connection for resisting block shear. In these equations, F_u is the minimum tension strength of the material (equal to 58 ksi for A36 steel, and 65 ksi for A992 steel); A_{nv} and A_{nt} are the net areas for shear and tension, respectively; A_{gv} is the gross shear area; and U_{bs} equals 1.0 for conditions that correspond to uniform tension stress, as in the coped beam with a single line of bolts shown in Figure 4.24a, while U_{bs} equals 0.5 for conditions that lead

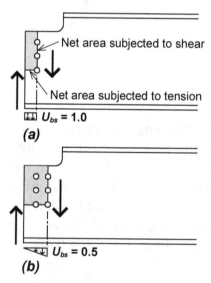

Figure 4.24: Block shear at coped beam with (a) coefficient U_{bs} =1.0 where tension stress is uniform (single line of bolts); and (b) U_{bs} = 0.5 where tension stress has a triangular distribution (double line of bolts)

to a triangular (non-uniform) tension stress, as in the coped beam with a two lines of bolts shown in Figure 4.24b. The available strength is then found by dividing the nominal capacity by the safety factor, $\Omega = 2.00$.

It is also possible that a mode of shear failure alone, with no tension component, could govern the connection design. In such a case, both yielding on the gross area of the cross section and rupture on the net area need to be checked. For yielding, the nominal capacity, R_n, equals $0.60F_y A_{gv}$, and the available strength, ΩR_n, is determined using a safety factor, $\Omega = 1.50$ (*not* $\Omega = 2.00$). For rupture on the net area, R_n equals $0.60F_u A_{nv}$, and the available strength, ΩR_n, is determined using a safety factor, $\Omega = 2.00$. All the parameters are as defined above for block shear. The lower safety factor for yielding reflects the relative safety of a yielding mode of failure compared with the more sudden and catastrophic type of failure associated with rupture.

Example 4.5 Find capacity of beam web based on block shear

Problem definition. Find the capacity of a bolted double-angle connection to the web of a coped W18 × 86 wide-flange beam, considering only block shear in the web. Assume A992 steel ($F_y = 50$ ksi and $F_u = 65$ ksi) for the beam, and ¾-in.-diameter bolts. The bolt spacing, $s = 3$ in., the vertical edge distance, $L_{ev} = 1.5$ in., and the horizontal edge distance, $L_{eh} = 1.5$ in. as defined in Figure 4.25.

Problem overview. Find the smaller of the capacities based on rupture and yielding of shear area, rupture of tension area, and bolt bearing on the web.

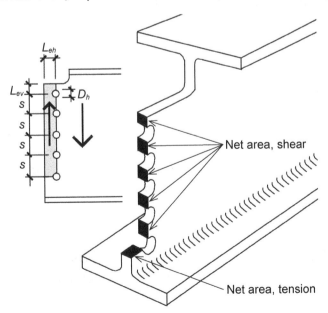

Figure 4.25: Block shear in a coped beam, for Example 4.5

Problem solution

1. Find capacity based on net areas subject to rupture. Lengths along net areas are found by subtracting the lengths of bolt hole diameters from the total (gross) dimension. The net area for shear, $A_{nv} = t_w(4s + L_{ev} - 4.5D_h) = 0.480(4 \times 3 + 1.5 - 4.5 \times 0.875) = 4.59$ in², where t_w is the web thickness (from Appendix Table A-4.3), s is the bolt spacing of 3 in., L_{ev} is the vertical edge distance of 1.5 in., and D_h is the bolt hole diameter (found by adding ⅛ in. to the bolt diameter of ¾ in.). The net area for tension, $A_{nt} = t_w(L_{eh} - 0.5D_h) = 0.480(1.5 - 0.5 \times 0.875) = 0.51$ in², where L_{eh} is the horizontal edge spacing and D_h is the bolt hole diameter.

   The capacity based on rupture of these net areas is defined as: $R_n = 0.6F_uA_{nv} + U_{bs}F_uA_{nt}$, where $U_{bs} = 1.0$ for a single line of bolt holes. Using the material properties defined above, we get: $R_n = 0.6(65)(4.59) + (1.0)(65)(0.51) = 212.2$ kips.

2. Find capacity based on gross area (yielding) for shear and net area (rupture) for tension. The gross area for shear, $A_{gv} = t_w(4s + L_{ev}) = 0.480(4 \times 3 + 1.5) = 6.48$ in², where t_w is the web thickness (from Appendix Table A-4.3); s is the bolt spacing of 3 in., and L_{ev} is the vertical edge distance of 1.5 in. The net area for tension, as in step 1, is 0.51 in².

   The capacity based on yielding of the shear area and rupture of the tension area is defined as: $R_n = 0.6F_yA_{gv} + U_{bs}F_uA_{nt}$, where $U_{bs} = 1.0$ as before. Using the material properties defined above, we get: $R_n = 0.6(50)(6.48) + (1.0)(65)(0.51) = 227.6$ kips.

3. The governing capacity is the smaller value from steps 1 and 2: $R_n = 212.2$ kips based on rupture of the net areas.

Deflection

Deflection is based on the same criteria discussed in Chapter 3 for wood beams and involves a comparison of an allowable deflection, typically set at span/240 for total loads and span/360 for live loads on floor beams, to the actual computed deflection. Actual deflections can be computed based on the coefficients in Appendix Table A-4.17 (which are the same coefficients used for wood in Appendix Table A-3.15). Allowable deflection guidelines can be found in Appendix Table A-1.3 (also summarized in Appendix Table A-4.17).

Example 4.6 Design steel beam

Problem definition. Using A992 steel, design the typical beam and girder for the library stack area shown in Figure 4.26. Use the generic dead load for steel floor systems. Assume that the beams are continuously braced by the floor deck, and that the girders are braced only by the beams framing into them.

Solution overview. Find loads; compute maximum bending moment and shear force; use appropriate tables to select beams for bending; then check for shear and deflection.

Problem solution

Find loads:
From Appendix Table A-2.1, the dead load, $D = 47$ psf.
From Appendix Table A-2.2, the live load, $L = 150$ psf

Beam design

1. Create load, shear and moment diagrams as shown in Figure 4.27 to determine critical (i.e., maximum) shear force and bending moment. The total distributed load, w = (dead + live)(tributary area for 1 linear foot) = $(47 + 150)(6) = 1182$ lb/ft = 1.18 kips/ft. Live load reduction would not apply even if the "influence" area was not less than 400 ft², because of the library stack occupancy (i.e., the probability of full loading makes live load reduction a dangerous assumption).

2. Find allowable bending stress: since the beam is laterally braced by the floor deck and the cross section is assumed to be compact, use

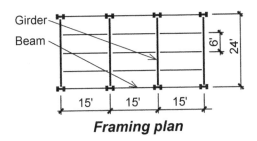

Framing plan

Figure 4.26: Framing plan for Example 4.6

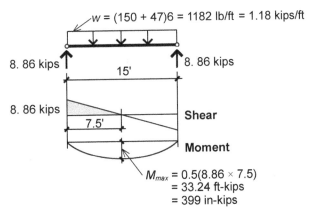

Figure 4.27: Load, shear, and moment diagrams for beam in Example 4.6

Equation 4.12 to find $Z_{req} = \Omega M_{max}/F_y = 1.67 M_{max}/F_y$. From Appendix Table A-4.1, $F_y = 50$ ksi for A992 steel, so $Z_{req} = 1.67(399)/50 = 13.33$ in^3.

3. From Appendix Table A-4.15, select a W12 × 14 with actual $Z_x = 17.4$ in$^3 \geq Z_{req}$. This section is, by definition, OK for bending.

4. Check section for shear: from Table A-4.3, the actual web area, $A_w = d \times t_w = 11.9 \times 0.20 = 2.38$ in^2.

5. From Equation 4.14, the required $A_w = V/F_v = 8.86/(0.36 \times 50) = 0.49$ in^2 where, from Appendix Table A-4.2, the allowable shear stress, $F_v = 0.36 F_y$ (and not the usual value of $F_v = 0.40 F_y$) because the beam web is unusually slender. Beams requiring such reduced allowable shear stresses are noted in Appendix Table A-4.3. Since the actual web area is greater than the required web area, the beam is OK for shear.

6. From Appendix Table A-1.3 (also summarized in Appendix Table A-4.17), find the allowable total-load deflection for a floor beam: $\Delta^T_{allow} =$ span/240 = 12(15)/240 = 0.75 in. and the allowable live-load deflection for a floor joist: $\Delta^L_{allow} =$ span/360 = 12(15)/360 = 0.5 in.

7. From Appendix Table A-4.17, the actual total load deflection, $\Delta^T_{act} = CP(L/12)^3/(EI)$ where:

   $C = 22.46$.

   $L = 15 \times 12 = 180$ in. (the term, L, is used for both span and live load).

   $P = w(L/12) = (150 + 47)(6)(180/12) = 17{,}730$ lb $= 17.73$ kips.

   $E = 29{,}000$ ksi (Appendix Table A-4.1, Note 1).

   $I = 88.6$ in^4 (Appendix Table A-4.3).

   $\Delta^T_{act} = 22.46(17.73)(180/12)^3/(29{,}000 \times 88.6) = 0.523$ in.

   Since $\Delta^T_{act} = 0.523$ in. $\leq \Delta^T_{allow} = 0.75$ in., the beam is OK for total-load deflection.

8. From Appendix Table A-4.17, the actual live load deflection, $\Delta^L_{act} = CP(L/12)^3/(EI)$ where:

   $C = 22.46$.

   $L = 15 \times 12 = 180$ in.

   $P = w(L/12) = (150 \times 6)(180/12) = 13500$ lb $= 13.5$ kips (Use live load only!).

   $E = 29{,}000$ ksi (Appendix Table A-4.1, Note 1).

   $I = 88.6$ in^4 (Appendix Table A-4.3).

   $\Delta^L_{act} = 22.46(13.5)(180/12)^3/(29{,}000 \times 88.6) = 0.398$ in.

   Since $\Delta^L_{act} = 0.398$ in. $\leq \Delta^L_{allow} = 0.5$ in., the beam is OK for live-load deflection.

9. *Conclusion:* The W12 × 14 section is OK for bending, shear and deflection. Therefore it is acceptable.

Girder design

1. Create load, shear and moment diagrams as shown in Figure 4.28 to determine the critical (i.e., maximum) shear force and bending moment. Each concentrated load is twice the typical beam reaction, or 17.73 kips. Alternatively, compute using tributary areas; that is, $P = (47 + 150)(15 \times 6) = 17,730$ lb $= 17.73$ kips. Live load reduction does not apply even though the "influence" area is greater than 400 ft², because of the library stack occupancy (i.e., the probability of full loading makes live load reduction a dangerous assumption).

2. Find allowable bending stress: The girder is not continuously braced by the floor deck; rather, it is braced every 6 ft by the beams framing into it, so the unbraced length, $L_b = 6$ ft. Use Appendix Table A-4.16 to directly find the lightest cross section for bending, based on $M_{max} = 212.76$ ft-kips, $L_b = 6$ ft, and assuming (conservatively) that the "lateral-torsional buckling modifier," $C_b = 1.0$. Find the intersection of moment and unbraced length (follow the dotted lines shown in Figure 4.29) and then move up

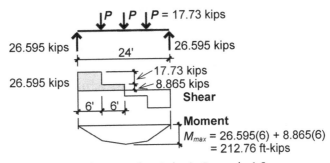

Figure 4.28: Load, shear, and moment diagrams for girder in Example 4.6

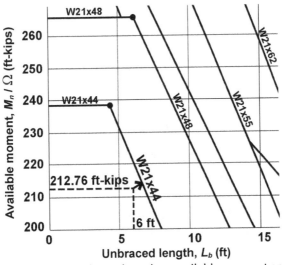

Figure 4.29: Selection of W21x44 beam based on available moment graphs (Appendix Table A-4.16) for Example 4.6

or to the right to the first solid line representing the available moment capacity of wide-flange beams. Select a W21 × 44.

3. Check section for shear: from Appendix Table A-4.3, the actual web area, $A_w = d \times t_w = 20.7 \times 0.35 = 7.25$ in^2.

4. From Equation 4.14, the required $A_w = V/F_v = 26.595/(0.40 \times 50) = 1.33$ in^2 where, from Appendix Table A-4.2, the allowable shear stress, $F_v = 0.40F_y$ (the usual value of $F_v = 0.40F_y$ applies in this case). Since the actual web area is greater than the required web area, the beam is OK for shear.

5. From Appendix Table A-1.3 (also summarized in Appendix Table A-4.17), find the allowable total-load deflection for a floor beam, $\Delta^T_{allow} =$ span/240 = 12(24)/240 = 1.2 in., and the allowable live-load deflection for a floor joist, $\Delta^L_{allow} =$ span/360 = 12(24)/360 = 0.8 in.

6. From Appendix Table A-4.17, the actual total-load deflection, $\Delta^T_{act} = CP(L/12)^3/(EI)$ where:

   $C = 85.54$.

   $L = 24 \times 12 = 288$ in.

   $P = (47 + 150)(15 \times 6) = 17,730$ lb $= 17.73$ kips.

   $E = 29,000$ ksi (Appendix Table A-4.1, Note 1).

   $I = 843$ in^4 (Appendix Table A-4.3).

   $\Delta^T_{act} = 85.54(17.73)(288/12)^3/(29,000 \times 843) = 0.86$ in.

   Since $\Delta^T_{act} = 0.86$ in. $\leq \Delta^T_{allow} = 1.2$ in., beam is OK for total-load deflection.

7. From Appendix Table A-4.17, the actual live-load deflection, $\Delta^L_{act} = CP(L/12)^3/(EI)$ where:

   $C = 85.54$.

   $L = 24 \times 12 = 288$ in.

   $P = 150(15 \times 6) = 13,500$ lb $= 13.5$ kips (Use live load only!).

   $E = 29,000$ ksi (Appendix Table A-4.1, Note 1).

   $I = 843$ in^4 (Appendix Table A-4.3).

   $\Delta^L_{act} = 85.54(13.5)(288/12)^3/(29,000 \times 843) = 0.65$ in.

   Since $\Delta^L_{act} = 0.65$ in. $\leq \Delta^L_{allow} = 0.80$ in., beam is OK for live-load deflection.

8. *Conclusion:* The W21 × 44 section is OK for bending, shear and deflection. Therefore it is acceptable.

Example 4.7 Analyze rectangular HSS (hollow structural section)

Problem definition. Determine whether an HSS12 × 4 × ¼ can be used as a typical beam for the library stack area shown in Example 4.6.

Solution overview. Find loads; compute maximum bending moment and shear force; check beam for bending, shear, and deflection.

Problem solution

1. Find loads and moment (same as Example 4.6):

   The dead load, D = 47 psf.

   The live load, L = 150 psf

   Maximum moment, M_{max} = 399 in-kips

2. Find allowable bending stress: Since the beam is laterally braced by the floor deck and the cross section is assumed to be compact, use Equation 4.12 to find $Z_{req} = \Omega M_{max}/F_y = 1.67 M_{max}/F_y$. From Appendix Table A-4.1, F_y = 46 ksi for HSS rectangular shapes (A500 grade B), so Z_{req} = 1.67(399)/46 = 14.49 in^3.

3. From Appendix Table A-4.6, the actual plastic section modulus for an HSS12 × 4 × 1/4, Z_x = 25.6 in^3. Since the actual Z_x is greater than Z_{req}, this HSS section is OK for bending.

4. Check section for shear: from Appendix Table A-4.2 (Note 3), the web area, A_w is taken as $2ht$ (where t is the wall thickness of the web and h can be assumed to equal the nominal depth minus $3t$). From Appendix Table A-4.4, this web area, $A_w = 2ht = 2(12 - 3 \times 0.233)(0.233)$ = 5.27 in^2.

5. From Equation 4.14, the required $A_w = V/F_v$ = 8.86/(0.36 × 50) = 0.49 in^2 where, from Appendix Table A-4.2, the allowable shear stress, $F_v = 0.36 F_y$ (and not the value of $F_v = 0.40 F_y$ used for most wide-flange beams). Since the actual web area is greater than the required web area, the HSS beam is OK for shear.

6. From Appendix Table A-1.3 (also summarized in Appendix Table A-4.17), find the allowable total-load deflection for a floor beam: Δ^T_{allow} = span/240 = 12(15)/240 = 0.75 in.; and the allowable live-load deflection for a floor joist: Δ^L_{allow} = span/360 = 12(15)/360 = 0.5 in.

7. From Appendix Table A-4.17, the actual total-load deflection, $\Delta^T_{act} = CP(L/12)^3/(EI)$ where:

   C = 22.46.

   L = 15 × 12 = 180 in.

   $P = w(L/12)$ = (47 + 150)(6)(180/12) = 17,730 lb = 17.73 kips.

   E = 29,000 ksi (Appendix Table A-4.1, Note 1).

   I = 119 in^4 (Appendix Table A-4.6).

   Δ^T_{act} = 22.46(17.73)(180/12)^3/(29,000 × 119) = 0.389 in.

   Since Δ^T_{act} = 0.389 in. ≤ Δ^T_{allow} = 0.75 in., the HSS beam is OK for total-load deflection.

8. From Appendix Table A-4.17, the actual live-load deflection, $\Delta^L_{act} = CP(L/12)^3/(EI)$ where:

   C = 22.46.

   L = 15 × 12 = 180 in.

   $P = w(L/12)$ = (150 × 6)(180/12) = 13500 lb = 13.5 kips (Use live load only!).

E = 29,000 ksi (Appendix Table A-4.1, Note 1).

I = 119 in⁴ (Appendix Table A-4.6).

Δ^T_{act} = 22.46(13.5)(180/12)³/(29,000 × 119) = 0.300 in.

Since Δ^L_{act} = 0.300 in. ≤ Δ^L_{allow} = 0.5 in., the HSS beam is OK for live-load deflection.

9. *Conclusion:* The HSS12 × 4 × ¼ section is OK for bending, shear and deflection. Therefore it is acceptable.

CONNECTIONS

Steel structural elements are typically connected to each other using high-strength bolts or welds. Especially in so-called field connections — those that take place at the construction site — bolts are preferred, as they are easier, and generally less expensive, to execute in such contexts (outdoors, with unpredictable weather conditions, and without convenient access to welding equipment). Often, when welding is found to be either necessary or expedient, it occurs at the fabricating shop, although field welding is sometimes unavoidable.

Steel connections are designated according to the types of forces and/or bending moments that are intended to be resisted, and that are symbolized by the hinges, rollers, or fixed constraints that populate load diagrams in statics texts (see Figure 1.14). In practice (see Figure 4.30), hinges and rollers become *simple* connections (previously designated as Type 2); fixed joints become *fully restrained*, or *FR*, connections (previously desginated as Type 1); and the intermediate conditions between simple and fully restrained, become *partially restrained*, or *PR*, connections (previosuly designated as Type 3).

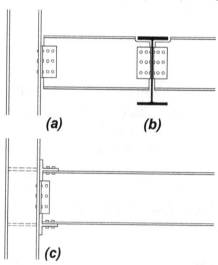

(a)   *(b)*

(c)

Figure 4.30: Typical bolted connections for steel members: (*a*) simple column-beam connection (formerly Type 2); (*b*) simple beam-girder connection (formerly Type 2); and (*c*) fully restrained, rigid frame connection between column and girder (formerly Type 1)

Bolted connections

High-strength bolts typically used to connect steel elements are stronger than the bolts most often used to connect wood elements: the two most commonly specified bolts used in steel structures are designated *Group A* (including A325 bolts with an ultimate strength, F_u = 105 ksi or 120 ksi, depending on the bolt diameter) and *Group B* (including A490 bolts with F_u = 150 ksi). In contrast, A307 bolts typically used in wood connections have an ultimate strength, F_u = 60 ksi. Bolts used to connect steel elements are stressed most commonly in shear, tension, or a combination of shear and tension, as illustrated in Figure 4.31.

For shear connections, most bolts are designed so that they "bear" against the edge of the bolt holes into which they are inserted. These are bearing-type, or "snug-tightened" joints, and a small amount of slip of the bolt within the slightly-larger bolt hole is permitted. In the less common cases where no slip is desired — for example, in structures subjected to repeated stress reversals — so-called *slip-critical* connections are designed on the basis of the clamping force that the bolts place on the steel elements being joined, so that friction between the surfaces clamped together resists the tendency of the bolts to slip within the bolt holes. In either case (bearing or slip-critical bolt design), two separate strength criteria must be satisfied: (1) the shear strength of the bolt itself; and (2) the compressive capacity of the elements being joined, as the bolts "bear" on the inside surface of the bolt holes.

Shear capacity. The nominal bolt shear stress can be taken as 68 ksi for *Group A* (A325) bolts and 84 ksi for *Group B* (A490) bolts: when divided by the safety factor for bolt shear, Ω = 2.00, the allowable stresses become 34 ksi for *Group A* and 42 ksi for *Group B* bolts. These values assume that the threaded part of the bolt shaft does not penetrate as far as the actual shear planes (designated as condition *X*, for threads *"eXcluded"* from the shear planes); in cases where the threaded portions of the shaft penetrate, or are included within,

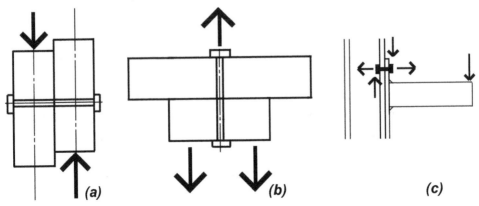

Figure 4.31: Bolts stressed in (*a*) shear; (*b*) tension; and (*c*) shear and tension

the shear planes (condition *N* for *"iNcluded"*), these available strengths are reduced by 80% to 27 ksi for *Group A* bolts and 34 ksi for *Group B* bolts. The capacity of a single bolt in shear is found by multiplying the appropriate available stress by the nominal bolt area, and then by the number of shear planes in the connection (typically either one or two corresponding to single or double shear). Typical values for the available shear strength of bolts can be found in Appendix Table A-4.18. While these values no longer include an implicit allowance (factor of safety) to account for unequal force distribution or eccentricities that may occur when groups of bolts are subjected to shear, we will assume in the examples that follow that all bolts are stressed equally. In such cases, the shear capacity of the connection is the sum of the capacities of the individual bolts, that is, the single-bolt capacity times the number of bolts in the connection. Slip-critical bolts are given a lower nominal shear stress, effectively requiring more bolts per connection, thereby ensuring that no slip will occur.

    Bearing capacity. The nominal bearing capacity of a bolt, $R_n = 3.0d_b t F_u$, depends on the strength of the material being bolted, measured by its minimum tensile strength, F_u, but may be reduced if the bolt holes are too closely spaced, or too close to the edge of the material being connected (when such clear spacing between bolt holes, or between a hole and the material edge, is less than 2 in., multiply R_n by $L_c/2$, where L_c is the smallest clear distance measured in the direction of the applied force). In this equation, d_b is the nominal bolt diameter and t is the thickness of the material upon which the bolt is bearing. The lowercase *d* in the abbreviation for bolt diameter, d_b, is consistent with steel industry practice, while the wood industry uses capital *D* to represent the diameter of nails and bolts (see Chapter 3). For bolts in single shear, the governing thickness is the thickness of the thinner element being joined. For bolts in double shear, the relevant thickness is either that of the middle piece, or the combined thicknesses of the two outer (side) pieces, whichever is less (assuming that all elements being joined are made from the same material). For connections made from different types of steel, bearing capacity should be computed for each element, based on its own thickness and material properties, with the smaller capacity governing the connection design for bearing.

    Dividing the nominal bearing capacity by the safety factor for bearing, $\Omega = 2.0$, we get the available strength for a bolt in bearing, $R_n/\Omega = 1.5d_b t F_u$, multiplied by $L_c/2$ as before, where the clear bolt hole spacing (or distance to the edge) is less than 2 in. The available strength is reduced by 80% for cases where the small deformations associated with bolt bearing, at ordinary service loads, are considered to be a design issue. Typical values for the available bearing strength of bolts can be found in Appendix Table A-4.19. The bearing capacity of the connection is the sum of the capacities of the individual bolts, that is, the single-bolt capacity times the number of bolts in the connection. The bolt hole diameter (assuming standard holes) used in the calculation of bolt hole spacing can be taken as $\frac{1}{16}$ in. greater than the nominal bolt diameter, rather than using a bolt hole diameter $\frac{1}{8}$ in. larger as is required in the calculation of net area for steel tension elements. For example, the clear bolt hole spacing for $\frac{3}{4}$-in.-diameter bolts spaced 3 in. on center in the direction of the force, $L_c = 2\frac{3}{16}$ in., is found by subtracting the bolt hole diameter ($\frac{3}{4} + \frac{1}{16} = \frac{13}{16}$ in.) from the centerline spacing (3 in.).

Minimum and maximum spacing. Bolts that are used to connect steel elements are also subjected to minimum and maximum spacing rules. The basic suggested minimum centerline spacing between bolts is 3 times the nominal bolt diameter, d_b, although a spacing no greater than $2\frac{2}{3}$ times d_b is permitted. The minimum centerline distance to any edge varies, depending on the bolt diameter. Minimum spacing and edge distance requirements are given in Appendix Table A-4.20 for typical bolt sizes.

In addition to these minimum spacing requirements, bolts are also subjected to maximum spacing rules, with 12 in. being the maximum centerline bolt spacing, in the direction of the applied load, permitted for plates bolted to another element (for example, to another plate, or to a rolled section). Where either element being joined is less than $\frac{1}{2}$ in. thick, this maximum spacing may be reduced to 24 times the thickness of the thinner element. Similarly, the maximum edge distance, measured from the bolt centerline, is 6 in., which may be reduced for elements less than $\frac{1}{2}$ in. thick to 12 times the element thickness. These requirements can be found in Appendix Table A-4.20 part C, for typical member thicknesses.

Tension, shear and block shear. Where bolt holes reduce the cross-sectional area of a tension element, the design of the tension element itself must account for this reduced net, or effective net, area, as described previously for steel tension elements. For coped beams bolted to the webs of girders, block shear must be checked, as described previously for steel beams.

Example 4.8 Design bolted connection for steel tension element

Problem definition. Examine the W8 × 24 wide-flange shape used as a tension element in a steel truss (the section's capacity was determined to be 148 kips in Example 4.1 when using two lines of $\frac{3}{4}$ in. diameter bolts). Find the required number of bolts so that their available strength is no less than the beam's tension capacity (Figure 4.32). Assume A36 steel for the W8 × 24 section, and A490 high-strength bearing-type bolts (threads included in the shear plane).

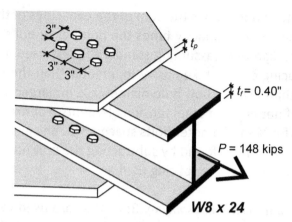

Figure 4.32: Connection of W8 × 24 tension element using two lines per flange of high-strength bolts for Example 4.8

Problem overview. Find the required number of bolts based on bolt shear; check for bolt bearing.

Problem solution

1. *Required number of bolts* (design based on shear): From Appendix Table A-4.18 part A, for A490 bolts and ¾ in. bolt diameter, the shear capacity per bolt is 18.6 kips, assuming threads excluded from the single shear plane. Based on Note 1 (for threads *included* in shear plane), this value is reduced by 80%, so the capacity per bolt becomes 0.80 × 18.6 = 14.88 kips per bolt. The required number of bolts is equal to the total capacity divided by the capacity per bolt, or 148/14.88 = 9.95 bolts. Clearly, this number must be rounded up to an integer that is divisible by 4, so that the four lines of bolts distributed on the two flanges all have the same number: therefore, we provisionally select 12 bolts, as shown in Figure 4.32.

2. Check required number of bolts (based on bearing capacity): From Appendix Table A-4.19, the bearing capacity per bolt, per inch of A36 material thickness, is 65.3 kips. As can be seen from Table A-4.3, the flange thickness of a W8 × 24 section is 0.40 in. Therefore, the capacity of a single bolt, based on bearing on the flange thickness, is 0.40 × 65.3 = 26.12 kips. The total capacity of the 12-bolt connection, again based on bearing, is 12 × 26.12 = 313 kips. Since this capacity is no smaller than the capacity determined in step 1 for shear, the provisional selection of 12 bolts is satisfactory. For a bearing capacity less than that determined for shear, the number of bolts would need to be increased accordingly, and the bolt design would be governed by bearing instead of shear.

Welded connections

Two pieces of steel may be welded together, not by directly melting one piece into the other, but rather by depositing melted steel contained in a separate electrode along the surfaces of the two steel pieces to be joined. Naturally, some melting of the joined pieces occurs as the "weld" steel is deposited; however, the weld and adjacent surfaces rapidly cool and harden as the electrode moves along the weld line, effectively connecting the pieces together. While there are numerous types of weld geometries — including groove welds, plug welds, and slot welds — the most common is the triangular *fillet* weld (pronounced ***fill-it***). In what follows, we will discuss the strength of fillet welds subjected to loads parallel, perpendicular, or angled to the weld line.

As can be seen in Figure 4.33, a fillet weld is assumed to fail along the surface defined by its throat, labeled t in Figure 4.33a, whether the weld itself is stressed in tension, compression, or shear. With symmetrical welds angled at 45° to the surfaces being joined, it can be seen that the throat dimension, t, equals $0.707w$ (where w is the hypotenuse of a 45° right triangle with both legs equal to t). For a weld of length, L, the surface area resisting either tension, compression, or shear is therefore $A_w = tL = 0.707wL$. A typical one-inch length of weld (that is, with $L = 1$), therefore has a failure surface area of $A_{w1} = 0.707w$. The nominal strength (capacity) of a weld loaded "longitudinally" — that is, as shown in Figure 4.33c — is found by multiplying this surface area by the weld strength, taken as $0.6F_{EXX}$, where F_{EXX} depends on the strength of the electrode used. For A36 ($F_y = 36$ ksi) and A992 ($F_y = 50$ ksi) steel, an electrode is typically specified with $F_{EXX} = 70$ ksi, designated generically as E70XX. Putting this all together, we can compute the nominal strength of a 1-in.-long longitudinal weld: $R_{wl} = 0.707(0.6 \times 70)(w) = 29.69w$ kips per inch of weld length. The available strength is found by dividing this nominal capacity by the safety factor, $\Omega = 2.0$, so that $R_{wl}/\Omega = 14.85w$ kips per inch of weld.

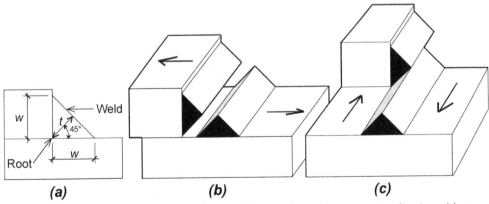

Figure 4.33: Three views of a typical fillet weld illustrating (*a*) the root, size (leg length), *w*, and throat dimension, *t*, as well as two modes of failure on the throat surface, based on either (*b*) tension or (*c*) shear

The general equation for all fillet welds, loaded longitudinally as shown in Figure 4.33c, transversely as shown in Figure 4.33b, or at any angle in between, is:

$$R_n/\Omega = 14.85w(1.0 + 0.50 \sin^{1.5} \theta) \tag{4.15}$$

where

R_n/Ω = the available strength of a one-inch-long weld (kips).

θ = the angle (from 0° to 90°) between the weld line and the direction of load.

w = the weld size, or leg length (in.).

It can be seen that for longitudinal welds, with $\theta = 0°$, the parenthetical term drops out, and Equation 4.15 is as derived earlier. For $\theta = 90°$ (a transverse weld), the capacity increases by a factor of $(1.0 + 0.50 \sin^{1.5} 90°) = 1.5$. The available strengths for longitudinal and transverse welds are therefore as follows: for a one-inch-long longitudinal weld, we get

$$R_{wl}/\Omega = 14.85w \tag{4.16}$$

while the available strength for a one-inch-long transverse weld is

$$R_{wt}/\Omega = 1.5(14.85w) = 22.27w \tag{4.17}$$

In these equations, R_{wl}/Ω and R_{wt}/Ω are the available strengths (kips) of a one-inch-long weld oriented, respectively, longitudinally or transversely to the load, and w is the weld size, or leg length (in.). Where both longitudinal and transverse welds occur in the same connection, the available strength is taken as either $(R_{wl}/\Omega + R_{wt}/\Omega)$ or $(0.85R_{wl}/\Omega + 1.5R_{wt}/\Omega)$, whichever is greater. Other constraints on fillet weld design are discussed below.

Weld size limits. Weld sizes cannot simply be determined on the basis of Equations 4.16 or 4.17 in order to satisfy the requirements for available strength of a connection. Rather, they are also constrained by the dimensions of the material welded together. Minimum weld sizes must be proportioned according to the thickness of the materials being joined; while maximum weld sizes must be no larger than the edge along which the weld is deposited or, where the edge is ¼ in. or more thick, must be at least ¹⁄₁₆ in. smaller than any such edge (these size constraints are summarized in Appendix Table A-4.21). For this reason, it is more common to first establish a provisional weld size according to these minimum and maximum limits, and then determine the required total weld length. For connections with combinations of longitudinal and transverse welds, the design process is necessarily iterative, unless one of the weld lengths, either for the longitudinal or transverse portion, can be initially determined from the connection geometry.

The minimum length of a fillet weld is required to be at least four times its leg size. Otherwise the effective size of the weld, used in calculations, must be taken as no more than one-fourth of the weld length. For example, the minimum weld length for a ½ in. leg size is 4 × ½ = 2 in. If a ½ in. weld size is used with a shorter weld length — say 1 in. — the effective weld size used in calculating the available strength of the weld would be no more than the actual length (1 in.) divided by 4, or ¼ in, even though the actual weld size is ½ in.

Longitudinal welds. For symmetrical and parallel longitudinal welds, the weld length, L, must be no smaller than the distance between the two weld lines, W, as shown in Figure 4.34.

Where such welds transmit force to the "end" of an element subject to tension or compression (that is, through an "end-loaded" weld), an effective length $L_e = 6L$ is used to compute the weld capacity, where 6 is defined as follows:

$$0.6 \leq \beta = 1.2 - 0.002(L/w) \leq 1.0 \qquad (4.18)$$

In other words, where the ratio of weld length to weld size, $L/w \leq 100$, $\beta = 1.0$, and the effective length equals the actual weld length. Otherwise, $\beta = 1.2 - 0.002(L/w)$, with a lower limit of $\beta = 0.60$ where the ratio of weld length to weld size, $L/w \geq 300$.

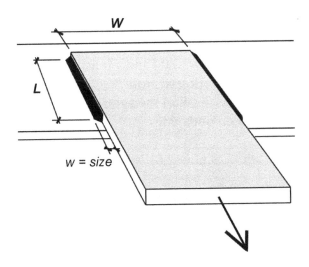

Figure 4.34: Parallel, longitudinal welds

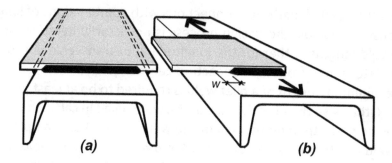

Figure 4.35: Termination of fillet welds where (*a*) welds occur on opposite sides of a common plane; and (*b*) a lap joint extends beyond a tension element

Fillet weld terminations. In certain cases, fillet welds must be terminated before reaching the edge of the steel elements they are connecting, to prevent damage (notching, gouging) of the element's edge. Figure 4.35*a* illustrates a condition where the fillet weld at the underside of a plate (shown as a dotted line) must be interrupted at the corners before turning 90° and being deposited on the opposite side of the same plate. Figure 4.35*b* illustrates a lap joint that extends beyond a tension element: in such cases, the fillet weld must terminate a distance equal to the weld size, *w*, from the edge of the tension element.

Shear strength of connecting elements. Where welded connecting elements such as gussets, angles, or other plates are subjected to shear, the required thickness, *t*, of such elements can be found by equating the available shear strength of the connector, per unit length, to the available longitudinal weld strength, again per unit length. The available shear strength of the connector is $0.6F_u t/\Omega$, while that of a single longitudinal weld, from Equation 4.16, is $R_{wl}/\Omega = 14.85w$. For a connector welded on both sides of the plate, the available strength of the weld doubles to $2 \times 14.85w = 29.69w$. Equating these strengths using a safety factor, $\Omega = 2.00$ and a tensile strength, $F_u = 58$ ksi (corresponding to a connector fabricated from A36 steel), we get the following required connector thickness, t_{min} (in.) for a given weld size, *w* (in.), where the connector plate is welded on both sides:

$$t_{min} = 29.69w(2.0)/(0.6 \times 58) = 1.71w \qquad (4.19)$$

Example 4.9 Find capacity of welded connectors with transverse or longitudinal welds

Problem definition. Find the capacities of the 6-in.-wide, ⅞-in.-thick plates shown in Figure 4.36, welded to (*a*) a wide-flange shape with transverse welds, and (*b*) an 8-in.-deep channel shape with longitudinal welds. In each case, assume that the plates are fabricated from A36 steel, and that the weld size is ⅜ in. Use an E70XX electrode with $F_u = 70$ ksi.

Solution overview. Find the capacity of the welds; confirm that the tensile capacity of the plates is no smaller than the weld capacity.

Problem solution
1. Based on Equations 4.16 and 4.17, we can express the capacity of the transverse and longitudinal welds as follows:
     For the transverse weld, the unit capacity, $R_{wt}/\Omega = 1.5(14.85w) = 1.5(14.85)(⅜) = 8.35$ kips per inch of weld. There is a total of $6 \times 2 = 12$ in. of transverse weld on the two plates (since the plate width, $W = 6$ in.), so the total capacity for the transverse welds, $P_t = 8.35(12) = 100.2$ kips.
     For the longitudinal weld, the unit capacity, $R_{wl}/\Omega = 14.85w = 14.85(⅜) = 5.57$ kips per inch of weld. Since this is an "end-loaded" condition, the ratio of weld length to weld size must be checked: $L/w = 8/(⅜) = 21.3$ is no greater than 100, so the effective weld length equals the actual length, which is 8 in. There is a total of $8 \times 2 = 16$ in. of longitudinal weld on the plate, so the total capacity for the longitudinal welds, $P_l = 5.57(16) = 89.1$ kips. The weld length, $L = 8$ in. cannot be smaller than the distance between the two weld lines, in this case equal to the plate width of 6 in.
2. The tensile capacity of both plates is based on the smaller of the following: either the capacity to resist tensile yielding on the gross area or to resist rupture on the net area. The capacity based on yielding (see previous section in this chapter) is $0.6F_y A_g = 0.6(36)(⅞ \times 6) = 113.4$ kips. The

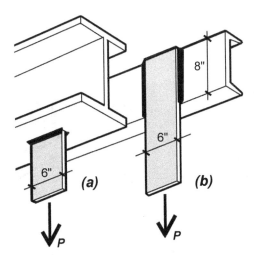

Figure 4.36: Connector plate capacity for Example 4.9 using (*a*) transverse welds and (*b*) longitudinal welds

capacity based on rupture is $0.5F_uA_n = 0.5(58)(\% \times 6) = 152.2$ kips. The governing tensile capacity, 113.4 kips, is larger than the actual capacity of either weld condition, so the strength of the welds governs both designs. For short gusset plates, the effective net area is taken as equal to the net area, so long as it is no bigger than 85% of the gross area.

3. *Conclusion:* the capacity of Plate *a*, P_t, equals 100.2 kips; and the capacity of Plate *b*, P_l, equals 89.1 kips.

Example 4.10 Find capacity of welded connector with angled load

Problem definition. Find the capacity of the ½-in.-thick plate shown in Figure 4.37, welded to a wide-flange column shape. Assume that the plate is fabricated from A36 steel, and that the weld size is ¾₆ in., on both sides of the plate. Use an E70XX electrode with $F_u = 70$ ksi.

Solution overview. Confirm that the shear capacity of the plate is greater than the capacity of the weld; compute the available strength of the weld.

Problem solution

1. From Equation 4.19, the required thickness of the plate (that is, the plate thickness consistent with the maximum available shear strength of a weld on both sides of a connector plate) is $t_{min} = 1.71w = 1.71(\%_{16}) = 0.32$ in. In this calculation, we have compared the weld and plate shear strength as if the load were parallel to the weld, even though the actual load on the connector is oriented at a 60° angle to the weld line.

2. Since the actual plate thickness of ½ in. is larger than the required thickness, $t_{min} = 0.32$ in., the weld will fail in shear before the plate does. For

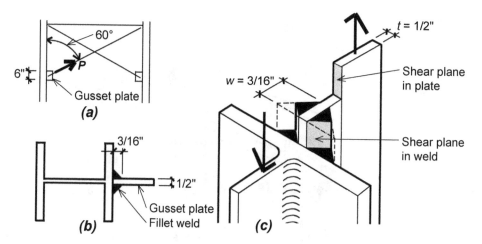

Figure 4.37: Connector plate capacity for Example 4.10: a gusset plate welded to a W-shape is shown (*a*) in elevation; (*b*) in section; and (*c*) in a schematic "cut-away" view showing the potential shear failure planes for the plate and fillet welds

this reason, we can find the capacity (available strength) of the connector by determining the available strength of the weld, per inch of length, according to Equation 4.15:

$R_n/\Omega = 14.85w(1.0 + 0.50 \sin^{1.5} \theta) = 14.85(\%_{16})(1.0 + 0.50 \sin^{1.5} 60) = 3.91$ kips per inch of weld.

3. The total weld length is $6 \times 2 = 12$ in., so the total available strength of the connector, $P = 12(3.91) = 46.9$ kips.

Example 4.11 Design a welded connector with both longitudinal and transverse welds

Problem definition. Find the required longitudinal weld length, L, on the two ½-in.-thick plates shown in Figure 4.38, to resist a load, $P = 80$ kips. Assume that the plate is fabricated from A36 steel. Use an E70XX electrode with $F_u = 70$ ksi.

Solution overview. Confirm that capacity of both plates is no less than 80 kips; find the required longitudinal weld length so that the total weld capacity is no less than 80 kips.

Problem solution
1. The tensile capacity of both plates is based on the smaller of the following: either the capacity to resist tensile yielding on the gross area or to resist rupture on the net area. The capacity based on yielding (see previous section in this chapter) is $0.6F_yA_g = 0.6(36)(\frac{1}{2} \times 4 \times 2) = 86.4$ kips. The capacity based on rupture is $0.5F_uA_n = 0.5(58)(\frac{1}{2} \times 4 \times 2) = 116$ kips. The governing tensile capacity, 86.4 kips, is larger than the actual load of 80 kips, so the plates are satisfactory. For short gusset plates, the effective net area is taken as equal to the net area, so long as it is no bigger

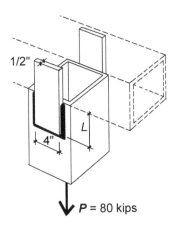

Figure 4.38: View of welded plate connectors for Example 4.11

than 85% of the gross area.

2. From Appendix Table A-4.21, for a ½-in.-thick plate, the minimum weld size is $\frac{3}{16}$ in., and the maximum weld size is $\frac{1}{2} - \frac{1}{16} = \frac{7}{16}$ in. For this example, we will choose a weld size of $w = \frac{3}{16}$ in.

3. Based on Equations 4.16 and 4.17, we can express the capacity of the longitudinal and transverse welds as follows:

   For the longitudinal weld, the unit capacity, $R_{wl}/\Omega = 14.85w = 14.85(\frac{3}{16}) = 2.784$ kips per inch of weld. There is a total of $4L$ in. of longitudinal weld on the two plates (where L is the length of each longitudinal segment), so the total capacity for the longitudinal welds, $P_l = 2.784(4L) = 11.138L$ kips.

   For the transverse weld, the unit capacity, $R_{wt}/\Omega = 1.5(14.85w) = 1.5(14.85)(\frac{3}{16}) = 4.177$ kips per inch of weld. There is a total of $4 \times 2 = 8$ in. of transverse weld on the two plates (since the plate width, $W = 4$ in.), so the total capacity for the transverse welds, $P_t = 4.177(8) = 33.413$ kips.

4. Where both longitudinal and transverse welds occur in the same connection, the available strength is taken as either (a) $R_{wl}/\Omega + R_{wt}/\Omega$; or (b) $0.85R_{wl}/\Omega + 1.5R_{wt}/\Omega$, whichever is greater. The terms R_{wl}/Ω and R_{wt}/Ω refer to the available strengths (capacities) of the longitudinal and transverse welds, respectively; therefore, we must test both alternatives, setting the capacities equal to the load, $P = 80$ kips and solving for the required length, L:

   $R_{wl}/\Omega + R_{wt}/\Omega = 11.138L + 33.413 = 80$; from which $L = 4.18$ in.

   $0.85R_{wl}/\Omega + 1.5R_{wt}/\Omega = 0.85(11.138L) + 1.5(33.413) = 80$; from which $L = 3.16$ in.

5. Since the *greater* capacity of the two alternatives may be used, the *smaller* length, $L = 3.16$ in. is acceptable. Looked at another way, if the length for both alternatives were set at $L = 3.16$ in., case (a) would have a capacity smaller than 80 kips, while case (b) would have a capacity exactly equal to 80 kips; it can be seen that case (b) has the greater capacity and therefore would govern the design. Increasing the length to 4.18 in. found in case (a) is not required. We round up the required length for the longitudinal weld to 3½ in.

CHAPTER 4 APPENDIX

Table A-4.1: Steel properties[1]

Category	ASTM designation	Yield stress, F_y (ksi)	(Ultimate) tensile stress, F_u (ksi)	Preferred for these shapes
Carbon	A36	36	58	M, S, C, MC, L, plates[4] and bars
	A500 Gr. B	42	58	HSS round
	A500 Gr. B	46	58	HSS rectangular
	A53 Gr. B	[2]35	60	Pipe
High-strength, low-alloy	A992	50	65	[3]W
	A572 Gr. 50	50	65	HP
Corrosion resistant, high-strength, low-alloy	A588	50	70	
	A242	42-50	63-70	
Low alloy reinforcing bars	A615	40	60	Rebar
		60	90	
		75	100	
Bolts	A325	n/a	120	High-strength bolts, 0.5 – 1 in. diameter
		n/a	105	High-strength bolts, over 1 – 1.5 in. diameter
	A490	n/a	150	High-strength bolts, 0.5 – 1.5 in. diameter
	A307 Gr. A	n/a	60	Common bolts
Cold-formed	A653 Gr. 33	33	45	Connector plates[4] in wood construction

Notes:

1. **The modulus of elasticity, *E*, for these steels can be taken as 29,000 ksi.**

2. Steel with F_y =35 ksi may be designed as if the yield stress is F_y = 36 ksi.

3. W-shapes have formerly been specified in A36; current practice in the U.S. is to use A992 with F_y = 50 ksi.

4. In wood fastener design, the dowel bearing strength of connector plates, F_e equals $1.5F_u$ (for A36 hot-rolled steel) and $1.375F_u$ (for A653 GR 33 cold-formed steel). These values are 1.6 times less than those permitted in steel structures so that they can be used in yield limit equations for wood members that have load duration adjustments (adjustments that may be as high as 1.6 for wind or seismic).

Table A-4.2: Steel allowable stresses and available strengths

Type of structural action	Allowable stress[1] (same units as F_y or F_u)	Available strength limit states (with safety factor, Ω)[4]
Tension	$F_t^{gross} = 0.60F_y$ (yielding)	$P_a \leq \dfrac{P_n}{\Omega} = \dfrac{F_y A_g}{1.67}$
	$F_t^{net} = 0.50F_u$ (rupture)	$P_a \leq \dfrac{P_n}{\Omega} = \dfrac{F_y A_g}{1.67}$
Compression	See Tables A-4.11 through A-4.14 (analysis) or A-4.10 (design)	
Bending[2], assuming laterally braced, compact section	$F_b = 0.60F_y$ (used with plastic section modulus, Z_x) or $F_b = 0.66F_y$ (used with elastic section modulus, S_x)	$M_a \leq \dfrac{M_n}{\Omega} = \dfrac{F_y Z_x}{1.67}$ The available strength method has no official limit state for the elastic moment
Shear[3]	$F_v = 0.40F_y$	$V_a \leq \dfrac{V_n}{\Omega} = \dfrac{0.6F_y A_w}{1.5}$

Notes:

1. Allowable stresses, although no longer officially sanctioned by the American Institute of Steel Construction, result in the same values that are obtained when considering available strength, except in the case of bending. For bending, the limit state defined by the elastic moment, formerly the basis of allowable stress design, is no longer applicable, although it can still be used with somewhat conservative results for laterally-braced, compact sections. On the other hand, an allowable stress equation can be formulated based on the plastic section modulus that is equivalent to the available strength equation for laterally-braced, compact sections.

2. The allowable stress for bending, $0.66F_b$, used with the elastic section modulus, S_x, gives a generally conservative value compared with using $\Omega = 1.67$ and the plastic section modulus, Z_x. To reconcile these two different safety factors, it is necessary to approximate the ratio of Z_x/S_x, which varies depending upon the cross section. This ratio can be taken conservatively as 1.1 for W shapes; therefore, $Z_x = 1.1S_x$, and the allowable moment, $M_p/\Omega = F_y Z_x/\Omega = 1.1F_y S_x/\Omega = 1.1F_y S_x/1.67 = 0.66F_b S_x$, which corresponds to the assumptions used for an allowable bending stress.

3. Both the allowable stress and available strength values for shear assume I-shaped rolled members meeting the slenderness criteria for beam webs. For beam webs that do not meet slenderness criteria for shear, a reduced allowable shear stress, $F_v = 0.36F_y$, is used. This is equivalent to using an increased allowable strength design safety factor, $\Omega = 1.67$, and applies to the following W-shapes: W12 × 14, W16 × 26, W24 × 55, W30 × 90, W33 × 118, W36 × 135, W40 × 149, and W44 × 230. For the rectangular HSS listed in Appendix Table A-4.6, the reduced shear stress, $F_v = 0.36F_y$, is also used, with a web area, A_w, equal to $2ht$ (where t is the wall thickness of the web and h can be assumed to equal the nominal depth minus $3t$). The value for the coefficient C_v is equal to 1.0 for all W-shapes, and is not included in the shear equations. For cross sections with very thin webs, this coefficient needs to be considered.

4. In these equations for various limit states, the subscript a refers to the available strength of the cross section, that is, the strength that is considered safe. The subscript n refers to the nominal strength of the cross section, that is, the actual limit state of the material. In other words, P_a is equivalent to the maximum tension force that the cross section can safely sustain; M_a equivalent to the maximum bending moment that the cross section can safely sustain; and V_a is equivalent to the maximum shear force that the cross section can safely sustain.

Table A-4.3: Dimensions and properties of steel W sections[5]

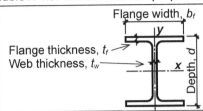

Flange width, b_f

Flange thickness, t_f
Web thickness, t_w

Depth, d

Cross-sectional area = A
Moment of inertia = I
Section modulus, $S_x = 2I_x/d$
Sectional modulus, $S_y = 2I_x/b_f$
Radius of gyration, $r_x = \sqrt{I_x/A}$
Radius of gyration, $r_y = \sqrt{I_y/A}$

Designation	A (in²)	d (in.)	t_w (in.)	b_f (in.)	t_f (in.)	S_x (in3)	Z_x (in3)	I_x (in4)	I_y (in4)	r_y (in.)
W4 × 13	3.83	4.16	0.280	4.06	0.345	5.46	6.28	11.3	3.86	1.00
W5 × 16	4.71	5.01	0.240	5.00	0.360	8.55	9.63	21.4	7.51	1.26
W5 × 19	5.56	5.15	0.270	5.03	0.430	10.2	11.6	26.3	9.13	1.28
W6 × 8.5[2]	2.52	5.83	0.170	3.94	0.195	5.10	5.73	14.9	1.99	0.890
W6 × 92	2.68	5.90	0.170	3.94	0.215	5.56	6.23	16.4	2.20	0.905
W6 × 12	3.55	6.03	0.230	4.00	0.280	7.31	8.30	22.1	2.99	0.918
W6 × 16	4.74	6.28	0.260	4.03	0.405	10.2	11.7	32.1	4.43	0.967
W6 × 15[1]	4.43	5.99	0.230	5.99	0.260	9.72	10.8	29.1	9.32	1.45
W6 × 20	5.87	6.20	0.260	6.02	0.365	13.4	14.9	41.4	13.3	1.50
W6 × 25	7.34	6.38	0.320	6.08	0.455	16.7	18.9	53.4	17.1	1.52
W8 × 10[2,4]	2.96	7.89	0.170	3.94	0.205	7.81	8.87	30.8	2.09	0.841
W8 × 13	3.84	7.99	0.230	4.00	0.255	9.91	11.4	39.6	2.73	0.843
W8 × 15	4.44	8.11	0.245	4.02	0.315	11.8	13.6	48.0	3.41	0.876
W8 × 18	5.26	8.14	0.230	5.250	0.330	15.2	17.0	61.9	7.97	1.23
W8 × 21	6.16	8.28	0.250	5.270	0.400	18.2	20.4	75.3	9.77	1.26
W8 × 24	7.08	7.93	0.245	6.50	0.400	20.9	23.1	82.7	18.3	1.61
W8 × 28	8.25	8.06	0.285	6.54	0.465	24.3	27.2	98.0	21.7	1.62
W8 × 31[2]	9.13	8.00	0.285	8.00	0.435	27.5	30.4	110	37.1	2.02
W8 × 35	10.3	8.12	0.310	8.02	0.495	31.2	34.7	127	42.6	2.03
W8 × 40	11.7	8.25	0.360	8.07	0.560	35.5	39.8	146	49.1	2.04
W8 × 48	14.1	8.50	0.400	8.11	0.685	43.2	49.0	184	60.9	2.08
W8 × 58	17.1	8.75	0.510	8.22	0.810	52.0	59.8	228	75.1	2.10
W8 × 67	19.7	9.00	0.570	8.28	0.935	60.4	70.1	272	88.6	2.12
W10 × 12[2,4]	3.54	9.87	0.190	3.96	0.210	10.9	12.6	53.8	2.18	0.785
W10 × 15[4]	4.41	10.0	0.230	4.00	0.270	13.8	16.0	68.9	2.89	0.810
W10 × 17[4]	4.99	10.1	0.240	4.01	0.330	16.2	18.7	81.9	3.56	0.845
W10 × 19	5.62	10.2	0.250	4.02	0.395	18.8	21.6	96.3	4.29	0.874
W10 × 22[4]	6.49	10.2	0.240	5.75	0.360	23.2	26.0	118	11.4	1.33
W10 × 26	7.61	10.3	0.260	5.77	0.440	27.9	31.3	144	14.1	1.36
W10 × 30	8.84	10.5	0.300	5.81	0.510	32.4	36.6	170	16.7	1.37
W10 × 33	9.71	9.73	0.290	7.96	0.435	35.0	38.8	171	36.6	1.94
W10 × 39	11.5	9.92	0.315	7.99	0.530	42.1	46.8	209	45.0	1.98
W10 × 45	13.3	10.10	0.350	8.02	0.620	49.1	54.9	248	53.4	2.01

(continued)

Table A-4.3 continued

Designation	A (in²)	d (in.)	t_w (in.)	b_f (in.)	t_f (in.)	S_x (in3)	Z_x (in3)	I_x (in4)	I_y (in4)	r_y (in.)
W10 × 49	14.4	10.0	0.340	10.0	0.560	54.6	60.4	272	93.4	2.54
W10 × 54	15.8	10.1	0.370	10.0	0.615	60.0	66.6	303	103	2.56
W10 × 60	17.7	10.2	0.420	10.1	0.680	66.7	74.6	341	116	2.57
W10 × 68	19.9	10.4	0.470	10.1	0.770	75.7	85.3	394	134	2.59
W10 × 77	22.7	10.6	0.530	10.2	0.870	85.9	97.6	455	154	2.60
W10 × 88	26.0	10.8	0.605	10.3	0.990	98.5	113	534	179	2.63
W10 × 100	29.3	11.1	0.680	10.3	1.120	112	130	623	207	2.65
W10 × 112	32.9	11.4	0.755	10.4	1.250	126	147	716	236	2.68
W12 × 14[3,4]	4.16	11.9	0.200	3.97	0.225	14.9	17.4	88.6	2.36	0.753
W12 × 16[4]	4.71	12.0	0.220	3.99	0.265	17.1	20.1	103	2.82	0.773
W12 × 19[4]	5.57	12.2	0.235	4.01	0.350	21.3	24.7	130	3.76	0.822
W12 × 22[4]	6.48	12.3	0.260	4.03	0.425	25.4	29.3	156	4.66	0.848
W12 × 26[4]	7.65	12.2	0.230	6.49	0.380	33.4	37.2	204	17.3	1.51
W12 × 30[4]	8.79	12.3	0.260	6.52	0.440	38.6	43.1	238	20.3	1.52
W12 × 35[4]	10.3	12.5	0.300	6.56	0.520	45.6	51.2	285	24.5	1.54
W12 × 40	11.7	11.9	0.295	8.01	0.515	51.5	57.0	307	44.1	1.94
W12 × 45	13.1	12.1	0.335	8.05	0.575	57.7	64.2	348	50.0	1.95
W12 × 50	14.6	12.2	0.370	8.08	0.640	64.2	71.9	391	56.3	1.96
W12 × 53	15.6	12.1	0.345	10.0	0.575	70.6	77.9	425	95.8	2.48
W12 × 58	17.0	12.2	0.360	10.0	0.640	78.0	86.4	475	107	2.51
W12 × 65[2]	19.1	12.1	0.390	12.0	0.605	87.9	96.8	533	174	3.02
W12 × 72	21.1	12.3	0.430	12.0	0.670	97.4	108	597	195	3.04
W12 × 79	23.2	12.4	0.470	12.1	0.735	107	119	662	216	3.05
W12 × 87	25.6	12.5	0.515	12.1	0.810	118	132	740	241	3.07
W12 × 96	28.2	12.7	0.550	12.2	0.900	131	147	833	270	3.09
W12 × 106	31.2	12.9	0.610	12.2	0.990	145	164	933	301	3.11
W12 × 120	35.2	13.1	0.710	12.3	1.11	163	186	1070	345	3.13
W12 × 136	39.9	13.4	0.790	12.4	1.25	186	214	1240	398	3.16
W12 × 152	44.7	13.7	0.870	12.5	1.40	209	243	1430	454	3.19
W12 × 170	50.0	14.0	0.960	12.6	1.56	235	275	1650	517	3.22
W12 × 190	56.0	14.4	1.06	12.7	1.74	263	311	1890	589	3.25
W12 × 210	61.8	14.7	1.18	12.8	1.90	292	348	2140	664	3.28
W12 × 230	67.7	15.1	1.29	12.9	2.07	321	386	2420	742	3.31
W12 × 252	74.1	15.4	1.40	13.0	2.25	353	428	2720	828	3.34
W12 × 279	81.9	15.9	1.53	13.1	2.47	393	481	3110	937	3.38
W12 × 305	89.5	16.3	1.63	13.2	2.71	435	537	3550	1050	3.42
W12 × 336	98.9	16.8	1.78	13.4	2.96	483	603	4060	1190	3.47
W14 × 22[4]	6.49	13.7	0.230	5.00	0.335	29.0	33.2	199	7.00	1.04
W14 × 26[4]	7.69	13.9	0.255	5.03	0.420	35.3	40.2	245	8.91	1.08

(continued)

Table A-4.3 continued

Designation	A (in²)	d (in.)	t_w (in.)	b_f (in.)	t_f (in.)	S_x (in3)	Z_x (in3)	I_x (in4)	I_y (in4)	r_y (in.)
W14 × 30[4]	8.85	13.8	0.270	6.73	0.385	42.0	47.3	291	19.6	1.49
W14 × 34[4]	10.0	14.0	0.285	6.75	0.455	48.6	54.6	340	23.3	1.53
W14 × 38[4]	11.2	14.1	0.310	6.77	0.515	54.6	61.5	385	26.7	1.55
W14 × 43[4]	12.6	13.7	0.305	8.00	0.530	62.6	69.6	428	45.2	1.89
W14 × 48	14.1	13.8	0.340	8.03	0.595	70.2	78.4	484	51.4	1.91
W14 × 53	15.6	13.9	0.370	8.06	0.660	77.8	87.1	541	57.7	1.92
W14 × 61	17.9	13.9	0.375	10.0	0.645	92.1	102	640	107	2.45
W14 × 68	20.0	14.0	0.415	10.0	0.720	103	115	722	121	2.46
W14 × 74	21.8	14.2	0.450	10.1	0.785	112	126	795	134	2.48
W14 × 82	24.0	14.3	0.510	10.1	0.855	123	139	881	148	2.48
W14 × 90[2]	26.5	14.0	0.440	14.5	0.710	143	157	999	362	3.70
W14 × 99[2]	29.1	14.2	0.485	14.6	0.780	157	173	1110	402	3.71
W14 × 109	32.0	14.3	0.525	14.6	0.860	173	192	1240	447	3.73
W14 × 120	35.3	14.5	0.590	14.7	0.940	190	212	1380	495	3.74
W14 × 132	38.8	14.7	0.645	14.7	1.03	209	234	1530	548	3.76
W14 × 145	42.7	14.8	0.680	15.5	1.09	232	260	1710	677	3.98
W14 × 159	46.7	15.0	0.745	15.6	1.19	254	287	1900	748	4.00
W14 × 176	51.8	15.2	0.830	15.7	1.31	281	320	2140	838	4.02
W14 × 193	56.8	15.5	0.890	15.7	1.44	310	355	2400	931	4.05
W14 × 211	62.0	15.7	0.980	15.8	1.56	338	390	2660	1030	4.07
W14 × 233	68.5	16.0	1.07	15.9	1.72	375	436	3010	1150	4.10
W14 × 257	75.6	16.4	1.18	16.0	1.89	415	487	3400	1290	4.13
W14 × 283	83.3	16.7	1.29	16.1	2.07	459	542	3840	1440	4.17
W14 × 311	91.4	17.1	1.41	16.2	2.26	506	603	4330	1610	4.20
W14 × 342	101	17.5	1.54	16.4	2.47	558	672	4900	1810	4.24
W14 × 370	109	17.9	1.66	16.5	2.66	607	736	5440	1990	4.27
W14 × 398	117	18.3	1.77	16.6	2.85	656	801	6000	2170	4.31
W14 × 426	125	18.7	1.88	16.7	3.04	706	869	6600	2360	4.34
W14 × 455	134	19.0	2.02	16.8	3.21	756	936	7190	2560	4.38
W14 × 500	147	19.6	2.19	17.0	3.50	838	1050	8210	2880	4.43
W14 × 550	162	20.2	2.38	17.2	3.82	931	1180	9430	3250	4.49
W14 × 605	178	20.9	2.60	17.4	4.16	1040	1320	10800	3680	4.55
W14 × 665	196	21.6	2.83	17.7	4.52	1150	1480	12400	4170	4.62
W14 × 730	215	22.4	3.07	17.9	4.91	1280	1660	14300	4720	4.69
W16 × 26[3,4]	7.68	15.7	0.250	5.50	0.345	38.4	44.2	301	9.59	1.12
W16 × 31[4]	9.13	15.9	0.275	5.53	0.440	47.2	54.0	375	12.4	1.17
W16 × 36[4]	10.6	15.9	0.295	6.99	0.430	56.5	64.0	448	24.5	1.52
W16 × 40[4]	11.8	16.0	0.305	7.00	0.505	64.7	73.0	518	28.9	1.57
W16 × 45[4]	13.3	16.1	0.345	7.04	0.565	72.7	82.3	586	32.8	1.57

(continued)

Table A-4.3 continued

Designation	A (in²)	d (in.)	t_w (in.)	b_f (in.)	t_f (in.)	S_x (in3)	Z_x (in3)	I_x (in4)	I_y (in4)	r_y (in.)
W16 × 50[4]	14.7	16.3	0.380	7.07	0.630	81.0	92.0	659	37.2	1.59
W16 × 57	16.8	16.4	0.430	7.12	0.715	92.2	105	758	43.1	1.60
W16 × 67[4]	19.6	16.3	0.395	10.2	0.665	117	130	954	119	2.46
W16 × 77	22.6	16.5	0.455	10.3	0.760	134	150	1110	138	2.47
W16 × 89	26.2	16.8	0.525	10.4	0.875	155	175	1300	163	2.49
W16 × 100	29.4	17.0	0.585	10.4	0.985	175	198	1490	186	2.51
W18 × 35[4]	10.3	17.7	0.300	6.00	0.425	57.6	66.5	510	15.3	1.22
W18 × 40[4]	11.8	17.9	0.315	6.02	0.525	68.4	78.4	612	19.1	1.27
W18 × 46[4]	13.5	18.1	0.360	6.06	0.605	78.8	90.7	712	22.5	1.29
W18 × 50[4]	14.7	18.0	0.355	7.50	0.570	88.9	101	800	40.1	1.65
W18 × 55[4]	16.2	18.1	0.390	7.53	0.630	98.3	112	890	44.9	1.67
W18 × 60[4]	17.6	18.2	0.415	7.56	0.695	108	123	984	50.1	1.68
W18 × 65	19.1	18.4	0.450	7.59	0.750	117	133	1070	54.8	1.69
W18 × 71	20.9	18.5	0.495	7.64	0.810	127	146	1170	60.3	1.70
W18 × 76[4]	22.3	18.2	0.425	11.0	0.680	146	163	1330	152	2.61
W18 × 86	25.3	18.4	0.480	11.1	0.770	166	186	1530	175	2.63
W18 × 97	28.5	18.6	0.535	11.1	0.870	188	211	1750	201	2.65
W18 × 106	31.1	18.7	0.590	11.2	0.940	204	230	1910	220	2.66
W18 × 119	35.1	19.0	0.655	11.3	1.06	231	262	2190	253	2.69
W18 × 130	38.3	19.3	0.670	11.2	1.20	256	290	2460	278	2.70
W18 × 143	42.0	19.5	0.730	11.2	1.32	282	322	2750	311	2.72
W18 × 158	46.3	19.7	0.810	11.3	1.44	310	356	3060	347	2.74
W18 × 175	51.4	20.0	0.890	11.4	1.59	344	398	3450	391	2.76
W18 × 192	56.2	20.4	0.960	11.5	1.75	380	442	3870	440	2.79
W18 × 211	62.3	20.7	1.06	11.6	1.91	419	490	4330	493	2.82
W18 × 234	68.8	21.1	1.16	11.7	2.11	466	549	4900	558	2.85
W18 × 258	76.0	21.5	1.28	11.8	2.30	514	611	5510	628	2.88
W18 × 283	83.3	21.9	1.40	11.9	2.50	565	676	6170	704	2.91
W18 × 311	91.6	22.3	1.52	12.0	2.74	624	754	6970	795	2.95
W21 × 44[4]	13.0	20.7	0.350	6.50	0.450	81.6	95.4	843	20.7	1.26
W21 × 50[4]	14.7	20.8	0.380	6.53	0.535	94.5	110	984	24.9	1.30
W21 × 57[4]	16.7	21.1	0.405	6.56	0.650	111	129	1170	30.6	1.35
W21 × 48[2,4]	14.1	20.6	0.350	8.14	0.430	93.0	107	959	38.7	1.66
W21 × 55[4]	16.2	20.8	0.375	8.22	0.522	110	126	1140	48.4	1.73
W21 × 62[4]	18.3	21.0	0.400	8.24	0.615	127	144	1330	57.5	1.77
W21 × 68[4]	20.0	21.1	0.430	8.27	0.685	140	160	1480	64.7	1.80
W21 × 73[4]	21.5	21.2	0.455	8.30	0.740	151	172	1600	70.6	1.81
W21 × 83[4]	24.4	21.4	0.515	8.36	0.835	171	196	1830	81.4	1.83
W21 × 93	27.3	21.6	0.580	8.42	0.930	192	221	2070	92.9	1.84

(continued)

Table A-4.3 continued

Designa-tion	A (in²)	d (in.)	t_w (in.)	b_f (in.)	t_f (in.)	S_x (in3)	Z_x (in3)	I_x (in4)	I_y (in4)	r_y (in.)
W21 × 101[4]	29.8	21.4	0.500	12.3	0.800	227	253	2420	248	2.89
W21 × 111	32.6	21.5	0.550	12.3	0.875	249	279	2670	274	2.90
W21 × 122	35.9	21.7	0.600	12.4	0.960	273	307	2960	305	2.92
W21 × 132	38.8	21.8	0.650	12.4	1.04	295	333	3220	333	2.93
W21 × 147	43.2	22.1	0.720	12.5	1.15	329	373	3630	376	2.95
W21 × 166	48.8	22.5	0.750	12.4	1.36	380	432	4280	435	2.99
W21 × 182	53.6	22.7	0.830	12.5	1.48	417	476	4730	483	3.00
W21 × 201	59.3	23.0	0.910	12.6	1.63	461	530	5310	542	3.02
W24 × 55[3,4]	16.2	23.6	0.395	7.01	0.505	114	134	1350	29.1	1.34
W24 × 62[4]	18.2	23.7	0.430	7.04	0.590	131	153	1550	34.5	1.38
W24 × 68[4]	20.1	23.7	0.415	8.97	0.585	154	177	1830	70.4	1.87
W24 × 76[4]	22.4	23.9	0.440	8.99	0.680	176	200	2100	82.5	1.92
W24 × 84[4]	24.7	24.1	0.470	9.02	0.770	196	224	2370	94.4	1.95
W24 × 94[4]	27.7	24.3	0.515	9.07	0.875	222	254	2700	109	1.98
W24 × 103[4]	30.3	24.5	0.550	9.00	0.980	245	280	3000	119	1.99
W24 × 104[4]	30.7	24.1	0.500	12.8	0.750	258	289	3100	259	2.91
W24 × 117[4]	34.4	24.3	0.550	12.8	0.850	291	327	3540	297	2.94
W24 × 131	38.6	24.5	0.605	12.9	0.960	329	370	4020	340	2.97
W24 × 146	43.0	24.7	0.650	12.9	1.09	371	418	4580	391	3.01
W24 × 162	47.8	25.0	0.705	13.0	1.22	414	468	5170	443	3.05
W24 × 176	51.7	25.2	0.750	12.9	1.34	450	511	5680	479	3.04
W24 × 192	56.5	25.5	0.810	13.0	1.46	491	559	6260	530	3.07
W24 × 207	60.7	25.7	0.870	13.0	1.57	531	606	6820	578	3.08
W24 × 229	67.2	26.0	0.960	13.1	1.73	588	675	7650	651	3.11
W24 × 250	73.5	26.3	1.04	13.2	1.89	644	744	8490	724	3.14
W24 × 279	81.9	26.7	1.16	13.3	2.09	718	835	9600	823	3.17
W24 × 306	89.7	27.1	1.26	13.4	2.28	789	922	10700	919	3.20
W24 × 335	98.3	27.5	1.38	13.5	2.48	864	1020	11900	1030	3.23
W24 × 370	109	28.0	1.52	13.7	2.72	957	1130	13400	1160	3.27
W27 × 84[4]	24.7	26.7	0.460	10.0	0.640	213	244	2850	106	2.07
W27 × 94[4]	27.6	26.9	0.490	10.0	0.745	243	278	3270	124	2.12
W27 × 102[4]	30.0	27.1	0.515	10.0	0.830	267	305	3620	139	2.15
W27 × 114[4]	33.6	27.3	0.570	10.1	0.930	299	343	4080	159	2.18
W27 × 129[4]	37.8	27.6	0.610	10.0	1.10	345	395	4760	184	2.21
W27 × 146[4]	43.2	27.4	0.605	14.0	0.975	414	464	5660	443	3.20
W27 × 161[4]	47.6	27.6	0.660	14.0	1.08	458	515	6310	497	3.23
W27 × 178	52.5	27.8	0.725	14.1	1.19	505	570	7020	555	3.25
W27 × 194	57.1	28.1	0.750	14.0	1.34	559	631	7860	619	3.29
W27 × 217	63.9	28.4	0.830	14.1	1.50	627	711	8910	704	3.32

(continued)

Table A-4.3 continued

Designation	A (in²)	d (in.)	t_w (in.)	b_f (in.)	t_f (in.)	S_x (in3)	Z_x (in3)	I_x (in4)	I_y (in4)	r_y (in.)
W27 × 235	69.4	28.7	0.910	14.2	1.61	677	772	9700	769	3.33
W27 × 258	76.1	29.0	0.980	14.3	1.77	745	852	10800	859	3.36
W27 × 281	83.1	29.3	1.06	14.4	1.93	814	936	11900	953	3.39
W27 × 307	90.2	29.6	1.16	14.4	2.09	887	1030	13100	1050	3.41
W27 × 336	99.2	30.0	1.26	14.6	2.28	972	1130	14600	1180	3.45
W27 × 368	109	30.4	1.38	14.7	2.48	1060	1240	16200	1310	3.48
W27 × 539	159	32.5	1.97	15.3	3.54	1570	1890	25600	2110	3.65
W30 × 90[3,4]	26.3	29.5	0.470	10.4	0.610	245	283	3610	115	2.09
W30 × 99[4]	29.0	29.7	0.520	10.5	0.670	269	312	3990	128	2.10
W30 × 108[4]	31.7	29.8	0.545	10.5	0.760	299	346	4470	146	2.15
W30 × 116[4]	34.2	30.0	0.565	10.5	0.850	329	378	4930	164	2.19
W30 × 124[4]	36.5	30.2	0.585	10.5	0.930	355	408	5360	181	2.23
W30 × 132[4]	38.8	30.3	0.615	10.5	1.00	380	437	5770	196	2.25
W30 × 148[4]	43.6	30.7	0.650	10.5	1.18	436	500	6680	227	2.28
W30 × 173[4]	50.9	30.4	0.655	15.0	1.07	541	607	8230	598	3.42
W30 × 191[4]	56.1	30.7	0.710	15.0	1.19	600	675	9200	673	3.46
W30 × 211	62.3	30.9	0.775	15.1	1.32	665	751	10300	757	3.49
W30 × 235	69.3	31.3	0.830	15.1	1.50	748	847	11700	855	3.51
W30 × 261	77.0	31.6	0.930	15.2	1.65	829	943	13100	959	3.53
W30 × 292	86.0	32.0	1.02	15.3	1.85	930	1060	14900	1100	3.58
W30 × 326	95.9	32.4	1.14	15.4	2.05	1040	1190	16800	1240	3.60
W30 × 357	105	32.8	1.24	15.5	2.24	1140	1320	18700	1390	3.64
W30 × 391	115	33.2	1.36	15.6	2.44	1250	1450	20700	1550	3.67
W33 × 118[3,4]	34.7	32.9	0.550	11.5	0.740	359	415	5900	187	2.32
W33 × 130[4]	38.3	33.1	0.580	11.5	0.855	406	467	6710	218	2.39
W33 × 141[4]	41.5	33.3	0.605	11.5	0.960	448	514	7450	246	2.43
W33 × 152[4]	44.9	33.5	0.635	11.6	1.06	487	559	8160	273	2.47
W33 × 169[4]	49.5	33.8	0.670	11.5	1.22	549	629	9290	310	2.50
W33 × 201[4]	59.1	33.7	0.715	15.7	1.15	686	773	11600	749	3.56
W33 × 221[4]	65.3	33.9	0.775	15.8	1.28	759	857	12900	840	3.59
W33 × 241[4]	71.1	34.2	0.830	15.9	1.40	831	940	14200	933	3.62
W33 × 263	77.4	34.5	0.870	15.8	1.57	919	1040	15900	1040	3.66
W33 × 291	85.6	34.8	0.960	15.9	1.73	1020	1160	17700	1160	3.68
W33 × 318	93.7	35.2	1.04	16.0	1.89	1110	1270	19500	1290	3.71
W33 × 354	104	35.6	1.16	16.1	2.09	1240	1420	22000	1460	3.74
W33 × 387	114	36.0	1.26	16.2	2.28	1350	1560	24300	1620	3.77
W36 × 135[3,4]	39.9	35.6	0.600	12.0	0.790	439	509	7800	225	2.38
W36 × 150[4]	44.3	35.9	0.625	12.0	0.940	504	581	9040	270	2.47
W36 × 160[4]	47.0	36.0	0.650	12.0	1.02	542	624	9760	295	2.50

(continued)

Table A-4.3 continued

Designation	A (in²)	d (in.)	t_w (in.)	b_f (in.)	t_f (in.)	S_x (in3)	Z_x (in3)	I_x (in4)	I_y (in4)	r_y (in.)
W36 × 170[4]	50.0	36.2	0.680	12.0	1.10	581	668	10500	320	2.53
W36 × 182[4]	53.6	36.3	0.725	12.1	1.18	623	718	11300	347	2.55
W36 × 194[4]	57.0	36.5	0.765	12.1	1.26	664	767	12100	375	2.56
W36 × 210[4]	61.9	36.7	0.830	12.2	1.36	719	833	13200	411	2.58
W36 × 232[4]	68.0	37.1	0.870	12.1	1.57	809	936	15000	468	2.62
W36 × 256	75.3	37.4	0.960	12.2	1.73	895	1040	16800	528	2.65
W36 × 231[4]	68.2	36.5	0.760	16.5	1.26	854	963	15600	940	3.71
W36 × 247[4]	72.5	36.7	0.800	16.5	1.35	913	1030	16700	1010	3.74
W36 × 262[4]	77.2	36.9	0.840	16.6	1.44	972	1100	17900	1090	3.76
W36 × 282[4]	82.9	37.1	0.885	16.6	1.57	1050	1190	19600	1200	3.80
W36 × 302	89.0	37.3	0.945	16.7	1.68	1130	1280	21100	1300	3.82
W36 × 330	96.9	37.7	1.02	16.6	1.85	1240	1410	23300	1420	3.83
W36 × 361	106	38.0	1.12	16.7	2.01	1350	1550	25700	1570	3.85
W36 × 395	116	38.4	1.22	16.8	2.20	1490	1710	28500	1750	3.88
W36 × 441	130	38.9	1.36	17.0	2.44	1650	1910	32100	1990	3.92
W36 × 487	143	39.3	1.50	17.1	2.68	1830	2130	36000	2250	3.96
W36 × 529	156	39.8	1.61	17.2	2.91	1990	2330	39600	2490	4.00
W36 × 652	192	41.1	1.97	17.6	3.54	2460	2910	50600	3230	4.10
W40 × 149[3,4]	43.8	38.2	0.630	11.8	0.830	513	598	9800	229	2.29
W40 × 167[4]	49.3	38.6	0.650	11.8	1.03	600	693	11600	283	2.40
W40 × 183[4]	53.3	39.0	0.650	11.8	1.20	675	774	13200	331	2.49
W40 × 211[4]	62.1	39.4	0.750	11.8	1.42	786	906	15500	390	2.51
W40 × 235[4]	69.1	39.7	0.830	11.9	1.58	875	1010	17400	444	2.54
W40 × 264	77.4	40.0	0.960	11.9	1.73	971	1130	19400	493	2.52
W40 × 278	82.3	40.2	1.03	12.0	1.81	1020	1190	20500	521	2.52
W40 × 294	86.2	40.4	1.06	12.0	1.93	1080	1270	21900	562	2.55
W40 × 327	95.9	40.8	1.18	12.1	2.13	1200	1410	24500	640	2.58
W40 × 331	97.7	40.8	1.22	12.2	2.13	1210	1430	24700	644	2.57
W40 × 392	116	41.6	1.42	12.4	2.52	1440	1710	29900	803	2.64
W40 × 199[4]	58.8	38.7	0.650	15.8	1.07	770	869	14900	695	3.45
W40 × 215[4]	63.5	39.0	0.650	15.8	1.22	859	964	16700	796	3.54
W40 × 249[4]	73.5	39.4	0.750	15.8	1.42	993	1120	19600	926	3.55
W40 × 277[4]	81.5	39.7	0.830	15.8	1.58	1100	1250	21900	1040	3.58
W40 × 297[4]	87.3	39.8	0.930	15.8	1.65	1170	1330	23200	1090	3.54
W40 × 324	95.3	40.2	1.00	15.9	1.81	1280	1460	25600	1220	3.58
W40 × 362	106	40.6	1.12	16.0	2.01	1420	1640	28900	1380	3.60
W40 × 372	110	40.6	1.16	16.1	2.05	1460	1680	29600	1420	3.60
W40 × 397	117	41.0	1.22	16.1	2.20	1560	1800	32000	1540	3.64
W40 × 431	127	41.3	1.34	16.2	2.36	1690	1960	34800	1690	3.65

(continued)

Table A-4.3 continued

Designa-tion	A (in²)	d (in.)	t_w (in.)	b_f (in.)	t_f (in.)	S_x (in3)	Z_x (in3)	I_x (in4)	I_y (in4)	r_y (in.)
W40 × 503	148	42.1	1.54	16.4	2.76	1980	2320	41600	2040	3.72
W40 × 593	174	43.0	1.79	16.7	3.23	2340	2760	50400	2520	3.80
W44 × 230[3,4]	67.8	42.9	0.710	15.8	1.22	971	1100	20800	796	3.43
W44 × 262[4]	77.2	43.3	0.785	15.8	1.42	1110	1270	24100	923	3.47
W44 × 290[4]	85.4	43.6	0.865	15.8	1.58	1240	1410	27000	1040	3.49
W44 × 335[4]	98.5	44.0	1.03	15.9	1.77	1410	1620	31100	1200	3.49

Notes:

1. Section not compact for steel with F_y = 36 ksi or F_y = 50 ksi.

2. Section compact for steel with F_y = 36 ksi, but not compact for steel with F_y = 50 ksi.

3. Section webs do not meet slenderness criteria for shear for which the allowable stress can be taken as F_v = 0.4F_y; instead, use a reduced allowable shear stress, F_v = 0.36F_y.

4. Section is slender for compression with F_y = 50 ksi.

5. W-shapes are grouped together with common inner roller dimensions (i.e., web "lengths" excluding fillets)

Table A-4.4: Dimensions and properties of steel C and MC channels

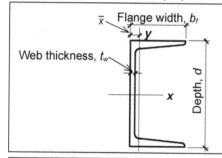

$\bar{x}$ ⟶ Flange width, b_f
↓ y
Web thickness, t_w
Depth, d
x

Cross-sectional area = A
Dimension to y-axis = $\bar{x}$
Moment of inertia = I
Section modulus, $S_x = 2I_x/d$
Radius of gyration, $r_x = \sqrt{I_x/A}$
Radius of gyration, $r_y = \sqrt{I_y/A}$

Designation	A (in²)	d (in.)	t_w (in.)	b_f (in.)	$\bar{x}$ (in.)	I_x (in⁴)	I_y (in⁴)
C3 × 3.5	1.09	3.00	0.132	1.37	0.443	1.57	0.169
C3 × 4.1	1.20	3.00	0.170	1.41	0.437	1.65	0.191
C3 × 5	1.47	3.00	0.258	1.50	0.439	1.85	0.241
C3 × 6	1.76	3.00	0.356	1.60	0.455	2.07	0.300
C4 × 4.5	1.38	4.00	0.125	1.58	0.493	3.65	0.289
C4 × 5.4	1.58	4.00	0.184	1.58	0.457	3.85	0.312
C4 × 6.25	1.77	4.00	0.247	1.65	0.435	4.00	0.345
C4 × 7.25	2.13	4.00	0.321	1.72	0.459	4.58	0.425
C5 × 6.7	1.97	5.00	0.190	1.75	0.484	7.48	0.470
C5 × 9	2.64	5.00	0.325	1.89	0.478	8.89	0.624
C6 × 8.2	2.39	6.00	0.200	1.92	0.512	13.1	0.687
C6 × 10.5	3.08	6.00	0.314	2.03	0.500	15.1	0.860
C6 × 13	3.81	6.00	0.437	2.16	0.514	17.3	1.05

(continued)

Table A-4.4 continued

Designation	A (in^2)	d (in.)	t_w (in.)	b_f (in.)	$\bar{x}$ (in.)	I_x (in^4)	I_y (in^4)
C7 × 9.8	2.87	7.00	0.210	2.09	0.541	21.2	0.957
C7 × 12.25	3.59	7.00	0.314	2.19	0.525	24.2	1.16
C7 × 14.75	4.33	7.00	0.419	2.30	0.532	27.2	1.37
C8 × 11.5	3.37	8.00	0.220	2.26	0.572	32.5	1.31
C8 × 13.75	4.03	8.00	0.303	2.34	0.554	36.1	1.52
C8 × 18.75	5.51	8.00	0.487	2.53	0.565	43.9	1.97
C9 × 13.4	3.94	9.00	0.233	2.43	0.601	47.8	1.75
C9 × 15	4.41	9.00	0.285	2.49	0.586	51.0	1.91
C9 × 20	5.87	9.00	0.448	2.65	0.583	60.9	2.41
C10 × 15.3	4.48	10.0	0.240	2.60	0.634	67.3	2.27
C10 × 20	5.87	10.0	0.379	2.74	0.606	78.9	2.80
C10 × 25	7.34	10.0	0.526	2.89	0.617	91.1	3.34
C10 × 30	8.81	10.0	0.673	3.03	0.649	103	3.93
C12 × 20.7	6.08	12.0	0.282	2.94	0.698	129	3.86
C12 × 25	7.34	12.0	0.387	3.05	0.674	144	4.45
C12 × 30	8.81	12.0	0.510	3.17	0.674	162	5.12
C15 × 33.9	10.0	15.0	0.400	3.40	0.788	315	8.07
C15 × 40	11.8	15.0	0.520	3.52	0.778	348	9.17
C15 × 50	14.7	15.0	0.716	3.72	0.799	404	11.0
MC3 × 7.1	2.11	3.00	0.312	1.94	0.653	2.72	0.666
MC4 × 13.8	4.03	4.00	0.500	2.50	0.849	8.85	2.13
MC6 × 6.5	1.95	6.00	0.155	1.85	0.513	11.0	0.565
MC6 × 7	2.09	6.00	0.179	1.88	0.501	11.4	0.603
MC6 × 12	3.53	6.00	0.310	2.50	0.704	18.7	1.85
MC6 × 15.1	4.44	6.00	0.316	2.94	0.940	24.9	3.46
MC6 × 16.3	4.79	6.00	0.375	3.00	0.927	26.0	3.77
MC6 × 15.3	4.49	6.00	0.340	3.50	1.05	25.3	4.91
MC6 × 18	5.29	6.00	0.379	3.50	1.12	29.7	5.88
MC7 × 19.1	5.61	7.00	0.352	3.45	1.08	43.1	6.06
MC7 × 22.7	6.67	7.00	0.503	3.60	1.04	47.4	7.24
MC8 × 8.5	2.50	8.00	0.179	1.87	0.428	23.3	0.624
MC8 × 18.7	5.50	8.00	0.353	2.98	0.849	52.4	4.15
MC8 × 20	5.88	8.00	0.400	3.03	0.840	54.4	4.42
MC8 × 21.4	6.28	8.00	0.375	3.45	1.02	61.5	6.58
MC8 × 22.8	6.70	8.00	0.427	3.50	1.01	63.8	7.01
MC9 × 23.9	7.02	9.00	0.400	3.45	0.981	84.9	7.14
MC9 × 25.4	7.47	9.00	0.450	3.50	0.970	87.9	7.57
MC10 × 6.5[1]	1.95	10.0	0.152	1.17	0.194	22.9	0.133
MC10 × 8.4[1]	2.46	10.0	0.170	1.50	0.284	31.9	0.326
MC10 × 22	6.45	10.00	0.290	3.32	0.990	102	6.40

(continued)

Table A-4.4 continued

Designation	A (in²)	d (in.)	t_w (in.)	b_f (in.)	$\bar{x}$ (in.)	I_x (in⁴)	I_y (in⁴)
MC10 × 25	7.35	10.0	0.380	3.41	0.953	110	7.25
MC10 × 28.5	8.37	10.0	0.425	3.95	1.12	126	11.3
MC10 × 33.6	9.87	10.0	0.575	4.10	1.09	139	13.1
MC10 × 41.1	12.1	10.0	0.796	4.32	1.09	157	15.7
MC12 × 10.6[1]	3.10	12.0	0.190	1.50	0.269	55.3	0.378
MC12 × 14.3	4.18	12.0	0.250	2.12	0.377	76.1	1.00
MC12 × 31	9.12	12.0	0.370	3.67	1.08	202	11.3
MC12 × 35	10.3	12.0	0.465	3.77	1.05	216	12.6
MC12 × 40	11.8	12.0	0.590	3.89	1.04	234	14.2
MC12 × 45	13.2	12.0	0.710	4.01	1.04	251	15.8
MC12 × 50	14.7	12.0	0.835	4.14	1.05	269	17.4
MC13 × 31.8	9.35	13.0	0.375	4.00	1.00	239	11.4
MC13 × 35	10.3	13.0	0.447	4.07	0.980	252	12.3
MC13 × 40	11.8	13.0	0.560	4.19	0.963	273	13.7
MC13 × 50	14.7	13.0	0.787	4.41	0.974	314	16.4
MC18 × 42.7	12.6	18.0	0.450	3.95	0.877	554	14.3
MC18 × 45.8	13.5	18.0	0.500	4.00	0.866	578	14.9
MC18 × 51.9	15.3	18.0	0.600	4.10	0.858	627	16.3
MC18 × 58	17.1	18.0	0.700	4.20	0.862	675	17.6

Note:

1. Section is slender for compression with $F_y = 36$ ksi.

Table A-4.5: Dimensions and properties of selected steel L angles

A. Angles with equal legs

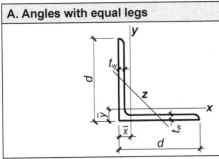

Cross-sectional area = A
Dimension to x- or y-axis = $\bar{x}$
Moment of inertia = I
Radius of gyration, $r_x = r_y = \sqrt{I_x/A}$
Radius of gyration, $r_z = \sqrt{I_z/A}$

Designation	A (in²)	d (in.)	t_w (in.)	x (in.)	I_x or I_y (in⁴)	I_z (in⁴)
L2 × 2 × 1/8[1,2]	0.491	2.00	0.1250	0.534	0.189	0.0751
L2 × 2 × 1/4	0.944	2.00	0.2500	0.586	0.346	0.141
L2 × 2 × 5/16	1.16	2.00	0.3125	0.609	0.414	0.173
L2 × 2 × 3/8	1.37	2.00	0.3750	0.632	0.476	0.203
L3 × 3 × 3/16[1,2]	1.09	3.00	0.1875	0.812	0.948	0.374
L3 × 3 × 1/4	1.44	3.00	0.2500	0.836	1.23	0.491
L3 × 3 × 3/8	2.11	3.00	0.3750	0.884	1.75	0.712
L3 × 3 × 1/2	2.76	3.00	0.5000	0.929	2.20	0.924
L4 × 4 × 1/4[1,2]	1.93	4.00	0.2500	1.08	3.00	1.18
L4 × 4 × 3/8	2.86	4.00	0.3750	1.13	4.32	1.73
L4 × 4 × 1/2	3.75	4.00	0.5000	1.18	5.52	2.25
L4 × 4 × 3/4	5.44	4.00	0.7500	1.27	7.62	3.25
L5 × 5 × 5/16[1,2]	3.07	5.00	0.3125	1.35	7.44	3.01
L5 × 5 × 7/16	4.22	5.00	0.4375	1.40	10.0	4.08
L5 × 5 × 5/8	5.90	5.00	0.6250	1.47	13.6	5.61
L5 × 5 × 7/8	8.00	5.00	0.8750	1.56	17.8	7.56
L6 × 6 × 5/16[1,2]	3.67	6.00	0.3125	1.60	13.0	5.20
L6 × 6 × 1/2	5.77	6.00	0.5000	1.67	19.9	8.04
L6 × 6 × 3/4	8.46	6.00	0.7500	1.77	28.1	11.6
L6 × 6 × 1	11.0	6.00	1.0000	1.86	35.4	15.0
L8 × 8 × 1/2[1,2]	7.84	8.00	0.5000	2.17	48.8	19.7
L8 × 8 × 5/8	9.69	8.00	0.6250	2.21	59.6	24.2
L8 × 8 × 7/8	13.3	8.00	0.8750	2.31	79.7	32.7
L8 × 8 × 1⅛	16.8	8.00	1.1250	2.40	98.1	40.9

(continued)

Table A-4.5 continued (Part *B*)

B. Angles with unequal legs

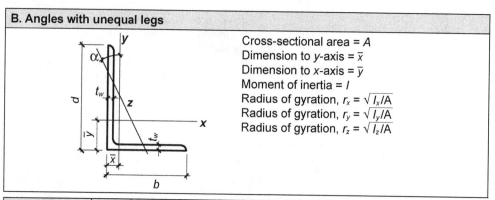

Cross-sectional area = A
Dimension to y-axis = $\bar{x}$
Dimension to x-axis = $\bar{y}$
Moment of inertia = I
Radius of gyration, $r_x = \sqrt{I_x/A}$
Radius of gyration, $r_y = \sqrt{I_y/A}$
Radius of gyration, $r_z = \sqrt{I_z/A}$

Designation	A (in²)	d (in.)	b (in.)	t_w (in.)	$\bar{x}$ (in.)	$\bar{y}$ (in.)	I_x (in⁴)	I_y (in⁴)	I_z (in⁴)	α (°)
L3 × 2 × 1/4	1.20	3.00	2.00	0.2500	0.487	0.980	1.09	0.390	0.223	23.6
L3 × 2 × 5/16	1.48	3.00	2.00	0.3125	0.511	1.01	1.32	0.467	0.271	23.4
L3 × 2 × 3/8	1.75	3.00	2.00	0.3750	0.535	1.03	1.54	0.539	0.318	23.1
L3 × 2 × 1/2	2.26	3.00	2.00	0.5000	0.580	1.08	1.92	0.667	0.409	22.4
L3 × 2½ × 1/4	1.32	3.00	2.50	0.2500	0.653	0.900	1.16	0.734	0.356	34.3
L3 × 2½ × 5/16	1.63	3.00	2.50	0.3125	0.677	0.925	1.41	0.888	0.437	34.2
L3 × 2½ × 3/8	1.93	3.00	2.50	0.3750	0.701	0.949	1.65	1.03	0.514	34.0
L3 × 2½ × 1/2	2.50	3.00	2.50	0.5000	0.746	0.995	2.07	1.29	0.666	33.7
L3½ × 2½ × 1/4[2]	1.45	3.50	2.50	0.2500	0.607	1.10	1.81	0.775	0.425	26.7
L3½ × 2½ × 5/16	1.79	3.50	2.50	0.3125	0.632	1.13	2.20	0.937	0.518	26.6
L3½ × 2½ × 3/8	2.12	3.50	2.50	0.3750	0.655	1.15	2.56	1.09	0.608	26.3
L3-½ × 2½ × 1/2	2.77	3.50	2.50	0.5000	0.701	1.20	3.24	1.36	0.782	25.9
L4 × 3 × 1/4[1,2]	1.69	4.00	3.00	0.2500	0.725	1.22	2.75	1.33	0.691	29.2
L4 × 3 × 3/8	2.49	4.00	3.00	0.3750	0.775	1.27	3.94	1.89	1.01	28.9
L4 × 3 × 1/2	3.25	4.00	3.00	0.5000	0.822	1.32	5.02	2.40	1.30	28.5
L4 × 3 × 5/8	3.99	4.00	3.00	0.6250	0.867	1.37	6.01	2.85	1.59	28.1
L4 × 3½ × 1/4[1,2]	1.82	4.00	3.50	0.2500	0.897	1.14	2.89	2.07	0.950	37.2
L4 × 3½ × 5/16	2.25	4.00	3.50	0.3125	0.923	1.17	3.53	2.52	1.17	37.1
L4 × 3½ × 3/8	2.68	4.00	3.50	0.3750	0.947	1.20	4.15	2.96	1.38	37.1
L4 × 3½ × 1/2	3.50	4.00	3.50	0.5000	0.994	1.24	5.30	3.76	1.808	36.9
L5 × 3 × 1/4[1,2]	1.94	5.00	3.00	0.2500	0.648	1.64	5.09	1.41	0.825	20.4
L5 × 3 × 5/16[1,2]	2.41	5.00	3.00	0.3125	0.673	1.67	6.24	1.72	1.01	20.2
L5 × 3 × 3/8[2]	2.86	5.00	3.00	0.3750	0.698	1.69	7.35	2.01	1.20	20.0
L5 × 3 × 1/2	3.75	5.00	3.00	0.5000	0.746	1.74	9.43	2.55	1.55	19.6
L5 × 3½ × 1/4[1,2]	2.07	5.00	3.50	0.2500	0.804	1.55	5.36	2.20	1.19	26.1
L5 × 3½ × 3/8[2]	3.05	5.00	3.50	0.3750	0.854	1.60	7.75	3.15	1.74	25.9
L5 × 3½ × 1/2	4.00	5.00	3.50	0.5000	0.901	1.65	9.96	4.02	2.25	25.6
L5 × 3½ × 3/4	5.85	5.00	3.50	0.7500	0.993	1.74	13.9	5.52	3.22	24.9

(continued)

Table A-4.5 continued (Part *B*)

Designation	A (in²)	d (in.)	b (in.)	t_w (in.)	$\bar{x}$ (in.)	$\bar{y}$ (in.)	I_x (in⁴)	I_y (in⁴)	I_z (in⁴)	α (°)
L6 × 3½ × 5/16[1,2]	2.89	6.00	3.50	0.3125	0.756	2.00	10.9	2.84	1.70	19.4
L6 × 3½ × 3/8[1,2]	3.44	6.00	3.50	0.3750	0.781	2.02	12.9	3.33	2.00	19.2
L6 × 3½ × 1/2	4.50	6.00	3.50	0.5000	0.829	2.07	16.6	4.24	2.58	18.9
L6 × 4 × 3/8[1,2]	3.61	6.00	4.00	0.3750	0.933	1.93	13.4	4.86	2.73	24.0
L6 × 4 × 1/2	4.75	6.00	4.00	0.5000	0.981	1.98	17.3	6.22	3.55	23.7
L6 × 4 × 5/8	5.86	6.00	4.00	0.6250	1.03	2.03	21.0	7.48	4.32	23.5
L6 × 4 × 7/8	8.00	6.00	4.00	0.8750	1.12	2.12	27.7	9.70	5.82	22.8
L7 × 4 × 3/8[1,2]	4.00	7.00	4.00	0.3750	0.861	2.35	20.5	5.06	3.05	18.7
L7 × 4 × 1/2[2]	5.26	7.00	4.00	0.5000	0.910	2.40	26.6	6.48	3.95	18.5
L7 × 4 × 5/8	6.50	7.00	4.00	0.6250	0.958	2.45	32.4	7.79	4.80	18.2
L7 × 4 × 3/4	7.74	7.00	4.00	0.7500	1.00	2.50	37.8	9.00	5.64	18.0
L8 × 4 × 1/2[1,2]	5.80	8.00	4.00	0.5000	0.854	2.84	38.6	6.75	4.32	14.9
L8 × 4 × 5/8	7.16	8.00	4.00	0.6250	0.902	2.89	47.0	8.11	5.24	14.7
L8 × 4 × 3/4	8.49	8.00	4.00	0.7500	0.949	2.94	55.0	9.37	6.13	14.4
L8 × 4 × 1	11.1	8.00	4.00	1.0000	1.04	3.03	69.7	11.6	7.87	13.9
L8 × 6 × 1/2[1,2]	6.80	8.00	6.00	0.5000	1.46	2.46	44.4	21.7	11.5	29.1
L8 × 6 × 5/8	8.41	8.00	6.00	0.6250	1.51	2.50	54.2	26.4	14.1	29.0
L8 × 6 × 7/8	11.5	8.00	6.00	0.8750	1.60	2.60	72.4	34.9	18.9	28.6
L8 × 6 × 1	13.1	8.00	6.00	1.0000	1.65	2.65	80.9	38.8	21.3	28.5

Notes:
1. Section not compact for steel with F_y = 36 ksi.
2. Section slender for steel with F_y = 36 ksi.

Table A-4.6: Dimensions and properties of selected steel rectangular and square hollow structural sections (HSS)

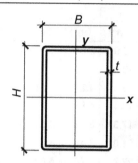

Cross-sectional area = A
Cross-sectional dimensions appear in designation as HSS $H \times B \times t$, where:
  Larger dimension (in.) = H
  Smaller dimension (in.) = B
  Nominal wall thickness (in.)[1] = t
Moment of inertia = I
Section modulus, $S_x = 2I_x/H$
Section modulus, $S_y = 2I_y/B$
Radius of gyration, $r_x = \sqrt{I_x/A}$
Radius of gyration, $r_y = \sqrt{I_y/A}$

Designation	A (in^2)	Design wall thickness, t (in.)[1]	S_x (in^3)	Z_x (in^3)	I_x (in^4)	I_y (in^4)	r_y (in.)
HSS2 × 2 × 3/16	1.19	0.174	0.641	0.797	0.641	0.641	0.733
HSS2 × 2 × 1/4	1.51	0.233	0.747	0.964	0.747	0.747	0.704
HSS2½ × 2½ × 3/16	1.54	0.174	1.08	1.32	1.35	1.35	0.937
HSS2½ × 2½ × 5/16	2.35	0.291	1.46	1.88	1.82	1.82	0.880
HSS3 × 3 × 3/16	1.89	0.174	1.64	1.97	2.46	2.46	1.14
HSS3 × 3 × 3/8	3.39	0.349	2.52	3.25	3.78	3.78	1.06
HSS3½ × 3½ × 3/16	2.24	0.174	2.31	2.76	4.05	4.05	1.35
HSS3½ × 3½ × 3/8	4.09	0.349	3.71	4.69	6.49	6.49	1.26
HSS4 × 3 × 3/16	2.24	0.174	2.47	3.00	4.93	3.16	1.19
HSS4 × 3 × 3/8	4.09	0.349	3.97	5.12	7.93	5.01	1.11
HSS4 × 4 × 1/4	3.37	0.233	3.90	4.69	7.80	7.80	1.52
HSS4 × 4 × 1/2	6.02	0.465	5.97	7.70	11.9	11.9	1.41
HSS6 × 4 × 1/4	4.30	0.233	6.96	8.53	20.9	11.1	1.61
HSS6 × 4 × 1/2	7.88	0.465	11.3	14.6	34.0	17.8	1.50
HSS6 × 6 × 1/4	5.24	0.233	9.54	11.2	28.6	28.6	2.34
HSS6 × 6 × 5/8	11.7	0.581	18.4	23.2	55.2	55.2	2.17
HSS8 × 4 × 1/4	5.24	0.233	10.6	13.3	42.5	14.4	1.66
HSS8 × 4 × 5/8	11.7	0.581	20.5	27.4	82.0	26.6	1.51
HSS8 × 8 × 1/4[2]	7.10	0.233	17.7	20.5	70.7	70.7	3.15
HSS8 × 8 × 5/8	16.4	0.581	36.5	44.7	146	146	2.99
HSS12 × 4 × 1/4	7.10	0.233	19.9	25.6	119	21.0	1.72
HSS12 × 4 × 5/8	16.4	0.581	40.8	55.5	245	40.4	1.57
HSS12 × 8 × 1/4[2]	8.96	0.233	30.6	36.6	184	98.8	3.32
HSS12 × 8 × 5/8	21.0	0.581	66.1	82.1	397	210	3.16
HSS12 × 12 × 1/4[2]	10.8	0.233	41.4	47.6	248	248	4.79
HSS12 × 12 × 5/8	25.7	0.581	91.4	109	548	548	4.62
HSS16 × 4 × 5/16	11.1	0.291	38.5	51.1	308	33.2	1.73
HSS16 × 4 × 5/8	21.0	0.581	67.3	92.9	539	54.1	1.60

(continued)

Table A-4.6 continued

Designation	A (in²)	Design wall thickness, t (in.)[1]	S_x (in³)	Z_x (in³)	I_x (in⁴)	I_y (in⁴)	r_y (in.)
HSS16 × 8 × 5/16	13.4	0.291	56.4	69.4	451	155	3.40
HSS16 × 8 × 5/8	25.7	0.581	102	129	815	274	3.27
HSS16 × 12 × 5/16[2]	15.7	0.291	74.4	87.7	595	384	4.94
HSS16 × 12 × 5/8	30.3	0.581	136	165	1090	700	4.80
HSS16 × 16 × 3/8	21.5	0.349	109	126	873	873	6.37
HSS16 × 16 × 5/8	35.0	0.581	171	200	1370	1370	6.25
HSS20 × 4 × 3/8	16.0	0.349	65.7	89.3	657	47.6	1.73
HSS20 × 4 × 1/2	20.9	0.465	83.8	115	838	58.7	1.68
HSS20 × 8 × 3/8	18.7	0.349	92.6	117	926	222	3.44
HSS20 × 8 × 5/8	30.3	0.581	144	185	1440	338	3.34
HSS20 × 12 × 3/8[2]	21.5	0.349	120	144	1200	547	5.04
HSS20 × 12 × 5/8	35.0	0.581	188	230	1880	851	4.93

Notes:

1. The nominal wall thickness, t, in the designation for an HSS shape (for example, ½ in. or ¼ in.) is different from the "design wall thickness," t, which is tabulated for each section and which is permitted to be smaller than the nominal value.

2. Section is not compact, based on flange slenderness: use reduced nominal bending strength, M_n, as follows:

$$M_n = M_p - (M_p - F_y S)\left[3.57\,\frac{b}{t}\sqrt{\frac{F_y}{E}} - 4.0\right] \leq M_p$$

Table A-4.7: Dimensions and properties of selected steel round hollow structural sections (HSS)

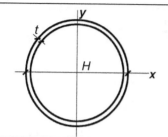

Cross-sectional area = A
Cross-sectional dimensions appear in designation as HSS $H \times t$, where:
    Diameter (in.) = H
    Nominal wall thickness (in.)[1] = t
Moment of inertia = I
Section modulus, $S = 2I/H$
Radius of gyration, $r = \sqrt{I/A}$

Designation	A (in²)	Design wall thickness, t (in.)[1]	I (in⁴)	r (in.)
HSS1.660 × 0.140	0.625	0.130	0.184	0.543
HSS1.990 × 0.120	0.624	0.111	0.251	0.634
HSS1.990 × 0.188	0.943	0.174	0.355	0.613
HSS2.375 × 0.125	0.823	0.116	0.527	0.800
HSS2.375 × 0.250	1.57	0.233	0.910	0.762
HSS2.500 × 0.125	0.869	0.116	0.619	0.844
HSS2.500 × 0.250	1.66	0.233	1.08	0.806
HSS3.000 × 0.125	1.05	0.116	1.09	1.02
HSS3.000 × 0.250	2.03	0.233	1.95	0.982
HSS3.500 × 0.125	1.23	0.116	1.77	1.20
HSS3.500 × 0.313	2.93	0.291	3.81	1.14
HSS4.000 × 0.125	1.42	0.116	2.67	1.37
HSS4.000 × 0.313	3.39	0.291	5.87	1.32
HSS6.000 × 0.250	4.22	0.233	17.6	2.04
HSS6.000 × 0.500	8.09	0.465	31.2	1.96
HSS8.625 × 0.250	6.14	0.233	54.1	2.97
HSS8.625 × 0.625	14.7	0.581	119	2.85
HSS10.000 × 0.250	7.15	0.233	85.3	3.45
HSS10.000 × 0.625	17.2	0.581	191	3.34
HSS12.750 × 0.375	13.6	0.349	262	4.39
HSS12.750 × 0.500	17.9	0.465	339	4.35
HSS14.000 × 0.375	15.0	0.349	349	4.83
HSS14.000 × 0.625	24.5	0.581	552	4.75
HSS16.000 × 0.375	17.2	0.349	526	5.53
HSS16.000 × 0.625	28.1	0.581	838	5.46
HSS18.000 × 0.500	25.6	0.465	985	6.20
HSS20.000 × 0.500	28.5	0.465	1360	6.91

Note:

1. The nominal wall thickness, t, in the designation for an HSS shape (e.g., 0.500 in. or 0.250 in.) is different from the "design wall thickness," t, which is tabulated for each section and which is permitted to be smaller than the nominal value.

Table A-4.8: Dimensions and properties of selected steel pipe

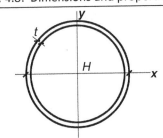

Cross-sectional area = A
Diameter (in.) = H
Moment of inertia = I
Section modulus, $S = 2I/H$
Radius of gyration, $r = \sqrt{I/A}$

Designation	A (in²)	Design wall thickness, t (in.)	Diameter (in.)	I (in⁴)	r (in.)
Standard weight steel pipe					
Pipe 2 Std.	1.02	0.143	2.38	0.627	0.791
Pipe 2½ Std.	1.61	0.189	2.88	1.45	0.952
Pipe 3 Std.	2.07	0.201	3.50	2.85	1.17
Pipe 3½ Std.	2.50	0.211	4.00	4.52	1.34
Pipe 4 Std.	2.96	0.221	4.50	6.82	1.51
Pipe 5 Std.	4.01	0.241	5.56	14.3	1.88
Pipe 6 Std.	5.20	0.261	6.63	26.5	2.25
Pipe 8 Std.	7.85	0.300	8.63	68.1	2.95
Pipe 10 Std.	11.5	0.340	10.8	151	3.68
Pipe 12 Std.	13.7	0.349	12.8	262	4.39
Extra strong steel pipe					
Pipe 2 x-Strong	1.40	0.204	2.38	0.827	0.771
Pipe 2½ x-Strong	2.10	0.257	2.88	1.83	0.930
Pipe 3 x-Strong	2.83	0.280	3.50	3.70	1.14
Pipe 3½ x-Strong	3.43	0.296	4.00	5.94	1.31
Pipe 4 x-Strong	4.14	0.315	4.50	9.12	1.48
Pipe 5 x-Strong	5.73	0.349	5.56	19.5	1.85
Pipe 6 x-Strong	7.83	0.403	6.63	38.3	2.20
Pipe 8 x-Strong	11.9	0.465	8.63	100	2.89
Pipe 10 x-Strong	15.1	0.465	10.8	199	3.64
Pipe 12 x-Strong	17.5	0.465	12.8	339	4.35
Double-extra strong steel pipe					
Pipe 2 xx-Strong	2.51	0.406	2.38	1.27	0.711
Pipe 2½ xx-Strong	3.83	0.514	2.88	2.78	0.854
Pipe 3 xx-Strong	5.17	0.559	3.50	5.79	1.06
Pipe 4 xx-Strong	7.66	0.628	4.50	14.7	1.39
Pipe 5 xx-Strong	10.7	0.699	5.56	32.2	1.74
Pipe 6 xx-Strong	14.7	0.805	6.63	63.5	2.08
Pipe 8 xx-Strong	20.0	0.816	8.63	154	2.78

Table A-4.9: Shear lag coefficient, U, for bolted and welded steel connections in tension[1]

Condition	Shear lag coefficient, U	Diagram
All parts of the element (e.g., web, flanges, legs) are connected by bolts or welds.	$U = 1.0$	
Transverse welds connecting some, but not all, of the cross-sectional "parts."	$U = 1.0$, but the net area, A_n, is taken as only that portion of the element cross section (consisting of flanges, webs, legs, and so on) that is directly connected by the transverse welds.	
Longitudinal welds connecting steel plates.	$U = 1.0$ where $l \geq 2w$ $U = 0.87$ where $2w > l \geq 1.5w$ $U = 0.75$ where $1.5w > l \geq w$	
Bolts connecting wide-flange (W) shapes; or M, S, HP shapes; or Tees made from any of those sections.	$U = 0.90$ where $b_f \geq 0.67d$ and flange is connected with at least 3 bolts per line. $U = 0.85$ where $b_f < 0.67d$ and flange is connected with at least 3 bolts per line. $U = 0.70$ where only the web is connected with at least 4 bolts per line.	
Bolts connecting single angles (L).	$U = 0.80$ where one leg of the angle is connected with at least 4 bolts per line. $U = 0.75$ where one leg of the angle is connected with 2 or 3 bolts per line.	

Note:

1. The shear lag coefficient, U, for all tension members except plates and HSS, can be taken as $U = 1 - \bar{x}/l$, where $\bar{x}$ is the distance measured from the connection plane to the centroid of the member and l is the length of the connection, measured either along the weld or measured from the first to the last bolt, in either case parallel to the direction of the tension force. For wide-flange shapes bolted through the flanges, the centroid is taken for half of the cross section, i.e., for the "tee" (WT shape), rather than for the whole W shape. Alternatively, the values for U listed in this table can be used in lieu of this equation.

Table A-4.10: Allowable axial loads (kips), A992 steel wide-flange columns (F_y = 50 ksi)

Designa-tion	Effective (unbraced) length, *KL* (ft)											
	6	7	8	9	10	11	12	13	14	15	16	17
W4 × 13	78.4	68.4	58.4	48.8	39.9	33.0	27.7	23.6	20.3	17.7	15.6	¹n/a
W5 × 16	111	101	92.2	82.4	72.6	63.2	54.2	46.1	39.8	34.6	30.4	27.0
W5 × 19	132	121	110	98.9	87.5	76.4	65.9	56.2	48.5	42.2	37.1	32.9
W6 × 8.5	46.7	39.3	32.2	25.7	20.8	17.2	14.4	12.3	10.6	¹n/a	¹n/a	¹n/a
W6 × 9	50.5	42.7	35.2	28.2	22.9	18.9	15.9	13.5	11.6	10.1	¹n/a	¹n/a
W6 × 12	67.7	57.6	47.7	38.5	31.2	25.8	21.6	18.4	15.9	13.8	¹n/a	¹n/a
W6 × 16	94.6	81.7	69.0	57.0	46.2	38.2	32.1	27.3	23.6	20.5	18.0	¹n/a
W6 × 20	148	139	130	120	110	99.7	89.5	79.6	70.2	61.2	53.8	47.7
W6 × 25	186	175	164	151	139	126	114	101	89.9	78.6	69.1	61.2
W8 × 31	248	240	231	221	210	199	188	176	164	152	141	129
W8 × 35	281	272	261	250	238	226	213	200	186	173	160	147
W8 × 40	319	309	297	285	271	257	243	228	213	198	183	168
W8 × 48	386	374	361	346	330	314	297	279	262	244	226	208
W8 × 58	469	455	439	421	403	383	363	341	320	299	277	256
W8 × 67	542	525	507	487	466	444	420	396	372	348	323	299
W10 × 33	262	253	243	231	219	207	194	181	168	154	142	129
W10 × 39	312	301	289	276	263	248	233	218	203	188	173	158
W10 × 45	362	350	337	322	306	290	273	256	238	221	204	187
W10 × 49	406	398	388	377	366	353	340	327	313	298	283	269
W10 × 54	446	437	426	415	402	389	375	360	345	329	313	297
W10 × 60	497	487	475	463	449	434	418	402	385	368	350	332
W10 × 68	565	554	541	527	511	495	477	459	440	420	400	380
W10 × 77	639	626	612	596	579	560	540	520	498	476	454	431
W10 × 88	734	719	703	685	665	645	622	599	575	550	525	499
W10 × 100	833	817	799	779	757	734	709	683	656	628	599	570
W10 × 112	934	916	896	874	850	824	797	768	739	708	676	644

(continued)

Table A-4.10 continued

Designa-tion	Effective (unbraced) length, KL (ft)											
	6	7	8	9	10	11	12	13	14	15	16	17
W12 × 40	316	305	292	279	264	249	234	218	202	186	171	156
W12 × 45	355	342	328	313	297	280	263	245	227	210	193	176
W12 × 50	396	382	366	350	332	313	294	275	255	235	216	197
W12 × 53	439	429	418	406	393	379	365	349	333	317	301	284
W12 × 58	479	468	457	444	430	415	400	383	366	349	331	314
W12 × 65	548	540	531	520	509	497	484	470	456	441	425	409
W12 × 72	606	597	587	576	563	550	536	521	505	488	471	454
W12 × 79	666	657	646	633	620	605	590	573	556	538	519	500
W12 × 87	736	725	713	700	685	669	652	634	615	596	575	554
W12 × 96	811	799	786	772	756	738	720	700	680	658	636	613
W12 × 106	898	885	871	855	837	818	798	777	754	731	706	681
W12 × 120	1016	1002	986	968	949	928	905	881	856	829	802	774
W12 × 136	1150	1134	1116	1096	1075	1051	1026	999	971	942	912	880
W12 × 152	1289	1272	1252	1230	1206	1180	1153	1123	1092	1060	1026	992
W12 × 170	1443	1424	1402	1378	1352	1323	1293	1260	1226	1191	1154	1116
W12 × 190	1611	1591	1567	1541	1512	1480	1447	1411	1374	1335	1294	1252
W12 × 210	1786	1763	1737	1709	1677	1643	1607	1568	1527	1484	1440	1394
W12 × 230	1958	1933	1906	1875	1841	1804	1764	1723	1678	1632	1584	1535
W12 × 252	2141	2115	2085	2052	2016	1976	1934	1888	1841	1791	1740	1686
W12 × 279	2372	2343	2311	2275	2236	2193	2147	2098	2046	1992	1936	1878
W12 × 305	2597	2566	2532	2493	2451	2405	2356	2304	2248	2190	2130	2068
W12 × 336	2866	2834	2797	2755	2710	2661	2608	2551	2492	2429	2364	2297

(continued)

Table A-4.10 continued

Designa-tion	Effective (unbraced) length, *KL* (ft)											
	6	**7**	**8**	**9**	**10**	**11**	**12**	**13**	**14**	**15**	**16**	**17**
W14 × 43	339	326	312	297	280	264	246	229	211	194	177	160
W14 × 48	380	366	350	334	316	297	278	259	239	220	201	183
W14 × 53	421	406	389	370	351	330	309	288	266	245	224	204
W14 × 61	503	491	479	464	449	433	416	398	380	361	342	322
W14 × 68	562	549	535	520	503	485	466	446	425	404	383	362
W14 × 74	613	600	584	568	550	530	510	488	466	444	421	397
W14 × 82	675	660	643	625	605	584	561	538	513	488	463	438
W14 × 90	771	764	755	745	734	722	710	696	682	667	651	635
W14 × 99	847	839	829	818	807	794	780	765	749	733	716	698
W14 × 109	932	923	912	901	888	874	859	843	826	808	789	769
W14 × 120	1028	1018	1007	994	980	964	948	930	911	892	871	850
W14 × 132	1130	1120	1107	1093	1078	1061	1043	1024	1003	982	960	936
W14 × 145	1248	1237	1225	1211	1196	1179	1161	1142	1122	1100	1078	1055
W14 × 159	1365	1353	1340	1325	1309	1291	1271	1251	1229	1205	1181	1156
W14 × 176	1514	1502	1487	1471	1453	1433	1412	1389	1364	1339	1312	1284
W14 × 193	1661	1647	1632	1614	1594	1573	1550	1525	1499	1471	1442	1412
W14 × 211	1814	1799	1782	1763	1741	1718	1693	1667	1638	1608	1577	1544
W14 × 233	2005	1988	1970	1949	1926	1901	1874	1844	1813	1781	1747	1711
W14 × 257	2213	2196	2175	2153	2127	2100	2070	2039	2005	1969	1932	1893
W14 × 283	2440	2421	2399	2374	2347	2317	2285	2251	2214	2176	2135	2093
W14 × 311	2678	2657	2633	2607	2577	2545	2511	2473	2434	2392	2348	2302
W14 × 342	2960	2938	2912	2883	2851	2817	2779	2738	2696	2650	2602	2553
W14 × 370	3196	3172	3145	3114	3080	3043	3003	2960	2914	2865	2814	2761
W14 × 398	3432	3407	3378	3345	3309	3270	3228	3183	3134	3083	3029	2973
W14 × 426	3667	3641	3610	3576	3539	3497	3453	3405	3354	3300	3243	3184
W14 × 455	3933	3905	3873	3837	3797	3754	3707	3656	3602	3545	3486	3423
W14 × 500	4317	4287	4252	4214	4171	4124	4073	4019	3961	3900	3836	3769
W14 × 550	4759	4727	4690	4649	4603	4553	4498	4440	4378	4312	4243	4170
W14 × 605	5232	5198	5158	5114	5065	5011	4952	4890	4823	4753	4678	4600
W14 × 665	5764	5728	5685	5638	5585	5528	5465	5398	5327	5251	5172	5088
W14 × 730	6327	6287	6242	6192	6136	6074	6008	5936	5860	5779	5694	5605

Note:
1. Slenderness ratio, *KL/r* > 200, for this effective length.

Table A-4.11: Allowable stresses for A992 steel columns (F_y = 50 ksi)

KL/r	F_c (ksi)	KL/r	F_c (ksi)	KL/r	F_c (ksi)	KL/r	F_c (ksi)
1	29.9	35	27.4	69	21.1	103	13.8
2	29.9	36	27.2	70	20.9	104	13.6
3	29.9	37	27.1	71	20.7	105	13.4
4	29.9	38	26.9	72	20.5	106	13.2
5	29.9	39	26.8	73	20.3	107	13.0
6	29.9	40	26.6	74	20.1	108	12.8
7	29.8	41	26.5	75	19.8	109	12.6
8	29.8	42	26.3	76	19.6	110	12.4
9	29.8	43	26.2	77	19.4	111	12.2
10	29.7	44	26.0	78	19.2	112	12.0
11	29.7	45	25.8	79	19.0	113	11.8
12	29.6	46	25.6	80	18.8	114	11.6
13	29.6	47	25.5	81	18.5	115	11.4
14	29.5	48	25.3	82	18.3	116	11.2
15	29.5	49	25.1	83	18.1	117	11.0
16	29.4	50	24.9	84	17.9	118	10.8
17	29.3	51	24.8	85	17.7	119	10.6
18	29.2	52	24.6	86	17.4	120	10.4
19	29.2	53	24.4	87	17.2	121	10.3
20	29.1	54	24.2	88	17.0	122	10.1
21	29.0	55	24.0	89	16.8	123	9.94
22	28.9	56	23.8	90	16.6	124	9.78
23	28.8	57	23.6	91	16.3	125	9.62
24	28.7	58	23.4	92	16.1	126	9.47
25	28.6	59	23.2	93	15.9	127	9.32
26	28.5	60	23.0	94	15.7	128	9.17
27	28.4	61	22.8	95	15.5	129	9.03
28	28.3	62	22.6	96	15.3	130	8.89
29	28.2	63	22.4	97	15.0	131	8.76
30	28.0	64	22.2	98	14.8	132	8.63
31	27.9	65	22.0	99	14.6	133	8.50
32	27.8	66	21.8	100	14.4	134	8.37
33	27.6	67	21.6	101	14.2	135	8.25
34	27.5	68	21.4	102	14.0	136	8.13

(continued)

Table A-4.11 continued

KL/r	F_c (ksi)	KL/r	F_c (ksi)	KL/r	F_c (ksi)	KL/r	F_c (ksi)
137	8.01	153	6.42	169	5.26	185	4.39
138	7.89	154	6.34	170	5.20	186	4.34
139	7.78	155	6.26	171	5.14	187	4.30
140	7.67	156	6.18	172	5.08	188	4.25
141	7.56	157	6.10	173	5.02	189	4.21
142	7.45	158	6.02	174	4.96	190	4.16
143	7.35	159	5.95	175	4.91	191	4.12
144	7.25	160	5.87	176	4.85	192	4.08
145	7.15	161	5.80	177	4.80	193	4.04
146	7.05	162	5.73	178	4.74	194	3.99
147	6.96	163	5.66	179	4.69	195	3.95
148	6.86	164	5.59	180	4.64	196	3.91
149	6.77	165	5.52	181	4.59	197	3.87
150	6.68	166	5.45	182	4.54	198	3.83
151	6.59	167	5.39	183	4.49	199	3.80
152	6.51	168	5.33	184	4.44	200	3.76

Table A-4.12: Allowable stresses for A500 Grade B HSS rectangular columns (F_y = 46 ksi)

KL/r	F_c (ksi)	KL/r	F_c (ksi)	KL/r	F_c (ksi)	KL/r	F_c (ksi)
1	27.5	35	25.4	69	20.0	103	13.5
2	27.5	36	25.2	70	19.8	104	13.3
3	27.5	37	25.1	71	19.6	105	13.1
4	27.5	38	25.0	72	19.4	106	12.9
5	27.5	39	24.9	73	19.2	107	12.8
6	27.5	40	24.7	74	19.1	108	12.6
7	27.5	41	24.6	75	18.9	109	12.4
8	27.4	42	24.5	76	18.7	110	12.2
9	27.4	43	24.3	77	18.5	111	12.0
10	27.4	44	24.2	78	18.3	112	11.8
11	27.3	45	24.0	79	18.1	113	11.7
12	27.3	46	23.9	80	17.9	114	11.5
13	27.2	47	23.7	81	17.7	115	11.3
14	27.2	48	23.6	82	17.5	116	11.1
15	27.1	49	23.4	83	17.3	117	11.0
16	27.1	50	23.3	84	17.1	118	10.8
17	27.0	51	23.1	85	16.9	119	10.6
18	27.0	52	23.0	86	16.7	120	10.4
19	26.9	53	22.8	87	16.6	121	10.3
20	26.8	54	22.6	88	16.4	122	10.1
21	26.7	55	22.5	89	16.2	123	9.94
22	26.7	56	22.3	90	16.0	124	9.78
23	26.6	57	22.1	91	15.8	125	9.62
24	26.5	58	22.0	92	15.6	126	9.47
25	26.4	59	21.8	93	15.4	127	9.32
26	26.3	60	21.6	94	15.2	128	9.17
27	26.2	61	21.4	95	15.0	129	9.03
28	26.1	62	21.3	96	14.8	130	8.89
29	26.0	63	21.1	97	14.6	131	8.76
30	25.9	64	20.9	98	14.4	132	8.63
31	25.8	65	20.7	99	14.2	133	8.50
32	25.7	66	20.5	100	14.1	134	8.37
33	25.6	67	20.4	101	13.9	135	8.25
34	25.5	68	20.2	102	13.7	136	8.13

(continued)

Table A-4.12 continued

KL/r	F_c (ksi)	KL/r	F_c (ksi)	KL/r	F_c (ksi)	KL/r	F_c (ksi)
137	8.01	153	6.42	169	5.26	185	4.39
138	7.89	154	6.34	170	5.20	186	4.34
139	7.78	155	6.26	171	5.14	187	4.30
140	7.67	156	6.18	172	5.08	188	4.25
141	7.56	157	6.10	173	5.02	189	4.21
142	7.45	158	6.02	174	4.96	190	4.16
143	7.35	159	5.95	175	4.91	191	4.12
144	7.25	160	5.87	176	4.85	192	4.08
145	7.15	161	5.80	177	4.80	193	4.04
146	7.05	162	5.73	178	4.74	194	3.99
147	6.96	163	5.66	179	4.69	195	3.95
148	6.86	164	5.59	180	4.64	196	3.91
149	6.77	165	5.52	181	4.59	197	3.87
150	6.68	166	5.45	182	4.54	198	3.83
151	6.59	167	5.39	183	4.49	199	3.80
152	6.51	168	5.33	184	4.44	200	3.76

Table A-4.13: Allowable stresses for A500 Grade B HSS round columns (F_y = 42 ksi)

KL/r	F_c (ksi)	KL/r	F_c (ksi)	KL/r	F_c (ksi)	KL/r	F_c (ksi)
1	25.1	35	23.3	69	18.8	103	13.1
2	25.1	36	23.2	70	18.6	104	12.9
3	25.1	37	23.1	71	18.5	105	12.8
4	25.1	38	23.0	72	18.3	106	12.6
5	25.1	39	22.9	73	18.1	107	12.4
6	25.1	40	22.8	74	18.0	108	12.3
7	25.1	41	22.7	75	17.8	109	12.1
8	25.1	42	22.6	76	17.6	110	12.0
9	25.0	43	22.4	77	17.5	111	11.8
10	25.0	44	22.3	78	17.3	112	11.6
11	25.0	45	22.2	79	17.1	113	11.5
12	24.9	46	22.1	80	17.0	114	11.3
13	24.9	47	22.0	81	16.8	115	11.2
14	24.8	48	21.8	82	16.6	116	11.0
15	24.8	49	21.7	83	16.5	117	10.8
16	24.8	50	21.6	84	16.3	118	10.7
17	24.7	51	21.4	85	16.1	119	10.5
18	24.7	52	21.3	86	16.0	120	10.4
19	24.6	53	21.2	87	15.8	121	10.2
20	24.5	54	21.0	88	15.6	122	10.1
21	24.5	55	20.9	89	15.5	123	9.93
22	24.4	56	20.7	90	15.3	124	9.78
23	24.3	57	20.6	91	15.1	125	9.62
24	24.3	58	20.5	92	15.0	126	9.47
25	24.2	59	20.3	93	14.8	127	9.32
26	24.1	60	20.2	94	14.6	128	9.17
27	24.0	61	20.0	95	14.4	129	9.03
28	24.0	62	19.9	96	14.3	130	8.89
29	23.9	63	19.7	97	14.1	131	8.76
30	23.8	64	19.6	98	13.9	132	8.63
31	23.7	65	19.4	99	13.8	133	8.50
32	23.6	66	19.2	100	13.6	134	8.37
33	23.5	67	19.1	101	13.4	135	8.25
34	23.4	68	18.9	102	13.3	136	8.13

(continued)

Table A-4.13 continued

KL/r	F_c (ksi)	KL/r	F_c (ksi)	KL/r	F_c (ksi)	KL/r	F_c (ksi)
137	8.01	153	6.42	169	5.26	185	4.39
138	7.89	154	6.34	170	5.20	186	4.34
139	7.78	155	6.26	171	5.14	187	4.30
140	7.67	156	6.18	172	5.08	188	4.25
141	7.56	157	6.10	173	5.02	189	4.21
142	7.45	158	6.02	174	4.96	190	4.16
143	7.35	159	5.95	175	4.91	191	4.12
144	7.25	160	5.87	176	4.85	192	4.08
145	7.15	161	5.80	177	4.80	193	4.04
146	7.05	162	5.73	178	4.74	194	3.99
147	6.96	163	5.66	179	4.69	195	3.95
148	6.86	164	5.59	180	4.64	196	3.91
149	6.77	165	5.52	181	4.59	197	3.87
150	6.68	166	5.45	182	4.54	198	3.83
151	6.59	167	5.39	183	4.49	199	3.80
152	6.51	168	5.33	184	4.44	200	3.76

Table A-4.14: Allowable stresses for A36[1] steel columns (F_y = 36 ksi)

KL/r	F_c (ksi)	KL/r	F_c (ksi)	KL/r	F_c (ksi)	KL/r	F_c (ksi)
1	21.6	35	20.2	69	16.8	103	12.3
2	21.6	36	20.1	70	16.7	104	12.2
3	21.5	37	20.1	71	16.5	105	12.1
4	21.5	38	20.0	72	16.4	106	11.9
5	21.5	39	19.9	73	16.3	107	11.8
6	21.5	40	19.8	74	16.2	108	11.7
7	21.5	41	19.7	75	16.0	109	11.5
8	21.5	42	19.6	76	15.9	110	11.4
9	21.5	43	19.6	77	15.8	111	11.3
10	21.4	44	19.5	78	15.6	112	11.1
11	21.4	45	19.4	79	15.5	113	11.0
12	21.4	46	19.3	80	15.4	114	10.9
13	21.4	47	19.2	81	15.3	115	10.7
14	21.3	48	19.1	82	15.1	116	10.6
15	21.3	49	19.0	83	15.0	117	10.5
16	21.3	50	18.9	84	14.9	118	10.4
17	21.2	51	18.8	85	14.7	119	10.2
18	21.2	52	18.7	86	14.6	120	10.1
19	21.2	53	18.6	87	14.5	121	9.97
20	21.1	54	18.5	88	14.3	122	9.85
21	21.1	55	18.4	89	14.2	123	9.72
22	21.0	56	18.3	90	14.1	124	9.59
23	21.0	57	18.2	91	13.9	125	9.47
24	20.9	58	18.1	92	13.8	126	9.35
25	20.9	59	17.9	93	13.7	127	9.22
26	20.8	60	17.8	94	13.5	128	9.10
27	20.7	61	17.7	95	13.4	129	8.98
28	20.7	62	17.6	96	13.3	130	8.86
29	20.6	63	17.5	97	13.1	131	8.73
30	20.6	64	17.4	98	13.0	132	8.61
31	20.5	65	17.3	99	12.9	133	8.49
32	20.4	66	17.1	100	12.7	134	8.38
33	20.4	67	17.0	101	12.6	135	8.25
34	20.3	68	16.9	102	12.5	136	8.13

(continued)

Table A-4.14 continued

KL/r	F_c (ksi)	KL/r	F_c (ksi)	KL/r	F_c (ksi)	KL/r	F_c (ksi)
137	8.01	153	6.42	169	5.26	185	4.39
138	7.89	154	6.34	170	5.20	186	4.34
139	7.78	155	6.26	171	5.14	187	4.3
140	7.67	156	6.18	172	5.08	188	4.25
141	7.56	157	6.10	173	5.02	189	4.21
142	7.45	158	6.02	174	4.96	190	4.16
143	7.35	159	5.95	175	4.91	191	4.12
144	7.25	160	5.87	176	4.85	192	4.08
145	7.15	161	5.80	177	4.80	193	4.04
146	7.05	162	5.73	178	4.74	194	3.99
147	6.96	163	5.66	179	4.69	195	3.95
148	6.86	164	5.59	180	4.64	196	3.91
149	6.77	165	5.52	181	4.59	197	3.87
150	6.68	166	5.45	182	4.54	198	3.83
151	6.59	167	5.39	183	4.49	199	3.80
152	6.51	168	5.33	184	4.44	200	3.76

Note:

1. Steel pipe fabricated with A53 Grade B steel and F_y = 35 ksi may be analyzed using this table for F_y = 36 ksi.

Table A-4.15: Plastic section modulus (Z_x) values: lightest laterally braced steel compact shapes for bending, F_y = 50 ksi

Shape	Z_x (in³)	^2L_p (ft)	Shape	Z_x (in³)	^2L_p (ft)	Shape	Z_x (in³)	^2L_p (ft)
W6 × 8.5[1]	5.59	3.14	W21 × 50	110	4.59	W36 × 182	718	9.01
W6 × 9[1]	6.23	3.20	W18 × 55	112	5.90	W40 × 183	774	8.80
W8 × 10[1]	8.77	3.14	W21 × 55	126	6.11	W40 × 199	869	12.2
W10 × 12[1]	12.5	2.87	W24 × 55	134	4.73	W40 × 211	906	8.87
W12 × 14	17.4	2.66	W21 × 62	144	6.25	W40 × 215	964	12.5
W12 × 16	20.1	2.73	W24 × 62	153	4.87	W44 × 230	1100	12.1
W10 × 19	21.6	3.09	W21 × 68	160	6.36	W40 × 249	1120	12.5
W12 × 19	24.7	2.90	W24 × 68	177	6.61	W44 × 262	1270	12.3
W10 × 22	26.0	4.70	W24 × 76	200	6.78	W44 × 290	1410	12.3
W12 × 22	29.3	3.00	W24 × 84	224	6.89	W40 × 324	1460	12.6
W14 × 22	33.2	3.67	W27 × 84	244	7.31	W44 × 335	1620	12.3
W12 × 26	37.2	5.33	W30 × 90	283	7.38	W40 × 362	1640	12.7
W14 × 26	40.2	3.81	W30 × 99	312	7.42	W40 × 372	1680	12.7
W16 × 26	44.2	3.96	W30 × 108	346	7.59	W40 × 392	1710	9.33
W14 × 30	47.3	5.26	W30 × 116	378	7.74	W40 × 397	1800	12.9
W16 × 31	54.0	4.13	W33 × 118	415	8.19	W40 × 431	1960	12.9
W14 × 34	54.6	5.40	W33 × 130	467	8.44	W36 × 487	2130	14.0
W18 × 35	66.5	4.31	W36 × 135	509	8.41	W40 × 503	2320	13.1
W16 × 40	73.0	5.55	W33 × 141	514	8.58	W36 × 529	2330	14.1
W18 × 40	78.4	4.49	W40 × 149	598	8.09	W40 × 593	2760	13.4
W21 × 44	95.4	4.45	W36 × 160	624	8.83	W36 × 652	2910	14.5
W21 × 48	107	6.09	W40 × 167	693	8.48			

Notes:

1. Section is just out of range to qualify as compact for F_y = 50 ksi steel. Because the nominal flexural strength of the section must be reduced a small percentage to account for slenderness of the noncompact flanges, the value for plastic section modulus has been reduced by the same percentage, so that it may be used, as is, in the bending strength equation: $Z_{req} = \Omega M_{max}/F_y$.

2. L_p, the largest unbraced length for which the section can be considered compact, is computed for F_y = 50 ksi steel. The comparable unbraced length for A36 steel is larger, and is equal to $4.16r_y$ (ft), where r_y is the section's radius of gyration about the y-axis (in.) — see Appendix Table A-4.3.

Table A-4.16: Available moment for A992 wide-flange (W) shapes[1,2]

A. Available moments from 0 to 100 ft-kips

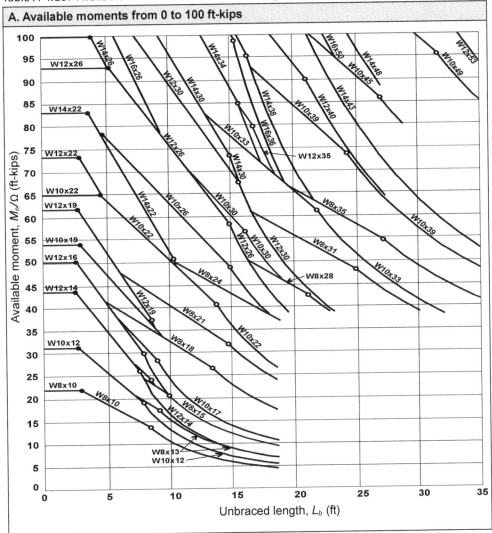

(continued)

Table A-4.16 continued (Part *B*)

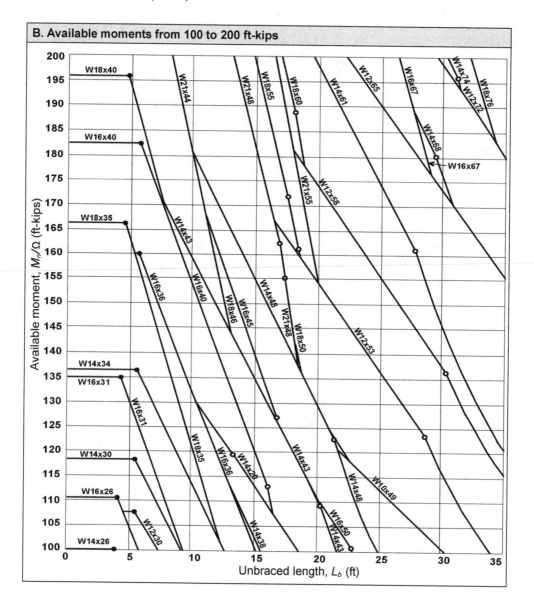

B. Available moments from 100 to 200 ft-kips

(continued)

Table A-4.16 continued (Part *C*)

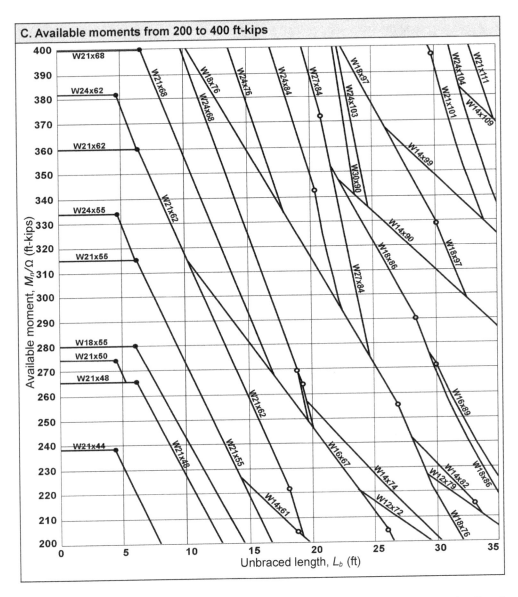

(continued)

Table A-4.16 continued (Part *D*)

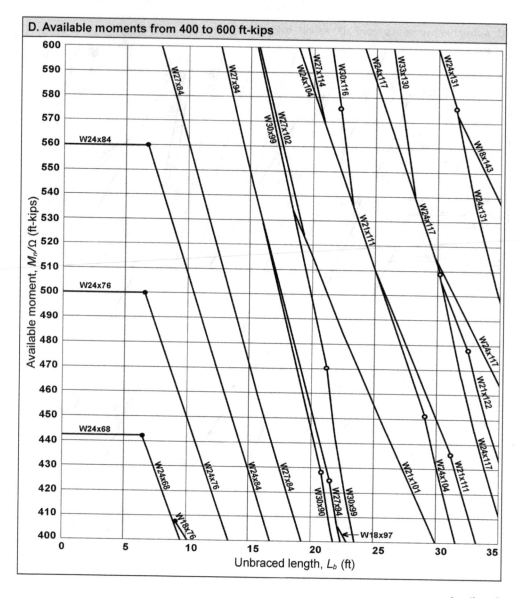

(continued)

Table A-4.16 continued (Part *E*)

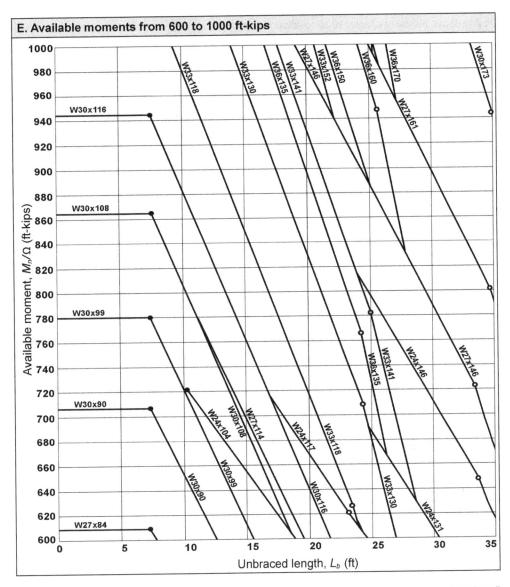

(continued)

Table A-4.16 continued (Part *F*)

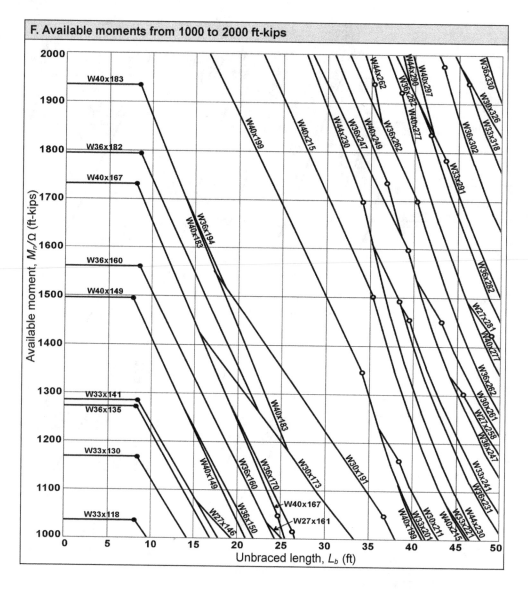

F. Available moments from 1000 to 2000 ft-kips

(continued)

Table A-4.16 continued (Part *G*)

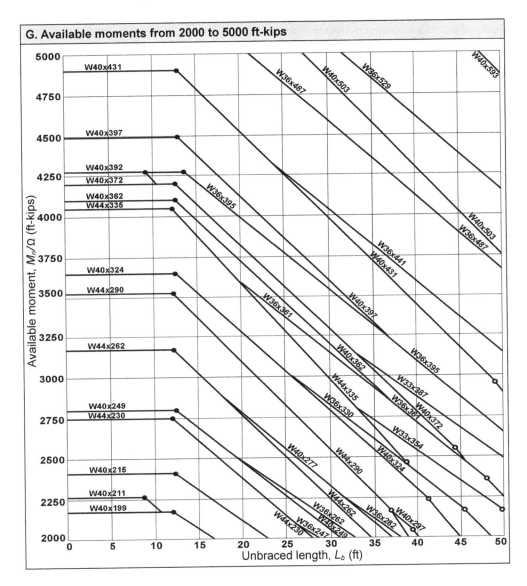

G. Available moments from 2000 to 5000 ft-kips

(continued)

Table A-4.16 continued (Part *H*)

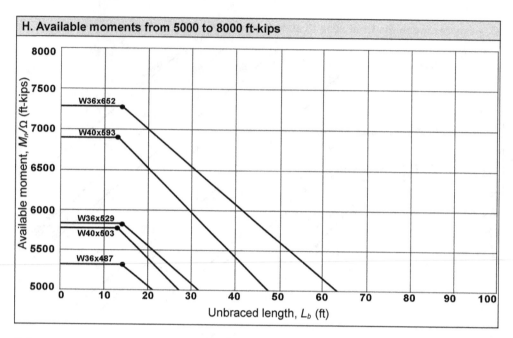

H. Available moments from 5000 to 8000 ft-kips

(Graph: Available moment, M_n/Ω (ft-kips), vertical axis from 5000 to 8000; Unbraced length, L_b (ft), horizontal axis from 0 to 100. Curves labeled: W36x652, W40x593, W36x529, W40x503, W36x487.)

Notes:

1. Values are based on the conservative assumption that the "lateral-torsional buckling modifier," $C_b = 1.0$. This conservative value of $C_b = 1.0$ is quite close to the actual value for simply-supported beams with equally spaced point loads of equal weight, where the beam is braced at those points only, except for the special case of a single point load at midspan, in which case $C_b = 1.364$. Actual values for C_b can be found for each unbraced beam segment by calculating the bending moments at the quarter-points along each segment (M_A, M_B, and M_C, with M_B being the moment at the midpoint of the segment), as well as the maximum moment, M_{max}, within each segment, and then inserting these values into Equation 4.13, reproduced as follows:

$$C_b = \frac{12.5M_{max}}{2.5M_{max} + 3M_A + 4M_B + 3M_C}$$

In any case, the available moment cannot exceed M_p/Ω, the value for braced, compact sections given in Appendix Table A-4.15.

2. Solid circles represent the maximum unbraced length, L_p, for which a plastic moment can be achieved before the onset of lateral-torsional buckling; open circles represent the maximum unbraced length, L_r, for which an elastic moment can be achieved before the onset of lateral-torsional buckling (see Figure 4.23).

Table A-4.17: Maximum (actual) deflection in a beam[1,2,3]

Deflection coefficient, C, for maximum (actual) deflection, Δ (in.), where $\Delta = \dfrac{CP(L/12)^3}{EI_x}$				
	simply-supported	one end pinned, one end continuous	both ends continuous	cantilever
$P = w(L/12)$	22.46	9.33	4.49	216
P	35.94	16.07	8.99	n/a
$P \quad P$	61.34	26.27	13.31	n/a
$P \, P \, P$	85.54	36.12	17.97	n/a
P	n/a	n/a	n/a	576

Notes:

1. Beam diagram symbols in top row of tables represent the following conditions (from left to right): simply-supported; one end pinned and one end continuous; both ends continuous; and cantilever.

2. Units for the maximum (actual) deflection equation are as follows:

Δ = maximum (actual) deflection (in.)

C = deflection coefficient

L = span (in.): The quantity ($L/12$) that appears in the deflection equation is therefore the span in feet

E = modulus of elasticity (psi when load is in lb; or ksi when load is in kips)

I_x = moment of inertia about axis of bending (in⁴)

P = concentrated load or resultant of uniformly-distributed load (lb or kips)

w = uniformly-distributed load (lb/ft or kips/ft)

3. Allowable deflections (from Appendix Table A-1.3) are as follows:

For live load only (or snow or wind only), the typical basic floor beam limit is $L/360$ while typical roof beam limits are $L/180$, $L/240$, or $L/360$ (for no ceiling, nonplaster ceiling, or plaster ceiling respectively).

For total loads (combined live and dead), the typical basic floor beam limit is $L/240$ while typical roof beam limits are $L/120$, $L/180$, or $L/240$ (for no ceiling, nonplaster ceiling, or plaster ceiling respectively).

Table A-4.18: Shear capacity, or available strength, for a high-strength bolt subjected to single shear with threads excluded from shear plane (kips)

A. Bearing-type connections[1]								
Bolt type	Nominal bolt diameter (in.)							
	5/8	3/4	7/8	1	1⅛	1¼	1⅜	1½
Group A (A325)	10.4	15.0	20.4	26.7	33.8	41.8	50.3	60.2
Group B (A490)	12.9	18.6	25.2	33.0	41.7	51.7	62.2	74.3

B. Slip-critical connections (based on strength rather than serviceability)[2]								
Bolt type	Nominal bolt diameter (in.)							
	5/8	3/4	7/8	1	1⅛	1¼	1⅜	1½
Group A (A325)	4.29	6.33	8.81	11.5	12..7	16.0	19.2	23.3
Group B (A490)	5.42	7.91	11.1	14.5	18.1	23.1	27.3	33.4

Notes:

1. Capacities are tabulated for single-shear connections, with bolt threads excluded from all shear planes (condition X). For double-shear, multiply values by 2; for threads included within shear planes (condition N), multiply values by 0.8. For double-shear and threads included, multiply by $2 \times 0.8 = 1.6$.

2. Slip-critical capacities are based on standard holes and single-shear. For double shear, multiply values by 2. Slip-critical bolts must also satisfy bearing capacity values in Appendix Table A-4.19.

Table A-4.19: Bearing capacity, or available strength, for a high-strength bolt bearing on material 1 in. thick, with clear spacing between bolts (or edge) ≥ 2 in. (kips)[1]

Material being connected	Nominal bolt diameter (in.)							
	5/8	3/4	7/8	1	1⅛	1¼	1⅜	1½
A36, $F_u = 58$ ksi	54.4	65.3	76.1	87.0	97.9	109	120	131
A992, $F_u = 65$ ksi	60.9	73.1	85.3	97.5	110	122	134	146

Note:

1. Capacity (available strength) is tabulated assuming that the bolt hole clear spacing (or clear spacing between bolt hole and material edge) in direction of force is no less than 2 in. For clear spacing less than 2 in., multiply capacity by $L_c/2$, where L_c is the actual clear spacing (in.). For cases where the small deformations associated with bolt bearing, at ordinary service loads, are considered to be a design issue, multiply capacity by 0.8. Where the thickness, t, of the material is other than 1 in., multiply the capacity by the thickness, t (in.). These multiplications are cumulative so that, for example, the capacity of a material with t = ⅝ in., clear spacing between bolts of 1.75 in., and consideration of bearing deformations, would be equal to the tabular value multiplied by (⅝)(1.75/2)(0.8) = (tabular value × 0.4375).

Table A-4.20: Minimum and maximum spacing and edge distance measured from bolt centerline for standard holes

A. Minimum bolt spacing (in.)	Nominal bolt diameter (in.)							
	5/8	3/4	7/8	1	1⅛	1¼	1⅜	1½
Suggested	1⅞	2¼	2⅝	3	3⅜	3¾	4⅛	4½
Required	1⅔	2	2⅓	2⅔	3	3⅓	3⅔	4

B. Minimum edge distance (in.)[1]	Nominal bolt diameter (in.)							
Type of edge	5/8	3/4	7/8	1	1⅛	1¼	1⅜	1½
Sheared edge	1⅛	1¼	[2]1½	[2]1¾	2	2¼	2¹³⁄₃₂	2⅝
Rolled or thermally cut edge	7/8	1	1⅛	1¼	1½	1⅝	1²³⁄₃₂	1⅞

C. Maximum bolt spacing and edge distance (in.)	Member thickness (in.)							
	1/4	3/8	1/2	5/8	3/4	7/8	1	1⅛
Centerline spacing[3]	6	9	12	12	12	12	12	12
Edge distance	3	4½	6	6	6	6	6	6

Notes:

1. Minimum edge distances, measured in the direction of force, may be reduced below these values, as long as bearing capacity is appropriately reduced (see Note 1 in Appendix Table A-4.19).

2. A value of 1¼ in. may be used for bolts at the ends of beam connection angles and shear end plates.

3. Maximum centerline spacing is measured in the direction of the applied load (longitudinally), and is valid for members not subject to corrosion, whether painted or not. For unpainted weathering steel, the maximum spacing is 7 in. or, where the thinner member is less than ½ in., 14 times that member's thickness.

Table A-4.21 Size limitations (leg size, w) for fillet welds (in.)

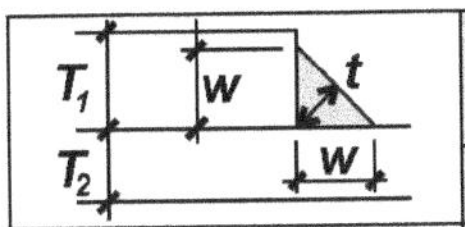	Thickness, T, of material being joined (in.)[1]				
	$T < 1/4$ in.	$T = 1/4$ in.	$1/4 < T \leq 1/2$ in.	$1/2 < T \leq 3/4$ in.	$3/4 < T$
Minimum weld size, w	1/8	1/8	3/16	1/4	5/16
Maximum weld size, w	T	3/16	$T - 1/16$ in.		

Note:

1. For minimum weld size, the thickness, T, is the thinner of the two plate thicknesses being joined (either T_1 or T_2); for maximum weld size, the thickness, T, is the smallest thickness (edge) that the weld leg actually comes into contact with (i.e., T_1).

CHAPTER 5

Reinforced concrete

Reinforced concrete is *plain concrete* in which steel bars have been strategically placed so that they compensate for the low tensile strength of the concrete. This allows concrete — historically (i.e., before the late nineteenth century) a material that was, like masonry, stressed primarily in compression — to become quite a bit more versatile. This versatility comes about not because reinforcing concrete with steel makes the concrete suitable for use in pure tension members, but rather because it opens up the possibility of using concrete where either *bending*, or other combinations of compression and tension are expected: not only in all sorts of slabs, beams, girders, and columns, but also in more exotic shell structures such as hyperbolic paraboloids.

For the record, it should be noted that steel bars added to concrete bending and compression elements may also be placed where *compression*, and not only tension, is expected. In columns, for example, buckling can cause bending in either of two directions about a column's weak axis, so the location of added tension and compression stresses is unknown. Therefore, reinforcing bars must be placed to resist tension on *both* sides of the column, even though one side will not be subjected to tension stress. In beams, compression steel is often provided for two reasons. First, it is convenient to provide at least a nominal amount of steel in all four corners of a rectangular concrete cross section, and not only in the tension zone. Doing so provides a framework (or *cage*) that enables the whole ensemble of necessary reinforcement to be tied together and lifted in one piece into formwork before the concrete is cast. Second, compression steel is often desired because it reduces deflection of beams, especially those with long spans and relatively narrow depths.

MATERIAL PROPERTIES

Concrete consists of aggregate (course aggregate, or gravel, and fine aggregate, or sand) that is bound together with hydraulic cement. "Hydraulic" refers to the fact that the cement reacts with and hardens (*cures*) in the presence of water. Water is therefore the third necessary ingredient in plain concrete.

Aggregate

While the Romans used all sorts of aggregate in their 2000-year-old plain concrete structures — including recycled brick rubble, tile, and relatively large hunks of rock — modern aggregate consists almost exclusively of stone and sand that are combined in precise proportions, using various sizes or grades to minimize voids between the aggregate particles.

The logic of grading can be understood by imagining a container filled with spherical stones, all of the same size (Figure 5.1a). Clearly the voids left between the spheres can be filled using smaller stones (Figure 5.1b); and the voids between those smaller stones can be filled with even smaller stones, or sands. The goal is to minimize such voids for two primary reasons. First, cement — which fills the voids and binds the aggregate together — is far more expensive than gravel and sand. Second, cement tends to shrink as it cures, so that large quantities of cement would result in unacceptably large amounts of shrinkage and cracking. Using only large stones is clearly less effective than adding a variety of smaller aggregate to a mix that includes large stones. On the other hand, using only small aggregate is also less effective, since a larger stone could displace not only a great deal of the smaller aggregate but also eliminate the voids (cement) between the small aggregate pieces that have been displaced.

So why not use really large rocks as aggregate, thereby displacing the most voids? In fact, the largest aggregate size used in any given mix is limited both by the spacing between bars of reinforcing steel (since the aggregate must be able to easily pass through the matrix of steel bars) and by the smallest dimension of the formwork or slab thickness. For this reason, maximum aggregate sizes of ¾ in. or 1 in. are fairly common. Aggregates graded in this way typically comprise about 60 to 80 percent of the volume (and 70 to 85 percent of the weight) of plain concrete, and consist of several grades of fine

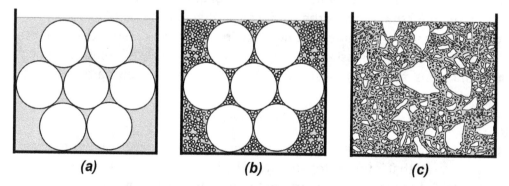

(a)   (b)   (c)

Figure 5.1: Schematic representation of (a) container filled with only large, spherical aggregate, (b) the same container with smaller, spherical aggregate partially filling the voids between the large aggregate and (c) the container with a more realistic representation of continuously graded aggregate; in all images, the gray tone represents the cement

aggregate (sand) and several grades of course aggregate (gravel), as represented in Figure 5.1c.

Cement

Modern cements — at least since 1824 when Joseph Aspdin patented a hydraulic mix whose color was similar to that of a stone found on the Isle of Portland in the English Channel (hence, *portland cement*) — contain a number of ingredients (calcium, silicon, aluminum and iron) which are ground, blended, and heated in a kiln to create a cement clicker which, in turn, is blended with gypsum and ground again into a fine powder. Cement ingredients come from rather commonplace materials such as limestone, shells, shale, clay, sand and iron ore.

Blended cements combine portland cement with other hydraulic materials including industrial by-products such as fly ash, blast furnace slag, and silica fume. These products can actually increase the durability and strength of concrete by reducing the amount of water necessary for the *workability* of the concrete mix. It turns out that more water is used in concrete than is needed for the chemical reaction between water and cement that results in the hardening of the cement; this "extra" water is required so that the concrete can be mixed and placed into forms; otherwise, it would be too stiff. When this extra water eventually evaporates, it leaves pores in the concrete that reduce the strength of the concrete (since a void cannot resist tensile or compressive forces) while providing a pathway for salts or other unwanted elements into the concrete, leading to various forms of damage or distress. Certain materials, such as fly ash — a by-product of coal-fired electric generating plants — are unusually smooth and spherical. For that reason, they act like ball bearings within the concrete mix, facilitating mixing and placing with reduced quantities of water.

The strength of concrete is quite sensitive to the water-cement (w/c) ratio: too little water makes the concrete hard to place, and encourages *honeycombing* — i.e., the appearance of voids when the formwork is stripped because the concrete was too stiff to fill the form properly, thereby reducing its strength. On the other hand, too much water leads to loss of strength and durability as described earlier. For ordinary concrete, a w/c ratio of about 0.6 (comparing the *weights* of the two materials) is typical, although in corrosive environments, the w/c ratio should be reduced to 0.5 or even 0.4. By using blended cements, the w/c ratio can be lowered — reducing voids and increasing both strength and durability — without compromising the workability of the mix. One also scores points with green building rating systems, since the use of recycled materials such as fly ash is considered beneficial.

There are some downsides to the use of such recycled material to replace a portion of the portland cement. In general, concrete cures faster when only portland cement is used, as blended cements slow down the curing process: this slower cure time could result in substantial losses (since time = money), especially in multistory buildings where each floor is cast sequentially only after the prior floor structure has cured sufficiently. Additionally, some of these recycled ingredients, such as silica fume, have actually become more expensive than standard cement; and some of the lower-priced options may contain unwanted ingredients (e.g., sulfur) that could increase the risk of cracking or corrosion of steel reinforcement.

Table 5.1: Types of portland cement

Type	Name	Common applications
Type I	General purpose	For ordinary construction of buildings, pavement, etc.
Type II	Moderate sulfate resistance	For concrete exposed to sulfate ions in soil or water
Type III	High early strength	For use in cold weather, or where rapid construction is desired
Type IV	Low heat of hydration	Rarely used; formerly used in massive structures like dams
Type V	High sulfate resistance	For concrete exposed to high levels of sulfate ions in soil or water

Five types of portland cement are manufactured, as shown in Table 5.1. In practice, Types I and II are often combined into a single product (Type I/II). Type III is more finely ground, which tends to accelerate the mostly exothermic chemical reactions associated with curing, providing more heat to keep these reactions going in cold weather. Type IV is no longer commonly used, but was designed to slow down the exothermic reactions associated with curing in order to minimize temperature differentials in massive structures like dams (Type II cement is now more commonly used for such purposes, as its moderate heat of hydration has proven to be acceptable in massive concrete construction). Type V is like Type II, but with even more resistance to sulfate attack.

Water

Water used in reinforced concrete should be free of organic matter and salts. Ordinary municipal water works well and is commonly used, but some forms of recycled water are also acceptable. When concrete is cast in either extremely hot or extremely cold conditions, ice may be added to the water, or the water may be heated, to compensate for these environmental conditions. This adds some expense to the process, but otherwise helps maintain an appropriate rate of curing.

Admixtures

Aside from the three main constituents of concrete — aggregate, cement, and water — other ingredients, called *admixtures*, are sometimes added to the concrete mix. The most commonly used are *air-entraining agents*. These admixtures increase the amount of air in concrete by forming tiny bubbles that are spread throughout the mix, allowing freezing water to expand (into these bubbles) without cracking the concrete. For this reason, air entrainment is almost always specified when concrete may be subject to freezing conditions. In fact, most cement types are available with such air-entraining agents already included.

Water reducers constitute a second class of admixtures that includes both mid-range and high-range variants, the latter also known as *plasticizers* or *superplasticizers*. These admixtures create workable, and in some cases highly "flowable," concrete at lower w/c ratios, thereby increasing the concrete's strength and durability. Some of these admixtures, such as fly ash, are precisely the ingredients used to create blended cements.

Corrosion inhibitors are a third type of admixture. These are designed to protect reinforcing steel from rusting in particularly corrosive environments; otherwise the inherently alkaline nature of concrete protects steel bars from corrosion without requiring any added ingredients.

Brittleness

Lack of ductility is an undesirable property for a structural material, and is associated with low tensile strength. This is because small cracks or imperfections in a brittle material tend to propagate when pulled apart under tension, leading to a characteristic type of brittle failure. To prevent sudden, catastrophic failure of reinforced concrete beams, for example, the amount of reinforcement must be kept *small* enough so that the steel will yield (in a ductile manner) before the concrete crushes (in a sudden, catastrophic, brittle manner). Where this is not possible — in structural elements controlled by compression — safety factors must be adjusted accordingly.

Mixing and testing

Concrete mixes are designed to achieve a desired compressive strength with the minimum amount of cement compatible with adequate workability. The primary variable in determining strength is the ratio of water to cement (w/c), where this ratio is based on the relative *weight*, not volume, of the two materials. A methodology for proportioning the constituent ingredients in concrete promulgated by the American Concrete Institute (ACI) is widely used in practice.

Concrete, however, poses unique challenges as a material because the constituent ingredients are often stored and put together at a batching plant, and then delivered to the job site in special trucks containing rotating drums in which the ingredients are mixed in transit. When the concrete is then *cast* (not "poured") into forms, there is no way to validate the strength of the mix unless portions of the mix are set aside and tested. Some tests can be performed immediately on the job site: for example, the percentage of entrained air in the mix can be measured with an air entrainment meter (Figure 5.2*a*) and the consistency of the mix — and by implication the workability — can be evaluated with a slump test (Figure 5.2*b*). The first of these tests is based on Boyle's law, with air pressure and volume being inversely proportional. The second test relies less on scientific equations and more on low-tech empirical evidence — when fresh concrete is placed in an inverted 12-in.-high cone and the cone is quickly removed, the concrete will "slump" down to an extent that can be correlated with its consistency and workability (which is, to some extent, related to the w/c ratio). A more accurate w/c measurement can be obtained by conducting a microwave oven test that determines this ratio by essentially heating a cylinder of fresh concrete until the water evaporates and then comparing the weight of evaporated water to that of the cement.

A test that is specified by the American Concrete Institute (ACI) and often mandated by building codes is a compressive strength cylinder test. Twelve-inch-high cylinders (Figure 5.2*c*) are filled with fresh concrete and cured in a testing lab for 28 days. At that time, they are crushed in a testing machine and their compressive strength is measured. Two cylinders are filled for every 150 cubic yards of concrete (or for every 5,000 ft^2 of slab surface) and, after

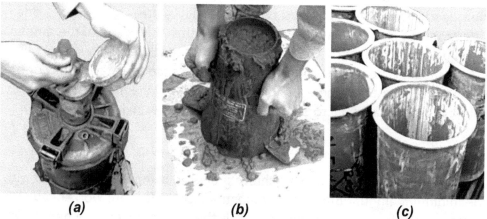

       (a)   *(b)*   *(c)*

Figure 5.2: Three tests commonly performed on concrete are (*a*) an air entrainment test to measure the percentage of entrained air, (*b*) a slump test to approximately measure the consistency, or workability, of the concrete, and (*c*) a cylinder test to measure the 28-day compressive strength (all images first screen-captured from the *Construction of Milstein Hall Part 4 Concrete* video by the author at http://impatientsearch.com/milstein/ and then photo-edited; the cylinders shown have not yet been filled with fresh concrete)

28 days of controlled curing, the average strength of any three consecutively tested cylinders must be greater or equal to the specified cylinder strength of the concrete. Alternatively, the concrete is considered acceptable — even if this first criterion is not met — as long as all tested cylinders are no more than 500 psi weaker than the specified cylinder strength.

Strength of concrete

Aside from concrete's relatively high compressive strength, the material properties that are most significant in terms of its structural behavior are low tensile strength, brittleness, and shrinkage.

The specified compressive strength of concrete, f'_c, is generally in the range of 3000 – 5000 psi for ordinary projects (Figure 5.3), although much higher values can be obtained, at greater expense, especially for high-rise applications. This compressive strength is not achieved immediately after the concrete is mixed, but only after 28 days of curing. Of course, if 28 days of waiting were required before a story could be cast on top of the story immediately below, completing the structure for a 12-story cast-in-place reinforced concrete building would take more than a year. In fact, concrete typically reaches more than half its specified strength after a week; at this time, formwork can be stripped and the next floor can be cast, even though the specified concrete strength has not yet been achieved. Concrete continues to get stronger for several years after the initial 28-day curing period, but this added strength is not considered explicitly in the design process.

Low tensile strength makes plain concrete unsuitable for most structural applications, since even elements subjected to compressive stresses generally

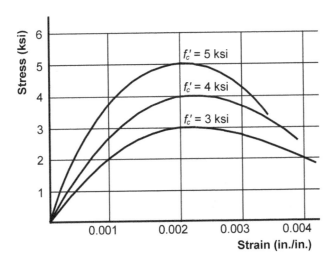

Figure 5.3: Compressive stress-strain curves are shown for 3000, 4000, and 5000 psi (3, 4, and 5 ksi) concrete

need sufficient tensile strength to inhibit buckling. For this reason, and to extend the range of its applications to beams and slabs as well as columns, concrete is reinforced with steel reinforcing bars, or "rebars," in regions of the cross section where tension is expected to occur.

Shrinkage

Concrete — actually cement within the concrete mix — shrinks as part of the curing process. Expansion and contraction due to temperature changes can also cause differential movement between concrete and adjacent materials. To reduce and control cracking in slabs where this movement is restrained, for example by perimeter beams containing steel reinforcement, additional temperature and shrinkage reinforcement is added to 1-way slabs. These are slabs where the concrete spans and is structurally reinforced in one direction only, so that temperature and shrinkage reinforcement must be placed perpendicular to this spanning direction. In beams, columns, or two-way slabs, no temperature and shrinkage reinforcement is needed since reinforcement is already present where cracking might otherwise occur.

Creep is a form of inelastic shrinkage of concrete. As opposed to elastic deformations, which are proportional to loads and reversible (i.e., the deformation goes away when the load is removed), creep is neither proportional to the load, nor is it entirely reversible. Instead, it represents an additional, and ongoing, shrinkage of concrete under load above and beyond the chemically-induced curing shrinkage mentioned earlier, or the elastic deformation under load described in Equation 1.18. For most beams and slabs, this phenomenon can be safely ignored; for multi-story buildings, however, the effects of creep can become important, especially when adjacent lower-story columns or shear walls experience different amounts of creep owing to different loading or reinforcement conditions. Such analysis is, however, beyond the scope of this book.

Long-term problems

In an ideal environment, the alkaline nature of concrete protects the steel reinforcing bars within from corrosion. In real environments, several problems may affect the durability of reinforced concrete structures.

Chloride-induced corrosion of reinforcing bars may occur for various reasons. The most obvious causal agents are de-icing salts that could get onto the surface of concrete slabs, e.g., in parking garages, and work their way into the concrete through cracks or pores. Remarkably, some older concrete has experienced this type of corrosion because of agents deliberately added to the concrete — either as "accelerating admixtures" to speed up the curing process or "etching agents" to remove cement at the surface of the concrete in order to reveal a more textured aggregate pattern.

Carbonation is a chemical process that occurs when cement reacts with "acid rain," causing the concrete to lose some of its alkalinity — this reduces the protection that the concrete ordinarily provides to reinforcing steel, and could lead to corrosion where concrete surfaces are exposed to such environmental conditions.

Sulfate attack is to some extent mitigated by the use of appropriate cements (Types II or V). Otherwise, where concrete comes into contact with sulfates in ground water or from ingredients in the concrete mix — e.g., some types of blast furnace slab or pulverized fuel ash — not only is alkalinity reduced (as in carbonation), but chemical reactions involving sulfates and concrete ingredients cause a volume increase that can lead to spalling of the concrete.

Alkali-silica reaction (ASR) occurs when alkalis in portland cement (or from other sources) react with certain aggregate in the concrete mix, forming an alkali-silica gel that expands — leading to cracking.

Related products

Precast concrete is reinforced concrete that is cast away from the building site, and assembled on site. Some (but not all) precast concrete is available in standard shapes and dimensions: floor and roof planks, tees and double-tees are examples. Otherwise, precast concrete may be fabricated in any shape and size consistent with the laws of statics, the strength and stiffness of the materials, and the constraints imposed by formwork, transportation, handling, and erection.

Precasting may imply a loss of structural continuity if connections are made with steel inserts bolted or welded together to create simple supports. On the other hand, it is possible, through emulative detailing, to design precast systems whose behavior is identical to that of site-cast systems. This is done by by maintaining the continuity of steel reinforcement from element to element. Special products are available to connect rebars that have been left exposed at the ends of the concrete pieces; non-shrinking grouts are then used to fill in the voids and complete the structural connection.

Precast concrete is also widely used as "nonstructural" cladding in addition to being used as primary structure, especially in the US. The quotation marks around nonstructural hint at the inadequacy of the term: in fact, all cladding is structural since it must resist wind, seismic, and impact loads and transfer these loads to the primary lateral-force resisting structural system of the building.

Autoclaved aerated concrete (AAC) has some of the ingredients characteristic of plain concrete — cement, fine aggregate, and water — but also contains aluminum powder that reacts chemically to release hydrogen gas. This gas creates a kind of foam out of the concrete mix, which is easily cut into blocks or other shapes and then hardened within a pressurized autoclave chamber. The resulting product is lightweight, the entrapped air makes it highly insulative, and the units can be stacked and mortared much like more conventional concrete masonry units (CMU).

SECTIONAL PROPERTIES

Because cast-in-place, or site-cast, concrete is literally made at the building site, the only real constraint on the sizes and shapes of concrete structural elements is the willingness of architects, engineers, owners, and contractors to design the structure, and assemble the formwork into which the concrete and reinforcement is placed. The history of reinforced concrete structures is thus filled with elaborate, structurally-expressive, one-of-a-kind projects in which the "plasticity" of the material is exploited. The costs of formwork can be significant, though, and many reinforced concrete structures are designed to minimize these costs by rationalizing the dimensions of the various concrete elements, in part by reusing standardized forms where possible. For these structures, the outside dimensions of beams, slabs and columns are often rounded up to the nearest ½ in., 1 in. or even-numbered inch, depending on how big the element is. Slabs 6 in. thick or less are rounded up to the nearest ½ in.; thicker slabs are rounded up to the nearest inch. The cross-sectional dimensions of beams and columns are rounded up to the nearest 1 in. or even-numbered inch (see Appendix Table A-5.1).

Reinforcing bar (rebar) spacing in reinforced concrete beams and columns is constrained by several factors. First, bars must be far enough apart so that aggregate in the concrete mix can pass freely between them — in general the largest aggregate size must be no more than ¾ the minimum distance between bars. Looked at from the opposite point of view (that is, with the maximum aggregate size set), the minimum space between bars must be 1⅓ times greater than the largest aggregate. For 1 in. aggregate, the minimum clear bar spacing would be 1⅓ in., or approximately 1½ in. Additional requirements relate bar spacing to bar size: for beams, the spacing must be not less than the nominal bar diameter, or 1 in.; for columns, the spacing must be not less than 1½ times the nominal bar diameter, or 1½ in.

In the U.S., rebars were designated and marked by a number corresponding to the bar's nominal diameter multiplied by eight: for example, a bar with a nominal diameter of ½ in. would be designated as a No. 4 bar (since ½ × 8 = 4). In an increasingly international marketplace, these designations have been

replaced with SI (international system) units, so the old No. 4 bar is now designated with the number 13 (since ½ in. = 12.7 mm, or approximately 13 mm).
Even so, the old U.S. system of bar numbering is still used by the American
Concrete Institute (ACI) in its structural concrete codes and commentaries,
and will be used in this text. Side-by-side listings of new and old designations
can be found in Appendix Tables A-5.2 and A-5.3.

For all commonly used beam reinforcing (No. 11 bars or smaller) and with
aggregate no larger than 1 in., the minimum bar *clear* spacing requirement
can be set at 1½ in. for beams. For column reinforcing of No. 8 bars or smaller
(that is, 1 in. diameter or smaller) and with aggregate no larger than 1 in., the
minimum spacing requirement can also be set at 1½ in. for columns. However,
for bar sizes larger than No. 8, the spacing requirement increases to 1½ times
the nominal bar diameter.

The implications for minimum width or diameter of reinforced concrete
columns and beams are shown in Figure 5.4 and summarized next, assuming
1½ in. cover and ½ in. diameter ties, stirrups, or spiral reinforcement. The specific function of these reinforcement types is explained later in this chapter
(ties and spirals for columns; stirrups for beams).

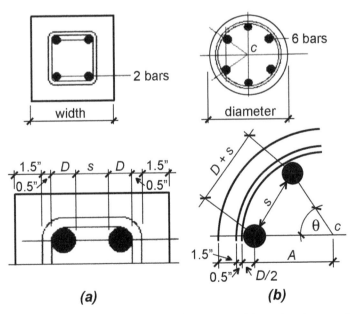

Figure 5.4: Minimum beam and column width (or diameter) based on bar spacing: (*a*) for
tied column or beam; and (*b*) for spiral column. The bar nominal bar diameter is *D*, the
required clear distance between bars is *s* and, for an angle, θ, between longitudinal bars in a
spiral column, the distance, $A = 2(\sin \theta/2)/(D + s)$

Rectangular columns or beams

1. For beams (with bar size of No. 11 or smaller) and for columns with bar size of No. 8 or smaller, with two bars along the beam or column face: the minimum width (in.) = 5.5 + 2D, where D is the bar diameter (in.). For beams or columns with more than two bars in a line, add 1½ in. + D for each additional bar.
2. For columns with bar size larger than No. 8, with two bars along the column face, the minimum width (in.) = 4 + 3.5D, where D is the bar diameter (in.). For columns with more than two bars in a line, add 2.5D for each additional bar.

Spiral columns

1. For spiral columns with six bars, No. 8 or smaller: the minimum column diameter (in.) = 7 + 3D, where D is the bar diameter (in.). For columns with bar sizes larger than No. 8: the minimum diameter = 4 + 6D.
2. Minimum widths for rectangular beams and columns, and minimum diameters for spiral columns, are given in Appendix Table A-5.3.

DESIGN APPROACHES

The so-called *strength design method* (originally called "ultimate strength design") was pioneered by the American Concrete Institute (ACI), which adopted a methodology in 1956 that both incorporated load factors and considered the ultimate (failure) stress, rather than an allowable stress, as an alternate and more rational strategy for design. A working (allowable) stress design method remained the dominant methodology, however, for many years. This latter method did not distinguish between uncertainties inherent in various load types (e.g., dead vs. live loads), and did not consider the actual strength of a structural element subjected to these loads. Instead, it accounted for risk using a single factor of safety based on an assumed elastic limit state. This is problematic for concrete on two counts: first, because the material itself does not exhibit clearly defined elastic behavior (see Figure 5.3) and second, because — in general and not just for concrete — the simple addition of load values without consideration of the probabilistic nature of their distribution within a structure is not entirely consistent with a risk-based approach to structural design.

By the early 1960s, strength design for reinforced concrete structures had matured to the point where both loads and resistances were given their own, independent sets of safety factors that were equivalent, at least in theory, to current versions of "Load & Resistance Factor Design" (LRFD) used for wood and steel. While the traditional working stress design method was, at that time, still the featured methodology for the design of reinforced concrete elements, strength design gradually began to displace the older method. The first incarnation of strength design did not yet have explicit strength reduction (resistance) factors and was presented somewhat tentatively in the 1956 edition of ACI 318, the "Building Code Requirements for Reinforced Concrete" that is updated by ACI every few years. A short note referred those willing to try this new method to the appendix, which contained a concise description of the requirements for "ultimate strength design." In 1963, working stress and strength methods achieved separate but equal status within the body of ACI 318. By 1971, strength design had become the featured method, with working stress design still included, but only as an "alternate design method." In 1989, working stress design no longer appeared in the main text of ACI 318 at all, but was moved to the appendix, where it remained as an alternate method for another decade: by the time ACI 318 was updated in 2002, working stress design had been consigned to a small note in the manual's *Commentary* stating that anyone still interested in it would need to consult the appendix of the 1999 edition, where it had last appeared.

Remarkably, it took 30 years after strength design was first presented in the ACI Code before the steel industry adopted its own version, called *load and resistance factor design (LRFD)*, in 1986. Up until quite recently, however, load factors differed between steel and reinforced concrete. Those adopted by ACI had been calculated on the basis of "engineering judgment" rather than on more solid empirical studies and probabilistic research. Initial values from 1963, for example, included load factors of 1.5 and 1.8 for dead and live loads respectively; these were "adjusted" to 1.4 and 1.7 in 1971, where they remained for more than 30 years. Meanwhile, dead and live load factors for steel structures were set at 1.2 and 1.6 respectively, values that appeared in the very first LRFD edition of the American Institute of Steel Construction's (AISC) *Manual of Steel Construction* in 1986, and that have been sanctioned by the American Society of Civil Engineers (ASCE) in their *Minimum Design Loads for Buildings and Other Structures* since 1988 and by the American National Standards Institute (ANSI) in the precursor to this standard dating from 1982. Since safety factors for loads ought to be completely independent of particular material properties, it was something of an embarrassment for the concrete and steel institutes to be seen arguing in this way, and something of a relief when the ACI finally reconciled their strength design load factors with those of the AISC and ASCE in the 2002 edition of ACI 318. In order to maintain a comparable level of safety with these newly reduced, and therefore *less* conservative, load factors, ACI 318-02 also adjusted its strength reduction factors — i.e., made them *more* conservative.

While LRFD, even today, is not universally used for steel design — and certainly not for wood design — strength design has almost completely superseded older working stress methods used to design reinforced concrete elements and is therefore the design method that will be considered exclusively in this chapter.

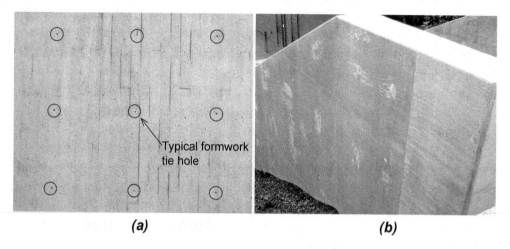

(a)   **(b)**

Figure 5.5: The pattern of formwork tie holes (*a*) can be considered as part of the architectural expression, as in the Johnson Museum, designed by I.M. Pei & Partners, or (*b*) can be filled solid in a utilitarian manner as in this stair adjacent to Gates Hall, designed by Morphosis Architects (photos at Cornell University by the author, Sept. 2014)

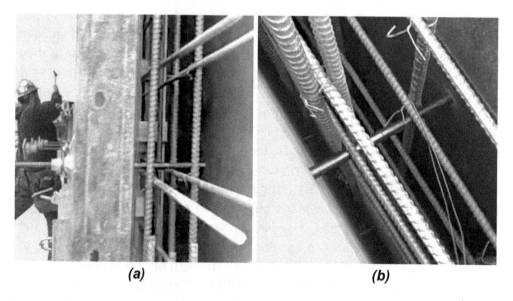

(a)   **(b)**

Figure 5.6: Formwork ties are inserted through the formwork to keep the two form surfaces aligned properly, to keep them from deforming due to the lateral pressure exerted by the concrete before it has cured, and to support reinforcing bars; these ties are shown (*a*) from the side and (*b*) from the top of a form before the concrete has been placed (all images screen-captured from the *Construction of Milstein Hall Part 2 Substructure* video by the author at http://impatientsearch.com/milstein/)

CONSTRUCTION SYSTEMS

Reinforced concrete buildings are built twice: first as an "inverse" building in which the desired content is made void and the space around this content is actually constructed; and then again as the real, intended structure consisting of concrete reinforced with deformed steel rods. Of course, the first building is not really a building at all, but rather the *formwork* in which the reinforced concrete building is cast. Still, the construction of extensive formwork as the inverse condition of the intended concrete structure has significant ramifications, not only in terms of structural costs but also in terms of formal constraints that are imposed on the concrete design by the necessity of first constructing the inverse forms from some other material.

Formwork

Historically, lumber was the primary material used to create forms into which concrete is placed, or cast. Now, other materials are also used, especially metal (reusable) forms and plywood (rather than boards), but also plastics and fiberglass. Formwork must be structurally able to withstand the lateral pressure of the "wet" concrete before it cures (hardens). Metal formwork ties are often provided for this purpose, leaving small circular marks in the surface of the concrete that may be organized and detailed for aesthetic purposes in so-called "architectural" concrete (i.e., concrete where the architect and client care about the surface qualities as in Figure 5.5*a*), or simply filled with grout in more utilitarian applications (or where the sloppiness of the finish is actually consistent with the aesthetic intentions as in Figure 5.5*b*). These ties can be configured so that they simultaneously support reinforcing bars, which are placed in the forms before the concrete is cast (Figure 5.6). Traditional formwork structures consist of ordinary dimension lumber arrayed in a gridded pattern of *soldiers* (vertical elements) and *wailers* (horizontal elements) that support two wooden surfaces (boards or plywood) between which a concrete wall is cast (Figure 5.7). Reusable metal forms are also commonly employed (Figure 5.8) and, in applications where concrete walls need to be insulated in any case, *insulating concrete forms (ICFs)* — consisting only of rigid insulation held together with metal ribs instead of formwork ties — can be used instead of wood- or metal-based systems of formwork (Figure 5.9). In such systems, the insulation-as-formwork remains in place permanently.

When reinforced concrete elements are exposed, the surface quality of the concrete may be problematic, since it is the cement — the least visually interesting component of the concrete — that rises to the surface. Many compensatory strategies have been employed to turn concrete into something more visually compelling. To remove the mottled gray surface of cement and expose aggregate, the surface can be sandblasted or acid etched; or the materials comprising the formwork itself can be carefully chosen to impart on the cement a mirror image of whatever the forms were made from — examples include the carefully spaced wooden boards shown in Figure 5.5*a*, or a rougher, "brutalist" aesthetic deriving from the use of construction-grade lumber, plywood, or even metal forms. Alternatively, form liners can be inserted into formwork to impart a texture or pattern onto the concrete that is independent of the formwork material itself (Figure 5.10).

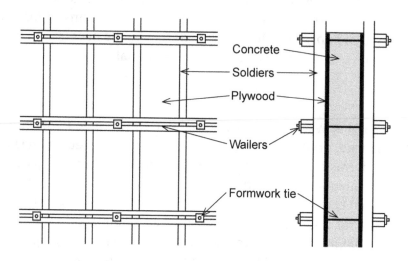

Figure 5.7: Typical formwork for reinforced concrete wall consists of soldiers and wailers supporting plywood surfaces, with formwork ties providing resistance to lateral pressure of the "wet" concrete

Figure 5.8: Reusable metal forms, these based on a 2-foot module, are assembled for a residential foundation wall (photos by the author)

Figure 5.9: Insulating concrete forms (ICFs) consist of rigid insulation tied together with metal ribs (photo by the author)

Figure 5.10: Form liner is peeled away to reveal ribbed concrete surface, Milstein Hall, Cornell University, designed by Rem Koolhaas-OMA (image screen-captured from the *Construction of Milstein Hall Part 2 Substructure* video by the author at http://impatientsearch.com/milstein/)

Conveying and placing concrete

Concrete is moved from mixer to formwork by various means, including wheel-barrows, buckets, pumping, or mere gravity (Figures 5.11 and 5.12). A danger in such movement is *segregation*, where heavier aggregate settles and water rises. Concrete is *placed* or *cast* rather than poured, although the latter term has insinuated itself into common construction vocabularies, and cannot be entirely avoided. In any case, try to say "cast-in-place" instead of "poured-in-place." To make sure that concrete has reached all parts of the formwork, it is often vibrated with special tools (yes, *vibrators* are used — see Figure 5.13). This prevents *honeycombing* (where voids appear after the formwork is removed). Concrete should be protected from moisture loss (evaporation) for at least 7 days, by sprinkling water on its surface, or by covering it with sheets such as polyethylene.

Frames and slabs

Reinforced concrete can be cast into an infinite variety of shapes, subject only to the laws of statics and the difficulty (expense) of creating the forms into which the concrete is cast. At one extreme can be found reinforced concrete structures whose forms are entirely unique, idiosyncratic, and expressive; at the other extreme are concrete structures made entirely from rationalized and reusable forms organized to produce buildings with relatively simple and repetitive geometries. In the latter category are framed structures consisting of columns and slabs, either with or without the hierarchically intermediate girders and beams characteristic of wood and steel structures. Reinforced concrete girders are never really omitted in such systems, but they can be subsumed within the thickness of floor or roof slabs so that the structure appears to consist only of a slab resting directly on columns. Figure 5.14 shows

(a)   *(b)*   *(c)*

Figure 5.11: Concrete can be placed in many ways including (*a*) by wheel barrow, (*b*) using pumps, and (*c*) down a chute directly from the ready mix truck (photo *a* by author; other images *b* and *c* screen-captured from construction video by the author — see http://impatientsearch.com/milstein/)

common structural slab systems for reinforced concrete-framed structures. Examples of one-way slab systems and grid (waffle) slab systems can be seen in Figure 5.15. Procedures for the design of reinforced concrete columns, one-way slabs, beams, and girders will be discussed later in this chapter.

Figure 5.12: Concrete for a slab is pumped from a remote vehicle

Figure 5.13: A vibrator is inserted into concrete from the top of the formwork

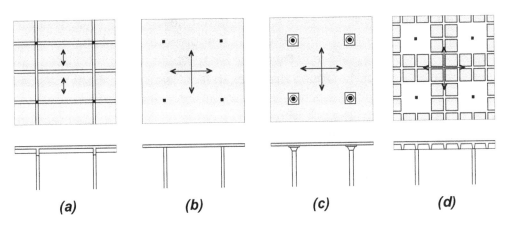

(a)   (b)   (c)   (d)

Figure 5.14: Reinforced concrete slabs take many forms including (a) 1-way slabs spanning between beams supported by girders, (b) 2-way flat plates in which all beams or girders are subsumed within the slab thickness, (c) 2-way flat slabs with articulated drop panels and/or column capitals to improve resistance to punching shear, and (d) 2-way grid (waffle) slabs created with reusable formwork with a pre-determined module (arrows indicate the direction of slab reinforcement)

(a)   *(b)*

Figure 5.15: (*a*) One-way slabs span directly between reinforced concrete girders supported on square columns, Teagle Hall, Cornell University, photo by the author; (*b*) two-way grid slabs are supported on cantilevered girders, Robert Purcell Community Center, Cornell University, photo by the author

TENSION ELEMENTS

Concrete, having very little tensile stress, is ordinarily not used for tension elements. Where it is used, its strength in tension can be taken as approximately 10% of its compressive strength, or $0.1f_c'$. The cylinder strength of concrete, f_c', is the ultimate (highest) compressive stress reached by a 6 in.×12 in. cylinder of concrete after 28 days of curing. Reinforced concrete, consisting of steel bars imbedded within a concrete element, would not normally be a good choice for a pure tension element, since the steel reinforcement would be doing all the work. In this case, one might wonder what would justify the added expense of casting concrete around the steel. In fact, two justifications are possible: first, in a reinforced concrete building consisting largely of compressive and bending elements, the use of reinforced concrete for occasional tension elements would allow a similar mode of expression and of detailing throughout the building; second, where the steel in tension requires fireproofing, the use of reinforced concrete in tension (where the concrete cover provides the fireproofing) might prove advantageous, compared to other solutions.

COLUMNS

Concrete columns are cast into forms containing a matrix of steel reinforcement. This reinforcement is distributed just inside the perimeter of the forms in a pattern designed to confine the concrete, much like sand would be confined when placed into a steel drum. In both cases (sand in a steel drum; concrete in a steel "cage"), the ability of the material to sustain an axial compressive stress is enormously increased by the presence of the confining steel, whether or not the steel contributes directly to the support of the external load.

Ties and spirals

Two patterns of steel reinforcement are commonly used for columns: a series of square or rectangular *ties* (Figure 5.16*a*) placed horizontally around a minimum of four longitudinal steel bars; or a continuous circular *spiral* wire (Figure 5.16*b*) wrapped around a minimum of six longitudinal bars. Tied columns are usually rectangular and spiral columns are usually circular, but either pattern of reinforcement can be used for any column cross section. In general, spiral reinforcement provides more reliable confinement of the concrete, and a more ductile type of failure than tied columns; strength reduction factors for spiral versus tied columns take this relative safety into account. The actual design of ties and spirals is based on fairly straight-forward guidelines, summarized in Appendix Table A-5.4. The design and analysis examples that follow do not include the calculation of tie or spiral spacing and size.

Design of concrete and longitudinal steel

The amount of longitudinal steel in reinforced concrete columns, measured according to the ratio of steel area to gross column area (*reinforcement ratio*), must fall between two limiting values. The lower limit of 1% provides a minimum amount of steel to protect against tension failures due to unanticipated

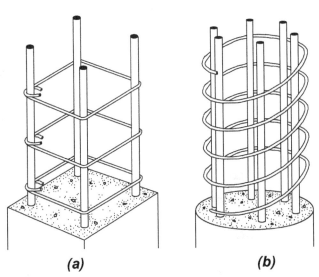

(a)   *(b)*

Figure 5.16: Containment of longitudinal bars using (*a*) ties; and (*b*) spiral reinforcement

bending moments; the upper limit of 8% prevents overcrowding of steel bars within the concrete formwork. The reinforcement ratio is defined as:

$$\rho_g = \frac{A_s}{A_g} \tag{5.1}$$

where ρ_g = the reinforcement ratio of longitudinal steel area to gross area; A_s = the cross-sectional area of longitudinal reinforcement; and A_g = the gross cross-sectional area of the concrete column, whether the column is rectangular or circular in section.

It is assumed in this chapter that reinforced concrete column stability is not a factor in the column's strength; that is, the column is not slender enough for buckling to be a problem. As a general rule of thumb, concrete columns braced against lateral misalignment ("sidesway"), with a slenderness ratio, KL/r, no greater than 40, are rarely influenced by stability considerations. Taking the radius of gyration of a rectangular column as approximately equal to 0.3 times the smaller cross-sectional column dimension, h (that is, assuming $r = 0.3h$), and taking the effective length coefficient, $K = 1.0$, we get $KL/r = 1.0L/(0.3h) \le 40$. Solving for the ratio of unbraced length, L, to minimum cross-sectional dimension, h, we find that slenderness effects may typically be neglected in axially-loaded reinforced concrete columns when $L/h \le 12$. For slender concrete columns, other techniques must be used to account for the possibility of buckling.

For columns, at least 1½ in. of concrete is left outside the matrix of reinforcement to protect it from corrosion and to provide fire resistance (2 in. for No. 6 or larger bars if the concrete is exposed to the weather, or the earth; 3 in. for all bars if the concrete is cast directly against the earth — see Appendix Table A-5.1). For typical reinforcement sizes, the distance from the outside of the concrete column to the centerline of the longitudinal reinforcement can be taken as about 2½ in. or 3 in. (Figure 5.17).

For a reinforced concrete column subjected to pure axial compression, the ultimate load at failure is simply the concrete strength (failure stress) times its

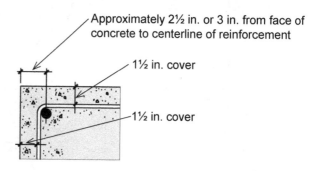

Figure 5.17: Detail of reinforced concrete element showing approximate distance from centerline of rebar to outside face of concrete

area, plus the yield stress of the longitudinal steel rebars times their area (Figure 5.18). The failure strength of concrete is taken as 85% of its cylinder strength, f_c', since the more rapid rate of loading of the test cylinders (Figure 5.19, curve a), compared to loading of actual structural columns (Figure 5.19, curve b), results in a higher measured strength than can be expected for real structures. The strain at which steel longitudinal reinforcement bars yield depends on their yield stress. For grade 60 rebars (f_y = 60 ksi), the yield strain (stress divided by modulus of elasticity) is 60/29,000 = 0.002. For grade 40 (f_y = 40 ksi), the yield strain is 40/29,000 = 0.001. In either case, the failure stress of the steel can be taken as its yield stress, f_y, since yielding would have already occurred when the concrete reaches its crushing strain (precipitating column failure) of about 0.003. Combining the failure stresses for concrete

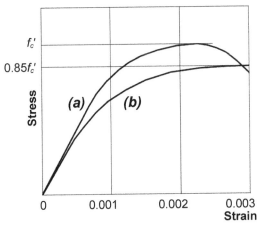

Figure 5.18: Nominal stresses at failure of axially loaded reinforced concrete column

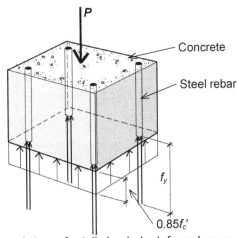

Figure 5.19: Stress-strain diagrams for plain concrete showing (a) fast loading characteristic of test cylinders; and (b) slow loading characteristic of actual structures

and steel, we get an ultimate failure load for an axially-loaded column of:

$$P_n = 0.85f_c'(A_c) + f_y A_s \qquad (5.2)$$

where A_s is the longitudinal steel area, and A_c is the net area of concrete, that is, the gross cross-sectional area minus the steel area.

There are two strength reduction safety factors for axially-loaded reinforced concrete columns: ϕ is the ordinary factor, while α accounts for the possibility of non-axial loading. Both factors depend on whether the column is tied or spiral (see Appendix Table A-5.5). Combining these strength reduction factors with factored loads (see Appendix Table A-5.4, which has been reproduced from Appendix Table A-2.7a), we get equations for the design and analysis of axially-loaded reinforced concrete columns. An example of such an equation for dead load (D) and live load (L) only, where P_u is the factored or "design" load, is:

$$P_u = 1.2D + 1.6L \le \phi\alpha(0.85f_c'A_c + f_y A_s) \qquad (5.3)$$

Example 5.1 Analyze axially-loaded reinforced concrete column

Problem definition. Assuming $f_c' = 4$ ksi and $f_y = 60$ ksi, find the nominal failure capacity of a 10 in. × 10 in. axially-loaded tied rectangular column with 4 No. 9 bars, as shown in Figure 5.20. Can this column support a live load of 100 kips and a dead load of 100 kips?

Solution overview. Find concrete and steel areas; multiply by failure stresses for concrete and steel and add together for ultimate capacity. Multiply ultimate capacity by strength reduction factors and compare with factored loads to determine whether capacity is adequate for given loads.

Problem solution
1. From Appendix Table A-5.2, the steel area for 4 No. 9 bars, $A_s = 4.00$ in².
2. The concrete area, $A_c = A_g - A_s = 10 \times 10 - 4.00 = 96$ in².

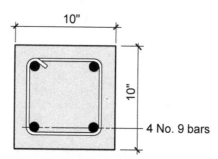

Figure 5.20: Column cross-section for Example 5.1

3. From Equation 5.2, the nominal capacity or failure load, $P_n = 0.85f_c'A_c + f_yA_s = 0.85(4)(96) + 60(4.00) = 566.4$ kips.

4. From Appendix Table A-5.2, strength reduction factors for a tied column are: $\phi = 0.65$ and $\alpha = 0.80$.

5. Based on Equation 5.3, check whether $P_u = 1.2D + 1.6L \leq \phi\alpha(P_n)$. We get: $P_u = 1.2D + 1.6L = 1.2(100) + 1.6(100) = 280$ kips; and $\phi\alpha(P_n) = (0.65)(0.80)(566.4) = 294.5$ kips. Therefore, since $P_u \leq \phi\alpha(P_n)$, the capacity is adequate and the column is OK.

6. In this example, all column parameters were given. However, we can still check that the column has an acceptable reinforcement ratio and that the bars fit within the cross section. Using Equation 5.1, we check that the reinforcement ratio is between 1% and 8% (that is, between 0.01 and 0.08): $\rho_g = A_s/A_g = 4.00/100 = 0.040$, so the reinforcement ratio is OK. Using Appendix Table A-5.3, we find that, for 2 No.9 bars in one line, we need 7.94 in. Since we actually have 10 in., the bars fit.

Example 5.2 Design axially-loaded reinforced concrete column with cross-sectional dimensions assumed

Problem definition. Assuming $f_c' = 3$ ksi and $f_y = 60$ ksi, find the required steel area for an axially-loaded 12-in.-square tied reinforced concrete column supporting a dead load (*D*) of 150 kips and a live load (*L*) of 100 kips. Select bar size.

Solution overview. Use Equation 5.3 relating reduced strength to factored loads and solve for steel area. The area of concrete within the column cross section is found by subtracting the steel area from the gross cross-sectional dimensions; that is, $A_c = A_g - A_s$. Check reinforcement ratio limits and bar fit.

Problem solution

1. From Equation 5.3: $P_u = 1.2D + 1.6L \leq \phi\alpha(0.85f_c'A_c + f_yA_s)$. Finding strength reduction factors, ϕ and α, from Table A-5.5, we get:

   $1.2(150) + 1.6(100) \leq (.65)(.80)[0.85(3)(144 - A_s) + 60A_s]$.
   $340 \leq (0.52)[367.2 - 2.55A_s + 60A_s]$.
   $653.85 \leq 367.2 + 57.45A_s$.
   $57.45A_s \geq 286.65$.
   $A_s \geq 4.99$ in². This is the required steel area for longitudinal bars.

2. From Appendix Table A-5.2, choose 4 No. 10 bars with actual $A_s = 5.08$ in². For symmetry, the number of bars is limited to 4, 6, 8, and so on.

3. Using Equation 5.1, check that the reinforcement ratio is between 1% and 8% (that is, between 0.01 and 0.08): $\rho_g = A_s/A_g = 5.08/144 = 0.035$, so

the reinforcement ratio is OK. Using Appendix Table A-5.3, we find that for two No. 10 bars in one line, we need 8.38 in. Since we actually have 12 in., the bars fit.

Example 5.3 Design axially-loaded reinforced concrete column with reinforcement ratio assumed

Problem definition. Assuming $f_c' = 5$ ksi and $f_y = 60$ ksi, select a diameter and find the required steel area for an axially-loaded spirally-reinforced circular reinforced concrete column supporting a dead load (D) of 150 kips and a live load (L) of 125 kips. Select bar size. Check reinforcement ratio and bar fit.

Solution overview. Use Equation 5.3 relating reduced strength to factored loads and solve for gross area. With the reinforcement ratio, ρ_g, assumed, the area of concrete within the column cross section, $A_c = (1.00 - \rho_g)A_g$ and the steel area, $A_s = \rho_g A_g$. Find the required gross area, select column dimensions (in this case, the column diameter), and proceed as in Example 5.2 with gross area known. Check reinforcement ratio limits and bar fit.

Problem solution

1. From Equation 5.3: $P_u = 1.2D + 1.6L \le \phi\alpha(0.85f_c'A_c + f_yA_s)$. Since $A_c = (1.00 - \rho_g)A_g$ and the steel area, $A_s = \rho_g A_g$, we get:

$$P_u = 1.2D + 1.6L \le \phi\alpha[0.85f_c'(1.00 - \rho_g)A_g + f_y\rho_g A_g]$$

The choice of a reinforcement ratio is somewhat arbitrary; we select $\rho_g = 0.04$; then, with strength reduction factors, ϕ and α, found from Appendix Table A-5.5, we get:

$1.2(150) + 1.6(125) \le (.75)(.85)[0.85(5)(1.00 - 0.04)A_g + 60(0.04)A_g]$.
$380 \le (0.6375)[4.08A_g + 2.40A_g]$.
$596.1 \le 6.48A_g$.

$A_g \ge 91.99$ in^2; since $A_g = \pi r^2$, the required radius for the concrete column, $r = \sqrt{91.11/\pi} = 5.41$ in. Therefore, the required diameter, $d = 2r = 2(5.41) = 10.8$ in.

The actual diameter that we select may be either bigger or smaller than this "required" diameter, since it was computed on the basis of a desired reinforcement ratio, which need not be — and cannot be — matched precisely in practice (since the actual bar area selected typically exceeds the required area, and since the actual diameter of the column is rounded to the nearest inch or "even" inch. We therefore select a column diameter close to the required value, say 10 in., and proceed as in Example 5.2, with the gross column area given.

2. From Equation 5.3: $P_u = 1.2D + 1.6L \leq \phi\alpha(0.85f_c'A_c + f_yA_s)$. The strength reduction factors, ϕ and α, from Appendix Table A-5.5, have already been found, the gross area of a circular column with a 10 in. diameter is $\pi r^2 = \pi 5^2 = 78.54$ in^2, and we get:

$1.2(150) + 1.6(125) \leq (.75)(.85)[0.85(5)(78.54 - A_s) + 60A_s]$.
$380 \leq (0.6375)[333.8 - 4.25A_s + 60A_s]$.
$596.1 \leq 333.8 + 55.75A_s$.
$55.75A_s \geq 262.3$.
$A_s \geq 4.71$ in^2. This is the required steel area for longitudinal bars.

3. From Appendix Table A-5.2, choose 6 No. 8 bars with actual $A_s = 4.74$ in^2. For spiral columns, the number of bars must be at least 6.

4. Using Equation 5.1, check that the reinforcement ratio is between 1% and 8% (that is, between 0.01 and 0.08): $\rho_g = A_s/A_g = 4.74/78.54 = 0.060$, so the reinforcement ratio is OK. Using Appendix Table A-5.3, we find that for 6 No.8 bars in the column, we need a 10.00 in. diameter. Since we actually have a 10 in. diameter, the bars fit.

The actual reinforcement ratio, $\rho_g = 0.060$, is much higher than our initial assumed value of $\rho_g = 0.04$. Had we selected a 12 in. diameter column instead of a 10 in. diameter column at the end of step 1, the actual steel ratio would have been much lower than 0.04. In other words, the practical requirement to use whole even numbers for column diameter, together with the need to select bar areas corresponding to actual rebar sizes, often makes it difficult to precisely define the reinforcement ratio in advance. This method does, however, lead to a reasonable size for the column in cases where a range of reasonable sizes is not initially known.

BEAMS AND SLABS

Concrete beams are reinforced with steel rods (reinforcing bars) in order to resist internal tension forces within the cross section. Unlike wood and steel, which can withstand substantial tension stress, concrete may be safely stressed only in compression. The pattern of steel reinforcement thus corresponds to the pattern of positive and negative bending moments within the beam: in regions of positive bending, steel is placed at the bottom of the cross section; in regions of negative bending, steel is placed at the top (Figure 5.21). Like concrete columns, 2½ in. to 3 in. of cover, measured from the outside face of the beam to the centerline of the reinforcing steel, is used to protect the steel from corrosion, provide fire resistance, and insure adequate bond

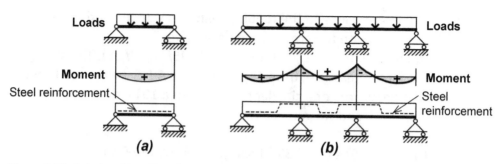

Figure 5.21: Relationship of bending moment and position of tension steel reinforcement with (*a*) simply-supported single-span beam and (*b*) multi-span beam

between the steel and concrete (see Figure 5.17).

The strength, or capacity, of a reinforced concrete beam can be determined by considering the equilibrium of tensile and compressive forces at any cross section. Failure of the beam occurs either with crushing of the concrete within the compression region; or yielding of the tension steel, followed by compressive crushing of the concrete. Since tension yielding is the preferred mode of failure — compressive crushing of the concrete would be sudden and catastrophic, whereas yielding of the steel provides warning signs of collapse — concrete beams are often deliberately *under-reinforced* to guarantee that, in the case of failure, the steel reinforcing bars begin to yield before the concrete in the compressive zone crushes.

At the point of failure, the stresses in a reinforced concrete cross section are as shown in Figure 5.22. The curved distribution of stresses within the compressive zone (above the neutral axis for "positive" bending) corresponds to the nonlinear stress-strain curves characteristic of plain concrete, with a value of $0.85f_c'$ taken for the strength of concrete corresponding to its behavior in an actual structure (Figure 5.19, curve *b*). Testing of many reinforced concrete beams has shown that the average stress within the compressive

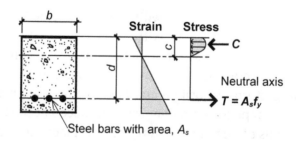

Figure 5.22: Strain and stress diagrams for tension-reinforced concrete beam at point of failure

zone is $0.85\beta_1 f_c'$, and the resultant location is $\beta_1 c/2$ from the face of the concrete beam, as shown in Figure 5.23a. The coefficient β_1 ranges from 0.85 for $f_c' \leq 4000$ psi, to 0.65 for $f_c' \geq 8000$ psi (Figure 5.24). Thus, for a cross section of width, b, the total compressive force, C, is

$$C = 0.85\beta_1 f_c' bc \qquad (5.4)$$

Since the steel yields before the concrete crushes (assuming that the beam has been designed to be under-reinforced), the steel stress is f_y and the total tensile force, T, is:

$$T = A_s f_y \qquad (5.5)$$

where A_s is the steel area. (As the steel is now used in the context of concrete design, the designation for its yield stress changes from F_y to f_y.)

Alternatively, a different, but equivalent, rectangular stress distribution can be used in place of the actual nonlinear distribution, as shown in Figure 5.23b. In this version, first formulated by C. S. Whitney and known as the

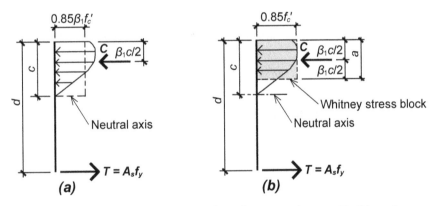

Figure 5.23: Comparison of (a) actual stresses in reinforced concrete beam with (b) equivalent rectangular ("Whitney") stress block

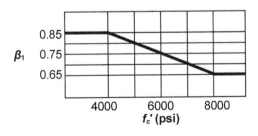

Figure 5.24: Relationship of coefficient β_1 to concrete cylinder strength, f_c'

"Whitney stress block," the dimensions of the rectangle are adjusted so as to be consistent with the empirically-determined resultant location. The definition of β_1 remains the same, as does the total compressive force, C.

Referring to the Whitney stress block diagram in Figure 5.23b, we can write equations of horizontal and moment equilibrium to determine the section's capacity. From horizontal equilibrium, the resultants of the compressive and tensile stresses must be equal in magnitude; that is: $T = C$, or:

$$A_s f_y = 0.85 f_c' \, ab \tag{5.6}$$

Solving for the stress block depth, a, we get:

$$a = \frac{A_s f_y}{0.85 f_c' b} \tag{5.7}$$

From moment equilibrium, the resisting moment within the cross section must equal the force T (or C) times the moment arm between T and C. This moment arm equals $d - a/2$, so we can write the moment at failure, $M_n = T(moment\ arm)$; or:

$$M_n = A_s f_y (d - a/2) \tag{5.8}$$

Substituting the expression for a from Equation 5.7, we get:

$$M_n = A_s f_y \left[d - \frac{A_s f_y}{(2)(0.85) f_c' b} \right] \tag{5.9}$$

We define a steel ratio, $\rho = A_s /(bd)$, so that

$$A_s = \rho bd \tag{5.10}$$

Then, substituting this expression for A_s into Equation (5.9), we get:

$$M_n = \rho f_y bd^2 [1 - 0.59 \rho f_y / f_c'] \tag{5.11}$$

This moment represents the nominal strength of the cross section when it fails. In the *strength design* method used for the design of reinforced concrete elements, we reduce this moment by a strength reduction factor, ϕ, so that the useful capacity of the section becomes:

$$\phi M_n = \phi bd^2 R \text{ or } M_u \leq \phi bd^2 R \tag{5.12}$$

where

   ϕ = capacity reduction factor, 0.9 for bending

M_n = the nominal strength of the cross section (in-kips)

M_u = the "design moment" based on factored loads (in-kips)

b = the width of the cross section (in.)

d = the effective depth of the cross section measured to the centerline of the steel reinforcement (in.)

R is "assembled" from terms in Equation 5.11 and defined in Equation 5.13, as follows:

$$R = \rho f_y (1 - 0.59 \rho f_y / f_c')$$ (5.13)

where

f_y = the yield stress of the steel reinforcement (we will use 60 ksi in all examples)

f_c' = the compressive cylinder strength of the concrete (ksi)

ρ = the steel ratio, $A_s /(bd)$

For given values of f_y and f_c', the relationship between R and ρ can be computed from Equation 5.13. Appendix Table A-5.9 gives typical values of R and ρ for f_y = 60 ksi, and f_c' ranging from 3000 psi to 5000 psi. Requirements for reinforcing bar cover and typical overall dimensions are the same as for reinforced concrete columns (see Table A-5.1).

Example 5.4 Analyze reinforced concrete beam

Problem definition. Check the capacity of the reinforced concrete cross section shown in Figure 5.25. Can it be safely used for the "service" (that is, unfactored) live load shown in Figure 5.25? Assume that the dead load, D, equals only the weight of the beam (assume 150 pcf for reinforced concrete, neglecting any other dead load); f_y = 60 ksi; and f_c' = 3000 psi. Reinforcing steel areas are listed in Appendix Table A-5.2; for minimum beam widths consistent with the number of bars selected, see Appendix Table A-5.3.

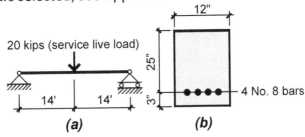

(a)   *(b)*

Figure 5.25: Reinforced concrete beam showing (*a*) loading diagram; and (*b*) cross section through beam for Example 5.4

Solution overview. Find factored loads and maximum moment; compute bending capacity.

Problem solution

1. From Appendix Table 5.4, the typical factored load combination for a floor beam is $1.2D + 1.6L$. The factored dead load consists of 1.2 times the beam weight, and is expressed in weight per linear foot of beam: $D = 1.2(150)(^{12}\!/_{12})(^{28}\!/_{12}) = 420$ lb/ft $= 0.42$ kips/ft. The factored live load, $L = 1.6(20) = 32$ kips.

2. Create load and moment diagrams as shown in Figure 5.26 to determine critical (i.e., maximum) bending moment. One can find the maximum moment for the concentrated and distributed loads separately, and then add them together (since they both occur at the beam's midpoint); or, as is shown in Figure 5.26b, the maximum moment may be computed directly by applying the equation of moment equilibrium to a free-body diagram cut at midspan.

3. Compute (bending) capacity of beam:

    From Appendix Table A-5.5, $\phi = 0.9$ for bending.

    From Appendix Table A-5.2, the area of four No. 8 bars is $A_s = 3.16$ in². The steel ratio, $\rho = A_s /(bd) = 3.16/(12 \times 25) = 0.0105$.

    From Appendix Table A-5.9 or from Equation 5.13, $R = 0.552$ ksi (this is obtained directly from Equation 5.13; when using Appendix Table A-5.9, interpolate between values for ρ, or, conservatively, use the closest but smaller value of ρ to find R).

    From Equation 5.12, $\phi M_n = \phi bd^2R = 0.9(12)(25^2)(0.552) = 3726$ in-kips

4. Check actual design moment: since the actual design moment = 3098 in-kips $\leq \phi M_n = 3726$ in-kips (the available moment capacity of the beam), the section is OK for bending.

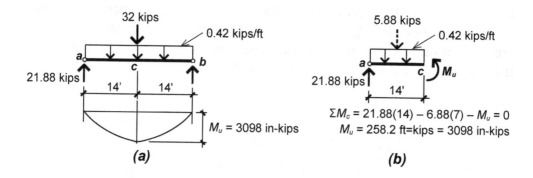

$$\Sigma M_c = 21.88(14) - 6.88(7) - M_u = 0$$
$$M_u = 258.2 \text{ ft=kips} = 3098 \text{ in-kips}$$

(a) **(b)**

Figure 5.26: To find maximum moment for Example 5.4, draw (*a*) loading and moment diagram; or (*b*) free-body diagram cut at midpoint with equation of moment equilibrium

Continuous beams and T-beams

For simply supported, determinate beams, no special guidelines are required for the calculation of shear and moment. In reality, though, reinforced concrete beams are rarely simply supported. Instead, concrete floor and roof structures are most often cast monolithically, and designed as indeterminate, continuous structures. As an aid in computing the maximum negative and positive bending moments characteristic of such structures (e.g., see Figure 1.61), approximate "moment values" have been tabulated for various support conditions. These can be used for uniformly-loaded floor structures with at least two more-or-less equal spans (differing in length by no more than 20%), as long as the dead load is greater or equal to one third of the live load (Appendix Table A-5.7).

Where slabs are cast monolithically with beams, as is most often the case (the use of precast elements being the most common exception), the beam thickness is measured to the top of the slab, as shown in Figure 5.27a. Where negative moments are being computed, corresponding to tension at the top, the beam width is not influenced by the presence of the slab (which is entirely in tension) and the capacity of the cross section is equivalent to that of a "pure" rectangular shape, as shown in Figure 5.27b. With positive bending, however, the compression zone is not limited by the web or stem of the beam, but extends out into the slab, as shown in Figure 5.27c. The effective width, b, of such a T-beam is considered to be the smaller of the following:

b = web width + ¼ beam span; or
b = centerline distance between beams; or   (5.14)
b = web width + 16 times slab thickness.

Positive moments can thus be resisted with a much greater effective cross-sectional width than can negative moments, by taking advantage of the concrete already present within the slab. As long as the entire compression zone

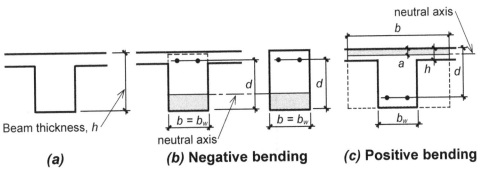

(a)   *(b)* **Negative bending**   *(c)* **Positive bending**

Figure 5.27: The total thickness of a T-beam (*a*) extends into the slab; such beams subjected to negative bending (*b*) can be designed as ordinary rectangular beams, while positive-moment T-beams (*c*) have a greater compressive "flange" width

(or the equivalent stress block depth, a) is within the slab, the design of such a "T-beam" is quite similar to the design of a rectangular beam of width, b. Whether the compressive stress block is, in fact, within the slab can be checked by computing the stress block depth, a (from Equation 5.7), substituting $\rho = A_s/(bd)$, and comparing a to the slab thickness, as follows:

$$a = \frac{A_s f_y}{0.85 f_c' b} = \frac{\rho f_y d}{0.85 f_c'} \qquad (5.15)$$

For $a \leq$ slab thickness, the effective beam width, b, can be used. Otherwise, the design of T-beams is somewhat more complex, since the compression zone extends into the web (Figure 5.28). The design of such beams is not considered in this text.

Where both positive and negative moments occur over the span of a beam, it is most common to first design the beam for negative moment (where only the beam web width is available to resist compression stresses), thereby establishing the cross-sectional dimensions for the entire span. The beam is then designed for positive moment as a T-beam with all cross-sectional dimensions given. Proceeding from the opposite direction, that is, positive moment first, would lead to a much smaller effective depth (since the T-beam is designed with a much larger effective width, b), which in turn could result in an inordinately high steel ratio within the regions of negative moment.

The question of whether a T-beam can be designed as a simple rectangular beam with effective width, b, is influenced to a considerable extent by the reinforcement ratio, ρ. Equation 5.15 for stress block depth shows that, for given values of f_y and f_c', the ratio of effective beam depth to stress block depth is inversely proportional to the steel ratio, ρ. That is, dividing both sides of Equation 5.15 by d, we get:

$$\frac{a}{d} = \frac{\rho f_y}{0.85 f_c'}; \text{ or } \frac{d}{a} = \frac{0.85 f_c'}{\rho f_y} \qquad (5.16)$$

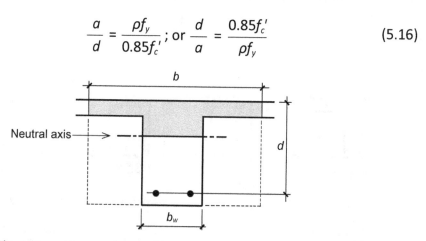

Figure 5.28: The compressive zone in a positive-moment T-beam rarely extends into the "web" of the beam

As an extreme example, for ρ taken as ρ_{max} (assume f_y = 60 ksi, f_c' = 4000 psi, and ρ_{max} taken with steel strain at 0.005), d/a = 3.13. This means that only beams and slabs proportioned so that the effective depth is no more than 3.13 times the slab thickness would be able to be designed as simple rectangular beams with effective width, b. For ρ taken as $0.5\rho_{max}$, d/a is 6.26; and the range of beam-slab proportions for which the compressive stress block remains within the slab thickness would be somewhat greater. For the very low steel ratios characteristic of real-world positive moment T-beam design, the stress block remains within the slab thickness for all but the most extreme proportions.

Design for bending (flexure)

To create under-reinforced beams, where yielding of the tension steel precedes crushing of the concrete in the event of failure, we first determine the amount of steel corresponding to the so-called "balanced" failure condition (where yielding and crushing occur simultaneously) and then provide an added margin of safety against brittle (concrete crushing) failure. Current code guidelines stipulate that the strain in the reinforcing steel be no less than 0.005 for so-called *tension-controlled members*, allowing a simple and uniform strength reduction factor, ϕ = 0.9 (design of non-tension-controlled beams requires a smaller strength reduction factor, and is beyond the scope of this book). As shown below, the tension-controlled strain of 0.005 is greater than the yield strain of steel, guaranteeing that the steel has already yielded when the concrete begins to crush. To determine the balanced steel area, or balanced steel ratio, $\rho_b = A_s/(bd)$, we assume that the concrete strain at failure is 0.003 as shown in Figure 5.19; and that the yield strain in the steel equals

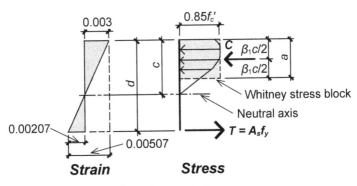

Figure 5.29: Balanced failure in a reinforced concrete beam

$f_y/E = 60/29,000 = 0.00207$ for 60-ksi reinforcing steel (Figure 5.29). From the linear strain diagram, we can express the ratio of c to d as $c/d = 0.003/0.00507$; from which we get $c = 0.5917d$. Since $a = \beta_1 c$ and $c = a/\beta_1$, we get:

$$\frac{a}{\beta_1} = 0.5917d; \text{ or } a = 0.5917\,\beta_1 d \qquad (5.17)$$

From horizontal equilibrium, $T = C$; or $A_s f_y = 0.85f_c' ab$. Substituting $A_s = \rho_b bd$; $a = 0.5917\beta_1 d$; and solving for ρ_b, we get:

$$\rho_b = 0.503\beta_1(f_c'/f_y) \qquad (5.18)$$

where ρ_b = the balanced steel ratio, $A_s/(bd)$; and $\beta_1 = 0.85$ for $f_c' \leq 4000$ psi (see Figure 5.24).

The maximum steel ratio (ρ_{max}), whether derived from the lowest permissible steel strain of 0.004 or the simpler value of 0.005, sets an upper limit to the amount of steel in a reinforced concrete beam where failure, should it occur, is initiated by yielding of the tensile reinforcement. By comparing the stress and strain diagrams of the balanced condition (Figure 5.29) with the condition where the steel strain at failure is 0.005, it can be shown that the steel ratio corresponding to a steel strain of 0.005 is $\rho_{max} = 0.63375\rho_b$. For beams, a lower limit for the steel ratio (ρ_{min}) is also prudent, and is set at $200/f_y$ for concrete strengths in the 3000- to 4000-psi range and $3\sqrt{f_c'}/f_y$ for 5000 psi or higher concrete (where f_c' and f_y are in psi units). A minimum slab steel ratio is set at $0.0018(h/d)$, consistent with slab requirements for minimum temperature and shrinkage reinforcement perpendicular to the direction of span, where h is the slab thickness and d is the effective depth. These lower bounds protect against a type of sudden failure that might otherwise occur in very lightly reinforced beams if the redistribution of stresses brought about by the initial cracking of concrete in the tension zone exceeds the capacity of the "cracked" cross section assumed in the calculation of steel area. Typical minimum and maximum values for the steel ratio, ρ, are shown in Appendix Table A-5.8.

There is a subtle, but important, difference between positive-moment T-beam design (with effective "flange" width, b, and web or stem width, b_w) and rectangular beam design (with constant width, b): the minimum steel ratio, ρ_{min}, is much lower for the T-beam when expressed in terms of width, b. This is because ρ_{min}, derived from a consideration of the beam's moment capacity before tensile cracking of the concrete, is defined in terms of the beam "web" width in the tension zone, b_w, and not the effective "flange" width, b. When using steel ratios expressed in terms of the effective width, b, the minimum steel ratio values computed with b_w must be divided by the ratio

b/b_w. To account for these lower minimum steel ratios in T-beam design, the R-ρ table provided (Appendix Table A-5.9) includes additional steel ratio values below those that would ordinarily be listed for rectangular beam design. Depending on the ratio of the effective width, b, to the web width, b_w, the minimum steel ratio, written in terms of b, can easily be determined; and the design can proceed as it would for a rectangular cross section.

It is permissible to design minimum steel areas for T-beams subjected to negative bending as if they were rectangular beams with $b = b_w$ in spite of the large area of concrete in the tension flange that could, in fact, sustain a much larger "uncracked" moment. The reason for this appears to have something to do with the redundancy of continuous (indeterminate) T-beam floor systems: redistribution of moments from supports to midspan is possible if failure at the negative-moment supports renders them incapable of sustaining bending stress, essentially turning the system into a series of simply-supported spans with positive moment only. This logic does not apply in the following two situations. First, for statically *determinate* T-beams (such as precast cantilevered tees) where redistribution of moments is not possible, the minimum negative steel is calculated based on the flange width or twice the web (stem) width, whichever is smaller (see keyed note c in Appendix Table A-5.9). Second, for any other negative moment where a T-beam cantilever occurs (i.e., where moment redistribution cannot occur), the minimum steel should be increased as it is for determinate T-beams.

Reinforced concrete beams can be safely designed within a range of sizes bracketed by these minimum and maximum steel ratios. Using ρ_{max} results in the smallest under-reinforced cross section; while ρ_{min} corresponds to the largest. Unlike wood and steel design, where the smallest, or lightest, cross section can usually be taken as the most economical, the best choice for a reinforced concrete beam is not necessarily the smallest cross section: the higher cost of steel relative to concrete, the potential difficulty of placing many steel reinforcing bars within a small cross-sectional area, and the reduced stiffness of a smaller cross section often suggest some intermediate steel ratio as the best choice. For example, steel ratios in the range of $0.5\rho_{max}$ seem to produce reasonably proportioned beams.

Steel ratio given

If the design of a reinforced concrete beam starts with the selection of a steel ratio, such as $0.5\rho_{max}$, we can solve for bd^2 in Equation 5.12 to get:

$$bd^2 \geq \frac{M_u}{\phi R} \qquad (5.19)$$

where

b = the width (in.) of the cross section

d = the effective depth (in.) of the cross section

M_u = the design moment found using factored loads (in-kips)

ϕ = 0.9 for bending

R = $\rho f_y(1 - 0.59\rho f_y /f_c')$, as defined in Equation 5.13 (ksi units; values can also be found in Appendix Table A-5.9)

While any values of width, b, and effective depth, d, consistent with the above equation are acceptable in principle, these cross-sectional dimensions are often constrained by three practical considerations. First, beam widths must be consistent with requirements for clear space between reinforcing bars and for concrete cover, as shown in Appendix Table A-5.3. Second, beam widths and depths are often made to align with other structural elements, such as column cross sections, other beams, or different sections of the same beam. Third, the actual depth of the cross section may be chosen to prevent excessive deflection, as indicated in Appendix Table A-5.13. It can be seen that one, but not both, of the cross-sectional dimensions must be assumed before the other dimension can be found. If the effective depth, d, is assumed as given, then:

$$b \geq \frac{M_u}{\phi R d^2} \tag{5.20}$$

If the width, b, is assumed as given, then:

$$d \geq \sqrt{\frac{M_u}{\phi R b}} \tag{5.21}$$

Given a steel ratio, and knowing both cross-sectional beam dimensions, the required steel area can then be found from Equation 5.10 — that is, $A_s = \rho bd$.

Cross-sectional dimensions given

Where both cross-sectional dimensions b and d are assumed as given, the steel ratio cannot also be selected, but must be calculated. From Equation 5.19, we found that: $bd^2 \geq M_u/(\phi R)$. We can find the steel ratio, ρ, by first solving for R as follows:

$$R \geq \frac{M_u}{\phi bd^2} \tag{5.22}$$

Then, the corresponding steel ratio can be determined from Appendix Table A-5.9. If the value of R does not appear in the table, two things are possible. Either the value is too low, corresponding to a required steel ratio, $\rho < \rho_{min}$; or the value is too high, corresponding to a required steel ratio, $\rho > \rho_{max}$. In the latter case, the cross-sectional dimensions must be changed and R recomputed. Where $\rho < \rho_{min}$, one can either adjust the cross-sectional dimensions, or simply use the larger quantity of steel corresponding to ρ_{min}. Alternatively, an acceptable steel ratio can be assumed, along with one cross-sectional dimension, and the procedures outlined earlier for "steel ratio given" can be followed.

Slabs

Reinforced concrete slabs, at least those designed to span in one direction, are no different conceptually from any other beams, with the following four caveats. First, only ¾ in. concrete cover is required (see Appendix Table A-5.1), so that the effective depth, d, measured to the centerline of the reinforcing steel, can generally be taken as the slab thickness minus one inch. Second, special shear reinforcement is rarely needed. Third, rather than computing the steel area for a slab, the required *spacing* of reinforcing bars is computed based on an assumed steel bar area. Finally, the minimum steel area is based on the gross slab dimensions (using the thickness, h, instead of the effective depth, d), so the minimum steel area, $A_{s,min} = 0.0018(h \times s)$, where s is the slab rebar spacing, and the minimum steel ratio, $\rho_{min} = 0.00180(h/d)$.

The calculation of rebar spacing for a one-way slab is facilitated by considering a typical 12-in.-wide strip of slab. Just as for a beam, the design moment, M_u, is found (or moment values are used), and R is computed based on Equation 5.22, with b set equal to 12 in. From Appendix Table A-5.9, ρ is found, and the required steel area for this 12-in. strip is computed just as for a beam: $A_s = \rho bd$ (where b = 12 in.). At this point, the design method for slabs diverges from that for beams, since the required steel area for a 12-in. wide strip is not, in itself, a useful piece of information. Instead, we prefer to find the required spacing for a selected rebar size, often choosing a No. 3, No. 4, or No. 5 bar size with a cross-sectional area of 0.11 in², 0.20 in², or 0.31 in² respectively (see Appendix Table A-5.2). Since the ratio of steel area per width of slab is now known ($A_s/12$ in.), we can establish the required width of slab — i.e., the required bar spacing — for any steel area. For example, choosing a No. 3 bar, we can equate the ratio of $A_s/12$ in. to the ratio of the No. 3 bar area to its required spacing, s: $A_s/12$ in. $= 0.11/s$, as shown in Figure 5.30. If a No. 4 bar were selected, the equation would be: $A_s/12$ in. $= 0.20/s$; for a No. 5 bar size, the equation would be $A_s/12$ in. $= 0.31/s$. For any of these cases, we solve for the spacing, $s = 12 \times$ (selected bar area)$/A_s$.

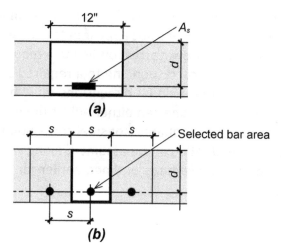

Figure 5.30: Steel in one-way slabs showing (*a*) equivalent steel area, A_s, for a given width, *b* = 12 in.; and (*b*) spacing, *s*, for a slab with a selected bar area (corresponding, typically, to a No. 3, No.4, or No. 5 rebar)

This reinforcement spacing can alternatively be determined more directly by substituting ρbd for A_s (where *b* = 12 in.) in this last equation. Doing so, we get: $s = 12 \times$ (selected bar area)/($12\rho d$), or:

$$s = \frac{\text{selected bar area}}{\rho d} \qquad (5.23)$$

where the "selected bar area" is typically that of a No. 3, No. 4, or No. 5 bar, and

   s = the centerline spacing between bars
   ρ = the computed steel reinforcing ratio
   d = the effective slab depth

The spacing, s, must not exceed 18 in. nor 3 times the slab thickness, in any case. It is also common practice to choose a bar size so that the bar spacing ends up being at least 1½ times greater than the slab thickness; bars that are more closely spaced may satisfy "code" requirements, but end up being more costly to put in place.

   Reinforcement may be required *perpendicular* to the main longitudinal slab reinforcement (i.e., perpendicular to the reinforcement placed parallel to the span) for two reasons. First, a minimum amount of perpendicular steel — with minimum steel area, $A_{s,min}$ = 0.0018($h \times s$) — is required to protect against cracking due to shrinkage of the concrete or thermal (temperature)

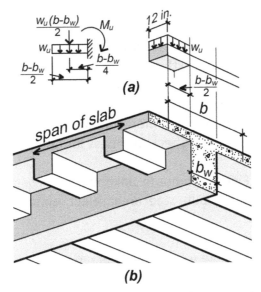

Figure 5.31: Slab steel for T-beams parallel to main slab reinforcement: (*a*) calculation of design moment, M_u = resultant force × distance = $[w_u(b - b_w)/2] \times [(b - b_w)/4] = w_u(b - b_w)^2/8$; and (*b*) view of T-beam with effective width, *b*, and web width, b_w

expansion. The spacing of such shrinkage-temperature steel cannot exceed 18 in. or 5*h*, where *h* is the slab thickness. Second, in cases where a T-beam is oriented so that it is parallel to the main slab reinforcement (for example, where a T-beam girder is supporting T-beams that in turn are supporting slabs, as shown in Figure 5.31), the overhanging flanges of the T-beam girder must be reinforced as if they were negative-moment cantilevers, with a design moment, $M_u = w_u(b - b_w)^2/8$. This reinforcement is not designed to improve the spanning capability of the slab itself, but rather to ensure that the effective width of the T-beam can function as assumed.

Deflection

The rigorous calculation of reinforced concrete beam or slab deflection is complicated by the difficulty of determining the stiffness, *EI*, of such bending elements that would be required in any deflection equation: in particular, the moment of inertia of a cracked section (cracked in the tension zone) containing two very different types of materials (steel and concrete) is complex and uncertain. While such procedures exist, we can control deflection — for preliminary design — by establishing minimum thicknesses for beam and slab elements based on their clear span, as shown in Appendix Table A-5.13. For example, the minimum thickness for a continuous reinforced concrete beam is set equal to its clear span divided by 21; while the minimum thickness for a continuous slab is set equal to its clear span divided by 28.

Example 5.5 Design reinforced concrete beam, with steel ratio assumed

Problem definition. Assuming a steel ratio, $\rho = 0.5\rho_{max}$, design a continuous rectangular concrete beam with a clear span of 36 ft to resist a positive design moment, M_u = 350 ft-kips. Assume f_y = 60 ksi; and f_c' = 3000 psi. The beam width is set at 16 in. to align with rectangular columns. Assume 3 in. cover, measured to the centerline of reinforcement, and use even numbers for both cross-sectional dimensions. Check thickness for deflection control.

Solution overview. Find R; compute unknown cross-sectional dimension; re-compute steel ratio; compute steel area; select reinforcement.

Problem solution

1. From Appendix Table A-5.8, find steel ratio:
   ρ_{max} = 0.0135.
   $\rho = 0.5\rho_{max}$ = 0.00675.

2. From Appendix Table A-5.9, find R based on ρ = 0.00675. Since this value of ρ falls between the tabular values of 0.00667 and 0.00700, we can interpolate by comparing ratios of the differences between ρ and R values as follows:

$$\frac{R - 0.369}{0.385 - 0.369} = \frac{0.00675 - 0.00667}{0.00700 - 0.00667}$$

from which R = 0.373. Alternatively, we can use Equation 5.13 directly to obtain $R = \rho f_y(1 - 0.59\rho f_y/f_c') = 0.00675(60)[1 - 0.59(0.00675)(60)/3)] = 0.373$.

3. From Equation 5.21, compute cross-sectional dimensions: since b = 16 in., we get:

$$d \geq \sqrt{\frac{M_u}{\phi R b}} = \sqrt{\frac{350 \times 12}{0.9(0.373)(16)}} = 28 \text{ in.}$$

4. Adjust the effective depth, d, so that the total thickness of the cross section is an even number. Since the assumed cover is 3 in., we can select an effective depth of either 27 in. (for a total thickness of 30 in.), or an effective depth of 29 in. (for a total thickness of 32 in.). Either choice is potentially correct, since even if the depth is less than what is required based on Equation 5.21, a revised steel ratio will be computed in the next step: a smaller depth will result in a larger steel ratio (more steel and less concrete), while a larger depth will result in a smaller steel ratio (less steel and more concrete). We will choose an effective depth, d = 29 in.

5. Find R using the actual cross-sectional dimensions, b = 16 in. and d = 29 in. From Equation 5.22, we get:

$$R \geq \frac{M_u}{\phi bd^2} = \frac{350 \times 12}{0.9(16)(29^2)} = 0.347$$

6. From Appendix Table A-5.9, we can either use R = 0.369 and a corresponding value of ρ = 0.00667; or we can interpolate between R = 0.335 and R = 0.369 to get:

$$\frac{0.347 - 0.335}{0.369 - 0.335} = \frac{\rho - 0.00600}{0.00667 - 0.00600}$$

from which ρ = 0.00624. We will use the more accurate value of ρ = 0.00624. Using the value of 0.00667 would work (and for preliminary design might save a few minutes of calculation time), but is needlessly conservative.

7. From Equation 5.10, compute steel area: $A_s = \rho bd = 0.00624(16)(29) = 2.90$ in^2.

8. From Appendix Table A-5.2, select reinforcement that will fit in the beam, as shown in Figure 5.32: two No. 11 bars (with actual A_s = 3.12 in^2) or three No. 9 bars (with actual A_s = 3.00 in^2).

9. From Appendix Table A-5.3, check whether either choice fits within the beam width of 16 in. Two No. 11 bars require 8.13 in. and three No. 9 bars require 10.04 in., so either choice works in a 16 in.-wide beam.

10. It is unlikely that our steel ratio will fall outside the limits for ρ_{min} and ρ_{max}, since our starting point was the selection of a steel ratio positioned between these two extremes. However, since the actual steel ratio being used is somewhat different from what we started with, a quick check is prudent. From Appendix Table A-5.8 (or A-5.9), the range of acceptable steel ratios is 0.0033 − 0.0135. For two No. 11 bars, the steel ratio, ρ = A_s/bd = 3.12/(16 × 29) = 0.0067, which falls between the two limiting values (the steel ratio for three No. 9 bars, ρ = 3.00/(16 × 29) = 0.0065, is also acceptable).

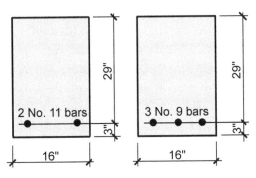

Figure 5.32: Alternate bar selection for Example 5.5

11. Check beam thickness for deflection control: from Appendix Table A-5.13, the minimum thickness for a continuous beam with clear span, L (in.), is $L/21 = (36 \times 12)/21 = 20.6$ in. This is no greater than the actual thickness of the beam, $h = d + 3 = 29 + 3 = 32$ in., so the beam is acceptable for deflection control.

Example 5.6 Design reinforced concrete slab with slab thickness assumed

Problem definition. Design a continuous 6 in.-thick reinforced concrete slab supporting a live load of 100 psf (and no live load reduction) with a clear span between supports of 14 ft. Assume $f_y = 60$ ksi; and $f_c' = 4000$ psi. Consider both negative and positive moment values on typical interior spans (Appendix Table A-5.7). Assume that the dead load consists of the reinforced concrete weight (150 pcf). Span dimensions are measured from the inside face of supporting elements, rather than from their centerlines, when computing shear and moment. Assume a 1 in. cover for slabs (measured to centerline of reinforcement).

Solution overview. Find factored loads; compute design moment; compute R; find ρ; compute rebar spacing. Check rebar spacing and deflection control.

Problem solution
Find loads:

> From Appendix Table A-2.1 (and as given in problem definition), the dead load, $D = 150$ pcf.
> The live load is given as $L = 100$ psf.

Slab design, negative moment

1. Find loads on 12-in-wide strip of slab:
   The live load, $L = 100$ psf = 100 lb/ft (for 1 linear foot of a 12-in.-wide strip of slab). Live load reduction is not being considered.
   The dead load, D (for 1 linear foot of a 12-in.-wide strip of slab) = $150(6/12) = 75.0$ lb/ft.
   From Appendix Table A-5.4, the factored (design) load, $w_u = 1.2 D + 1.6 L = 1.2(75) + 1.6(100) = 250$ lb/ft = 0.250 kips/ft.
2. Using moment values from Appendix Table A-5.7, compute the negative design moment for a typical interior span. Because the clear span of the slab is greater than 10 ft (see Note 2, Appendix Table A-5.7), the moment value is $M_u = w_u l_n^2 /11 = 0.250 \times 14^2/11 = 4.455$ ft-kips = 53.455 in-kips. The initial calculation used kips/ft units for w_u and foot units for l_n, with the resulting moment value in ft-kips units. This value was then multiplied by 12 to convert the moment value to in-kips units.

3. From Equation 5.22, $R \geq M_u/(\phi bd^2) = 53.455/(0.9 \times 12 \times 5^2) = 0.198$. In this equation, the effective slab depth, d, is taken as 1 in. less than the given slab thickness, $h = 6$ in., consistent with typical requirements for slab cover.

4. From Appendix Table A-5.9, we can either use $R = 0.232$ and a corresponding value of $\rho = 0.00400$, or we can interpolate between $R = 0.0194$ and $R = 0.232$. A value for ρ will be found by interpolation:

$$\frac{0.198 - 0.194}{0.232 - 0.194} = \frac{\rho - 0.00333}{0.00400 - 0.00333}$$

from which $\rho = 0.00340$.

5. From Appendix Table A-5.2, we select a value for A_s: assuming No. 4 reinforcing bars for the slab, $A_s = 0.20$ in^2.

6. From Equation 5.23, find rebar spacing: $s = A_s/(\rho d) = 0.20/(0.00340 \times 5) = 11.76$ in.

   The maximum permitted bar spacing for a slab is the smaller of 18 in. or three times the slab thickness, $3h = 18$ in. Rounding down, negative slab moments are resisted by No. 4 bars at 11 in. on center (a value that is also greater than the "practical" minimum of 1½ times the slab thickness).

7. Checking the steel ratio, we find the limits from Appendix Table A-5.9 to be $\rho_{min} = 0.00180(h/d) = 0.00180(6/5) = 0.00216$ (see keyed note d for slabs in Appendix Table A-5.9) and $\rho_{max} = 0.01810$. The actual steel ratio can be found by dividing a single bar area by the gross concrete area determined by its spacing, s, and effective depth, d:
   $\rho = 0.20/(11 \times 5) = 0.00364$, which falls between these limiting values.

8. Deflection control can be checked using Appendix Table A-5.13: for a continuous slab, the minimum thickness equals the clear span divided by 28, or $(14 \times 12)/28 = 6.00$ in. The actual slab thickness, $h = 6$ in., corresponds exactly to this minimum, so the slab is thick enough for deflection control.

Slab design, positive moment

1. Find loads: same as for negative moment: $w_u = 0.250$ kips/ft.

2. From Appendix Table A-5.7, compute the positive design moment value, $M_u = w_u l_n^2/16 = 0.250 \times 14^2/16 = 3.063$ ft-kips $= 36.75$ in-kips. The initial calculation used kips/ft units for w_u and foot units for l_n, with the resulting moment value in ft-kips units. This value was then multiplied by 12 to convert the moment value to in-kips units.

3. From Equation 5.22, $R \geq M_u/(\phi bd^2) = 36.75/(0.9 \times 12 \times 5^2) = 0.136$. In this equation, the effective slab depth, d, is taken as 1 in. less than the given

slab thickness, h = 6 in., consistent with typical requirements for slab cover.

4. From Appendix Table A-5.9, we see that the value for R = 0.136 actually appears in the table (we got lucky!), so we can use the corresponding value of ρ = 0.00231 without interpolating.

5. From Appendix Table A-5.2, we select a value for A_s: assuming No. 4 reinforcing bars for the slab, A_s = 0.20 in².

6. From Equation 5.23, find rebar spacing: $s = A_s /(\rho d) = 0.20/(0.00231 \times 5) =$ 17.3 in.

   The maximum permitted bar spacing for a slab is the smaller of 18 in. or three times the slab thickness, $3h$ = 18 in. Rounding down, negative slab moments are resisted by No. 4 bars at 17 in. on center (a value that is also greater than the "practical" minimum of 1½ times the slab thickness).

7. Checking the steel ratio, we find the limits from Appendix Table A-5.9 to be ρ_{min} = 0.00180(h/d) = 0.00180(6/5) = 0.00216; we can also find this value directly for a slab with h = 6 in. by examining the "ρ" column in the table (see keyed note d for slabs in Appendix Table A-5.9) and ρ_{max} = 0.01810. The actual steel ratio can be found by dividing a single bar area by the gross concrete area determined by its spacing, s, and effective depth, d:

   ρ = 0.20/(17 × 5) = 0.00235, which falls between these limiting values.

8. Deflection control need not be checked again, as it proved acceptable in the calculations for negative steel.

Example 5.7 Design reinforced concrete slab and T-beam, with cross-sectional dimensions assumed

Problem definition. Design a continuous reinforced concrete slab and typical beam to accommodate light manufacturing, as shown in Figure 5.33. Assume f_y = 60 ksi; and f_c' = 5000 psi. Consider both negative and positive moment values on typical interior spans (Appendix Table A-5.7). Assume a beam width

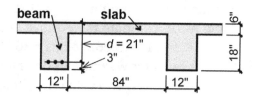

Figure 5.33: Cross section through slab and T-beam for Example 5.7

of 12 in., and a slab thickness of 6 in. as shown. The beams have a clear span of 30 ft. Assume that the dead load consists of the reinforced concrete weight (150 pcf). Span dimensions are measured from the inside face of supporting elements, rather than from their centerlines, when computing shear and moment. Design beam and slab for typical interior spans. Assume 3-in. cover for beams, and 1 in. for slabs (measured to centerline of reinforcement).

Solution overview. For slab: find factored loads; compute design moment; compute R; find ρ; compute rebar spacing. *For beam:* find factored loads; compute design moment; compute R; find ρ; compute steel area, A_s; select reinforcement. Check bar fit for beam and deflection control for both beam and slab.

Problem solution
Find loads:

    From Appendix Table A-2.1 (and as given in problem definition), the dead load, D = 150 pcf.

    From Appendix Table A-2.2, the live load, L = 125 psf (light manufacturing).

Slab design, negative moment

1. Find loads on 12-in-wide strip of slab:
   The live load, L = 125 psf = 125 lb/ft (for 12-in.-wide strip of slab). Live load reduction does not apply for live loads greater than 100 psf.
   The dead load, D (for 12-in.-wide strip of slab) = 150(⁶⁄₁₂) = 75.0 lb/ft (see Figure 5.34).
   From Appendix Table A-5.4, the factored (design) load, $w_u = 1.2\,D + 1.6\,L = 1.2(75) + 1.6(125) = 290$ lb/ft = 0.290 kips/ft.
2. Using moment values from Appendix Table A-5.7, compute the negative design moment for a typical interior span. Because the clear span of the slab is no greater than 10 ft (see Note 2, Appendix Table A-5.7), the moment value is $M_u = w_u\,l_n^2 / 12 = 0.290 \times 7^2/12 = 1.184$ ft-kips = 14.21 in-kips. The initial calculation used kips/ft units for w_u and foot units for l_n, with

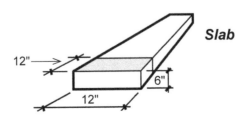

Figure 5.34: Tributary area for calculation of slab weight, Example 5.7

the resulting moment value in ft-kips units. This value was then multiplied by 12 to convert the moment value to in-kips units.

3. From Equation 5.22, $R \geq M_u/(\phi b d^2) = 14.21/(0.9 \times 12 \times 5^2) = 0.0526$. In this equation, the effective slab depth, d, is taken as 1 in. less than the given slab thickness, $h = 6$ in., consistent with typical requirements for slab cover.

4. From Appendix Table A-5.9, we can either use $R = 0.0661$ and a corresponding value of $\rho = 0.00111$, or we can interpolate between $R = 0.0495$ and $R = 0.0661$. In this case, the minimum steel ratio for a slab, $\rho_{min} = 0.00180(h/d) = 0.00180(6/5) = 0.00216$, so there is no point interpolating: the result — as can be seen by examining Appendix Table A-5.9 — will be less than ρ_{min}. Therefore, *we use the minimum value*, $\rho = 0.00216$.

5. From Appendix Table A-5.2, we select a value for A_s: assuming No. 3 reinforcing bars for the slab, $A_s = 0.11$ in^2.

6. From Equation 5.23, find rebar spacing: $s = A_s/(\rho d) = 0.11/(0.00216 \times 5) = 10.19$ in.

The maximum permitted bar spacing for a slab is the smaller of 18 in. or three times the slab thickness, $3h = 18$ in. Rounding down, negative slab moments are resisted by No. 3 bars at 10 in. on center (a value that is also greater than the "practical" minimum of 1½ times the slab thickness).

7. Checking the steel ratio, we find the limits from Appendix Table A-5.9 to be $\rho_{min} = 0.00216$ (see keyed note d for slabs in Appendix Table A-5.9) and $\rho_{max} = 0.02130$. The actual steel ratio can be found by dividing a single bar area by the gross concrete area determined by its spacing, s, and effective depth, d:

$\rho = 0.11/(10 \times 5) = 0.00220$, which falls between these limiting values.

8. Deflection control can be checked using Appendix Table A-5.13: for a continuous slab, the minimum thickness equals the clear span divided by 28, or $(7 \times 12)/28 = 3.00$ in. The actual slab thickness, $h = 6$ in., exceeds this minimum, so the slab is thick enough for deflection control.

Slab design, positive moment

1. Find loads: same as for negative moment: $w_u = 0.290$ kips/ft.

2. From Appendix Table A-5.7, compute the positive design moment value, $M_u = w_u l_n^2/16$. Rather than going through the computation process, notice that the positive moment is smaller than the negative moment already computed; since the negative moment in this case was governed by the minimum steel ratio, the positive moment (which is even smaller) will have the same result. Therefore, use the same bars and spacing computed for the negative moment: No. 3 bars at 10 in. on center.

Beam design, negative moment

1. Find distributed load on beam:
   We found that the live load, L = 125 psf, so the distributed load per foot of beam = 125 × tributary area = 125(8) = 1000 lb/ft. Live load reduction does not apply since the live load is greater than 100 psf.
   The dead load can be found by adding the slab and beam-stem weight as shown in Figure 5.35: D = slab weight + beam-stem weight = 150($\frac{6}{12}$)(8) + 150($\frac{18}{12}$)($\frac{12}{12}$) = 600 + 225 = 825 lb/ft.
   From Appendix Table A-5.4, the factored (design) load = 1.2 D + 1.6 L = 1.2(825) + 1.6(1000) = 2590 lb/ft = 2.59 kips/ft.

2. Using moment values from Appendix Table A-5.7, compute the negative design moment for a typical interior span: $M_u = w_u l_n^2 / 11 = 2.59 \times 30^2/11 = 211.9$ ft-kips = 2542.9 in-kips.

3. From Equation 5.22, $R \geq M_u /(\phi bd^2)$ = 2542.9/(0.9 × 12 × 21²) = 0.534. In this equation, the effective beam depth, d, is taken as 3 in. less than the total beam thickness, h = 24 in., measured from the bottom of the beam "web" or "stem" to the top of the slab.

4. From Appendix Table A-5.9, we can either use R = 0.558 and a corresponding value of ρ = 0.01000, or we can interpolate between R = 0.506 and R = 0.558 to get:

$$\frac{0.534-0.506}{0.558-0.506} = \frac{\rho - 0.00900}{0.01000 - 0.00900}$$

from which ρ = 0.00954. We will use the more accurate value of ρ = 0.00954.

5. From Equation 5.10, compute steel area: $A_s = \rho bd$ = 0.00954(12)(21) = 2.40 in².

6. From Appendix Table A-5.2, select reinforcement that will fit in the beam,

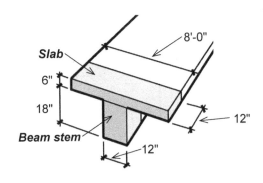

Figure 5.35: Tributary area for calculation of slab and beam stem weight, Example 5.7

as shown in Figure 5.36: two No. 10 bars (with actual A_s = 2.54 in²) *or* three No. 9 bars (with actual A_s = 3.00 in²).

7. From Appendix Table A-5.3, check whether either choice fits within the beam web (or stem) width of 12 in. Two No. 10 bars require 7.83 in. and three No. 9 bars require 10.04 in., so either choice works in a 12-in.-wide beam.

8. Checking the steel ratio, we find the limits from Appendix Table A-5.9 to be ρ_{min} = 0.00354 (see keyed note *a* in Appendix Table A-5.9 for negative-moment T-beams) and ρ_{max} = 0.02130. The actual steel ratio can be found by dividing the bar area by the gross concrete area determined by width and effective depth: for the two No. 10 bars, ρ = 2.54/(12 × 21) = 0.0101, which falls between these limiting values (the steel ratio for three No. 9 bars, ρ = 3.00/(12 × 21) = 0.0119, is also acceptable).

9. Deflection control can be checked using Appendix Table A-5.13: for a continuous beam, the minimum thickness equals the clear span divided by 21, or (30 × 12)/21 = 17.14 in. The actual beam thickness, h = 24 in., is greater than this minimum, so the beam is thick enough for deflection control.

Beam design, positive moment (T-beam design)

1. Find distributed load on beam: same as for negative-moment design.
2. Using moment values from Appendix Table A-5.7, compute positive de-sign moment for a typical interior span: $M_u = w_u \, l_n^2 \, /16 = 2.59(30^2)/16 =$ 145.69 ft-kips = 1748.3 in-kips.
3. From Equation 5.14, the effective width, b is the smaller of the following:
   b = web width + ¼ span = 12 + (30 × 12)/4 = 102 in.
   b = centerline distance between beams = 96 in.
   b = web width + 16 times slab thickness = 12 + (16 × 6) = 108 in.
   The effective width, b = 96 in.

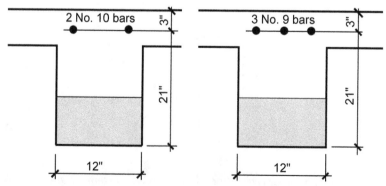

Figure 5.36: Bar selection options for negative moment in T-beam, Example 5.7

4. From Equation 5.22, $R \geq M_u / (\phi b d^2) = 1748.3/(0.9 \times 96 \times 21^2) = 0.0459$. In this equation, the effective beam depth, d, is taken as 3 in. less than the total beam thickness, $h = 24$ in., measured from the bottom of the beam web or stem to the top of the slab.

5. From Appendix Table A-5.9, we can either use $R = 0.0459$ and a corresponding value of $\rho = 0.00083$, or we can interpolate between $R = 0.0400$ and $R = 0.0495$ to get:

$$\frac{0.0459 - 0.0400}{0.0495 - 0.0400} = \frac{\rho - 0.00067}{0.00083 - 0.00067}$$

from which $\rho = 0.00077$. We will use the more accurate value of $\rho = 0.00077$.

For positive moment T-beams, the minimum steel ratio is determined by dividing 0.00354 by the ratio $b/b_w = 96/12 = 8$, from which $\rho_{min} = 0.00354/8 = 0.00044$ (see keyed note b in Appendix Table A-5-9). Our value of ρ is *not* smaller than ρ_{min}, so it is acceptable. Because a value for ρ was actually found in Appendix Table A-5.9 (no values greater than ρ_{max} are listed in that table) and because steel ratios for positive moment T-beams tend to be quite small, the maximum steel ratio need not be checked.

6. From Equation 5.15, check that the stress block depth, a, falls within slab thickness:
$a = \rho f_y d / (0.85 f_c') = 0.00077(60)(21)/(0.85 \times 5) = 0.23$ in. $\leq$ slab thickness = 6 in., so T-beam assumptions are valid.

7. From Equation 5.10, compute steel area: $A_s = \rho b d = 0.00077(96)(21) = 1.55$ in^2.

8. From Appendix Table A-5.2, steel reinforcement is selected, as shown in Figure 5.37: two No. 8 bars with $A_s = 1.58$ in^2.

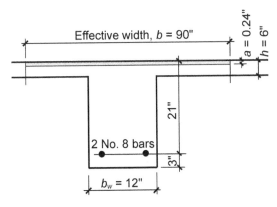

Figure 5.37: Bar selection for positive moment in T-beam, Example 5.7

9. From Table A-5.3, check whether this choice fits within the beam web (or stem) width of b_w = 12 in. Two No. 8 bars require 7.33 in., so the choice works in a 12-in.-wide beam.

10. The steel ratio has already been checked (step 5). The check for deflection control is the same as for negative moment and need not be repeated.

Shear

Wood and steel beams are generally designed for bending and checked for shear. If a beam selected for bending cannot safely resist the shear stresses, a larger section must be used. Reinforced concrete beams are almost never acceptable for shear after they are designed for bending, because shear stresses, combined with bending stresses, produce diagonal tension within the beam. Since concrete is so weak in tension, excessive shear (really diagonal tension) would cause the beam to fail catastrophically. Rather than increase the size of the cross section to the point where the concrete can safely resist all diagonal tension stresses, shear (web) reinforcement is used where the shear stress exceeds the capacity of the concrete.

Web reinforcement, consisting of U- or rectangular-shaped steel stirrups, is generally made from No. 3 or No. 4 bars, bent as shown in Figure 5.38. The force resisted by each stirrup is based on an area twice the size of the bent bar, or $2A_s$, since two prongs of each stirrup are present at any diagonal tension crack (Figure 5.39). Thus, assuming that diagonal tension cracks form at a 45° angle, the number of stirrups resisting tension within each crack is d/s, where d = the effective depth of the beam and s = the stirrup spacing.

At failure, corresponding to yielding of the stirrups, the total force resisted by the steel web reinforcement is therefore equal to the number of stirrups times the force resisted by each; that is: $V_s = (d/s)(2A_s f_y)$ or:

$$V_s = 2A_s f_y\, d/s \qquad\qquad\qquad (5.24)$$

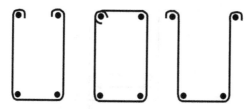

Figure 5.38: Typical web steel (stirrups) to resist diagonal tension associated with shear stress in beams

where

V_s = the total force resisted by web reinforcement, which can be no larger than $4 \times V_c$ (see Equation 5.26 for definition of V_c)

d = the effective depth of the beam

s = the stirrup spacing

A_s = the area of the reinforcing bar from which the stirrup is made

f_y = the yield stress of the reinforcing bar, 60 ksi in all text examples.

Solving for the stirrup spacing, we get:

$$s = 2A_s f_y d / V_s \qquad (5.25)$$

The concrete itself also inhibits the formation of diagonal tension cracks; its contribution can be taken as:

$$V_c = 2\sqrt{f_c'}\, bd \qquad (5.26)$$

where

V_c = the total force resisted by the concrete (lb)

f_c' = the cylinder strength of the concrete (psi)

b = the width of the beam, or "web" width for T-beams (in.)

d = the effective depth of the beam (in.)

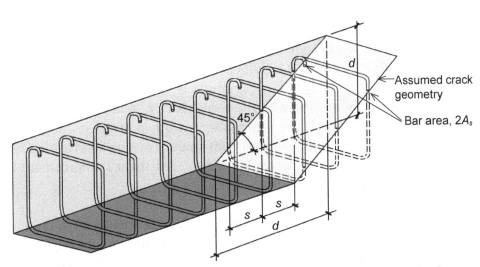

Figure 5.39: Assumed crack geometry for calculation of web steel capacity to resist shear forces (at diagonal tension cracks)

The value for concrete capacity shown in Equation 5.26 presumes concrete of normal weight ("normalweight" is one word in the ACI 318 reference). For lightweight concrete, this value is multiplied by 0.85 (sand-lightweight concrete) or 0.75 (all-lightweight concrete).

The strength design method for shear in concrete beams stipulates that the design shear force, V_u, at any section (produced by factored loads) not exceed the available capacity of the concrete and web steel combined. When the strength reduction factor for shear, ϕ, is included, we get:

$$V_u \le \phi(V_c + V_s) \tag{5.27}$$

where

$\quad V_u$ = the design shear force.

$\quad \phi$ = capacity reduction factor = 0.75 for shear (Appendix Table A-5.5)

V_s and V_c = the values defined in Equations 5.24 and 5.26

There are several limitations that affect the deployment of web steel, as follows:

The closest practical stirrup spacing is 3 to 4 in.

The first stirrup is generally placed at a distance $s/2$ from the face of the support.

A minimum amount of web steel is required when $V_u > 0.5\phi V_c$, even if the calculated shear force to be resisted by web steel is less than or equal to zero, i.e., for $V_u \le \phi V_c$. This required minimum web steel can be written in terms of a required maximum stirrup spacing: $s = 2A_s f_y /(0.75b \times \sqrt{f_c'}) \le 2A_s f_y /(50b)$. For certain beams with small total depth or thickness, this requirement is waived, in which case stirrups are only needed when $V_u > \phi V_c$. Both f_y and f_c' are expressed in psi units; b (in.) is the beam "stem" width in this case and d is the effective depth (in.). This minimum amount of web steel is required, even if $V_u < \phi V_c$; only when $V_u < 0.5\phi V_c$ can shear reinforcement be discontinued.

When $V_s \le 2V_c$, stirrup spacing cannot exceed the smaller of $d/2$, 24 in., or the maximum spacing governed by the requirement for minimum web steel. When $V_s > 2V_c$, the first two criteria are reduced by half (to the smaller of $d/4$ or 12 in.).

A single stirrup size is used throughout a given beam; the spacing of these stirrups varies to account for changing values of shear along the span of the beam. For uniformly loaded spans, except as noted below, the maximum shear force at the face of the support is:

$$V_u = w_u l_u / 2 \tag{5.28}$$

where w_u is the uniformly distributed factored, design load (lb/ft or kips/ft); and l_u is the clear span (ft). This applies to plan geometries with relatively equal spans and unfactored live loads that are no more than 3 times the unfactored

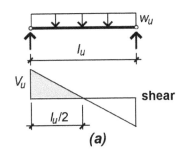

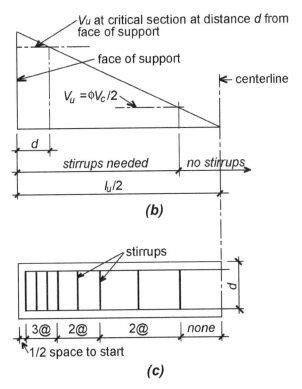

Figure 5.40: Shear diagram (*a*) for a uniformly loaded beam; with (*b*) half of the shear diagram enlarged; and (*c*) beam elevation showing typical stirrup spacing

dead loads, just as for the moment values listed in Appendix Table A-5.7. The one exception is at the "interior" support of end spans in continuous structures, for which the design shear should be taken as 1.15 times the value in Equation 5.28. Since the point of critical (maximum) shear is actually measured at a distance d from the face of the beam's support — whether that support consists of wall, column, or girder — it makes no difference if the span used in Equation 5.28 is measured from face of support or support centerline. In either case, the "theoretical" value shown in Equation 5.28 must be reduced to the value computed at the critical section. Figure 5.40b shows such a critical section measured from the face of support as well as a typical pattern of shear force and web reinforcement for a uniformly-loaded beam (Figure 5.40c). The stirrup spacing is symmetrical; only half is shown. Equations for web steel are reproduced in Appendix Table A-5.6.

Example 5.8 Design shear reinforcement (stirrups) for reinforced concrete beam

Problem definition. Design the distribution of web steel (use No. 3 bars) for the cross section shown in Figure 5.41, assuming a factored design load, $w_u = 6$ kips/ft on a clear interior span, $l_u = 30$ ft. Use $f_c' = 4000$ psi and $f_y = 60$ ksi.

Solution overview. Compute concrete capacity; find minimum, maximum and intermediate (optional) spacing for stirrups; sketch distribution of stirrups along length of beam.

Problem solution

All equations can be found in Appendix Table A-5.6 with lb or psi units; these have been converted to kips or ksi units in what follows, except where lb or psi units are specifically required (Appendix Table A-5.6 parts C and F).

   1. Compute concrete shear capacity (Appendix Table A-5.6 part C):

$$V_c = 2bd\sqrt{f_c'} = 2(12 \times 24)\sqrt{4000} = 36{,}429 \text{ lbs} = 36.43 \text{ kips}$$

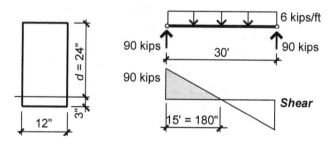

Figure 5.41: Cross section, load, and shear diagrams for Example 5.8

2. Find minimum spacing of No. 3 stirrups at critical V_u (at distance d from support), as shown in Figure 5.42:

   The maximum design shear at the face of support, V_u, can be taken as $w_u l_u/2 = 90$ kips for interior spans. The design shear at the critical distance, d, from the face of support can be found using similar triangles or, more directly, by reducing the maximum value of V_u by the ratio of the small to large triangle legs, as shown in Figure 5.42: V_u at distance, d, equals 90(156/180) = 78 kips.

   From Appendix Table 5.6 part E: the steel capacity, $V_s \geq V_u/\phi - Vc = 78/0.75 - 36.43 = 67.57$ kips.

   From Appendix Table A-5.2, the area of a No. 3 bar is $A_s = 0.11$ in^2. From Appendix Table 5.6 part B: the required spacing, $s \leq 2A_s f_y d/V_s = 2(0.11)(60)(24)/67.57 = 4.69$ in. Round down the required spacing to the first half-inch increment: $s = 4.5$ in.

3. Find maximum spacing of No. 3 stirrups:

   From Appendix Table A-5.6 part F, and since $V_s = 67.57$ kips $\leq 2V_c = 2(36.43) = 72.86$ kips, the maximum stirrup spacing is governed by the smaller of $d/2 = 12$ in., 24 in., or the spacing corresponding to the requirement for minimum web steel: $2A_s f_y/(0.75b \times \sqrt{f_c'}) \leq 2Asf_y/(50b)$ or 22 in. (f_y and f_c' must be in psi units in this equation!) The maximum spacing is therefore 12 in.

   The location along the beam elevation where this maximum stirrup spacing can begin is found as follows. First find the steel capacity corresponding to the maximum spacing from Appendix Table 5.6 part A: $V_s = 2A_s f_y d/s = 2(0.11)(60)(24)/12 = 26.4$ kips. Next, find the total design shear corresponding to the steel and concrete capacities at this location from Appendix Table 5.6 part D: $V_u = \phi(V_c + V_s) = 0.75(36.43 + 26.4) = 47.12$ kips.

   Finally, use similar triangles to determine the distance from the beam

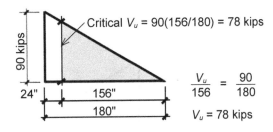

Figure 5.42: Shear diagram for calculation of critical design shear for Example 5.8

centerline corresponding to the location where maximum stirrup spacing can begin, as shown in Figure 5.43. The starting point for maximum spacing is no further than 94.24 in. from the beam centerline.

4. Find location where no stirrups are needed:

From Appendix Table 5.6 part G, $V_u = 0.5\phi V_c = 0.5(0.75)(36.43) = 13.66$ kips.

The location along the beam elevation where no stirrups are required can be found by using similar triangles, as shown in Figure 5.44. The starting point for no stirrups is no further than 27.32 in. from the beam centerline.

5. (Optional) Select intermediate spacing between minimum and maximum values determined earlier:

Choose a spacing between the smallest required at the support (4.5 in.) and the maximum (12 in.), for example, $s = 8$ in.

Determine starting point for intermediate spacing as follows. First, find the steel capacity corresponding to the chosen spacing: from Appendix Table A-5.6 part A, $V_s = 2A_s f_y d/s = 2(0.11)(60)(24)/8 = 39.6$ kips. Next, find the total design shear corresponding to the steel and concrete capacities at this location from Appendix Table 5.6 part D: $V_u = \phi(V_c + V_s) = 0.75(36.43 + 39.6) = 57.02$ kips. Finally, use similar triangles to

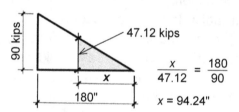

Figure 5.43: Shear diagram for calculation of location where maximum stirrup spacing can begin, for Example 5.8

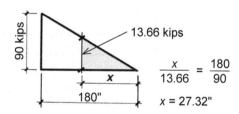

Figure 5.44: Shear diagram for calculation of location where no stirrups are required, for Example 5.8

determine the distance from the beam centerline corresponding to the location where this intermediate stirrup spacing can begin, as shown in Figure 5.45. The starting point for intermediate spacing, $s = 8$ in., is no further than 114 in. from the beam centerline.

6. Sketch the distribution of web steel (stirrups) for one half of the beam. The first stirrup is generally placed at a distance $s/2 = 4.5/2 = 2.25$ in. from the face of the support (round down to 2 in.). The remaining stirrups are arranged within the zones of minimum, intermediate (optional) and maximum spacing, as shown in Figure 5.46. In this example, the middle 38 inches (that is, twice 19 in.) of the beam are not required to have stirrups.

Depending on the beam's cross-sectional dimensions, span, load, and material properties, the distribution of stirrup spacing can sometimes become

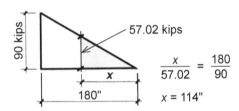

Figure 5.45: Shear diagram for calculation of location where intermediate stirrup spacing may begin, for Example 5.7

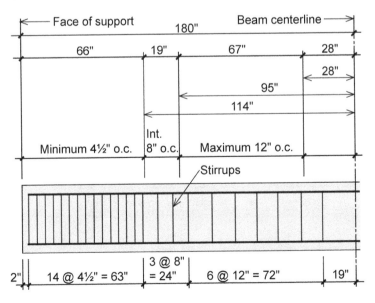

Figure 5.46: Elevation of beam showing spacing of stirrups for Example 5.8

even more complex for uniformly loaded beams with a triangular shear force pattern. As can be seen in Figure 5.47, there are four possible zones where the maximum shear force might occur, these zones bounded by values of V_u/ϕ equal to 0, $0.5V_c$, V_c, $3V_c$, and $4V_c$. These bounded areas are significant since they define four zones with different criteria for stirrup spacing. In zone I, no stirrups are needed; in zone II, only minimum web steel is needed; in zone III, stirrup spacing cannot exceed the limits of "regular" maximum spacing (the smaller of $d/2$, 24 in., or the value determined by minimum web steel); and in zone IV, stirrup spacing cannot exceed the limits of "reduced" maximum spacing (the smaller of $d/4$, 12 in., or the value determined by minimum web steel). The upper limit of $5V_c$ corresponds to the maximum acceptable value of V_u/ϕ — beyond that point, the shear force resisted by web steel is considered too high, and is not permitted.

Aside from the added cost and inefficiency of using too much steel, nothing prevents a designer from deploying stirrups at the minimum spacing, corresponding to the largest shear force, throughout the length of the beam. And there is also no prohibition against creating a greater number of spacing conditions, using any number of "intermediate" spacings, to minimize the amount of steel used in the beam. Finally, stirrup spacing over regions with constant shear force, V_u — commonly encountered in girders with concentrated loads — can be found with the same equations used in Example 5.7 and summarized in Appendix Table A-5.6.

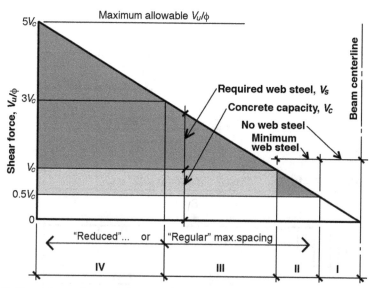

Figure 5.47: Shear force diagram showing four zones where the maximum shear force might occur; the shear force, V_u is divided by the strength reduction factor, ϕ, in order to more clearly show the concrete and web steel contributions in relation to the total shear force at any point: $V_u/\phi = V_c + V_s$

Connections

Reinforced concrete elements are not ordinarily "connected" in the usual sense of the term; rather, they are most often cast together into a monolithic assembly. Of course, there are construction joints between sections of the structure cast separately, but even at such joints, opposite faces of concrete brought together in compression bear against each other just as if they had been monolithically cast; and steel reinforcement in tension is made to extend through each construction joint so that tensile forces in the bars continue from one side of the joint to the other.

The following discussion therefore does not include any reference to the types of welds, bolts, screws, or nails commonly found in wood or steel construction, where discrete structural elements subjected to tension, compression, or bending must be explicitly connected in order to function together as a coherent structural system. Instead, two "quasi-connections," both typical of reinforced concrete construction, shall be examined: the end condition of a continuous beam, and the lapped splicing of reinforcing bars where the bottom of one column is cast against the top of another column.

Development length, tension

The fact that much reinforcing steel is subjected to tension raises an important question: what prevents such steel bars from being pulled out of, or slipping within, the concrete into which they have been placed? As can be seem in Figure 5.48, any bending of a structural element literally stretches the tension region while the compression region shortens.

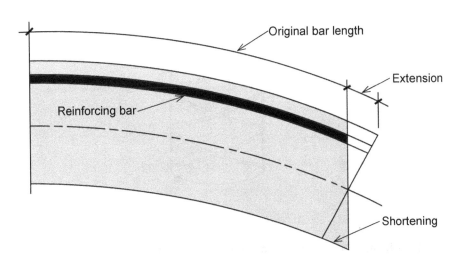

Figure 5.48: Extension of rebar in tension zone of reinforced concrete element

If the surface between the reinforcing bars and adjacent concrete were smooth and frictionless, the bars would remain "unstretched" as the beam bent; in general, it is the bond between the steel bars and concrete that guarantees that such slippage will not occur. This bond is primarily a result of bumps, or deformations, placed on the surface of the reinforcement that create a mechanical interlocking of the steel and concrete surfaces, as shown schematically in Figure 5.49.

The strength of this bond, per unit of bar length, has been measured experimentally, so the total necessary bar length required to resist any tendency for the bar to be pulled through the concrete can be determined for any given tension stress. This required bar length is called the development length, l_d, and is shown in Equation 5.29 for No. 7 or larger uncoated bars with normal-weight concrete and adequate bar spacing, or adequate spacing plus confinement with ties or stirrups, to prevent splitting of the concrete. Specifically, as illustrated in Figure 5.50, the bars must have a clear space between them at least equal to twice the bar diameter, that is, at least equal to $2d_b$, and clear cover at least equal to the bar diameter, d_b. Alternatively, if adequate stirrups or ties are used throughout the development length region to confine the bars and prevent splitting of the concrete, the minimum clear spacing requirement may be reduced to d_b.

$$l_d = \frac{f_y \psi_t}{20\sqrt{f_c'}} d_b$$

(5.29)

Figure 5.49: Schematic representation of a deformed reinforcing bar (rebar)

In Equation 5.29, l_d is the development length for tension (in.), f_y is the yield stress of the steel reinforcement (psi), f_c' is the compressive strength of the concrete (psi), ψ_t is a coefficient equal to 1.0 except when there is at least 12 in. of freshly cast concrete below the steel bars, in which case $\psi_t = 1.3$ (accounting for the negative impact on the bond between steel and concrete caused by rising air and water within a large mass of freshly-cast concrete), and d_b is the reinforcing bar diameter (in.). Where the minimum conditions for spacing and stirrups (or ties) described above are not met, the development length must be increased by a factor of 1.5. Where the bar size is smaller than No. 7, the development length is multiplied by 0.8. In no case may the development length be less than 12 in. Typical values for development length are tabulated in Appendix Table A-5.10 for common bar sizes.

Development length is influenced primarily by three factors: assuming adequate bar spacing and/or ties to prevent splitting of the concrete, the required development length becomes larger if the tensile strength of the concrete decreases (concrete's tensile strength is proportional to the square root of its compressive strength); the required development length also increases if the stress in the bar increases (that stress being at most equal to the yield stress of the steel); and the development length increases as well if the surface area of the bar decreases (the surface area being proportional to the bar diameter). These three parameters can all be found in Equation 5.29.

If we imagine an isolated and discrete concrete beam within a continuous concrete structure, it is easier to see where and how the concept of

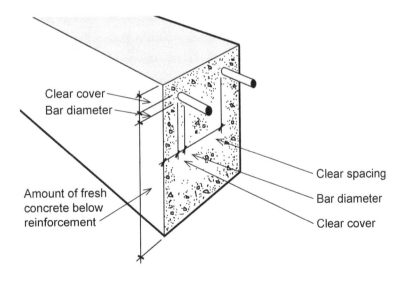

Figure 5.50: Clear cover and spacing requirements for reinforced concrete beams

development length becomes important. As can be seen in Figure 5.51, a typi-cal reinforced concrete beam-girder "connection" must resist the shear force and bending moment that occur at the surface where they come together. The shear force is resisted through the shear resistance of the concrete itself, the longitudinal steel bars, and the steel ties or stirrups provided for that purpose (the latter not shown in Figure 5.51 for clarity). The bending moment, in turn, is resolved into a compressive force (the resultant of the stress distribution shown below the neutral axis for "negative" bending) and a tensile force (car-ried by the longitudinal steel reinforcement shown above the neutral axis). The compressive force presents no particular problems, as the concrete in the beam "pushes" against the concrete in the girder. The tensile force, however, could pull the bars out of the girder and beam, unless those bars develop sufficient bond with the concrete to resist that tendency or are otherwise anchored into the concrete. In the case of the beam, sufficient space is avail-able to develop that bond strength by making sure that the bars extend into the beam for a distance at least as great as the required development length, l_d (see Equation 5.29). For an exterior girder, however, it is likely that sufficient space is not available, and a 90° or 180° hook is often required.

As shown in Figure 5.51c, a 90° hook must be extended a distance of $12d_b$ below the bent portion of the bar, which in turn is defined by an inner radius that cannot be less than $3d_b$ for bars smaller than No. 9; $4d_b$ for No. 9, No. 10, and No. 11 bars; and $5d_b$ for No. 14 and No. 18 bars. In these guidelines, d_b refers to the bar diameter. The required development length for such hooks, l_{dh}, is given by the following equation for uncoated bars and normalweight concrete:

$$l_{dh} = \frac{0.2f_y}{\sqrt{f_c'}} d_b \tag{5.30}$$

In this equation, l_{dh} is the development length for hooks (in.), f_y = the yield stress of the steel reinforcement (psi); f_c' is the compressive strength of the concrete (psi); and d_b is the bar diameter (in.). In no case may the develop-ment length for a hook be less than $8d_b$ or 6 in. Typical values are tabulated in Appendix Table A-5.11 for common bar sizes.

It is possible to reduce this length even further, if certain requirements are met that increase the level of confinement of the hook, making it less likely to split the concrete:

l_{dh} may be multiplied by 0.7 for all bar hooks (except those with No. 14 and No. 18 bars) with side cover of at least 2.5 in. and, for 90-degree hooks only, cover beyond the hook of at least 2 in.

l_{dh} may be multiplied by 0.8 for all bar hooks (except those with No. 14 and No. 18 bars) where perpendicular ties or stirrups, spaced no more than $3d_b$ along the development length, enclose them; or, for

90-degree hooks only, where parallel ties or stirrups enclose the "vertical" and "bent" parts of the hook, also spaced no more than $3d_b$.
l_{dh} may also be multiplied by the ratio of required steel bar area to provided steel bar area, except in cases where the yield stress, f_y, must be specifically accounted for.

These reduction factors are cumulative; that is, they may be combined.

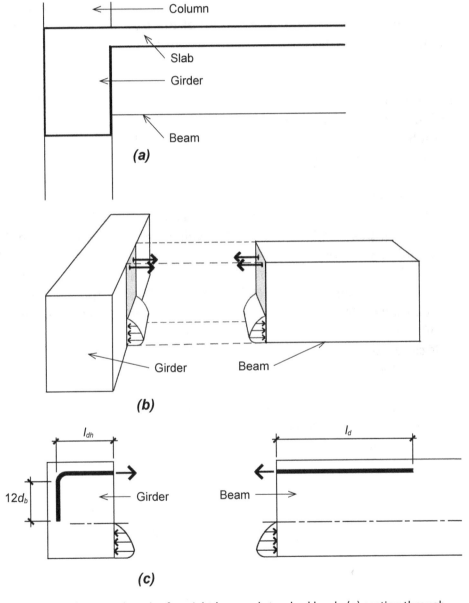

(a)

(b)

(c)

Figure 5.51: Development length of straight bars and standard hook: (*a*) section through typical slab and girder; (*b*) exploded view showing "connection" between beam and girder (with slab omitted for clarity); and (*c*) required development length of hook (in girder) and straight bar (in beam)

Example 5.9 Find required development length for straight bar and 90-degree hook in reinforced concrete structure

Problem definition. A reinforced concrete beam frames into an exterior girder, as shown in Figure 5.52, and the negative moment at the connection is resisted using No. 8 bars with 2 in. clear spacing between them. The required area for each bar = 0.74 in². Perpendicular ties (not shown) are provided along the development length of the hook within the girder, spaced at 3 in. on center, and side cover of 3 in. is provided. Assume $f_c' = 4000$ psi and $f_y = 60,000$ psi. Find the required development length, l_d, of the bars within the beam, the hook development length, l_{dh}, and hook extension beyond the bend, within the girder.

Solution overview. Find the nominal development lengths for a No. 8 bar, using 4000-psi concrete, in Appendix Table A-5.10 (for the beam) and Appendix Table A-5.11 (for the hook in the girder). Multiply these base values by the appropriate factors shown in the notes below each table.

Problem solution

1. The nominal development length required for the No. 8 bar in the beam is 48 in. (Appendix Table A-5.10). This value is multiplied by 1.3 (see Note 2) and by the ratio of required steel bar area to provided steel bar area = 0.74/0.79 = 0.937 (see Note 3), so that the final value for the required development length, $l_d = 48(1.3)(0.937) = 58.5$ in. or, rounded up to the nearest inch, 59 in. The required area for each bar = 0.74 in² was given (or otherwise would be computed); the value for the provided steel bar area is simply the actual area of a No. 8 bar (see Appendix Table A-5.2). The computed development length exceeds the absolute minimum of 12 in. (see Note 5 in the table).

2. The nominal development length for the 90-degree hook in the beam is 19 in.(Appendix Table A-5.11). This value is multiplied by 0.7 (see Note 1 in the table), 0.8 (see Note 2 in the table), and the ratio of required steel

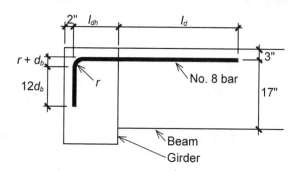

Figure 5.52: Required rebar development length for Example 5.9

bar area to provided steel bar area = 0.74/0.79 = 0.937 (see Note 3 in the table), so that the final value for the required hook development length, l_{dh} = 19(0.7)(0.8)(0.937) = 9.97 in. or, rounded up to the nearest inch, 10 in. The actual dimensions of the girder would need to be able to accommodate this required length. The computed development length for hooks exceeds the two absolute minimums (see Note 6): $8d_b$ = 8(1.0) = 8 in., or 6 in. Checking the minimum radius and minimum length of the "vertical" portion of the hook (see Note 5 in the table), we see that the required extension of the bar below the bend is $12d_b$ = 12(1.0) = 12 in. and the minimum inner radius for a No. 8 bar is $3d_b$ = 3(1.0) = 3 in.

There are two other requirements for tension reinforcement in continuous beams. First, for so-called positive-moment reinforcement — where tension occurs at the *bottom* of reinforced concrete beams — one-fourth of the rebars need to be extended at least 6 in. into the supports at each end of the beam. Second, for negative-moment reinforcement — where tension occurs at the *top* of the beam, typically in the vicinity of supports — at least one-third of the rebars need to extend beyond the point of inflection (where the negative moment becomes zero and the curvature changes from negative to positive) a distance of either d, $12d_b$, or $l_n/16$, whichever is greater: d is the effective depth of the beam; d_b is the rebar diameter; and l_n is the clear span, measured between the faces of supports.

Development length, compression

For a steel reinforcing bar in compression, much of the stress in the steel can be transferred to the concrete through direct bearing of the bar end on the concrete. For that reason, the required development length in compression, l_{dc}, is smaller than that required when bars are stressed in tension, and is given by the greater of the following values:

$$l_{dc} = \frac{0.02f_y}{\sqrt{f_c'}} d_b \text{ and } l_{dc} = 0.0003f_y d_b \tag{5.31}$$

In these equations, l_{dc} is the development length (in.) for normalweight concrete in compression; f_y = the yield stress of the steel reinforcement (psi); f_c' is the compressive strength of the concrete (psi); and d_b is the bar diameter (in.). As with bars in tension, it is possible to reduce this required length by multiplying the greater value found in Equation 5.31 by the ratio of required steel bar area to provided steel bar area. In addition, the required development length may be multiplied by 0.75 in columns with adequate spirals or ties (specifically, with a minimum ¼ in. spiral at no more than a 4 in. pitch; or with No. 4 ties spaced at no more than 4 in. on center). In no case can the development length for compression be less than 8 in. Typical values are tabulated in Appendix Table A-5.12 for common bar sizes.

Bar splices in tension

Since the length of reinforcing bars is limited by manufacturing and transportation constraints, it is often necessary to splice them together, at least in cases where the continuity assumed in design indicates lengths greater than those available from a single bar. While it is possible to weld bars together, or to use special mechanical splicing devices, the most common method for creating continuity between two bars in tension is by lapping them a sufficient distance so that tensile stresses can be transferred through the bond developed between the steel bars and adjacent concrete. For virtually all tension splices, the required lap distance is taken as $1.3l_d$, where the development length, l_d, is defined as in Equation 5.29 (or as tabulated in Appendix Table A-5.10), except that the 12 in. minimum length for l_d does not apply (but there is still a minimum *splice* length of 12 in.), and a reduction of the development length based on the ratio of provided to required steel area is not permitted. There are some limits placed on larger bar sizes: No. 14 and No. 18 bars cannot be lap spliced in tension.

Bar splices in compression

Columns are almost always cast floor by floor, with longitudinal reinforcement left extending vertically beyond the current floor level, so that it can be spliced into the column steel for the next floor being cast. For $f_y \leq 60$ ksi and $f_c' \geq 3000$ psi, the required lap distance for compression is taken as:

$$\text{required compressive lap distance} = 0.0005f_y d_b \qquad (5.32)$$

This required lap distance equals $30d_b$ for 60 ksi steel bars, with an absolute minimum lap distance of 12 in. In these equations, f_y = the yield stress of the steel reinforcement (psi); f_c' is the compressive strength of the concrete (psi); and d_b is the bar diameter (in.). It should be emphasized that in many reinforced concrete columns, especially those explicitly designed to resist bending moment as well as compressive force, a given lap splice may need to resist tension, compression, or both tension and compression, under different loading scenarios. For bars that resist only compression, and where confinement is provided by ties or spirals, it is possible to create splices, not by lapping the bars, but instead by placing their ends in contact so that they bear directly upon each other. However, even in such cases where no tension is anticipated, all columns must maintain some ability to resist unexpected tension forces, so that either additional "tension" steel must be provided in such cases, or else compressive lap splices must be used (since compressive lap splices provide sufficient resistance to unexpected tension forces in the bars). The required length of column lap splices in compression may be reduced where sufficient confinement, in the form of ties or spirals, is provided. Specifically, where the bar area of a tie (taken as the total tie area cut in section, as shown in Figure 5.53) is greater or equal to $0.0015(h \times s)$ — where h = the greater column cross-sectional thickness in inches, and s = the tie spacing in inches — the required lap distance may be multiplied by 0.83; with spirals, the required lap length may be multiplied by 0.75. In any case, the lap length can never be taken less than 12 in. Limits placed on larger bars are relaxed somewhat for lap splices in compression: No. 14 and No. 18 bars cannot be lap spliced to each other, but may be lap spliced to No. 11 and smaller bars. In cases where

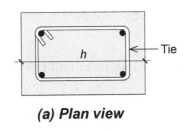

(a) Plan view

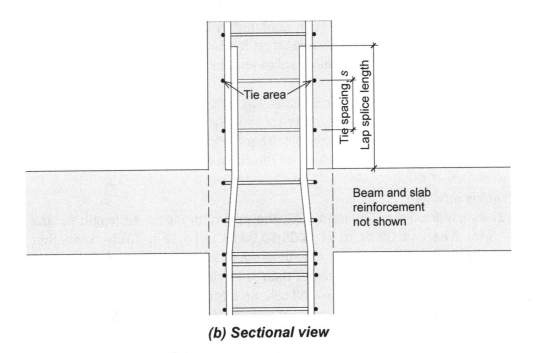

(b) Sectional view

Figure 5.53: Column lap splice parameters

two different bar sizes are lap spliced together in compression, the required splice length is found by (1) computing the required development length for the larger bar, (2) computing the required lap splice length for the smaller bar, and (3) using the larger of these two values.

For a column resisting only compressive forces, the required lap length is determined for the bars originating in the upper column; the bars extended upwards from the lower column that terminate in the upper column must satisfy the requirements for compressive development length (Equation 5.31). In practice, the larger of these two criteria (compressive development length for the lower bars and required lap splice length for the upper bars) determine the minimum splice length. Since loads typically are smaller in upper-level columns, it is possible that smaller bars sizes can be used in the upper columns; these smaller bars can be spliced with larger bars extending upward from the lower column. In such cases, different bar diameters, d_b, must be used in determining lap splice length and development length.

Example 5.10 Find required length of compression column splice in reinforced concrete structure

Problem definition. A 12 in. × 16 in. reinforced concrete column is configured as shown in Figure 5.53. The longitudinal (vertical) bars in the lower column consist of four No. 9 bars, which extend into the upper column. Four No. 8 bars originate in the upper column, and are spliced to the lower column bars as shown. The longitudinal steel is confined by No. 3 ties spaced at 9 in. on center. Assuming only compressive stress in the column, with f_y = 60 ksi and f_c' = 3000 psi, what is the required splice length?

Solution overview. Find the compressive lap splice length based on the diameter of the No. 8 bars in the upper column. Find the required compressive development length based on the No. 9 bars extended into the upper column. Use the larger of these two values for the column splice length.

Problem solution
1. *Lap splice.* From Equation 5.32, the minimum lap splice length for the No. 8 bars = $0.0005f_y d_b$ = 0.0005(60,000 × 1.0) = 30 in. To check whether the 0.83 reduction factor may be used, it is necessary to see if the No. 3 bar area for the ties is greater than or equal to 0.0015(h × s), where h = 16 in. (the larger of the overall column dimensions) and s = 9 in. (the tie spacing). Using twice the area of a single tie (Appendix Table A-5.2), we find that 2(0.11) = 0.22 ≥ 0.0015(16 × 9) = 0.216, so the lap splice length may be reduced to 30 × 0.83 = 24.9 in. or, rounding up, 25 in.

2. *Development length.* From Equation 5.31, we get:

$$l_{dc} = \frac{0.2 \times 60,000}{\sqrt{3000}}(1.128) = 21.9 \text{ in. and}$$

$$l_{dc} = 0.0003(60,000 \times 1.128) = 20.3 \text{ in.}$$

The bar diameter, d_b, is found in Appendix Table A-5.2. Using the larger value and rounding up, the minimum development length, $l_{dc} = 22$ in. Because the tie spacing is greater than 4 in. on center, no reduction in development length may be taken.

3. Comparing the requirements for lap splice length and development length, the larger of the two values will be used: 25 in.

CHAPTER 5 APPENDIX

Table A-5.1: Dimensions of reinforced concrete beams, columns, and slabs

A. Cover requirements (from outside face of concrete to face of closest rebar)	
Interior	1½ in. (or ¾ in. for slabs)
Exterior or exposed to ground	2 in. (or 1½ in. for No.5 bars or smaller)
Formed directly to ground	3 in.

B. Typical gross dimensions	
Beams and columns	Round to the nearest inch, or 2 in. increment, for all outside (gross) dimensions
Slabs	Round to ½ in. increment (or 1 in. increment if over 6 in. thick)

Table A-5.2: Steel reinforcement — rebar — areas (in²) for groups of bars

Designation and diameter			Number of bars									
Bar No.[1]	SI Bar No.[2]	Dia. (in.)	1	2	3	4	5	6	7	8	9	10
3	10	0.375	0.11	No. 3 (10) bars are used primarily for ties and in slabs								
4	13	0.500	0.20	0.40	0.60	0.80	1.00	1.20	1.40	1.60	1.80	2.00
5	16	0.625	0.31	0.62	0.93	1.24	1.55	1.86	2.17	2.48	2.79	3.10
6	19	0.750	0.44	0.88	1.32	1.76	2.20	2.64	3.08	3.52	3.96	4.40
7	22	0.875	0.60	1.20	1.80	2.40	3.00	3.60	4.20	4.80	5.40	6.00
8	25	1.000	0.79	1.58	2.37	3.16	3.95	4.74	5.53	6.32	7.11	7.90
9	29	1.128	1.00	2.00	3.00	4.00	5.00	6.00	7.00	8.00	9.00	10.00
10	32	1.270	1.27	2.54	3.81	5.08	6.35	7.62	8.89	10.16	11.43	12.70
11	36	1.410	1.56	3.12	4.68	6.24	7.80	9.36	10.92	12.48	14.04	15.60
[3]14	43	1.693	2.25	4.50	6.75	9.00	11.25	13.50	15.75	18.00	20.25	22.50
[3]18	57	2.257	4.00	8.00	12.00	16.00	20.00	24.00	28.00	32.00	36.00	40.00

Notes:

1. Rebars in the US were traditionally designated by the nominal diameter (in.) multiplied by eight, so that a No. 3 bar, for example, has a nominal diameter of ⅜ in. Rebars are no longer marked using this designation (see Note 2).

2. Rebars are currently marked by the approximate number of millimeters in their diameter (SI units), although designation by nominal diameter (in.) multiplied by eight is still widely used in the US.

3. No. 14 and No. 18 bars are used primarily in columns.

Table A-5.3: Reinforced concrete minimum width or diameter (in.) based on bar spacing

A. Minimum width (in.) for beams[3]

Designation		Number of bars in one line				
Bar No.[1]	SI Bar No.[2]	2	3	4	5	6
4	13	6.33	8.17	10.00	11.83	13.67
5	16	6.58	8.54	10.50	12.46	14.42
6	19	6.83	8.92	11.00	13.08	15.17
7	22	7.08	9.29	11.50	13.71	15.92
8	25	7.33	9.67	12.00	14.33	16.67
9	29	7.58	10.04	12.50	14.96	17.42
10	32	7.83	10.42	13.00	15.58	18.17
11	36	8.13	10.88	13.63	16.38	19.13

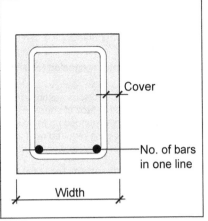

B. Minimum width (in.) for tied columns[3]

Designation		Number of bars in one line				
Bar No.[1]	SI Bar No.[2]	2	3	4	5	6
4	13	6.50	8.50	10.50	12.50	14.50
5	16	6.75	8.88	11.00	13.13	15.25
6	19	7.00	9.25	11.50	13.75	16.00
7	22	7.25	9.63	12.00	14.38	16.75
8	25	7.50	10.00	12.50	15.00	17.50
9	29	7.94	10.75	13.56	16.38	19.19
10	32	8.38	11.50	14.63	17.75	20.88
11	36	8.81	12.25	15.69	19.13	22.56
14	43	10.13	14.50	18.88	23.25	27.63
18	57	11.88	17.50	23.13	28.75	34.38

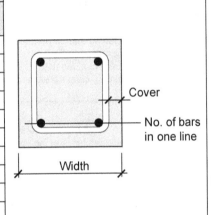

C. Minimum diameter (in.) for spiral columns[3]

Designation		Total number of bars in column				
Bar No.[1]	SI Bar No.[2]	6	8	10	12	14
4	13	8.50	9.73	10.97	12.23	13.49
5	16	8.88	10.18	11.50	12.84	14.17
6	19	9.25	10.63	12.03	13.44	14.86
7	22	9.63	11.08	12.56	14.05	15.55
8	25	10.00	11.53	13.09	14.66	16.23
9	29	10.75	12.47	14.23	15.99	17.76
10	32	11.50	13.42	15.36	17.32	19.29
11	36	12.25	14.36	16.50	18.66	20.82
14	43	14.50	17.18	19.91	22.65	25.41
18	57	17.50	20.95	24.45	27.98	31.53

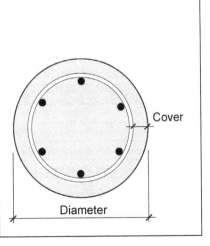

(continued)

Table A-5.3 continued (Notes)

Notes:

1. Rebars in the United States were traditionally designated by the nominal diameter (in.) divided by eight. Rebars are no longer marked using this designation.

2. Rebars are currently designated (and marked) by the approximate number of millimeters (SI units) in their diameter.

3. These minimum dimensions assume 1 in. maximum aggregate; 1½ in. cover (measured from outside face of rebar or spiral to face of concrete); and ½ in.-diameter stirrups, ties, or spiral. Minimum widths or diameters are typically rounded up to nearest inch, or to the nearest even inch. The amount of column steel is also limited by the required reinforcement ratio, ρ_g, between 0.01 and 0.08.

Table A-5.4: Specifications for steel ties and spirals in reinforced concrete columns

Ties	
Use minimum No. 3 bars to confine longitudinal steel up to No. 10; use minimum No. 4 bars for No. 11, 14, and 18 longitudinal steel. Center-to-center spacing of ties is the smaller of: • 16 × longitudinal bar diameter • 48 × tie bar diameter • Smallest column dimension Clear spacing of ties cannot be less than 4/3 of maximum aggregate size. Ties must be arranged so that corner bars are bounded by a tie bent at a 90° angle, and alternate longitudinal bars (between the corners) are restrained by a tie bent to at least 135°. No unsupported longitudinal bar shall be farther than 6 in. clear on either side of a laterally supported bar.	
Spirals	
Use a continuous bar or wire of at least ⅜-in. diameter, with the clear space measured between turns of the spiral no more than 3 in. and no less than 1 in or 4/3 of maximum aggregate size. A minimum ratio, ρ_s, of the volume of spiral steel to the volume of concrete inside the spiral (the "core") is also specified: $\rho_s = 0.45(A_g/A_c - 1)(f_c'/f_y)$ with $f_y \le 60$ ksi, A_g being the gross concrete area, and A_c being the area of the "core" within the spiral.	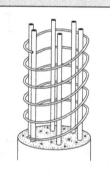

Table A-5.5: Reinforced concrete strength reduction factors, ϕ and α

Type of behavior	ϕ	α^1
Bending	[2]0.9	n/a
Axial tension	0.9	n/a
Axial compression: spiral columns	[3]0.75	0.85
Axial compression: tied columns	[3]0.65	0.80
Shear	0.75	n/a

Notes:

1. α accounts for unintended eccentricity or bending moment.

(continued)

Table A-5.5 continued (Notes)

2. ϕ decreases linearly from value listed above at $\varepsilon_t = 0.005$ to 0.65 or 0.75 (for tied or spiral lateral reinforcement respectively) at $\varepsilon_t = 0.002$, where ε_t is the net tensile strain in the extreme tension steel (we assume "tension-controlled" sections in this text, with values of $\phi = 0.9$ as shown).

3. ϕ increases linearly from value listed above at $\varepsilon_t = 0.002$ to 0.9 at $\varepsilon_t = 0.005$, where ε_t is the net tensile strain in the extreme tension steel for elements with combined compression and bending (this type of combined loading is beyond the scope of this book; in the problems considered herein, with only compressive stresses, the value of ϕ is as shown).

Table A-5.6: "Shear" equations for reinforced concrete beams[1]

	Equation
A. Capacity of steel stirrups[2] (lb)	$V_s = \dfrac{2A_s f_y d}{s}$
B. Required stirrup spacing[2] (in.)	$s \leq \dfrac{2A_s f_y d}{V_s}$
C. Capacity of concrete (lb)[3]	$V_c = 2bd\sqrt{f_c'}$
D. Strength design equation[2]	$V_u \leq \phi(V_c + V_s)$
E. Required steel capacity (lb) from strength design equation[2]	$V_s \geq \dfrac{V_u}{\phi} - V_c$
F. Maximum stirrup spacing[3] (in.)	For $V_s \leq 2V_c$, the smaller of: • $d/2$ • 24 in. • $2A_s f_y/(0.75b \times \sqrt{f_c'}) < 2A_s f_y/(50b)$ [see note 4] For $V_s > 2V_c$, the smaller of: • $d/4$ • 12 in. • $2A_s f_y/(0.75b \times \sqrt{f_c'}) < 2A_s f_y/(50b)$ [see note 4]
G. Design shear where no stirrups are needed[2] (lb)	$V_u = 0.5\phi V_c$

Notes:

1. Units are as follows:

b = cross section width, or "web" width for T-beams (in.)

d = cross section effective depth (in.)

s = stirrup spacing (in.)

A_s = stirrup bar area, one "prong" only (in^2)

f_y = yield stress of steel stirrup (psi)

f_c' = cylinder strength of concrete (psi)

V_u = design (factored) shear force (lb)

V_c = capacity of concrete to resist shear (lb)

V_s = capacity of steel stirrups to resist shear (lb)

ϕ = 0.75 for shear (see Appendix Table A-5.5)

2. Pound (lb) and pound per square inch (psi) units specified according to Note 1 may be changed to kips and ksi in these equations only.

3. The concrete cylinder strength f_c' must be in psi units in Appendix Table 5.6 part C (with the resulting value of V_c in lb units) and both the steel yield stress f_y and the concrete cylinder strength f_c' must be psi units in part F (with in. units resulting).

4. This limiting value for maximum spacing corresponds to the *minimum* amount of web steel required when $V_u > 0.5\phi V_c$, except that it does not apply when the total beam depth (thickness, h) is less than 10 in. or, for T-beams, when the total beam depth is less than 24 in. and is also less than the larger of 2.5 × flange depth or 0.5 × the beam stem width.

Table A-5.7: Approximate moment values for continuous reinforced concrete beams and slabs[1]

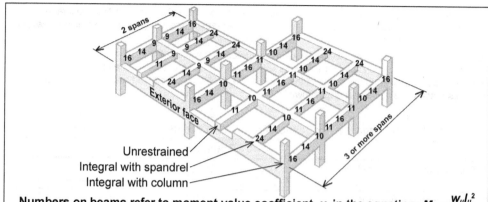

Exterior face
Unrestrained
Integral with spandrel
Integral with column

Numbers on beams refer to moment value coefficient, x, in the equation: $M_u = \dfrac{w_u l_u^2}{x}$

End restraints for two spans	Positive moment	Negative moment	
	End span	End span	
		At interior support[2]	At exterior support[2]
Discontinuous end unrestrained	$w_u l_n^2/11$	n/a	n/a
Discontinuous end re-strained by spandrel girder	$w_u l_n^2/14$	$w_u l_n^2/9$	$w_u l_n^2/24$
Discontinuous end restrained by column	$w_u l_n^2/14$	$w_u l_n^2/9$	$w_u l_n^2/16$

End restraints for three or more spans	Positive moment		Negative moment		
	Interior span	End span	Typical interior support[2]	End span	
				At interior support[2]	At exterior support[2]
Discontinuous end unrestrained	$w_u l_n^2/16$	$w_u l_n^2/11$	n/a	n/a	n/a
Discontinuous end re-strained by spandrel girder	$w_u l_n^2/16$	$w_u l_n^2/14$	$w_u l_n^2/11$	$w_u l_n^2/10$	$w_u l_n^2/24$
Discontinuous end restrained by column	$w_u l_n^2/16$	$w_u l_n^2/14$	$w_u l_n^2/11$	$w_u l_n^2/10$	$w_u l_n^2/16$

Notes:

1. The units for uniformly distributed design load, w_u, are typically lb/ft or kips/ft; the units for clear span, l_n, are feet; and the resulting moment value, M_u is in ft-lb or ft-kips depending on the units chosen for the distributed load. These moment values are valid only for continuous reinforced concrete beams or slabs when the following conditions are met:

   a. Lengths of adjacent spans do not differ by more than 20%.

   b. The unfactored live load is less than or equal to 3 times the unfactored dead load.

2. The negative moment (at the face of support) can be taken as $w_u l_n^2/12$ for slabs with clear spans no greater than 10 ft, and for beams framing into relatively stiff columns (specifically, the sum of column stiffness divided by the sum of beam stiffness at each end of the beam must be greater than 8). Stiffness is the product of modulus of elasticity and moment of inertia, neither of which are straightforward quantities for structural elements consisting of two materials bonded together. For normalweight concrete, the modulus of elasticity, E_c (psi), may be taken as $57,000\sqrt{f_c'}$, where the cylinder strength of concrete, f_c', is in

(continued)

Table A-5.7 continued (Notes)

psi units. The calculation of moment of inertia is left to the designer, with the American Concrete Institute (ACI) permitting any "reasonable and consistent assumptions." One suggestion is to use gross $E_c I$ values for both beams and columns. Where E_c is the same for all members, a typical joint with columns and beams at all four orthogonal points, and constant width for column and beam sections, would qualify for the $w_u l_n^2/12$ negative beam moment only when the column thickness at that joint becomes more than twice the beam thickness.

Table A-5.8: Limits on steel ratio for "tension-controlled" reinforced concrete beams[1,2]

f_c' (psi)	Limits on steel ratio, $\rho_{min} - \rho_{max}$
3000	0.00333 – 0.01350
4000	0.00333 – 0.01810
5000	0.00354 – 0.02130

Note:

1. Values are for $f_y = 60$ ksi, $\phi = 0.9$, and steel strain, $\varepsilon_t = 0.005$ for ρ_{max}.

2. Values for maximum steel ratio apply to all beams and one-way slabs; values for minimum steel ratio apply only to "tension-controlled" rectangular beams and negative-moment indeterminate T-beams; the minimum steel ratio for positive moment T-beams is $\rho_{min} = 0.00333/(b/b_w)$ and the minimum steel ratio for one-way slabs is $\rho_{min} = 0.00180/(h/d)$. For details, see Appendix Table A-5.9 keyed notes.

Table A-5.9: Values of R and ρ for reinforced concrete beams, T-beams, and one-way slabs (using 60 ksi steel)[1,2]

R (ksi)			ρ	$\dfrac{b}{b_w}$
$f_c' = 3$ ksi	$f_c' = 4$ ksi	$f_c' = 5$ ksi		
0.0197	0.0197	0.0198	[b]0.00033	10
0.0221	0.0221	0.0221	[b]0.00037	9
0.0251	0.0251	0.0251	[b]0.00042	8
0.0286	0.0287	0.0287	[b]0.00048	7
0.0334	0.0334	0.0335	[b]0.00056	6
0.0399	0.0400	0.0400	[b]0.00067	5
0.0493	0.0494	0.0495	[b]0.00083	4
0.0657	0.0659	0.0661	[b]0.00111	3
0.0982	0.0987	0.0990	[b]0.00167	2
0.1151	0.1158	0.1162	[b,d]0.00196 (ρ_{min} for slab h = 12")	1.70
0.1160	0.1167	0.1171	[b,d]0.00198 (ρ_{min} for slab h = 11")	1.68
0.1172	0.1179	0.1183	[b,d]0.00200 (ρ_{min} for slab h = 10")	1.67
0.1186	0.1193	0.1198	[b,d]0.00203 (ρ_{min} for slab h = 9")	1.64
0.1204	0.1212	0.1216	[b,d]0.00206 (ρ_{min} for slab h = 8")	1.62
0.1229	0.1237	0.1241	[b,d]0.00210 (ρ_{min} for slab h = 7")	1.59
0.1263	0.1271	0.1276	[b,d]0.00216 (ρ_{min} for slab h = 6")	1.54
0.1286	0.1294	0.1300	[b,d]0.00220 (ρ_{min} for slab h = 5.5")	1.51
0.1314	0.1323	0.1329	[b,d]0.00225 (ρ_{min} for slab h = 5")	1.48
0.1351	0.1360	0.1366	[b,d]0.00231 (ρ_{min} for slab h = 4.5")	1.44
0.1399	0.1410	0.1416	[b,d]0.00240 (ρ_{min} for slab h = 4")	1.39
0.1467	0.1478	0.1485	[b,d]0.00252 (ρ_{min} for slab h = 3.5")	1.32
0.1569	0.1581	0.1589	[b,d]0.00270 (ρ_{min} for slab h = 3")	1.23
0.192	0.194	0.195	[a]0.00333	1
0.229	0.232	0.233	[c]0.00400	0.83
0.282	0.287	0.289	[c]0.00500	0.67
0.335	0.341	0.345	[c]0.00600	0.56
0.369	0.377	0.381	[c]0.00667	0.50
0.385	0.394	0.399	0.00700	—
0.435	0.446	0.453	0.00800	—
0.483	0.497	0.506	0.00900	—
0.529	0.547	0.558	0.01000	—
0.575	0.596	0.609	0.01100	—
0.618	0.644	0.659	0.01200	—
0.661	0.691	0.708	0.01300	—
0.681	0.714	0.733	[e]0.01350	—
—	0.736	0.757	0.01400	—
—	0.781	0.805	0.01500	—
—	0.824	0.852	0.01600	—
—	0.867	0.898	0.01700	—
—	0.908	0.943	0.01800	—
—	0.913	0.947	[e]0.01810	—
—	—	0.987	0.01900	—
—	—	1.031	0.02000	—
—	—	1.073	0.02100	—
—	—	1.086	[e]0.02130	—

(continued)

Table A-5.9 continued (Keyed Notes)

Keyed notes for minimum and maximum steel ratio, ρ_{min} and ρ_{max}

a. Minimum steel ratio for rectangular beams and negative-moment, indeterminate T-beams:

$b/b_w = 1.0$
For $f_c' = 3$ or 4 ksi, $\rho_{min} = 0.00333$
For $f_c' = 5$ ksi, $\rho_{min} = 0.00354$

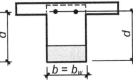

Positive moment rectangular beam   Negative moment rectangular beam   Negative moment indetermiate T-beam

---

b. Minimum steel ratio for positive-moment T-beams:

For $f_c' = 3$ or 4 ksi $\rho_{min} = \dfrac{0.00333}{b/b_w}$ and is tabulated for b/b_w between 1 and 10

For $f_c' = 5$ ksi, $\rho_{min} = \dfrac{0.00354}{b/b_w}$

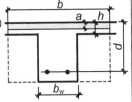

The effective width, b, of a positive-moment T-beam is smaller of the following:

b = web width + ¼ beam span
b = centerline distance between beams
b = web width + 16 times slab thickness

---

c. Minimum steel ratio for negative-moment determinate T-beams (e.g., precast sections and cantilevers):

For $f_c' = 3$ or 4 ksi $\rho_{min} = \dfrac{0.00333}{b/b_w}$ and is tabulated for b/b_w between 0.5

and 1.0 (with $\rho_{min} = 0.00667$ for values of $b/b_w < 0.5$)

For $f_c' = 5$ ksi, $\rho_{min} = \dfrac{0.00354}{b/b_w}$ (with $\rho_{min} = 0.00707$ for values of $b/b_w < 0.5$)

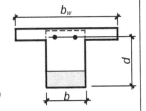

---

d. Minimum steel ratio for 1-way slabs:
$\rho_{min} = 0.00180(h/d)$ for slabs where h = slab thickness and d = slab effective depth; the same steel ratio applies to shrinkage and temperature control steel perpendicular to slab longitudinal bar. Tabulated values assume 1 in. cover from face of slab to rebar centerline, i.e., $d = h - 1$. Values of ρ_{min} for slab thicknesses from 3 in. to 12 in. are noted in the table.

---

e. Maximum steel ratio:
$\rho_{max} = 0.01350$ for $f_c' = 3$ ksi
$\rho_{max} = 0.01800$ for $f_c' = 4$ ksi
$\rho_{max} = 0.02130$ for $f_c' = 5$ ksi

Note:

1. $M_u \leq \phi b d^2 R$, where $\phi = 0.9$, $R = \rho f_y (1 - 0.59 \rho f_y / f_c')$, and $\rho = A_s/bd$. When using this table, R, f_y, and f_c' are in ksi units; b is the compressive zone cross-sectional width (or effective width); b_w is the tension zone width; and d is the effective depth, all in inch units. For positive-moment T-beams, results are valid only when the compressive stress block depth, $a = \rho f_y d/(0.85 f_c') \leq$ slab thickness, h. Steel strain at failure, $\varepsilon_t = 0.005$ for ρ_{max} (that is, only tension-controlled sections are considered).

Table A-5.10: Development length in inches, l_d, for deformed bars in tension, uncoated, normalweight concrete, with adequate spacing and/or stirrups[1,2,3,4,5]

f_c' (psi)	Bar number ["in-lb" designation, with nominal diameter (in.) = bar number/8]										
	3	4	5	6	7	8	9	10	11	14	18
3000	17	22	28	33	48	55	62	70	78	93	124
4000	15	19	24	29	42	48	54	61	67	81	108
5000	13	17	22	26	38	43	48	54	60	72	96

Notes:

1. Bars must have a clear space between them at least equal to twice the bar diameter, that is, at least equal to $2d_b$, and a clear cover at least equal to the bar diameter, d_b. Alternatively, if adequate stirrups or ties are used throughout the development length region to confine the bars and prevent splitting of the concrete, the minimum clear spacing requirement may be reduced to d_b. For bars not meeting these conditions, multiply values by 1.5.

2. Values assume "bottom" bars in tension (that is, bars placed for positive moment in beams); for "top" bars in tension with at least 12 in. of freshly-placed concrete below them, multiply values by 1.3.

3. Values may be multiplied by the ratio of required steel bar area to provided steel bar area, except in cases where the anchorage is required to reach the yield stress, f_y, or in certain high-risk seismic zones.

4. All of the modifications mentioned in Notes 1, 2, and 3 are cumulative; that is, a value may be multiplied by one or more of the applicable modification factors.

5. In any case, the development length, l_d, cannot be less than 12 in.

Table A-5.11: Development length for standard hooks in inches, l_{dh}, for uncoated bars, normalweight concrete[1,2,3,4,5,6]

f_c' (psi)	Bar number ["in-lb" designation, with nominal diameter (in.) = bar number/8]										
	3	4	5	6	7	8	9	10	11	14	18
3000	17	22	28	33	48	55	62	70	78	93	124
4000	15	19	24	29	42	48	54	61	67	81	108
5000	13	17	22	26	38	43	48	54	60	72	96

Notes:

1. Values may be multiplied by 0.7 for all bar hooks (except those fabricated with No. 14 and No. 18 bars) with side cover of at least 2.5 in. and, for 90° hooks only, cover beyond the hook of at least 2 in.

2. Values may be multiplied by 0.8 for all bar hooks (except those fabricated with No. 14 and No. 18 bars) where perpendicular ties or stirrups, spaced no more than $3d_b$ along the development length, enclose them; or, for 90° hooks only, where parallel ties or stirrups enclose the "vertical" and "bent" parts of the hook, also spaced no more than $3d_b$.

3. Values may be multiplied by the ratio of required steel bar area to provided steel bar area, except in cases where the anchorage is required to reach the yield stress, f_y, or in certain high-risk seismic zones.

4. All of the modifications mentioned in Notes 1, 2, and 3 are cumulative; that is, a value may be multiplied by one or more of the applicable modification factors.

5. A 90° hook must be extended a distance of $12d_b$ below the bent portion of the bar, which in turn is defined by an inner radius that cannot be less than $3d_b$ for bars smaller than No. 9; $4d_b$ for No. 9, No. 10, and No. 11 bars; and $5d_b$ for No. 14 and No. 18 bars.

6. In any case, the development length for hooks, l_{dh}, cannot be less than $8d_b$ or 6 in.

Table A-5.12: Development length in inches, l_{dc}, for deformed bars in compression[1,2,3,4]

f_c' (psi)	Bar number ["in-lb" designation, with nominal diameter (in.) = bar number/8]										
	3	4	5	6	7	8	9	10	11	14	18
3000	9	11	14	17	20	22	25	28	31	38	50
4000	8	10	12	15	17	19	22	25	27	33	43
5000	8	9	12	14	16	18	21	23	26	31	41

Notes:

1. Values may be multiplied by 0.75 where adequately confined by a spiral or ties (specifically, with a minimum ¼ in. spiral at no more than a 4 in. pitch; or with No. 4 ties spaced at no more than 4 in. on center).

2. Values may be multiplied by the ratio of required steel bar area to provided steel bar area, except in cases where the anchorage is required to reach the yield stress, f_y, or in certain high-risk seismic zones.

3. All of the modifications mentioned in Notes 1 and 2 are cumulative; that is, a value may be multiplied by one or both of the applicable modification factors.

4. In any case, the development length for compression, l_{dc}, cannot be less than 8 in.

Table A-5.13: Recommended minimum thickness (in.) of reinforced concrete beams and slabs for deflection control[1,2]

Beams	L/16	L/18.5	L/21	L/8
Slabs	L/20	L/24	L/28	L/10

Notes:

1. Beam diagram symbols in top row of tables represent the following conditions (from left to right): simply-supported; one end pinned and one end continuous; both ends continuous; and cantilever.

2. L = span (in.)

Unit abbreviations and conversion

Unit abbreviations

SI (international system) units	Inch-pound units
m = meter mm = millimeter MPa = megapascal N = newton kN = kilonewton kg = kilogram km/h = kilometers per hour	in. = inch ft = foot kip *is unabbreviated* lb = pound psi = pounds per square inch ksi = kips per square inch psf = pounds per square foot pcf = pounds per cubic foot mph = miles per hour

Conversions from SI (international system) to inch-pound units

Length, area, volume, section modulus, and moment of inertia	Weight, moment, and speed	Pressure, load per unit length, and density
1 m = 3.2808 ft 1 mm = 0.03934 in. 1 mm^2 = 0.00155 in^2 1 m^2 = 10.7639 ft^2 1 m^3 = 35.3147 ft^3 1 mm^3 = 6.1024 x 10^{-5} in^3 1 mm^4 = 2.4025 x 10^{-6} in^4	1 N = 0.2248 lb 1 kN = 0.2248 kips 1 N-m = 0.738 ft-lb 1 kN-m = 0.738 ft-kips 1 N-m = 8.8450 in-lb 1 kN-m = 8.850 in-kips 1 km/h = 0.6214 mph	1 MPa = 145.0377 psi 1 MPa = 0.1450 ksi 1 kN/m = 0.0685 kips/ft 1 kN/m2 = 20.8854 psf 1 kg/m3 = 0.0624 pcf

Conversions from inch-pound to SI (international system) units

Length, area, volume, section modulus, and moment of inertia	Weight, moment, and speed	Pressure, load per unit length, and density
1 ft = 0.3048 m 1 in = 25.40 mm 1 in^2 = 645.16 mm^2 1 ft^2 = 0.0929 m^2 1 ft^3 = 0.0283 m^3 1 in^3 = 16,387 mm^3 1 in^4 = 416,231 mm^4	1 lb = 4.4482 N 1 kip = 4.4482 kN 1 ft-lb = 1.3558 N-m 1 ft-kip = 1.3558 kN-m 1 in-lb = 0.11298 N-m 1 in-kip = 0.11298 kN-m 1 mph = 1.609 km/h	1 psi = 0.006895 MPa 1 ksi = 6.895 MPa 1 kip/ft = 14.59 kN/m 1 psf = 0.0479 kN/m^2 1 pcf = 16.03 kg/m^3

References

American Concrete Institute, *Building Code Requirements for Structural Concrete* (ACI 318-14), 2014

American Forest & Paper Association and American Wood Council, *National Design Specification for Wood Construction*, 2015 Edition, ANSI/AWC NDS-2012 (including revised values for visually-graded Southern Pine, effective June, 2013)

American Institute of Steel Construction, *Steel Construction Manual*, Fourteenth Edition, 2011

American Society of Civil Engineers, *Minimum Design Loads for Buildings and Other Structures* (ASCE/SEI 7-10), 2010

Glossary

about [as in: compute moment about the neutral axis] *prep.* the term "about" is equivalent to saying: "by measuring moment arms perpendicularly from each force to."

aggregate *n.* Stone selected for use in concrete, consisting of various grades, or sizes, from course (gravel) to fine (sand).

axial force *n.* A force parallel to the longitudinal axis of a structural element.

balloon frame *n.* A type of light wood-frame construction characterized by the use of dimension lumber for continuous vertical studs (2x4 or 2x6 at 16 in. or 24 in. on center) and closely spaced joists and rafters; largely superseded by platform frame construction.

beams and stringers *n.* A subcategory of "timbers," refers to lumber whose smaller nominal cross-sectional dimension exceeds 4 in. and whose larger nominal cross-sectional dimension is at least 4 in. bigger than the smaller dimension, thereby forming a rectangular shape appropriate for use as a beam, but not limited to that use.

bearing *ger.* The force exerted, in compression, by the surface of a structural element in contact with (that is, pressing against) the surface of another element.

bending moment *n.* An effect on a structural element caused by the action of at least two parallel force components that are not co-linear, and resulting in a distribution of stress within the element's cross section characterized by maximum stress at the "extreme fibers" (opposite edges) and zero stress at the neutral axis.

bolt *n.* A type of fastener used in both wood and steel construction consisting of a head and threaded shank, onto which is placed a nut; bolts are first inserted into a bolt hole before being tightened.

brittle *adj.* Lacking ductility, that is, lacking the ability to absorb energy, therefore being susceptible to catastrophic and sudden failure, especially under dynamic loading.

cantilevered beam *n.* A beam which extends beyond one or both of its supports.

cast iron *n.* An alloy of iron with very high carbon content; used most famously in the nineteenth century for structural columns, but largely superseded by steel in the early twentieth century.

cellulose *n.* An organic compound consisting of hundreds of linked and linear glucose units comprising about half the content of wood.

compact section *n.* Steel shapes proportioned so that, when used in bending, the strength and reserve capacity of the element will not be compromised by local flange or web buckling within those portions of the cross section subjected to compressive stress; this is primarily a function of the relative thickness of flanges and webs; for noncompact shapes, the available strength is reduced.

conifer *n.* A type of cone-bearing tree, one of the gymnosperms, including the most common structural lumbers: firs, pines, hemlocks, redwoods, larches, etc.

continuous beam *n.* Any beam that extends over more than two supports, and is therefore statically indeterminate.

couple [of equal and opposite forces on a cross section in bending] *n.* Two equal and opposite forces, F, separated by a moment arm, τ (that is., two such forces that are not co-linear), and therefore causing a moment, $M = F \times \tau$.

curing [of concrete] *ger.* The chemical process by which concrete hardens; the reaction of portland cement and water within the concrete mix.

cylinder strength [of concrete] *n.* The compressive stress at which a 6 in. × 12 in. cylinder of concrete, which has cured for 28 days, fractures.

decay *n.* The deterioration of wood caused by fungi; occurs when wood is wet or moist, temperatures are suitable, and oxygen (air) is available.

deflection *n.* The movement measured perpendicular to the longitudinal axis of a structural element under load, typically a beam; the term usually refers to the maximum deflection, often at midspan.

determinate *adj.* Pertaining to a class of structures whose reactions can be determined using only equations of equilibrium; includes simply-supported beams, cables, three-hinged arches, and pinned trusses formed from simple triangles.

development length *n.* For reinforcement in reinforced concrete structures, the minimum bar length such that any tendency for the bar to slip relative to the concrete is counteracted.

dimension lumber *n.* Lumber whose smaller nominal cross-sectional dimension is 4 in. or less; used extensively in light wood framing.

ductile *adj.* Having the capacity to absorb energy without fracturing; a quality of steel, but not of cast iron; of wood (in compression), but not of unreinforced concrete or masonry; see *brittle*.

elastic [behavior of material] *adj.* A material property characterized by a return to the initial shape after a load is first applied and then removed; associated with linear stress-strain behavior.

elastic moment *n.* The largest bending moment that can be sustained by a structural element such that all stresses within a given cross section are within the elastic range; in steel, the distribution of stresses coinciding with an elastic moment are linear, with a maximum value equal to the yield stress, F_y.

equilibrium *n.* A state of "rest," or balance, characterized by the sum of all forces in any direction being zero and the sum of all moments about any axis being zero; in a "plane" (two-dimensional) structure, conditions of static equilibrium are met when all forces in the x- and y-directions (that is, those axes that define the plane in which the structural element exists) equal zero, and all moments about the z-axis equal zero.

free-body diagram *n.* [FBD] A diagram of a structural element (or portion thereof) abstracted from its context, together with all forces and moment acting on the element, both externally (ordinary loads and reactions) and internally (at cross sections where the element has been "cut," representing internal shears, axial forces, and bending moments).

force *n.* A vector with magnitude and direction represented by an arrow, ordinarily described as a load or weight, and measured in units of pounds or kips.

graded [lumber] *adj.* Having a mark that describes the quality of a given piece of lumber; typical grades include select structural, No. 1, No. 2, No. 3, stud, construction, standard, and utility.

grain [of lumber] *n.* The directional pattern observed on the surface of lumber (or manufactured products such as plywood) corresponding to the groups of cellulose fibers originally running longitudinally up the trunk of the tree.

hardwood *n.* Wood from broad-leafed, deciduous angiosperm trees, such as oak, elm, and maple; not necessarily harder than "softwoods."

hydraulic *adj.* Referring to cement, having the ability to harden due to a chemical reaction with water.

indeterminate *adj.* Pertaining to a class of structures whose reactions cannot be determined using only equations of equilibrium; analysis of such structures requires, in addition to equilibrium, consideration of compatibility of displacements, and therefore of the relative stiffness of structural elements; such structures are also described as redundant, in that they contain elements, or constraints, beyond what is required for equilibrium.

influence area *n.* The area in plan within which a load will have an effect upon (that is, influence) a structural element, formerly used in the calculation of live load reduction; not to be confused with tributary area, but rather equal to the tributary area times the live load element factor, K_{LL}.

internal hinge *n.* A connecting device within a structural form that prevents translation (vertical or horizontal moment) of one side relative to the other, but allows rotation; present in three-hinged arches and multi-span determinate beams.

joist [steel or wood] *n.* One of a series of closely spaced and parallel beams supporting a floor; in wood-frame construction, joists are commonly made from dimension lumber and spaced at 16 in. or 24 in. on center.

knot [in lumber] *n.* A defect in a piece of lumber characterized by the interruption of the board's parallel grain by circular rings corresponding to the former position of a branch.

lag screw *n.* A type of fastener used in wood construction consisting of a head, shank, and tapered tip; part of the shank and tapered tip are threaded; sometimes called lag bolts.

leeward *adj.* Referring to the side of a building on the far side relative to the direction of the wind; see *windward*.

lignin *n.* The "glue" binding cellulose fibers together within a wood cross section.

linear [for example, stretching and shortening on a cross section subjected to bending] *adj.* In a straight line; referring to the straight-line stress-strain (or load-deformation) curves of certain materials, within their elastic ranges.

live load reduction *n.* The permitted reduction of live loads assumed to be present on relatively large areas, justified by the probabilistic argument that the worse-case live load values found in building codes (determined for relatively small areas) are increasingly less likely to be valid as the areas being considered get larger; calculations for live load reduction were formerly based on the so-called influence area, but now are based on the tributary area multiplied by a live load element factor, K_{LL}.

live load element factor [see *influence area*]

main member *n.* Where two structural elements are connected using nails or lag screws, the member into which the fastener end terminates; with bolts, the thicker of the two members, if any; or the middle member in three-member (usually bolted) connections.

moisture content *n.* A measure of the water within a piece of wood, defined as the weight of water divided by the dry weight of the wood and expressed as a percentage; the moisture content (m.c.) separating dry ("seasoned") and wet ("green") lumber is about 19%.

modulus of elasticity *n.* A material property defined as the change in stress divided by the change in strain; therefore, the slope of a stress-strain curve; implicated in the "stiffness," but not the strength, of a material.

moment of inertia *n.* For structural elements subjected to bending, a cross-sectional property indicating the section's contribution to stiffness; calculated by finding the sum of the products of areas and the square of their distances to the centroidal axis of the section.

nail *n.* A type of fastener used to connect two pieces of wood consisting of a head, shank, and tapered tip; typically driven into the wood by means of a hammer or pneumatic device.

penetration *n.* For nails and lag screws, the length of the fastener within the main member.

plane structure *n.* A structure or structural element that can be modeled as existing, and moving under the application of loads, on a two-dimensional (plane) surface.

plastic [behavior of material] *adj.* A material property characterized by a failure to return to the initial shape after a load is first applied and then removed; steel, for example, has a distinct plastic range beyond its elastic range.

plastic moment *n.* In steel, the bending moment at a cross section within a structural element corresponding to a stress distribution in which all stresses are assumed to be equal to the yield stress, F_y, half in tension and half in compression.

platform frame *n.* A type of light wood-frame construction characterized by the use of dimension lumber for 1-story-high vertical studs (2x4 or 2x6 at 16 in. or 24 in. on center) and closely spaced joists and rafters which, after a subfloor has been installed, provide a "platform" for the construction of additional stories; derived from, but has largely superseded balloon frame construction.

point of inflection *n.* A point along a structural element subject to bending marking the transition from positive to negative moment; a point of zero moment between regions of bending with opposite curvature.

ponding *ger.* A phenomenon associated with flat or low-slope roofs in which rain water, collecting in the deflected areas at the midspan of roof beams, causes increased deflection as it accumulates, leading to progressively large deflections and, potentially, structural failure; can be prevented by providing adequate slope, proper drainage, and camber for large spans.

portland cement *n.* The most commonly used cement used to make concrete.

posts and timbers *n.* A subcategory of "timbers," refers to lumber whose smaller nominal cross-sectional dimension exceeds 4 in. and whose other nominal cross-sectional dimension is the same or no more than 2 in. bigger than the smaller dimension, thereby forming a relatively square shape appropriate for use as a column (post), but not limited to that use.

reaction *n.* For any structural element, the forces and moments at its supports necessary to resist the action of applied loads, thereby maintaining a condition of equilibrium.

redundant [see *indeterminate*]

reinforcement (steel) ratio [in reinforced concrete] *n.* The ratio of the area of reinforcing steel to the gross area, for columns; for beams, the ratio of the area of reinforcing steel to the area defined by the beam width times the beam depth measured from the face of concrete in the compression zone to the centerline of tensile steel reinforcement.

relative stiffness *n.* The stiffness of one element (stiffness defined for elements subjected to bending as the modulus of elasticity times the moment of inertia; for elements subjected to axial force, as the modulus of elasticity times the cross-sectional area) compared to that of another; where two or more elements combine to resist the same loads, those loads are resisted by each element in proportion to its relative stiffness. Stiffness is sometimes used as a convenient shorthand to describe a load-deformation relationship which includes both the actual element stiffness (involving only material and cross-sectional properties) as well as element length or span.

residual stress *n.* Stress "locked in" to a structural element, usually as an unintended but unavoidable result of heating and cooling during the manufacturing process (for example, hot-rolled steel sections), but sometimes as a deliberate technique for improving material qualities (for example, tempered glass).

sag [of a cable] *n.* The vertical distance measured from the low-point of a cable to the level of the supports.

sag point *n.* The position along the length of a gable corresponding to the lowest point; see sag.

seasoning *ger.* The process of drying out wood after it has been cut into boards (lumber); both air-drying or kiln-drying are used.

section modulus *n.* A cross-sectional property indicating that section's relative strength in bending; equals the moment of inertia divided by half the height of the section (for symmetrical sections).

shear force *n.* An internal force within a cross section perpendicular to the longitudinal axis of the structural element.

side member *n.* Where two structural elements are connected using nails or lag screws, the member into which the fastener is first inserted; with bolts, the thinner of the two members, if any; or the two outside members in three-member (usually bolted) connections.

sign [of a bending moment or shear force] *n.* An arbitrary assignment of "positive" or "negative" corresponding to rotational direction (for a bending moment), or vertical direction (for shear in a beam); for beams, positive bending corresponds to tension on the bottom and compression on the top of the cross section, with a counterclockwise moment acting on the right side of a free-body diagram; while positive shear corresponds to an downward-acting force on the same free-body diagram.

simply supported beam *n.* A beam supported by a hinge and a roller, the hinge preventing all translation but allowing rotation, and the roller preventing translation perpendicular to the longitudinal axis of the beam while allowing "horizontal" translation and rotation; such a model is commonly applied to ordinary steel and wood beams and joists, which both approximates their actual behavior, and allows them to be analyzed as statically determinate structures.

shear lag *n.* A phenomenon encountered when a connection is made to only a portion of a steel element in tension, so that the cross section in the vicinity of that connection is only partially, and incompletely, stressed.

slenderness ratio *n.* A dimensional property of a structural element subjected to axial compression indicating its susceptibility to buckling, and defined as the effective length divided by the radius of gyration; the more "slender" the element, the greater the tendency to buckle.

softwood *n.* Wood from cone-bearing gymnosperm trees, such as pines, firs, larches, etc., and comprising the majority of structural lumber; not necessarily softer than "hardwoods."

spandrel [beam or girder] *adj.* At the outside face of a building.

specific gravity *n.* A material property equal to the relative density of the material compared to that of water.

spiral [in a reinforced concrete column] *n.* A continuous steel wire in the shape of a spiral used to confine both longitudinal reinforcing steel and concrete within a round cross section.

stagnation pressure [see *velocity pressure*]

statically determinate [see *determinate*]

statically indeterminate [see *indeterminate*]

stud [steel or wood] *n.* One of a series of closely-spaced and parallel posts comprising a wall; in wood-frame construction, studs are commonly made from dimension lumber and spaced at 16 in. or 24 in. on center.

tension-controlled member *n.* A reinforced concrete element in which failure is initiated by yielding of reinforcing steel in tension, rather than by crushing of concrete in compression.

thickness [of wood cross section] *n.* The smaller dimension of a wood cross section.

tie [in a reinforced concrete column] *n.* One of a series of steel reinforcing bars placed around the perimeter of reinforced concrete columns and used to confine both longitudinal reinforcing steel and concrete within rectangular cross sections.

timbers *n.* Lumber whose smaller nominal cross-sectional dimension is greater than 4 in.

torsion *n.* An effect on a structural element caused by the action of a moment about the element's longitudinal axis; also referred to as torque or twisting.

tributary area *n.* The area in plan assigned to each structural element, measured from the centerlines between those elements; used to determine the distribution of loads; results in accurate load values only in special cases without cantilevers or continuous (indeterminate) elements, and with symmetrical placement of loads; otherwise still useful as an approximate means for assigning loads.

unbraced length [between lateral supports on a beam] *n.* The distance between lateral supports on a beam, used to determine the beam's susceptibility to lateral-torsional buckling, and therefore the reduction in allowable bending stress.

under-reinforced [concrete beams] *adj.* Having the desirable property that failure is initiated by yielding of reinforcing steel in tension rather than by crushing of concrete in compression; such behavior is implemented by requiring a minimum steel strain at failure of 0.004 (or 0.005 to take advantage of the highest "strength reduction" factor for bending).

uniformly distributed [load] *adj.* Spread out evenly over a floor or roof (in which case it is measured in units of pounds per square foot), or over a linear element such as a beam (in which case it is measured in units of pounds or kips per linear foot).

unserviceable *adj.* Not useful or adequate for its intended purpose, due to such things as excessive vibration or deflection under normal loads.

velocity (or stagnation) pressure *n.* The pressure (uniformly distributed load) assumed to act on the surface of a building, caused by the force of a constant wind; proportional to the square of the wind's speed.

weld *n.* A type of fastening used in steel construction in which molten steel deposited by an electrode cools and joins two structural steel elements together. *v.* To engage in the activity of depositing such electrode-steel in order to connect two steel structural elements together.

width [of wood cross section] *n.* The larger dimension of a wood cross section.

windward *adj.* Referring to the side of a building directly in the path of the wind; see *leeward*.

withdrawal *n.* The capacity of a nail or lag screw to remain in place when subjected to a tension force that would otherwise pull it out.

workability [of concrete] *n.* Being of a consistency that permits proper mixing and placement; not too stiff.

wrought iron *n.* An alloy of iron with very low carbon content; in many ways a precursor to modern steel, but no longer commonly used.

yielding [of steel] *ger.* A characteristic property of steel in the plastic range in which the material is able to strain without any increase in stress, that is, deformations can increase at a constant load; the stress at which yielding occurs, marking the end of the elastic range, is called the yield stress.

Index

CPSIA information can be obtained
at www.ICGtesting.com
Printed in the USA
FSHW011109300620
71491FS

9 781612 298016